Actionable Gamification

Beyond Points, Badges, and Leaderboards

Yu-kai Chou and Erik van Mechelen

Actionable Gamification

Beyond Points, Badges, and Leaderboards

Yu-kai Chou and Erik van Mechelen

ISBN 978-0-692-85890-5

Octalysis Media

3444 Ellery Common.

Fremont, CA, 94538.

USA.

Octalysis Media is the publishing branch of The Octalysis Group, specialized in content related to gamification, motivational psychology and behavioral design.

Wall of Awesome

"I've been following Yu-kai's work on gamification for years and have enjoyed his deep insights and actionable recommendations. Octalysis is a powerful and pragmatic framework to understand human nature and positive motivators that encourage people to do their best work. It should be required reading for anyone building, managing, or collaborating with a team, community, or ecosystem."
-Susie Wee, CTO of Networked Experiences at Cisco Systems

"Yu-kai is the real deal. His experience, expertise and passion make this a "must read" for those looking to grasp the possibilities available through applied gamification."
-Jeff Gates, formal counsel to U.S. Senate Committee on Finance and Author of *The Ownership Solution*, *Democracy at Risk*, and *Guilt By Association*

"Yu-kai's Insights were instrumental in helping Lucky Diem supercharge our client La Quinta's bookings per user by 206% and incremental revenue per user by $157 (132% Lift) against *the control group. Being able to achieve a viral coefficient of 530%, I would recommend any business to work with Yu-kai and learn his Octalysis Framework."*
-Andrew Landis, Founder & CEO of Lucky Diem

"Yu-kai's book makes gamification practical. It is chock full of specific examples, suggestions for implementations, and pitfalls to avoid. Actionable Gamification is a gold mine of insights, and those who study and practice what it offers will have a powerful toolkit of incentives for business and personal contexts. Run, don't walk, to get your copy — I highly recommend it."
-Chuck Pickelhaupt, VP of Emerging Technologies R&D for Fidelity Investments

"This book is probably the most important and well researched guide to Gamification that is on the market today. If you think Gamification is about gaming stuff them you are dead wrong. It's about how your brain works and is motivated. This is probably one of the best values on Amazon today if you are a business manager, marketing expert or entrepreneur. I can't wait for his next book."
-Bob Garlick, Host of Business Book Review Podcast

""I've been tracking the development of Octalysis for over 2 years now, and It's become a comprehensive framework for enterprise gamification. Psychology is at the core of every activity, and game designers are masters at it. Yu-kai's framework has mapped out the various dimensions for reasoning about and optimizing a gamified enterprise process. I have no doubt that it will make its way into business school text books soon."
-Moataz Rashad, Former Head of Software Architecture at Sony Mobile

This book is dedicated to those who passionately believe in something and have the courage to pursue it in the face of circumstantial obstacles. We are surrounded by social and economical systems that are designed by others long ago to fulfill their own dreams, but some individuals manage to take a leap of faith, risk social rejection and even persecution in order to create more meaning in their own lives and the lives of those around them.

You inspire the world and move humanity forward. I salute you for doing what I continuously strive for but may never fully reach. I hope this book will help you on your journey towards making a difference.

Contents

Introduction

This book is not about why gamification is amazing. It is not about how gamification is the future and how inspiring life could be with it. It is not necessarily for the late adopters who are simply curious about what gamification is. It also does not focus on what the gamification industry is doing as a whole, especially when that is continuously changing every month. Rather, this book is about *implementing good gamification design* into your products, workplace, and lifestyle.

It is a deep exploration into what makes a game fun and how to apply those fun and engaging elements in real-life productive activities. It is about how you can use gamification and scientifically proven methods to improve your company, your life, and the lives of those around you.

Effective gamification is a combination of game design, game dynamics, behavioral economics, motivational psychology, UX/UI (User Experience and User Interface), neurobiology, technology platforms, as well as ROI-driving business implementations. This book explores the interplay between these disciplines to capture the core principles that contribute to good gamification design. I will be sharing my observations in multiple industries and sectors based on my 12-year journey of passionately and relentlessly pursuing the craft of Gamification.

Chapters in this book tend to build on previous chapters, so skipping around is not suggested. That said, if you have been an avid reader of my work and viewer of my videos, you might already have a firm grasp of the 8 Core Drives within the Octalysis Framework. In that case, feel free to skip to a section that you want to home in on.

If you are extremely busy and aren't sure if you want to commit to this book, I recommend starting off with Chapters 3, 5, 10, 14, and 15 to decide whether you would like to read the entire book.

Within the book, there will be many everyday scenarios to illustrate the potential of these Core Drives and the flexibility of their applications beyond traditional "gamification" examples. I myself still constantly gain new insights and revelations when I reflect and speculate upon the various possibilities contained in the 8 Core Drives. I hope you do too.

As this book is titled "Actionable Gamification," my goal is for it to become a strategy guide in helping my readers master the games that truly make a difference in their lives. If you absorb the contents of this book, you will have literally obtained what many companies pay tens of thousands of dollars to acquire.

My ultimate aim is to enable the widespread adoption of good gamification and *human-focused design* in all types of industries. I care deeply about creating a world that is sustainably more enjoyable and productive. In that world, there no longer will be a great divide between what people have to do and what they want to do - our lives become better as we spend time enjoying everything we do.

I'm excited for you to dive into the contents of this book so that we can start to build a world that harnesses the *power of play together*. Let's begin.

Yu-kai Chou (Written February 14th 2014)

Chapter 1: When the Surreal Blends into our World

How a Game changed my Life

On a seemingly regular morning in 2003, I woke up feeling different. I felt utterly unenthusiastic about the new day. There was nothing to look forward to – no demons to slay, no gears to perfect, no drops to loot and no Excel spreadsheets to strategize on. That was the first morning after I decided to quit Diablo II, a computer based role-play-game (RPG) developed by Blizzard Entertainment.

And I felt extremely empty.

Little did I know that I was going through one of the most treacherous effects stemming from black hat game design. Something I now call the "Sunk Cost Prison."

But it was that morning, that I also had the most impactful epiphany in my life, something that propelled me from a slightly-above-average student, to go on to start my first business during my first year of college at UCLA; to become a guest lecturer at Stanford University by twenty-three, raise over $1 million a year later, and finally become an international keynote speaker and recognized consultant in the field of gamification by my late twenties.

More importantly, this deep revelation ensured that I would become passionate and excited about my work every single day since.

I am sharing this with you not to sound conceited (after all, you are already reading my book), but because I truly believe if anyone was to take what I have learned during this epiphany to heart, they would likely do even better in a shorter amount of time, without all the fumbling and stumbling I went through.

Diablo II: my Epiphany

In 2003, like many students of my generation, I was a heavy gamer. In each game I played, I was very competitive and always strived to obtain the highest score. I was almost incapable of playing a game casually. It was either all or nothing.

As part of my obsession, I would generate complex spreadsheets to help me determine the exact combos I would need for playing optimally. (In Chapter 7 we will explore how many gamers do this.) I would read strategy guides while in the restroom and post regularly on forums, becoming a known leader within various gaming communities. Once I even broke into my college buddy, Jun Loayza's apartment while he was still in class, entering through the window after removing the screen, just to practice a game he owned called "Super Smash Bros Melee." (Eventually, Jun and I became Co-Founders of many exciting projects in the years to come). As you can see, I was fairly obsessed with gaming.

Back then however, most of my time was heavily invested in playing Diablo II. My friends and I would spend hours every day leveling up. I had more than 5 characters above Level 90 and a couple above level 96. In the game world this means I've likely logged over a thousand hours on this one game. If I played for two hours every single day for two straight years, it would still just barely exceed fourteen hundred hours. Quite intense, I know.

But at one point, as most gamers do, my friends began to quit playing Diablo II and moved on to other new games. Eventually I decided to quit as well since I didn't want to play alone. It was during this transition that a sudden sense of ennui (or weariness) caught me by surprise.

I felt depressingly empty. I thought to myself, "I've spent thousands upon thousands of hours getting more experience, leveling up, accumulating more gold, collecting better gear...and now I end up with nothing." *Was there really no meaning to all the hours I had spent playing in the past few years?* What if I had spent all this time learning a new language, or playing the violin instead? I would be "high level" in real life, instead of in some digital world of escapism.

This emptiness brought a rude, but important awakening. How could I instead, play a game that everyone is playing but the outcomes would actually mean something in the real world?

The First Game I Designed

I realized the game I was looking for was simply *life* itself.

If I were my own role-playing game character, I would never just stay in town, be idle and do nothing – the real life equivalent of watching TV, "hanging out" and leaving dreams unfulfilled. Of course not! I would go out into the wilderness, defeat monsters, gain experience, learn new skills, accumulate resources, ally myself with those who have complementary skills, learn from those who were of a higher level than I, and seek to conquer exciting quests.

The only problem is, unlike most games with a computer interface, life does not have clear objectives, visual cues to tell me what to do, or feedback mechanics to show me how I have advanced in it. I had to design my own game, along with clear goals, meaningful quests, and creative feedback systems. Effectively, I had to transform life into an entire adventure where I, the player, could advance and grow in.

This realization started my journey of personal growth and entrepreneurial pursuits. My life became my game and I was determined to become a high-level player in it. Despite being young, I felt my years as a competitive gamer had taught me how to master this new game of life.

Designing my life then became a decade long journey of addressing two intriguing design questions:

1. How to make games more meaningful?
2. How to make life more fun?

Little did I know back then that this lonely passion from 2003 would become one of the hottest new industries and buzzwords that people now commonly throw around as the term "Gamification."

Why Gamification?

Gamification, or the act of making something game-like, is certainly not something new. Throughout history, humans have tried to make existing tasks more intriguing, motivating, and even "fun." When a small group of people casually decide to compete against each other in hunting and gathering, or simply start keeping score of their activities and comparing it to their past records, they are adopting principles that are prevalent in modern games to make tasks more engaging.

One of the earlier works done on adapting gameplay practices within the workplace can be traced back to 1984, when Charles Coonradt explored the value of adding game-play elements at work through his book The Game of Work. [1]

Coonradt addressed the question, "Why would people pay for the privilege of working harder at their chosen sport or recreational pursuit than they would work at a job where they were being paid?"

---

[1] Charles Coonradt. *The Game of Work*. Paperback. Gibbs Smith. Layton, Utah. 07/01/2012.

He then boiled it down to five conclusions that led to hobbies being more preferable to work.

- Clearly defined goals
- Better scorekeeping and scorecards
- More frequent feedback
- A higher degree of personal choice of methods
- Consistent coaching

As we dive deeper into our journey together, we will learn about how these factors boil down to specific motivation Core Drives that can be intently designed for.

On the other hand, some early forms of marketing gamification can also be seen in the form of (regrettably) "shoot the duck" banner ads on websites, where an image ad tempts users to click on it by displaying a duck flying around. These tactics have probably tricked many people, myself included, into clicking on them once or twice upon seeing them. Later on, eCommerce sites like eBay and Woot.com all adapted sound gamification principles to become hugely popular examples of how game mechanics and dynamics can really make a process fun and engaging (in later chapters, we will examine how both eBay and Woot.com utilize great gamification design to make purchases exciting and urgent).

Of course, as "games" evolved throughout the centuries, the art of "making things game-like" naturally evolved too. Through the advent of the Internet, Big Data, pluggable frameworks, and stronger graphics, our ability to design and implement better gamification experiences has drastically improved to the point where we can now bring sophisticated and subtle game-like experiences into every aspect of our lives.

In recent years, the term "gamification" became a buzzword because the gaming industry shifted from making simple games that only target young boys, to social and mobile games like *Farmville* and

Angry Birds that also appeal to middle-aged executives as well as senior retirees alike.

As people discover that everyone from their nieces to their grandmas are playing games, while companies like *Zynga*, *King*, and *Glu Mobile* are having impressive Initial Public Offerings (IPOs), they begin to see the social power of gamification. At the same time, gamification has also been damaged by the lack of sustaining success from companies like Zynga, largely due to bad design, which we will examine closely in Chapter 14 on White Hat vs Black Hat Gamification.

The term "gamification" rose to prominence when organizations such as *Bunchball* and *Gamification.co* branded their services with the exotic word, which spurred a whole new industry: one that gives managers, marketers, and product designers tools for creating engagement and loyalty in their experiences.

Human-Focused Design: The Better Term for Gamification

In my own view, *gamification* is the craft of deriving fun and engaging elements found typically in games and thoughtfully applying them to real-world or productive activities. This process is what I call "Human-Focused Design," in opposition to what we normally find in society as "Function-Focused Design." Human-Focused Design optimizes for human motivation in a system as opposed to optimizing for pure functional efficiency within the system.

Most systems are inherently "function-focused," that is, designed to get the job done quickly. This is like a factory that assumes its workers will do their jobs because they are required to, not because they necessarily want to perform the associated tasks. However, at its core, Human-Focused Design emphasizes that people aren't rudimentary cogs in a system.

We have feelings, ambitions, insecurities, and reasons for whether or not we want to do certain things. Human-Focused Design optimizes for these feelings, motivations, and engagement as the basic foundation for designing the overall system as well as its functions. (Note: I originally created the term "Human-Focused Design" to contrast with "Function-Focused Design" in 2012, but it should not be confused with "Human Centered Design[2]," or "User-Centric Design" by IDEO[3].)

The reason we call this design discipline "Gamification" is because the gaming industry was the first to master Human-Focused Design.

Games have no other purpose than to please the humans playing them. Yes, there are often "objectives" in games, such as killing a dragon or saving the princess. But those are all excuses to simply keep the player happily entertained inside the system, further engaging them enough to stay committed to the game.

The harsh reality of game designers is that, no one ever *has* to play a game. They *have to* go to work, do their taxes, and pay medical bills, but they don't have to play a game. The *moment* a game is no longer fun, users leave the game and play another game or find other things to do.

Since game designers have spent decades learning how to keep people consistently engaged with repetitive activity loops towards "purposeless" goals, games are a great source of insight and understanding into Human-Focused Design. Indeed, depending on how you qualify a game (think of *chess, hide-and-seek,* and *Monopoly*), you could stretch back centuries to learn what game designers can teach us on creating compelling, playful experiences.

---

[2]Wikipedia Entry "User-Centered Design": http://en.wikipedia.org/wiki/User-centered_design

[3]Human Centered Design Tookit by IDEO. URL: http://www.ideo.com/work/human-centered-design-toolkit/

Through gamification, we can look through the lens of games to understand how to combine different game mechanics and techniques to form desired and joyful experiences for everyone.

The Conquests of Gamification

Games have the amazing ability to keep people engaged for long periods of time, build meaningful relationships between people, and develop their creative potential. Unfortunately, most games these days are simply focused on escapism – wasting your life away on something that does not improve your own life nor the lives of others - besides the game makers of course.

Now imagine if there is a truly addictive game, where the more time you spend on it, the more productive you become. You would be playing and enjoying it all day. Your career would improve as your income increased, you would experience better relationships with your family, create value for your community, and solve the world's most challenging problems. That is the promise I believe Gamification can fulfill, and it is the vision I continuously strive for throughout my life.

In a few short years, gamification has reached a social tipping point and is starting to creep into every aspect of our lives - from education, work, marketing, parenting, sustainability, all the way to healthcare and scientific research:

- The U.S. Armed Forces now spends more money on recruitment games than any other marketing platform.
- Volkswagen generated 33 million web visits and 119,000 new ideas through its People's Car Project to design the "perfect car".
- Nike used gamified feedback to drive over 5,000,000 users to beat their personal fitness goals every day of the year.

- With *Beat the GMAT*, students increased the time they spent on the website improving their test scores by 370% through a gamified platform.
- In 10 days, Foldit gamers solved an AIDS virus protein problem that had confounded researchers for 15-years.
- According to the Entertainment Software Association, 70% of major employers are already using gamification to enhance performance and training at their companies.
- In a similar report, the market research firm Gartner predicted that 70% of Fortune 500 firms would use Gamification by the end of 2014.

The list goes on and on. In fact, I have compiled a list of over "90 Gamification Case Studies with ROI Stats" from reputable and "serious" firms like SAP and Cisco on my blog *YukaiChou.com*. This list has been one of my most viewed pages to date because enthusiasts and practitioners are constantly looking for actual metrics that prove that gamification can create a return beyond simple aesthetics. The page can be accessed at YukaiChou.com/ROI.

In my own experience, I also see the trend on the rise too. Just a few years ago, only a handful of people approached me to talk about gamification. Nowadays, I am starting to get invitations to speak or consult in a variety of verticals and industries from every continent except Antarctica.

Unfortunately, in the same report, Gartner also predicted that 80% of those gamified efforts will fail due to bad design, which we will also explore in depth in this book.

So the question still remains: what exactly can gamification do? Does it actually create value and return measurable results, or is it just a new gimmicky fad without lasting impact? More importantly, how can my own company improve our metrics just like all those case studies mentioned above, instead of failing miserably like the 80% predicted by Gartner?

As stated in the Introduction, this book is not about explaining why gamification is valuable and why you should use it. I won't be devoting much time in explaining its validity because there are enough books out there that already do that quite well. My goal is to explain exactly how to be successful in applying gamification principles and techniques to real world situations. I aim to address these pressing questions and help you design experiences that actually motivate behavior, instead of simply adding some "game shells" on top of a failed idea in the hopes of a miracle. Life is too short to waste on playing bad games.

On that fateful day in 2003 when I decided to quit playing computer games, I never would have guessed that I would end up devoting my life's work to studying it so many years later. The value games can provide us far exceeds simply killing time. Now is the time to harness that value and make the most out of our time.

The journey begins here.

Chapter 2: The PBL Fallacy

A Story about Social Media

The landscape of gamification development must be viewed within a historical context to see why gamification mechanics themselves don't ultimately lead to effective design. Let's start by taking a look at social media[4].

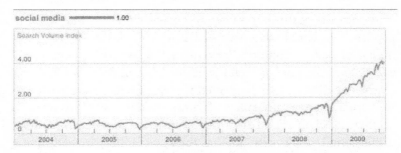

Google Trends search for "Social Media"

Due to the proliferation of blogs, Facebook, and Twitter, the versatile term "social media" overtook "social networking" in 2007 and became a new buzzword. When enough interest and excitement in an industry hits critical mass, there will always be people and agencies proclaiming themselves as experts, to capitalize on the trending buzz. It really doesn't matter what the new buzzword is – SEO, SaaS, Cloud, Big Data, you name it - the terms are so new that while no one can truly be an expert, everyone is in the running to be considered as one.

And so these "experts" saw the growth in "social media" platforms and services as heralding the dawn of a new era in technology, busi-

---

[4]Google Trends search, "social media", accessed 12/15/2014.

ness, and culture. They made sure to demonstrate the importance of its influence through viral growth models and by collecting case studies that show companies obtaining huge successes due to their social media savviness. "Everyone is now a publisher" became the motto, and how companies leveraged the phenomenon became the focus. The pitch was very inspiring and logical.

Unfortunately, being an "expert" only went so far. When companies actually hired these social media services to run their marketing campaigns, they found that all these "experts" could do was create Twitter profiles and Facebook Fan Pages (I've even seen services that charge thousands of dollars just to create these accounts).

However, the real question wasn't *how* to publish but *what* to publish. Content strategy was still a mystery in the early days of the social media revolution. For content, the "experts" would simply ask their companies to send them worthy updates for posting. Every once in a while they might even provide some customer support using the companies' Twitter accounts or share pictures on their Facebook Fan Pages. But overall, the industry felt a little disillusioned by this new "fad," as the miracle they were expecting in ROI (Return on Investments) just wasn't being realized.

What most people didn't recognize then was that social media is much deeper than simply possessing and posting on profile accounts. That's just the outer shell of its influence and impact. Today, we know that great social media campaigns focus on how to create value for the audience by sharing information that is insightful and engaging, has a personal voice, engages and sincerely interacts with each potential customer, and much, much more. In essence, the beauty of social media was in how you designed and implemented a campaign, not in the bells and whistles you used. It was the informal and formal dialogue you had with your community that ultimately taps into the platform's unique possibilities.

Having knowledge of good social media principles does not necessarily mean someone can execute them correctly. Take popularity for example. Most people know the principles of being a"popular" person – be outgoing, funny, confident, in some cases compassionate, etc. But when you look around your community or network, you find that there are still only a few people who are truly "popular," while some may even appear to be sleazy as they try. Helping a brand become popular is exactly what true social media experts would be doing if both principles and execution were aligned.

Fortunately, social media does have the power to make a company radically successful and the trend stuck around. (There are still dozens of successful social media case studies appearing on a monthly basis.) Today, most companies now subscribe to the belief of, "If your company doesn't have a social strategy, it will become irrelevant."

What connection does this have with gamification? We will soon see that the early days of social media almost completely mirror the gamification industry today.

An Obsession with Grunt Work

As I mentioned in the last chapter, games have the amazing ability to keep people engaged for a long time, build relationships and communities among players, and cultivate their creative potential. Still people often ask, "Do games really have the power to motivate people?" Consider this: many feel that children today do not have strong work ethics. They complain that kids nowadays don't have discipline, are easily distracted, and don't show persistence when encountering challenges.

But when it comes to playing games, these same kids have what most people would consider amazing work ethics. Many of them wake up secretly behind their parents' back at 3AM in the morning, just to play a game and level up their fictional characters.

What's the motivation behind this? If you have ever played RPGs (Role-Playing Games) before, you would know that the act of "leveling up" often requires defeating the same monsters over and over again in the same stage for hours on end. Even mobile games like Candy Crush or Angry Birds require the same repetitive action (bird-throwing and gem-matching) for weeks or months in order to level up and progress. In the gaming world, this is appropriately called "grinding," and it is fun and addictive for children and adults alike.

In the real world, this is often defined as "grunt work." Generally, no one likes to do grunt work, and it requires strong work ethic and will power to complete it. But kids, who again are assumed to have no discipline or work ethic, are somehow sacrificing sleep and risking punishment to complete seemingly pointless grunt work for fun.

Why? Because they are excited about leveling their character up. They want to get that extra +5 strength and gain a new game skill to beat a challenging boss that they couldn't defeat until they reached a high enough level. They do it because they see the big picture, the "why" they are doing it. They like that sense of accomplishment, as well as the use of their creativity in developing and optimizing certain strategies. They desire these feelings so much that anything that stands in the way, be it grunt work or otherwise, is worth doing and doing urgently.

Now, imagine a world where there is no longer a divide between what you need to do and what you want to do. Where everything is fun and engaging, and you actually want to wake up each morning to tackle the challenges ahead. Grunt work takes on a new meaning when understood as an affect of powerful motivational factors. This is the promise and vision that good gamification design can create.

Secondhand Sushi Making

Despite the many case studies on gamification that demonstrate the potential and promise of its great impact in the world, there are still many more examples of poor practices, failed attempts, and misconceptions. When I started my gamification career in 2003, it was a topic that no one really understood or believed in. People thought I was just creating more excuses to play video games

Fast-forward twelve years and gamification is now a leading design methodology for industries across the globe. Though it gives me great pleasure to see that my once lonely passion became mainstream, it troubled me that experts who were working in gamification didn't seem to understand games very much. Yes, they might have played Candy Crush a little, or even Angry Birds and Fruit Ninja. But if you ask them what games have they been completely immersed in and obsessed with for long periods of time, you get very short answers.

As with social media, once gamification became a buzzword, it attracted many who saw it as an opportunity to corner an emerging industry. I'm a firm believer that you should immerse yourself in an experience in order to best understand it. Yes, you can derive insight by closely observing those who are going through the experience. But that is like watching someone eat sushi and asking them to take a survey about it, rather than eating the sushi yourself. You're not going to get the same findings, and if you try to replicate that experience simply based on the survey, you're going to impart a "superficial sushi taste" to the product you're designing.

As a result, many gamification professionals focus only on developing the superficial layer of games. I call this the shell of a game experience. This is most often manifested in the form of what we call the PBLs: Points, Badges, and Leaderboards. Many gamification professionals seem to believe that if you put points on something boring, add some badges, and provide a competitive leaderboard, that once boring product will automatically become exciting.

Of course that's also what a lot of gamification platforms specialize in: adding PBLs into various products in a scalable manner. And as a result, many people who are less informed but curious about gamification start to believe that the sum total of gamification methodology and philosophy is merely the process of adding points, badges, and leaderboards to products. Justifiably, this leads them to believe that gamification is a shallow fad and not very impactful.

This has also generated a backlash from the game development community, as they claim that gamification is a bastardization of the true essence intrinsic to good gaming. And who can blame them? Foursquare seems to be nothing more than points, badges, and leaderboards based on going to places, while Nike+ seems to be the same thing based on running. Is this as deep as gamification goes?

Of course, points, badges, and leaderboards do have a place in game design. That's why you see them in so many different games. They have the ability to motivate behavior and push people towards certain actions. But gamification is so much more than PBLs. Many gamification professionals are only familiar with how to implement PBL mechanics and even though these do create value, most of them completely miss the point of engaging the user. It is not unusual for users to feel insulted by shallow shell mechanics.

If you ask any gamer what makes a game fun, they will not tell you that it is because of the PBLs. They play it because there are elements of strategy and great ways to spend time with friends, or they want to challenge themselves to overcome difficult obstacles. The points and badges are often an added bonus that's nice to have depending on the context. This is the difference between extrinsic motivation, where you are engaged because of a goal or reward, and intrinsic motivation, where the activity itself is fun and exciting, with or without a reward. We'll dive deeper into these distinctions in Chapter 13 on Left Brain vs Right Brain Motivations.

A Trojan Horse without Greek Soldiers

Generic game mechanics and poorly constructed game elements such as levels, boss fights, or quests often fall into the same hole as PBLs. Simply put, applying traditional "game elements" ubiquitous in popular gameplay without diving deeper into user motivation contributes to shallow user experience: it's all flash and no bang. An almost humorous example of this is when people I meet call something a "quest" instead of a "task" thinking that this automatically makes the same original actions fun and engaging. Sure, having a playful attitude can make a big difference, but it only goes so far, especially when your customers and employees may already distrust your motives.

The truth is, simply incorporating game mechanics and game elements does not make a game fun.

Games aren't necessarily fun because of high quality graphics or flashy animations either. There are many unpopular, poor-selling games with state-of-the-art 3D high- resolution graphics. There are also games with very basic graphics such as Minecraft, or even no graphics, such as the purely text-based multi-user dungeon games (MUDs), that have large communities of players addicted to them. Clearly, there are more to games than "meets the eye."

Unfortunately, a lot of people who work in gamification incorrectly think that applying game mechanics like points, badges, and leaderboards – elements that you can also find in boring and unsuccessful games - will automatically make the product or experience fun and engaging. Unfortunately, it's not just what game elements you put in - it's how, when, and most importantly, why these game elements appear.

It would be foolish for a modern army commander to say, "Hey! The Greeks sent a big wooden horse to the Trojans and won the war. Lets send our enemies a big wooden horse too!" In this case, he clearly doesn't understand the true design behind the Trojan Horse, but he only copied the outer shell of it. Instead, it would be much more effective if he created a virus that pretended to be a normal file to corrupt enemy computers. Learn from the design; don't copy the shell.

The Threat and Opportunities in Gamification

Even though gamification has become accepted in the mainstream, poorly designed applications threaten its long-term viability and impact development. I am genuinely afraid that in a few years, companies will look at gamification and say, "Hey, we tried the points stuff and it didn't work out. I guess gamification was just a short-term fad."

That would be a huge loss for the world.

Based on my years of research, observation, and design in gamification, I am a hundred percent certain that good gamification design can unlock tremendous potential and improve many lives in the process. There are hundreds of case studies that illustrate this also. And so it is my job (and hopefully yours one day) to continue protecting and innovating the core essence and the promise of gamification.

In the long run, the term "gamification" might actually fade and eventually disappear. Currently, no one describes a website's design as being "so Web 2.0!" Gamification may just become the normal way we design, implement, and interact with the world around us. It's my hope that the principles that optimize for human motivation becomes the standard for good design across the board.

Fortunately, there are enough good gamification examples that continue to show how thoughtful design can improve core business metrics and inspire new ways of thinking and execution. Besides the 90+ Gamification Case Studies listed on my site, as mentioned in the last chapter, it is interesting to note that some of the best historical examples of gamification, such as eBay or Woot.com, have not been categorized as gamification by most people in the industry. There are dozens, if not hundreds of companies that became extremely successful because, regardless of what it was called, they applied great game mechanics and gameplay dynamics to their processes. Some of these examples are illustrated in the following chapters.

Because of these success stories, I believe that gamification will continue to evolve and meet real needs if practitioners and the general gamification community also evolve in their understanding of its principles and practice.

So if "game mechanics" alone are not the true reason why games are so engaging and sometimes addictive, then what is?

The Story of the Good Designer vs. Bad Designer

To understand the core of good gamification design, let's start with an example of how a bad game designer might design a game.

In designing a game, a bad designer might start off thinking, "Okay, what popular game mechanics and game elements should I use? Well, of course we need monsters in the game. We also need swords so where should I place those? How about crops that friends can fertilize? What about some birds that show a lot of attitude? I'm sure people will love it!"

As you can see from the exaggerated depiction above, a game might have all the "right game elements" but still be incredibly boring or stupid if they do not focus on their users' motivations first. It is worth remembering that every single game in the market has what we call game mechanics and game elements. However, most are still boring and are financial losers. Only a few well-designed games become engaging and even addictive. Are you designing your experience to be the failing game or the successful game? How would you know?

So let us look at how a good game designer might tackle the problem. Instead of starting with what game elements and game mechanics to use, the good game designer may begin by thinking, "Okay, how do I want my users to *feel*? Do I want them to feel inspired? Do I want them to feel proud? Should they be scared? Anxious? What's my goal for their intended experience?

Once the designer understands how she wants her users to feel, *then* she begins to think, "Okay, what kind of game elements and mechanics can help me accomplish my goals of ensuring players feel this way." The solution may lie in swords, plants, or perhaps word puzzles, but the whole point here is that game elements are just a means to an end, instead of an end in itself. Game elements are simply there to push and pull on their users' behavioral core drives.

As a result, in order to further explore, systemize, and scale methods of combining game mechanics with our motivational core drives, in 2012 I decided to share my original gamification design framework called Octalysis to the world. The Octalysis Framework embodies my life's work, and the majority of this book will be about how to use Octalysis to design experiences that are fun, engaging, and rewarding.

Chapter 3: The Octalysis Framework

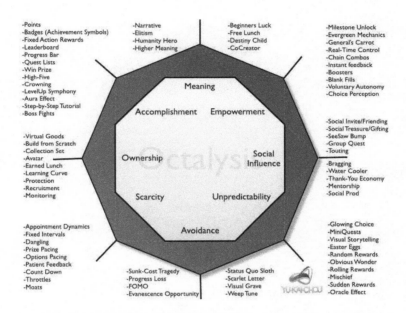

-Points
-Badges (Achievement Symbols)
-Fixed Action Rewards
-Leaderboard
-Progress Bar
-Quest Lists
-Win Prize
-High-Five
-Crowning
-LevelUp Symphony
-Aura Effect
-Step-by-Step Tutorial
-Boss Fights

-Virtual Goods
-Build from Scratch
-Collection Set
-Avatar
-Earned Lunch
-Learning Curve
-Protection
-Recruitment
-Monitoring

-Appointment Dynamics
-Fixed Intervals
-Dangling
-Prize Pacing
-Options Pacing
-Patient Feedback
-Count Down
-Throttles
-Moats

-Narrative
-Elitism
-Humanity Hero
-Higher Meaning

-Sunk-Cost Tragedy
-Progress Loss
-FOMO
-Evanescence Opportunity

-Beginners Luck
-Free Lunch
-Destiny Child
-CoCreator

-Status Quo Sloth
-Scarlet Letter
-Visual Grave
-Weep Tune

-Milestone Unlock
-Evergreen Mechanics
-General's Carrot
-Real-Time Control
-Chain Combos
-Instant feedback
-Boosters
-Blank Fills
-Voluntary Autonomy
-Choice Perception

-Social Invite/Friending
-Social Treasure/Gifting
-SeeSaw Bump
-Group Quest
-Touting
-Bragging
-Water Cooler
-Thank-You Economy
-Mentorship
-Social Prod

-Glowing Choice
-MiniQuests
-Visual Storytelling
-Easter Eggs
-Random Rewards
-Obvious Wonder
-Rolling Rewards
-Mischief
-Sudden Rewards
-Oracle Effect

Meaning

Accomplishment   Empowerment

Ownership   Social Influence

Scarcity   Unpredictability

Avoidance

YUKAICHOU

A Gamification Design Framework for Everyone

Because of the issues discussed in the last chapter, I spent the past decade working to create a complete framework to analyze and build strategies around the various systems that make games engaging. I saw that almost every successful game appeals to certain Core Drives within us and motivates us towards a variety of decisions and activities. I also noticed that different types of game techniques push us forward differently; some through inspiration and empowerment, some through manipulation and obsession. I drilled down to find what differentiates one type of motivation from another. The end result is a gamification design framework called *Octalysis*, which derives its name from an octagonal shape with 8 Core Drives representing each side.

Octalysis with only 8 Core Drives Present

In the past decade, I have been blessed in many more ways than I could anticipate. My lonely passion in gamification became something that various industries paid attention to. I could have easily stumbled upon a passion that remained a desert land throughout my life. Similarly, when I published the Octalysis Framework on my blog *YukaiChou.com*, it was also extremely well-received by the industry. Many brilliant pieces of work remain unnoticed or unappreciated for most of the creator's life, let alone a design framework I simply put up on my personal blog. To my delight, within a year the Octalysis Framework was organically translated into over fourteen different languages - I had to stumble upon most of them one at a time. I quickly received many opportunities to speak, teach, and consult globally.

Through many years of experiments and adjustments, I realized that everything we do is based on one or more of the 8 Core Drives within Octalysis. This is important to keep in mind because it also suggests that if there are none of these Core Drives behind a Desired Action, there is no motivation, and no behavior happens.

Let us quickly examine what these 8 Core Drives are.

The 8 Core Drives of Gamification

Core Drive 1: Epic Meaning & Calling

Epic Meaning & Calling is the Core Drive that is in play when a person believes they are doing something greater than themselves and/or were "chosen" to take that action. An example of this is when a player devotes a lot of their time to contribute to projects such as Wikipedia. We are familiar with the fact that people don't contribute to Wikipedia to make money, but they don't even do it to pad their resumes. People contribute to Wikipedia because they believe they are protecting humanity's knowledge – something much bigger than themselves. This also comes into play when someone has "Beginner's Luck" – an effect where people believe they have some type of gift that others don't or believe they are "lucky" getting that amazing sword at the very beginning of the game.

Core Drive 2: Development & Accomplishment

Development & Accomplishment is our internal drive for making progress, developing skills, achieving mastery, and eventually over-coming challenges. The word "challenge" here is very important, as a badge or trophy without a challenge is not meaningful at all. This is also the core drive that is the easiest to design for and, coincidently, is where the majority of the PBLs: points, badges, leaderboards mostly focus on.

Core Drive 3: Empowerment of Creativity & Feedback

Empowerment of Creativity & Feedback is expressed when users are engaged in a creative process where they repeatedly figure new things out and try different combinations. People not only need ways to express their creativity, but they need to see the results of their creativity, receive feedback, and adjust in turn. This is why playing with Legos and making art is intrinsically fun. If these techniques are properly designed and integrated to empower users to be creative, they often become Evergreen Mechanics: where a game designer no longer needs to continuously add additional content to keep the activity fresh and engaging. The brain simply entertains itself.

Core Drive 4: Ownership & Possession

Ownership & Possession is where users are motivated because they feel like they own or control something. When a person feels ownership over something, they innately want to increase and improve what they own. Besides being the major core drive for the desire to accumulate wealth, it deals with many virtual goods or virtual currencies within systems. Also, if a person spends a lot of time customizing their profile or avatar, they automatically feel more ownership towards it also. Finally, this drive is also expressed when the user feels ownership over a process, project, and/or the organization.

Core Drive 5: Social Influence & Relatedness

Social Influence & Relatedness incorporates all the social elements that motivate people, including: mentorship, social acceptance, social feedback, companionship, and even competition and envy. When you see a friend that is amazing at some skill or owns something extraordinary, you become driven to attain the same. This is further expressed in how we naturally draw closer to people, places, or events that we can relate to. If you see a product that reminds you of your childhood, the sense of nostalgia would likely increase the odds of you buying the product.

Core Drive 6: Scarcity & Impatience

Scarcity & Impatience is the Core Drive of wanting something simply because it is extremely rare, exclusive, or immediately unattainable. Many games have Appointment Dynamics or Torture Breaks within them (come back 2 hours later to get your reward) – the fact that people can't get something right now motivates them to think about it all day long. As a result, they return to the product every chance they get. This drive was well utilized by Facebook when it launched: at first it was just for Harvard students, then it opened up to a few other prestigious schools, and eventually all colleges. When it finally opened up to everyone, many people wanted to join simply because they previously couldn't get in.

Core Drive 7: Unpredictability & Curiosity

Unpredictability is the Core Drive of constantly being engaged because you don't know what is going to happen next. When something does not fall into your regular pattern recognition cycles, your brain kicks into high gear and pays attention to the unexpected. This is obviously the primary Core Drive behind gambling addictions, but it is also present in every sweepstake or lottery program that companies run. On a lighter level, many people watch movies or read novels because of this Core Drive. The very controversial Skinner Box experiments, where an animal irrationally presses a lever frequently because of unpredictable results, are exclusively referring to the core drive of Unpredictability & Curiosity - although many have misunderstood it as the driver behind points, badges, and leaderboard mechanics in general.[5]

Core Drive 8: Loss & Avoidance

This Core Drive should come as no surprise – it's the motivation to avoid something negative from happening. On a small scale, it could be to avoid losing previous work or changing one's behavior. On a larger scale, it could be to avoid admitting that everything you did up to this point was useless because you are now quitting. Also, opportunities that are fading away have a strong utilization of this Core Drive, because people feel if they didn't act immediately, they would lose the opportunity to act forever (e.g. "Special offer for a limited time only!")

Left Brain (Extrinsic Tendency) vs. Right Brain (Intrinsic Tendency) Drives

I will repeat multiple times in this book that, because everything you do is based on one or more of these 8 Core Drives, when there are none of these 8 Core Drives behind a Desired Action, there is *zero* motivation and no action takes place. In addition, each of these 8 Core Drives have different *natures* within them. Some make the user feel powerful, but do not create urgency, while others create urgency, obsession, and even addiction, but make the user feel

---

[5]Skinner, B. F. (1983). *A Matter of Consequences*. p116, 164. Alfred A. Knopf, Inc. New York, NY.

bad. Some are more short-term extrinsically focused, while some are more long-term intrinsically focused. As a result, these 8 Core Drives are charted on an Octagon not simply for aesthetic purposes, but because the placement determines the *nature* of the motivation.

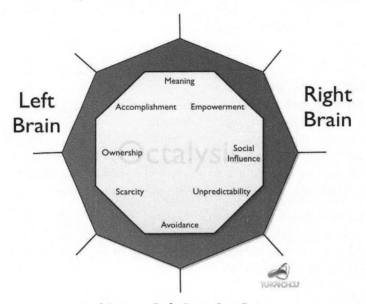

Left Brain vs Right Brain Core Drives

The Octalysis Framework is arranged so that the Core Drives that focus on creativity, self-expression, and social dynamics are organized on the right side of the octagon. In my framework, I call them Right Brain Core Drives. The Core Drives that are most commonly associated with logic, analytical thought, and ownership are graphed on the left side of the Octagon and are termed Left Brain Core Drives.

It is worth noting (especially for the "sciencey" readers who are now shaking their heads) that the Left Brain and Right Brain references are not literal in terms of actual brain geography but merely a symbolic differentiation between two distinct functions of the brain.

Interestingly, Left Brain Core Drives tend to rely on Extrinsic Motivation – you are motivated because you want to obtain something, whether it be a goal, a good, or anything you cannot obtain. On the other hand, Right Brain Core Drives are mostly associated with Intrinsic Motivations – you don't need a goal or reward to use your creativity, hangout with friends, or feel the suspense of unpredictability – the activity itself is rewarding on its own.

This is important, because many companies emphasize designing for Extrinsic Motivators, such as providing users a reward when they complete a task. However, many studies have shown that extrinsic motivation impairs intrinsic motivation. Why? Because once the companies stop offering the extrinsic motivator, user motivation will often plummet to a level much lower than when the extrinsic motivator was first introduced. We will examine this tendency, termed the *overjustification effect*, in Chapter 13.

It is much better for companies to design experiences that motivate the Right Brain Core Drives, making something in of itself fun and rewarding so users can continuously enjoy and engage in the activity. Motivation is often better when it sticks.

White Hat vs Black Hat Gamification

White Hat vs Black Hat Core Drives

Another factor to note within the Octalysis Framework is that the top Core Drives in the octagon are considered very positive motivations, while the bottom Core Drives are considered to be more negative. I call techniques that heavily use the top Core Drives "White Hat Gamification," while techniques that utilize the bottom Core Drives are called "Black Hat Gamification."

If something is engaging because it lets you express your creativity, makes you feel successful through skill mastery, and gives you a higher sense of meaning, it makes you feel very good and powerful. On the other hand, if you are always doing something because you don't know what will happen next, you are constantly in fear of losing something, or because you're struggling to attain things you can't have, the experience will often leave a bad taste in your mouth- even if you are consistently motivated to take these actions.

From an Octalysis perspective, the problem with Zynga games (as of 2015) is that they have been very successful with implementing many Black Hat Game Techniques. Of course, they don't have the framework to understand it as "black hat," but they refer to it as "Data Driven Design."[6] Because of the Black Hat Motivation, for a long period of time their games drove great numbers off each user in terms of retention, addiction, and monetization. However, because most Zynga games do not make users *feel* good when playing, when the user is finally able to wean themselves from the system, they will.

This is similar to the situation with gambling addictions - they don't feel like they are in control of themselves, and when they quit they actually feel empowered. In recent years, Zynga further validated my theories based on Octalysis by "double-downing" on a suite of gambling games such as the Slot Machine Game *Treasures of Olympus,* which further draws their design methodology away from White Hat Core Drives. [7]

It's important to note that just because something is called Black Hat doesn't necessarily mean it is bad. These are just motivators and they can also be used for productive and healthy results. Many people voluntarily submit themselves to Black Hat Gamification in order to go to the gym more often, eat healthier, or avoid hitting the snooze button on their alarm clock every morning. We will talk about the ethics and positive Black Hat Gamification Design in Chapter 14.

---

[6] Mike Williams. GameIndustry.biz. "Zynga's high-speed, data-driven design vs console development". Posted 08/06/2012

[7] Vikas Shukla. Valuewalk.com. "Zynga Inc (ZNGA) Unveils 'Riches of Olympus' Slots Game". Posted 02/07/2014.

Based on the Octalysis Framework, a good Gamification practitioner should consider all 8 Core Drives in promoting positive and productive activities so that everyone ends up happier and healthier afterwards.

The Hidden Ninth Core Drive: Sensation

Beyond the 8 Core Drives that will be explored in depth within this book, there is in fact a hidden ninth Core Drive called "Sensation," which is the physical pleasure one obtains from taking an action. People do drugs, get massages, or have sex (hopefully along with many other Core Drives) because of the *sensation* Core Drive. If you choose one food over another, it is often merely because one tastes better than the other, which is primarily *sensation*. They key differentiation here compared to other Core Drives is that *sensation* deals with physical feelings that bring pleasure to our touch, hearing, sight, smell, and even taste. The other Core Drives bring pleasure to us through psychological means - the meaning and context behind what we see, hear, or taste.

The reason why I don't have it included in the main set of the framework is that the Octalysis Framework primarily focuses on psychological motivators instead of physical ones. For instance, in *most* cases I cannot design an interactive experience where the user gets the feeling of physical acceleration while being on a roller coaster. Massages can be designed as rewards or *feedback mechanics* within the Octalysis Strategy Dashboard (covered in Chapter 16), but the behaviors will usually be motivated through Core Drives such as Scarcity, Accomplishment, and Ownership.

Even though we don't include sensation as part of the 8 Core Drives of Octalysis, we recognize its presence and understand how certain behaviors are driven by it. However, *sensation* by itself also has limitations without the 8 Core Drives accompanying it. Even pleasurable activities such as sex, when lacking *curiosity*, *relatedness*, *creativity*, and *scarcity*, can potentially become rather unappealing.

How to Apply Level 1 Octalysis to Actual Systems

Now that we have the Octalysis Framework laid out, the next step is to determine how to utilize it. Since everything a person does is based on one or more of the Core Drives, generally any engaging product or system will have at least one of the Core Drives listed above. If none of the Core Drives are present within a system, there is no motivation, and users will drop out.

The first application of Octalysis is to use it in analyzing the strengths and weaknesses of various products and experiences with respect to motivation. The key here is to start thinking about how that product or experience utilizes each of the 8 Core Drives, and identify all the game mechanics and techniques that are used to activate them.

A few Gamification examples with Octalysis

Here's an Octalysis done for a few games and online products:

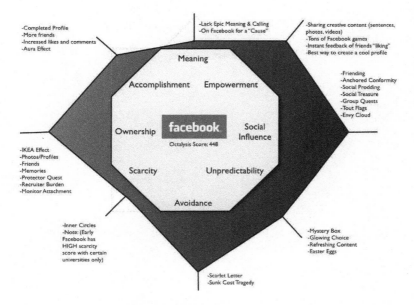

-Completed Profile
-More friends
-Increased likes and comments
-Aura Effect

-Lack Epic Meaning & Calling
-On Facebook for a "Cause"

-Sharing creative content (sentences, photos, videos)
-Tons of Facebook games
-Instant feedback of friends "liking"
-Best way to create a cool profile

Meaning

Accomplishment   Empowerment

-Friending
-Anchored Conformity
-Social Prodding
-Social Treasure
-Group Quests
-Tout Flags
-Envy Cloud

Ownership   facebook   Social Influence

Octalysis Score: 448

-IKEA Effect
-Photos/Profiles
-Friends
-Memories
-Protector Quest
-Recruiter Burden
-Monitor Attachment

Scarcity   Unpredictability

Avoidance

-Inner Circles
-Note: (Early Facebook has HIGH scarcity score with certain universities only)

-Mystery Box
-Glowing Choice
-Refreshing Content
-Easter Eggs

-Scarlet Letter
-Sunk Cost Tragedy

As you can see from the chart, Facebook is very strong in many of the 8 Core Drives, but rather weak on Core Drive 1: Epic Meaning & Calling - there is generally no higher purpose on using Facebook unless you are one of the few who are actively contributing to a cause on Facebook.

It is also weak on Core Drive 6: Scarcity & Impatience, as these days there are very few things that users want to do on Facebook but are barred from doing it.

The illustration tells us that Facebook mostly focuses on Right Brain Core Drives, which focus on Intrinsic Motivation. It also trends more into the Black Hat zone, which means that it is more prone to drive obsessive behavior that encourages users to return on a daily basis.

Among the Left Brain Core Drives, we see that people are extrinsically motivated on Facebook, not so much to feel accomplished or gain exclusivity, but because of Core Drive 4: Ownership & Possession - to collect, customize, and improve what is theirs.

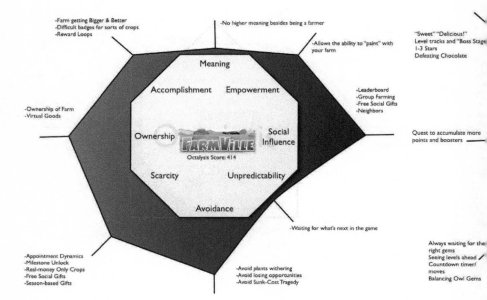

Here we see a couple game examples that contrast against each other.

Like Facebook, Farmville and Candy Crush also lack Core Drive 1: Epic Meaning & Calling within, but Farmville also lacks Core Drive 7: Unpredictability & Curiosity - there are not that many surprises in the game. You go back on Farmville simply to harvest the crops that you planted a few hours earlier. Candy Crush is a little more balanced, but a little skewed towards the Right Brain Core Drives.

Previously, I crafted each Octalysis shape by hand on Keynote. Fortunately, a fan of Octalysis, Ron Bentata from Israel, graciously offered to build an easier Octalysis Tool for everyone.

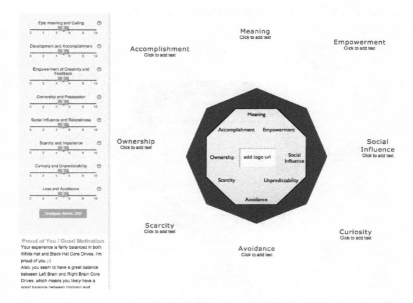

(Accessed from www.yukaichou.com/octalysis-tool)

With the Octalysis Tool, let's see a few more examples with Octalysis.

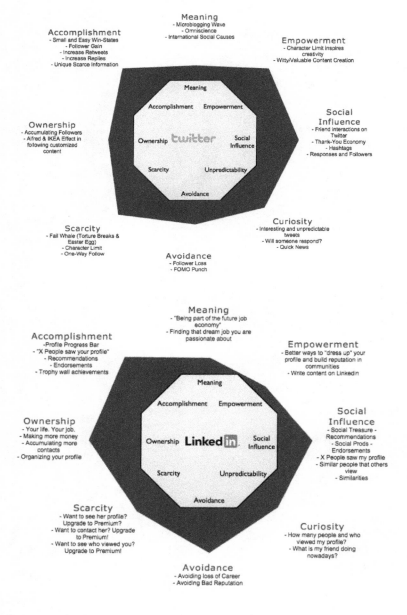

Here we can see that Twitter is also fairly well balanced but skews more towards Right Brain Core Drives. In contrast, LinkedIn is heavily focused on the Left Brain Core Drives, with a White Hat emphasis. This makes sense, because LinkedIn is all about your career, your life, your accomplishment. Those are very extrinsic goals, and as a result, everyone feels like they need to have a LinkedIn Account. However, because it lacks Right Brain (intrinsic tendency) Core Drives, there's not a lot of enjoyable activities on LinkedIn. And this has been the challenge that they have been faced with for many years. Users create their profiles, and then there is nothing left to *do* on LinkedIn. The account just sits there.

In the past couple of years, LinkedIn has been working very hard to increase engagement on the site, especially on Core Drive 5: Social Influence & Relatedness through Game Techniques such as Social Prods and Social Treasures - we will talk about how LinkedIn uses these Game Techniques in Chapter 9. However, through the Octalysis Framework we can see that LinkedIn could benefit massively if they put more effort into Core Drive 3: Empowerment of Creativity & Feedback, as well as Core Drive 7: Unpredictability & Curiosity.

Quick Intro to Level II Octalysis and Beyond

Ten years of Gamification study and implementations result in a fairly robust framework that can become actionable towards driving better motivation and metrics. As you can see, creating a rich gamified experience is much more than simply slapping on various game-mechanics to existing products. It is a craft that requires a nontrivial amount of analysis, thinking, testing, and adjusting.

As you become more and more advanced in Octalysis beyond the contents of this book, you will start to learn the higher levels of Octalysis design. (Up to *five levels*. There are only a handful of people in the world who know what is Level IV and above). These advanced levels incorporate much more sophisticated design principles and in-depth analysis.

Once one has achieved mastery in Level I Octalysis, they can then apply it to Level II Octalysis, where we try to optimize experiences throughout all four phases of the player/user journey. These phases are: *Discovery* (why people would even want to try out the experience), *Onboarding* (where users learn the rules and tools to play the game), *Scaffolding* (the regular journey of repeated actions towards a goal) and *Endgame* (how do you retain your veterans).

Level 2 Octalysis
Design for All 4 Phases

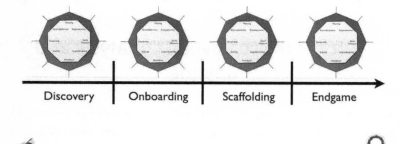

Level II Octalysis: Factoring in the 4 Phases of a Player's Journey

Most people treat their product as one experience, which seems reasonable. But in terms of motivation, I believe this is a mistake because the reason you are using a product on Day 1 is often very different from that of Day 100. Since everything you do is because of one of these 8 Core Drives (besides the 9th hidden Core Drive -

Sensation), if at any phase none of the 8 Core Drives are present, there is no reason for the user to move on to the next phase, and the user simply drops out.

Level 2 Octalysis
Design for All 4 Phases

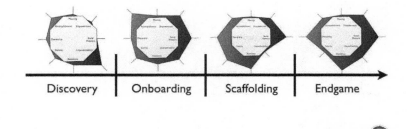

| Discovery | Onboarding | Scaffolding | Endgame |

Sensing the pulse of what players feel across the journey

In the above illustration, you can evaluate how different Core Drives are more prominent during each Experience Phase of the player's journey - whether it would be *unpredictability, accomplishment,* or *social influence.* For instance, most people *Discover* a product because of Core Drive 7: Unpredictability & Curiosity – they read about it on the news or hear others talking about it.

During *Onboarding,* they might be motivated by Core Drive 2: Development & Accomplishment – feeling smart and competent during the early stages. During the *Scaffodling* Phase, they might be motivated because of the social dynamic (Core Drive 5) as well as trying to go after the goal they could not reach yet (Core Drive 6: Scarcity & Impatience). In the *Endgame,* they might continue to be engaged because they don't want to lose their status and achievements (Core Drive 8: Loss & Avoidance).

How you design for all four Experience Phases through the 8 Core Drives will strongly demonstrate your ability as an Octalysis Gamification Designer. Of course, never forget to design for the proper *nature* of the Core Drives, understanding when you want to have more Black Hat, when to have more White Hat, and when to use Extrinsic/Intrinsic motivators.

Once you have mastered Level II Octalysis, you can then push on to Level III and factor in the different player types. This will allow you to see how different types of people are motivated at different stages of the experience.

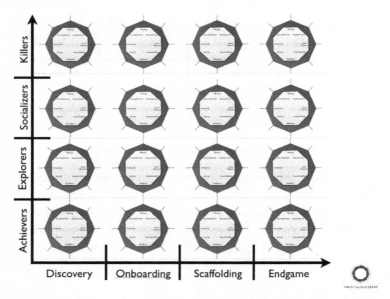

Pushing up a level further: Level 3 Octalysis with Bartle's Player Types

In the above diagram, I applied Richard Bartle's Four Player Types (Achievers, Socializers, Explorers, and Killers) to Level III Octalysis primarily because it is the most recognized model in game design. However, Level III Octalysis does not need to use Bartle's Player

Types[8]. In fact, Richard Bartle himself claims that his Four Player Types may not be suitable for gamification environments[9]. It could be Sales vs. Marketing Staff, Male vs. Female, Loyal Customers vs. Nonchalant Customers vs. New Customers etc. The point here is that different types of people are motivated differently, so Level III Octalysis allows the designer to understand and design for how everyone is feeling at different stages. We will also examine Richard Bartle's Four Player Types with Octalysis in Chapter 15.

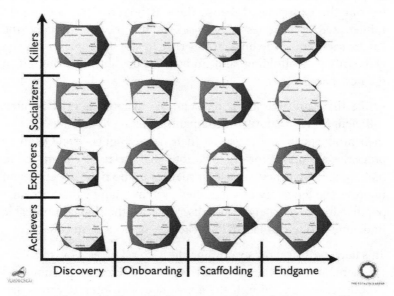

Sensing how each Player Type is motivated at each Experience Phase

It is incredibly difficult to design something that pleases everyone. But with this framework, you can start to identify where the weaknesses are within your system and work on improving for motivation at various points. Once you become familiar with Level III Octalysis, you can almost *feel* how motivation moves within

---

[8]Richard Bartle, "Hearts, Clubs, Diamonds, Spades: Players Who suit MUDs". 04/1996.
[9]Gabe Zichermann. Slideshare: "A game designer's view of gamification" by Richard Bartle. Posted 06/24/2012.

your system and recognize where motivation is lacking or whether there is too much Black Hat or Extrinsic Motivation in the system.

For instance, through Level III Octalysis, one can reach conclusions such as, "Looks like the Achievers start the experience in Discovery well, Onboarding is fine, but in Scaffolding they lose motivation and drop out. The Explorers will try out the product because of Core Drive 7: Unpredictability & Curiosity, but during Onboarding they feel confused and would leave. Socializers wouldn't even try out the experience because there is no Core Drive 5: Social Influence & Relatedness advertised in the product. Finally, the Killers seem to be the ones in this case to stay through Discovery, Onboarding, Scaffolding, and Endgame - possibly showing off to the new players."

While there are five levels of Octalysis in total, Level I is often sufficient for the majority of companies seeking to understand why their products are not engaging their users. Higher-level Octalysis processes are useful for organizations that are truly committed to making sure that they push their metrics in the right direction and improve the longevity of a gamified system. Many games are only popular for three to eight months, but ones that have impeccable Endgame design can last over decades — or even centuries.

This book will be about examining the 8 Core Drives, how to design for them, and how they all come together to create a phenomenal experience for any user. If the above does not interest you so far, it is safe for you to put the book down and do better things with your time. But if the above excites you and you choose to go on, I promise you there will be an exhilarating journey of discovery, empowerment and awakening ahead. I'm even feeling excited just thinking about it.

To get the most out of the book, Choose only ONE of the below options to do right now:

Easy: Think of a game that you have enjoyed playing for a very long time. Can you identify which of the 8 Core Drives are present in the game?

Medium: Think about why you are reading this book. What Core Drives have motivated you to read this book over other activities?

Share what you come up with on Twitter or your preferred social network with the hashtag #OctalysisBook and see what ideas other people have.

Chapter 4: Putting Gamification in its Place

Before we jump further into deeper experience and engagement design through the 8 Core Drives, I'd like to take a moment to resolve some pressing questions regarding the various forms of gamification campaigns.

While the topic of Gamification is exciting and productive, many people new to the industry have a hard time figuring out what gamification means and how to categorize it.

What if our employees don't want to play games? Is calling something a quest considered gamification? Is the gamification BlendTech uses to promote its blenders the same as the gamification that eBay uses to make its platform addictive? How do I know what type of gamification works for my company?

All this can be quite confusing to the average reader (which of course, you are not). As Gamification is such an all-encompassing umbrella term for "making things game-like" (by the way, the popular Wikipedia definition is, "the use of game thinking and game mechanics in non-game contexts"[10]), there are almost no bounds for what it can or cannot be. This allows gamification to be far reaching into all sorts of fields and industries. However, it also invites many critics who are upset about how broad the term can be. They especially criticize that, due to the broad nature of the term, gamification enthusiasts are claiming everything good, fun, motivating, or immersive as something they perform on a professional level.

---

[10]Wikipedia Article: "Gamification", accessed 12/13/2014. URL: http://en.wikipedia.org/wiki/Gamification

Before you read on, I want to make a disclaimer that this chapter does not teach you how to gamify an experience towards better results but merely addresses some issues on the language and semantics within the field and my own opinion on the matter. I can't promise you a definitive conclusion to the debate over what is and what isn't gamification, but I do hope you leave the chapter with a more rounded understanding of the field.

There are many more fascinating topics on human behavior and good design that excite me more in the chapters to come. Even though it breaks my heart to spend precious time writing about this non-productive topic, I don't want my readers to be unaware of the greater "Gamification World."

The War on Words

Back in 2011, gamification notables Gabe Zichermann and Sebastian Deterding had a public debate on gamification concepts.

Some background info: Gabe Zichermann is a brilliant marketer, speaker, CEO of the largest Gamification conference in the industry, the GSummit, and is one of the leading evangelists of Gamification and its commercial use.

Sebastian Deterding is the Ph.D. academic that studies the deep theories and motivations of game design and Gamification. He is considered one of the most respected thought leaders in the space.

In this debate of epic proportions, Sebastian Deterding publicly examined each chapter of Gabe Zichermann's book *Gamification by Design*, and explained why he considered each chapter to be flawed and/or inaccurate[11]. Hyperbolically speaking, his blog post on the subject was almost longer than the book itself.

---

[11]Deterding, Sebastion. "A Quick Buck by Copy and Paste", *Gamification Research Network*, Posted 09/15/2011.

One of Deterding's critiques was that, contrary to what Zichermann states in Gamification by Design, serious games and advergames should not be considered examples of Gamification. For those who are unfamiliar with these terms, Wikipedia defines serious games as, "a game designed for a primary purpose other than pure entertainment." In other words, games that are generally built for a productive purpose, such as training, education, healthcare, and the like (Hence, the term "serious").[12].

BusinessDictionary.com defines advergames as, "A video game which in some way contains an advertisement for a product, service, or company."[13] These are games that basically act as interactive advertisement campaigns which draw potential customers onto a website or into a business. When I refer to "shoot-the-duck banner ads" as early and embarrassing forms of marketing gamification, those banner ads are technically classified as Advergames.

As you can see, both definitions have the word "a [video] game" in them, which seems to go against the core essence of what "gamifying" something means. In my own writings, I talk about how you can gamify anything that involves human motivation, as long as it is not already a game, just like how you can't liquefy liquid. You can however, apply better game design to games.

So because advergames and serious games are "games," by that standard you can't really gamify them. Right?

Semantics vs. Value

To me this discussion is non-productive. I would rather spend my time learning about and harnessing the power of games to change the world for the better, instead of debating over classifications of

---

[12]Zichermann, Gabe. "A Teachable Moment" by Gabe Zichermann, Gamification.co, Posted 09/20/2011.

[13]BusinessDictionary entry: "advergames". Accessed 12/13/2014.

terms. What good have you created in the world when you spend your day arguing if something is "a game made for traveling" or "travel gamified"?

But there are people who would say, "No. That great example is a serious game! Gamification is just limited to these things that are really lame." Why do people first define gamification as something lame, and then call it lame? For many years I have also worked on serious game projects and advergames, and if I can utilize that knowledge and experience to help the world, why limit what I can do as a gamification professional just because of some definitions?

I'll share a little secret with you: For the most stringent academics out there, though I claim to have twelve years of gamification experience, I'm actually a fraud. Technically, I have three years of *serious games* experience, three years of *loyalty program* experience, and six years of *gamification* experience, consisting of two distinct periods. Throughout the entire time, I was driven by the exact same vision of applying game principles to impact the world. Call me lazy, but I'd rather just refer to my work as gamification and start producing results that make a difference in the world instead of arguing about what I can and cannot do as a gamification professional.

I've written about how I (along with many "gamification professionals") am not a big fan of the word "Gamification." This is mostly the term that the industry has adopted. I have preferred the term "Human-Focused Design" (as opposed to Function-Focused Design), which is a design process that remembers the human motivations within the system.

On a similar note, I also dislike the term "serious games," as it implies that pure games are not serious – something that millions of serious gamers out there would heavily disagree with. Think how many sports athletes would be offended if they played basketball for a charitable cause, and people called that the "Serious Sports" industry.

Then there are the more "corporate-appealing" terms like Motivational Design, Behavioral Economics, or Loyalty Programs, which have many blends and overlaps with the vague term "gamification." Many out there claim that Loyalty Programs are not considered gamification but would then argue that airline reward miles are one of the best examples of gamification.

Further following the battle semantics, many game-based solution enthusiasts like Sebastian Deterding and Jane McGonigal disagree with so many principles from most of the "mainstream" gamification experts and platforms, that they came out and expressed that, if that was gamification, they wanted nothing to do with it. They prefer the term "Gameful Design" to the word Gamification, which they sometimes regard as the ascended form of gamification[14][15]. Along with Deterding and McGonigal, many other critics of gamification claim that implementations of mainstream gamification are uninspiring and manipulative.

At the end of the day, instead of arguing about what is and isn't included in umbrella terminologies, wouldn't it be much more productive for everyone to say, "Lets make everything better with the lessons we've learned through so many hours of game-play in our lives"?

Of course, people inevitably have long discussions on semantics, and therefore it makes sense to have a structured way of thinking through the entire conversation so you can communicate with your colleagues or superiors.

---

[14]Mcgonigal, Jane. Slideshare: "We don't need no stinkin' badges: How to re-invent reality without gamification", posted 2/17/2011.

[15]Deterding, Sebastian. "The Lens of Intrinsic Skill Atoms: A Method for Gameful Design", *Game Design, College of Arts, Media, and Design, Northeastern University*, 06/27/2014.

Tomato: Fruit or Vegetable

In my opinion, serious games and advergames should actually be included in gamification, as they are utilizing game design to achieve a non-game productive result.

There's often a blurry line between the "is a game" versus the "is not a game" spectrum. For instance, sometimes it is difficult to say whether something is a "game" that trains people, or rather just "training that is gamified." You could say that a game that trains employees to have good conduct is a "serious game," but you can also say that they decided to gamify their training program. According to my own definition, it feels like you could "gamify" training by introducing a "serious game," but you can't gamify that very serious game once it is created. Now since it is already a game, you can only apply better game design to it instead of "gamifying" it. You can see how this conversation can quickly become non-constructive.

In my own TEDx talk in Lausanne, Switzerland, I brought up 8 world-changing concepts in gamification, each representing one of the Core Drives in the previous chapter[16]. I mentioned that my favorite gamification example for Core Drive 3: Empowerment of Creativity & Feedback was the "Serious Game" FoldIt. To some, that statement might have caused a heart attack.

My example for Core Drive 5: Social Influence & Relatedness was DragonBox, which is a learning game; for Core Drive 8: Loss & Avoidance, it was "Zombies, Run!" which is a fitness game to motivate you to run more. Some don't consider them gamification examples since they are already games (as opposed to just plastering badges on something boring).

Again, if there is a way to utilize things we have learned from games to make the world better, why work so hard to limit yourself in

---

[16]TEDx Talks, Chou. "Gamification to Change the World" by Yu-kai Chou. Posted 2/26/2014. URL: http://www.yukaichou.com/tedx

how you approach it? The audience clearly did not care and were inspired about the potentials of evolving everything in our lives into something fun and dynamic, or more game-like.

And for the record, a tomato is biologically classified as a fruit, but is culinarily treated as a vegetable. It probably matters more to the expert horticulturist than to people who just care about preparing and eating a healthy and delicious meal.

Explicit Gamification: Games that Fulfill Non-Game Purposes

Moving away from what is and isn't gamification, I think it is more productive to differentiate types of gamification into two ways based on how they are executed and how different types of players respond to them. The two types of gamification implementations in my own work are "Implicit Gamification" and "Explicit Gamification."

Explicit Gamification involves strategies that utilize applications that are obviously game-like. Users acknowledge they are playing a game, and generally need to opt into playing. An example would be *Dikembe Mutombo's 4 ½ weeks to Save the World*[17]. This is an interesting and quirky "Advergame" launched by Old Spice, where a reknowned basketball legend tries to save the world by accomplishing a series of challenges in an 8-bit video game world before the anticipated "end of the world" in 2012. Of course, Old Spice powerups and placements can be seen repeatedly within the game. This is a clear example of not only applying game design techniques into marketing, but using a game itself to do the marketing.

---

[17] Pro Basketball Talk, NBC Sports, "New online game: Dikembe Mutombo's 4½ weeks to save the world", posted 11/28/2014.

McDonald's Monopoly Game is also a good example of explicit gamification[18]. Everyone knows they are playing a game but the key purpose of the game is to get people to return to McDonald's and eat more french fries - nothing subtle there. We will examine McDonald's Monopoly game in more detail in Chapter 9 regarding Game Technique #16: Collection Sets.

Other interesting examples of Explicit Gamification include the famous serious game *FoldIt* that facilitated AIDS research[19], as well as AutoDesk's *Undiscovered Territory*[20], a game created for selling their very expensive 3D imaging software. There are also explicit gamification examples such as Repair the Rockaways[21], which is a game similar to Farmville, but the number of bricks that are available is determined by how much is donated to support Hurricane Sandy repairs.

Again, these examples are all *games* where people play and opt into, hence "explicit" gamification. The advantage of designing for explicit gamification is that the product is generally more playful and it allows the designer to have more freedom of creativity. The disadvantage is that it could be seen as childish, non-serious, or distracting to some target users such as enterprise firms, banks, or manufacturers. Some corporate managers, upon seeing graphical game-play, immediately feel an aversion to it, though if designed well, the interactive "game" can keep the target user engaged for longer and lead to better business results. Also, more often than not, implementing great explicit gamification usually requires more resources in order to create a high quality game.

---

[18]MentalFloss.com. "13 Things You Might Not Know About McDonald's Monopoly", posted 10/7/2014.

[19]FoldIt Website: http://fold.it

[20]Undiscovered Territory by Autodesk: http://area.autodesk.com/undiscoveredterritory

[21]"Repair the Rockaways", Mother New York.

Implicit Gamification: Human-Focused Design that Utilizes Game Elements

Implicit Gamification is a form of design that subtly employs gamification techniques and the 8 Core Drives of Octalysis into the user experience. Implicit Gamification techniques are filled with game design elements that are sometimes even invisible to the user. This is like a doorknob, where the best designs are the ones that you aren't even aware of but simply use to open the door.

Implicit Gamification examples are often discussed in gamification literature, such as the LinkedIn Progress Bar[22], the intrinsic motivation that drives Wikipedia[23], competitive bidding and feedback system via eBay[24], social comparison and motivation in OPower[25], and Unpredictability and Scarcity within Woot![26].

Upon seeing the progress bar on LinkedIn, most people won't say, "Ah, they're making me play a game! I don't want to play games." The Progress Bar just gently builds a Win-State for the user to see and motivates them to get closer and closer towards the goal. Of course, many of the points, badges, leaderboards, and levels are seen commonly in implicit gamification.

The advantages of implicit gamification is that it is technically easier to implement and can be appropriate in most contexts. The disadvantage of implicit gamification is that this very convenient implementation can often lead to "lazy" design where the subtle game dynamics are incorrectly designed for and sloppily put

[22]Taige Zhang. KISSMetrics Blog. "The Power of The Progress Bar". Accessed 03/01/2015.

[23]Don Tapscott & Anthony D. Williams. *Wikinomics: How Mass Collaboration Changes Everything.* p70. Portfolio Trade. 2006.

[24]Equimedia. "Using gamification to improve website engagement and increase revenue", posted 09/30/2013.

[25]oPower Blog. "Gamification and Energy Consumption", 08/30/2012. Accessed 12/15/2014.

[26]2CO Blog. "E-Commerce & Gamification: Increase Your Sales Like These 3 Pros", posted 6/13/2014.

together. This would lead to something completely ill-formed or ineffective in terms of driving business metrics.

Implicit vs. Explicit Gamification

At the end of the day, one type of gamification is not inherently better than the other. The proper use of Implicit or Explicit Gamification depends on the purpose of the project as well as your target market. Some groups like participating in games; some don't. Some want to have that adrenaline rush when purchasing, while others want to expand their creativity and master a learning curve. Of course, all 8 Core Drives can be implemented into Implicit and Explicit Gamification campaigns, which we will explore in the following chapters.

While it is not useful to argue what gamification includes and excludes, it is very important to understand what types of implementations are most appropriate for your design project based on the objectives, the contextual landscape, and cultural expectations. Again, at the end of the day, gamification should never be a cookie-cutter solution. All games have game elements and game mechanics in them, but most games are not successful, and only a few well-designed games become highly engaging. Gamification requires sophisticated design to actually be effective and create a long lasting relationship between the player and the game maker.

4 Application Fields of Gamification

Now that we have covered the different implementation methods for gamification, we will explore the various applications of gamification in several industries.

In general, the majority of my clients represent four fields that

I consistently see innovating time and time again, indicating a tremendous amount of application and growth in these sectors:

- Product Gamification
- Workplace Gamification
- Marketing Gamification
- Lifestyle Gamification

Product Gamification

Product Gamification is about making a product, online or offline, more engaging, fun, and inspirational through game design. Most companies struggle to create products that customers fall in love with, continue using, and passionately share with their friends. Some of these products have great "functional" purposes, but don't focus on the motivation and Core Drives of their users.

In a previous era, consumers didn't have adequate information and were accustomed to slow gratification. Along with immense barriers for starting new companies, it was not as detrimental for a company to simply assume that customers would use their products - provided that they were marketed correctly. However, people today are spoiled with instant gratification through the Internet, with immersive empowerment and real-time feedback through games, and the constant connection to their social network. Your users, customers, and employees are becoming less tolerant of badly designed products that do not take into account their motivations, especially when they have a variety of competitive alternatives they can choose from.

Many corporations and startups excitedly tell me, "Our product is great! Users can do this; users can do that; and they can even do these things!" And my response to them has been, "Yes, you are telling me all the things your users *can* do. But you have not explained to me *why* the user would do it."

That's the problem with a majority of company products – great technology and functionalities, but no traction. People don't have a reason to go out of their way to use the product. Sometimes, a startup founder tells me, "Hey, Yu-kai, there's no reason why people wouldn't use our product. We save them money, we save them time, and we make their lives better." On lucky days, customers themselves would even say, "Yeah, there's no reason why I wouldn't use your product. It saves me money, it saves me time, and it makes my life better. I'll definitely sign-up sometime tomorrow."

For those who have run startups or launched products before, you know the crucial part of the entire phrase is the ending. When people say they will do it "tomorrow," more often than not it means "never." This is because at this point they are motivated by Core Drive 8: Loss & Avoidance, and specifically by something I call Status Quo Sloth (Game Technique #85) – they are avoiding a change in their habits and behavior.

Remember how we talked about how Gamification is actually Human-Focused Design learned from decades, even centuries of game design experience? When you are launching a new product, its motivational standing is very similar to a game. No one *has* to play a game. You have to do your taxes; you have to go to work; and you really should go to the gym. But you never have to play a game, and let's be honest, oftentimes you shouldn't.

Because games have invested an amazing amount of creativity, innovation, and resources into figuring out how to get people to want to spend more time on them, there are definitely many great lessons you can learn from games for your own products. The key here is to make a product so exciting that customers become obsessed with using your product and are compelled to share how exciting their experiences were to their friends.

Workplace Gamification

Workplace Gamification is the craft of creating environments and systems that inspire and motivate employees towards their work. More often than not, employees show up to work every day just so they can earn a paycheck (Core Drive 4: Ownership & Possession) and to not lose their jobs (Core Drive 8: Loss & Avoidance). As a result, employees only work hard enough to earn their paychecks and to not lose their jobs (if you recall, Core Drives 4 and 8 are great examples of Left Brain, Extrinsic and Black Hat Motivation).

In fact, Gallup's 142-country study shows that only 13% of employees are categorized as "engaged" with their work[27]. In comparison, 24% of the workforce is categorized as "Actively Disengaged," which means they are so unhappy with their work that they minimize their productivity, spread negativity, and even sabotage productive efforts that require them to do more work to keep their jobs.

That is something pretty scary to think about. It means that, chances are, a quarter of your company is poisonous! How can any organism be competitive at anything if 24% of its body is composed of cancer cells?

Contrary to popular self-denial, it is actually not the employees' fault they are disengaged. Companies like Zappos and Google (especially in the old days) are known to get their employees motivated, driven, and excited about their work on a daily basis[28][29]. I firmly believe that everyone has the capacity and the longing to become motivated and driven for something that is worth their cause. It is bad environmental and cultural design that turns good employees into toxic cells.

Of course, you don't need a Gallup study to know how disengaged

---

[27] Gallup. "Worldwide, 13% of Employees Are Engaged at Work", posted 10/8/2013.

[28] David Vise & Mark Malseed. *The Google Story*. p96. Random House, New York, NY. 2005.

[29] Great Place to Work Institute. White Paper: "How Zappos Creates Happy Customers and Employees", 2011.

employees are at work. Just think about how often people close to you complain about their work or their bosses. Think about the movie Office Space, the quintessential comedy about life in a typical bland, rigid, and oppressive company in America[30]. The movie was such a great hit and now a cult classic because people can actually relate to the frustration and disengagement of the characters in the movie (a good example of the "relatedness" piece within Core Drive 5 at work).

Why does that matter? Because research has shown that on average, the companies with disengaged and unmotivated employees only obtain 50% of profits and only 40% of revenue growth when compared to companies with engaged and motivated employees.[31] If I told you that you could double your profits and improve your revenue growth by 250% without opening new markets and without introducing new breakthrough technologies but by simply making your workplace more engaging and motivating, would you do it? Most people would say yes. But from my own personal experience, there will still be people who say no, simply because, "I don't want my employees playing games. It's a distraction!"

Workplace Gamification is critical for today's economy and the future of creative innovation. The Gen-Ys entering the workforce (and they are thirty now) are used to being in environments that provide them Epic Meaning, Relatedness, Autonomy, and more. This will only get worse as the even-younger generation enters the workforce, so it is wise for companies to start setting up the correct motivations systems as early as possible to avoid the devastation of having a surplus in labor but a shortage in talent.

---

[30] SpliceToday. "Five Reasons Office Space is a Cult Classic", 08/01/2013.

[31] Aon Hewitt. "2013 Trends in Global Employee Engagement". 2013.

Marketing Gamification

Marketing Gamification is the art of creating holistic marketing campaigns that engage users in fun and unique experience designed for a product, service, platform, or brand. Not too long ago, people clicked on online ads because, more often than not, they couldn't tell the difference between ads and content. But nowadays, users are becoming more sophisticated in filtering out unwanted promotions, decreasing the effectiveness of many advertisement campaigns (thanks in large part to ad blocker apps too).

Then you have TV commercials, where everyone simply tunes them out, switches the channel away, or just fast-forwards if they have a TiVo. As for other traditional methods like ads on billboards or newspapers...don't even get me started.

In the past decade, Search Engine Marketing (SEM) and Search Engine Optimization (SEO) have proven to be fairly effective techniques for gaining exposure and improving sales. In fact, a search engine is just a large leaderboard, and the industry of Search Engine Optimization is simply the game to climb to the top of that leaderboard. This works because 1) you can target the right people who are searching for your exact solution, and 2) you can target them at the right time they are searching.

However, SEO and SEM still lack the *trust* component in online marketing. If a website you trust and have followed for two years sells something you need, you are likely not going to go searching for a random site on a search engine to purchase from.

Enter Social Media Marketing. Through platforms like blogs, Facebook, Twitter, and Youtube, brands are able to build relationships with potential customers, create unique value, and establish trust that leads to future engagement. Unfortunately, social media platforms are just the delivery channels for engaging content; in and of themselves, they do not motivate or successfully engage with users.

This is where Gamification comes in. Marketing Gamification specifically utilizes game elements and strategies throughout a player's journey by first focusing on why a user would engage with you in the first place. Marketing shouldn't just be one action done from the marketer and one response back from the customer, but should be an entire ecosystem where both the marketer and customer are able to experience fun and feel continuously engaged through a variety of interactions.

Marketing Gamification utilizes the platforms and vehicles described above as well as others: SEO, Social Media, Blogging, Email Marketing, online/offline competitions, viral vehicle strategies, and reward schedules to continuously engage users throughout an engaging and gamified experience.

Lifestyle Gamification

I mentioned in Chapter 1 that my life completely changed when I was struck by an epiphany that I should treat everything like a game. Since gamification is great at motivating people towards certain activities, why wouldn't you apply that to motivate yourself?

Lifestyle Gamification involves applying gamification principles and the 8 Core Drives into daily habits and activities, such as managing your to-do list, exercising more often, waking up on time, eating healthier, or learning a new language.

There are also many technological enablers that make Lifestyle Gamification more popular, including big buzzword trends such as Big Data, Wearable Tech, Quantified Self, and The Internet of Things[32]. The interesting thing about all these trends is that it enables all your activity to be tracked allowing you the ability to manage your Feedback Mechanics and Triggers.

Games have historically been able to track every single action that a player makes. A game would automatically know that this

---

[32] Mckinsey Quarterly. "The Internet of Things", 03/2010 edition.

particular player is on Level three, she has picked up these four items, learned these three skills, talked to these six characters, but not those other three characters, and because of that, this door does not open for the player.

A game remembers everything you have done and customizes your experience based on that. In real-life, most of your "data" is not recorded, and so it is hard to craft a optimized lifestyle. The trend with wearable tech and quantified self finally allows us to track more of our own behavior on a daily basis. Of course, even companies that claim they wield the power of Big Data don't yet compare to the level of customization that gamers take for granted. Many still stick to generalized demographics and non-actionable reports, instead of creating a unique experience for each user in real-time[33].

Lifestyle Gamification branches into a few sectors such as Career Gamification, Health Gamification, Productivity Gamification, and Education Gamification. It can be utilized to gamify big picture activities such as accomplishing your life goals, or very tactical activities such as using a dice to determine how you should reward yourself (which is derived from Core Drive 7: Unpredictability & Curiosity).

Since Lifestyle Gamification fundamentally changed my life, I am extremely passionate about how it can help people achieve their dreams through 1. Finding their game, 2. Analyzing their initial stats 3. Formulating their skill trees, 4. Connecting with allies, 5. Finding the right quests, and 6. Beating the game. Since this is a huge topic that warrants its own book, I won't be spending time in this book covering the topic in detail.

So far we have laid out a wide net that covers many terms, concepts, Core Drives, Experience Phases, natures of motivation, and implementations of design. Don't feel intimidated. For the next

---

[33]Business2Community. "Deliver an Excellent Customer Experience Using Big Data". posted 11/10/2014.

few chapters, we begin to dive deeper into all the things we already talked about, which will allow you to have an even better grasp of the foundation of the Octalysis Framework.

To get the most out of the book, Choose only ONE of the below options to do right now:

Easy: Think about what areas in your life that you would like gamification to help you improve. Is it Product, Workplace, Marketing, or Lifestyle Gamification?

Medium: Identify a gamification example you have encountered before. Is it Explicit or Implicit Gamification? What are the pros and cons for using that type of implementation?

Share what you come up with on Twitter or your preferred social network with the hashtag #OctalysisBook and see what ideas other people have.

Chapter 5: The First Core Drive - Epic Meaning & Calling

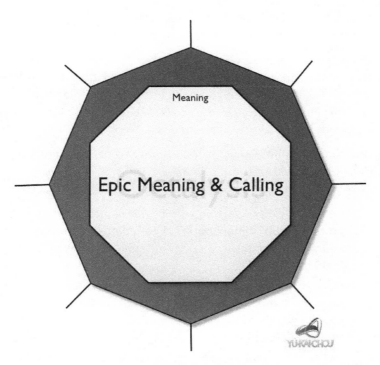

Now that we have established a foundational overview of the Octalysis Framework, it is time to dive deeper into each Core Drive and discover the power and enchantment within.

If there is only one thing you remember after reading this book, it should be to focus on motivation by thinking through the 8 Core Drives instead of focusing on features and functionalities. Of course to do that, you need to be familiar with the 8 Core Drives to wield them correctly, otherwise you may even end up hurting user motivation.

The Core Drive High Above

Epic Meaning & Calling is the First Core Drive of Octalysis Gamification. This is the drive where people are motivated because they believe they are engaged in something bigger than themselves.

Games often trigger the Epic Meaning & Calling Core Drive. In many games, an intro narrative communicates that the world is about to be destroyed, and somehow, you as the player are the only one qualified to save the world. That immediately creates excitement and motivation towards the adventure.

What about real life? Do we ever encounter scenarios where we are driven by Epic Meaning & Calling?

- Have you ever wondered why people contribute to the non-profit website Wikipedia? What would make someone spend hours updating a site that doesn't pay her or even help her build her resume?
- Why are people so loyal to Apple products, to the extent that they know they want to buy the next product, even before they know what it is?
- Why are school rivalries so engaging, driving radical behaviors such as pranks, streaking, violence, while also leading to profit for the schools?
- Can higher purpose also be designed into parenting styles beyond the usual reward and punishment system?

Interestingly, these questions can all be answered by the powerful White Hat Core Drive of Epic Meaning & Calling. In this chapter, we'll attempt to address many of these questions and provide more understanding of this selfless Core Drive.

The Encyclopedia that Pwned Me

"Pwn is a leetspeak slang term derived from the verb own, as meaning to appropriate or to conquer to gain ownership. The term implies domination or humiliation of a rival used primarily in the Internet-based video game culture to taunt an opponent who has just been soundly defeated (e.g., "You just got pwned!")." - Wikipedia[34].

When I founded my first startup company in 2004, I was really excited about finally being an entrepreneur and wanted to promote it everywhere. I learned that anyone can update Wikipedia because it is user-generated, and thought it would be a stellar idea to have my company included within the vast knowledge of Wikipedia. I excitedly spent an entire day crafting a great and informative section about my company - describing when it was founded, by which amazing prodigies, and the problems it set out to solve.

Once completed, I proudly clicked the "publish" button. And there it was: I saw my own company as a Wikipedia article. Woohoo! We were officially on Wikipedia now! What an Epic Win!

However, my bliss of "finally making it in life" was short-lived.

About three minutes after my posting, my post was flagged by a "member of the Wikipedia community," stating that this entity was not significant enough and therefore does not deserve to be on Wikipedia. Five minutes later, a couple others agreed to that point of view, and my post was deleted.

Just like that, my full day's worth of work disappeared within ten minutes.

---

[34]Wikipedia Entry: "pwn": http://en.wikipedia.org/wiki/Pwn. Accessed 12/18/2014.

The first question that came to my mind after the many "dot dot dot" moments and the three ||| lines across my forehead was, "Who are these people? Do they even have lives??"

It sure seems odd that a fairly large group of volunteers go on Wikipedia regularly, not to be enlightened with mind-blowing knowledge, but to police the platform for pests like me who are trying to sneak irrelevant or unimportant content into the Wikipedia.

If you have ever hired interns or entry-level employees and have paid attention to their motivations and feelings, you may know that asking people to do "auditing work" on mountains of pages and to flag outdated content can present an awkward situation. You know that no one enjoys this type of grunt work. These bright young interns and employees really want to learn great skills from you and your company so they can grow as professionals. But there is negligible learning associated with such mundane work. *Someone* in the company has to do the work, and the entry level interns naturally should be the ones that perform the tasks that no one else wants to do.

As a result, you try to tell them to do it as a matter-of-fact, so they may go with the flow without thinking about the demoralizing nature of it. Or you may choose to spend a lot of time explaining to them how this is important to the company and how their work creates great impact. You could also try to make the project sound fun and exciting. At the end of the day, you know in your heart that this is dreadful work, and the young colleague simply needs to "pay their dues" before they can get other interns to do the same.

But when it comes to Wikipedia, people are volunteering their precious time outside of their jobs to do the exact same thing without getting any "real" benefits! When you come home from work, there are lots of things you can do - practice your daily boss-complaining ritual, watch TV, Skype with your significant other, or even play games. People choose to police Wikipedia above all those other activities because they feel like they are protecting humanity's knowledge - something greater than themselves.

When it comes to Epic Meaning & Calling, it's not about what you want as an individual nor about what makes you feel good. Individuals participate in the system and take action not because it necessarily benefits them, but because they can then see themselves as heroes of a grander story. It's about playing your part for the greater good.

And if playing my part does not require me to sacrifice my life as a martyr but simply involves me to spend a couple hours a day monitoring weird activities on Wikipedia, that's a huge bargain and something worth doing.

According to an MIT study, obscenities that are randomly inserted on Wikipedia are removed in an average of 1.7 minutes[35]. These unpaid guardians are definitely keeping *humanity's knowledge* in check diligently.

However, based on my later acquired understanding in human motivation, I also had the hunch that instead of getting paid for pouring hours of their precious labor into Wikipedia, they are also more likely to *pay* Wikipedia instead.

After some research, *whoopee,* I discovered that people who have spent time editing Wikipedia are almost nine times more likely to donate to Wikipedia compared to people who only benefit off it by consuming the valuable information (28% vs 3%)[36]. What's more, donors who don't edit the site have all donated far fewer than three times, while a whopping 80% of donors who have also put labor into Wikipedia have donated five times or more.

Time and time again, we see that, when your system or product demonstrates deep and sincere passion towards a higher vision, others will want to believe in it and get on the journey with you,

[35]Don Tapscott and Anthony D. Williams. *Wikinomics.* P75. Portfolio Publishing. September 28, 2010.

[36]Wikimedia Blog. "Who are Wikipedias Donors". 02/05/2012.

even if it means foregoing financial compensation (which is Core Drive 4: Ownership & Possession).

Even to this day, when people ask me, "Why don't you enter yourself and your Octalysis model onto Wikipedia? You're fairly well-known in your industry right?" I usually try to sidetrack the conversation, as the mere thought of doing so brings back scarring memories of having such an authoritative community unanimously vote that I was not worthy of being mentioned.

"Nah, I'm not that well-known."

Newton's Legacy is Beyond a Fruit

Core Drive 1: Epic Meaning & Calling is generally best communicated during the Discovery and Onboarding Phase of a Player's Journey. You want to communicate very early on exactly why the user should participate in your mission and become a player.

Apple is one of the rare companies that understand this Core Drive, and they managed to instill this into consumers without being user-generated, being an open platform, or pushing for "a charitable cause." Every once in a while, I'll have friends who excitedly tell me, "Hey Yu-kai, I am saving up to buy the next *iPhone*." I would respond, "But you don't even know what's in the new iPhone! What if it sucks?" My friends would then respond with, "I don't care. I'm going to buy the next *iPhone*."

Isn't that a strange phenomenon in a world where electronic consumers are spoiled by a plethora of options out there, with many alternatives touting the same or better capabilities than the iPhone but only a fraction of the cost?

Why are people so crazy about Apple products?

What we are seeing here is that these friends of mine (and I suspect yours too) have first self-identified as an "Apple Person." Therefore, they need to do what "Apple People" do, which is to buy the newest iPhones and Macbooks, as well as act like "Apple Snobs" by walking around and making comments such as, "Oh, I never have that problem because I use a Mac." I myself have also been guilty of this.

When confronted with the topic of many Android phones having better specs and lower prices than the iPhone, my response has usually been, "Well, I don't know about the specs, but I do know that, when I'm using an Android phone, I feel frustrated; but when I'm using an iPhone, I feel happy. That's probably worth something." (By the way, in my opinion, it is often unfair to compare the market share of iPhones to Android Phones as a success measurement, since the iPhone is sold by one company, while Android Phones are sold by over a dozen companies throughout the world. When people freak out about "Oh look! There are more Android users than iPhone users now!", that's basically saying that all these non-Apple smartphone companies combined have surpassed Apple. Big deal.)

So the multi-billion dollar question is: So, how did Apple do this?

Besides offering stellar products with elegant design and meticulous engineering, Apple has been one of the few electronics companies that actually try to sell a higher meaning.

Lets examine two of the most successful commercials in history - both from Apple.

The Crazy Ones in 1984

The first Apple commercial that reached massive fame and success, is the "1984" commercial, aired in 1984's Super Bowl XVIII on CBS[37].

---

[37] Maney, Kevin. "Apple's '1984' Super Bowl Commercial Still Stands as Watershed Event". USA Today. January 28, 2004.

This is a build-up of the popular novel "Nineteen Eighty-Four" by George Orwell, published in 1948 about a futuristic dystopian world where a unified society is controlled and brainwashed by a centralized government[38].

The ad presents a drab, depressive setting - representing a diabolical, yet orderly society; seemingly under the repressive control of a totalitarian influence. In a large room filled with gray, cheerless individuals dress in monotonous grey uniforms, an authoritative voice booms. The masses stare blankly at a huge screen displaying the colossal image of a "dictatorial figure". "Big Brother" is addressing the minions, demanding their obedience, their loyalty, their minds.

Suddenly, a woman in full color runs in and throws a sledgehammer at the big screen, completely shattering it. Then, a deep male voice says, "On January 24th, Apple Computer will introduce Macintosh. And you'll see why 1984 won't be like '1984.'"[39]

Through this commercial, Apple reassures viewers that the world wouldn't be controlled by "Big Brother" - IBM, but would be liberated by Apple's computers.

Though Apple's Board did not really approve of this commercial and it was almost thrown into the garbage bin, when finally aired, it became one of the most successful commercials in history. In his book, *Electric Dreams: Computers in American Culture*, Ted Friedman discusses how powerful the commercial was:

Super Bowl viewers were overwhelmed by the startling ad. The ad garnered millions of dollars worth of free publicity, as news programs rebroadcast it that night. It was quickly hailed by many in the advertising industry as a masterwork. Advertising Age named it the 1980s Commercial of the Decade, and it continues to rank high on lists of the most influential commercials of all time. [40]

---

[38] Orwell, George. Nineteen Eighteen-Four. Secker & Warburg. 1949.

[39] Youtube, "Apple - 1984" URL: http://www.yukaichou.com/1984

[40] Friedman, Ted. *Electric Dreams: Computers in American Culture*, 2005.

Afterwards, Apple's internal team calculated the amount of free airtime that the commercial garnered. They estimated that the total value was about $150 million worth of derived airtime. Within three months of the commercial's appearance, Apple would sell $155 million worth of Macintoshes, establishing itself as the revolutionary computer company on the block.

The second extraordinarily successful Apple marketing campaign to resonate with people was the "Think Different" campaign. This commercial ran in 1998, not long after Apple's Founder, Steve Jobs returned to the board at the end of 1996. [41]

At the time, Apple was a struggling company, and a dying brand. Jobs not only trimmed Apple's product line from over 350 items down to 10, he knew he had to reinvent the Apple brand.

While there are many shorter versions of the ad, the original full text runs:

Here's to the crazy ones. The misfits. The rebels. The troublemakers. The round pegs in the square holes. The ones who see things differently. They're not fond of rules. And they have no respect for the status quo. You can quote them, disagree with them, glorify or vilify them.

But the only thing you can't do is ignore them. Because they change things. They invent. They imagine. They heal. They explore. They create. They inspire. They push the human race forward. Maybe they have to be crazy.

How else can you stare at an empty canvas and see a work of art? Or sit in silence and hear a song that's never been written? Or gaze at a red planet and see a laboratory on wheels? We make tools for these kinds of people.

While some see them as the crazy ones, we see genius. Because the people who are crazy enough to think they can change the world,

---

[41]Hormby, Tom. Low End Mac. "Think Different: The Ad Campaign that Restored Apple's Reputation". 8/10/2013.

are the ones who do.[42]

The series of commercials was a gigantic success. It won dozens of prestigious advertisement awards and made the Apple brand "cool" again. It tangibly spearheaded the transformation of Apple from a dying company into literally the most valuable company in the world within a decade.

Have you noticed something unique and interesting about these ads?

Neither of these campaigns actually talks about computers or electronics. They don't talk about specs, RAM, color screens, or computers. You're not even sure what they sell if you are unfamiliar with the company.

They sold a vision.

When people connect with a statement like, "Because of Apple Computers, 1984 will not be like Nineteen Eighty-Four," many started to think, "Wow! That's amazing! I don't know what they do, but I want to be part of this!"

How do you "be part of it"? You buy the Macintosh computer.

Similarly, when people hear the deep wise voice concluding with, "Because the people who are crazy enough to think they can change the world, are the ones who do," they become inspired and think, "Yes! I've always been hiding my true passions to conform with what people expected of me. I want to be one of the crazy ones that changes the world!" And of course, the way to think different and change the world is to buy an iPod and have a thousand songs in your pocket.

See the power of Epic Meaning & Calling? When every other company is selling how amazing their computers are, Apple sells a vision worth believing in. Interestingly, when Apple was developing

---

[42] Siltanen, Rob. Forbes. "The Real Story Behind Apple's 'Think Different' Campaign". 12/14/2011.

the Think Different campaigns, the first rule was that there would be no products in the commercials. This is so counterintuitive, yet so *Human-Focused.*

As long as Apple can continue to make people think that it is a vision worth believing in, their customers will continue to be "Apple People" and buy Apple products. But if one day Apple does something stupid and breaks the trust of being a vision worth believing in, people will stop blindingly purchase their products and will begin to look at the specs again.

Mjolnir is Not Just a Tool

Some companies have approached me during my all-too-good-sounding soapbox, and asked me, "Yu-kai, this Epic Meaning & Calling thing is great and all, but our product is just a tool. It's not meant to change the world and solve global warming. How can we add Epic Meaning & Calling to a simple tool?"

For this, one of my favorite examples is the mobile app Waze[43]. Waze is a GPS-based mobile navigation app that provides a wealth of user-generated information about travel conditions from the Waze community.

When you think of a GPS, it is purely functional as a tool. You turn left, turn right, and get to your destination - very functional as a tool, but not very epic. So how does an app like Waze create Epic & Meaning & Calling? And how do you instill that meaning without giving users long videos to watch or huge amounts of text to read?

What Waze did was brilliant. In the early days of Waze, when you first download the app, it would show you one image. On the left side of that image, there is a huge snake monster, consisting of a street with many cars stuck on it. This snake monster's name was

---

[43]Waze Website: waze.com

Traffic. On the right side of the image, there were cute little Waze knight characters with swords, shields, and armor, working together to fight this big snake monster.

So now, when you are driving with Waze, you are not just getting to your destination, you are helping a community of brave Wazers fight this Traffic monster! This resonates on a subconscious level because, deep in our hearts, everyone hates traffic with a passion.

Of course, the actual way to beat this Traffic monster is to drive with Waze on. Since Waze is a user-generated system, as you drive with the app on, it will start to gather valuable information about the road conditions that will help the overall driving experience of the community.

The powerful thing about Epic Meaning & Calling, is that it turns otherwise passive users into powerful evangelists of your mission. They are even highly forgiving of your flaws. Because Waze is user-generated, sometimes it is not as accurate. Consequently, in its early days, it took me to the wrong location about three times, and I became apologetically late for my meetings.

You would think that the only purpose of a GPS is to take you to the correct destination, and when it fails in that one purpose, most users would say, "This is a piece of crap. I'm going to delete it!" However, because of the Epic Meaning & Calling Waze has instilled in the hearts and minds of people, when it takes people to the wrong location: instead of deleting it in anger, many people start to panic. "Oh no! The map is broken! I need to go fix it!"

How powerful is that? When you fail in your core competency, instead of deleting the app in anger, users actually rush to solve the problem for you. Again, when it comes to Epic Meaning & Calling, what makes you happy is irrelevant. It's about the bigger meaning and higher vision. And when you see a crack in that higher vision you believe in, you become fearful that others will see that crack and lose faith in the vision. As a result, you take it upon yourself to fix it.

This ties back to the core of Human-Focused Design. You play a game not because you have to, but because you enjoy doing so. You use Waze not because there aren't any other good GPS apps out there that can report to you traffic conditions, hazards, and watchful policemen; you use it because it's fun and you enjoy the experience the most. And just like Mjolnir, Thor's mighty hammer known for leveling mountains[44], this is no ordinary tool- it evens slays traffic!

Despite the many errors and frustrations leading to inaccuracy, within a few years of its founding, the company was acquired by Google for over $1 Billion Dollars. Not bad for selling a vision.

Your Parents are Bigger Than You!

Some people mistake Octalysis and Gamification as technology solutions that are expensive to implement. In reality, they are

---

[44]In Norse mythology and the Comic Book Marvel Universe, Mjolnir is the divine thunder hammer of Thor.

design systems focused on motivation. So if the activity relates to motivation, you can apply gamification to it. Just like games – you can play with a complex 3D Virtual World technology like World of Warcraft, or you can play Hide-And-Seek, something that requires no technology at all. Children these days have both World of Warcraft and Hide-And-Seek available, and the last time I checked they still enjoy Hide-And-Seek.

Because of that, we can even apply Octalysis Gamification to things a bit more abstract, such as parenting. Parents often use two main Core Drives to motivate their children to behave well - Core Drive 2: Development & Accomplishment (reward when the child behaves), as well as Core Drive 8: Loss & Avoidance (punish/ground when the child does not behave).

However, the Chinese culture has "figured out" how to implement Core Drive 1: Epic Meaning & Calling into parenting, through the meaning behind a term known as "孝" . Pronounced "Sheeow," (or "Xiao" in correct Pinyin spelling, but most people don't know what to do with the X). It has no direct English translation, but it is a concept that translates into a belief that since the first day of your birth, you are indebted to your parents who you owe your life and existence to. As a result, "孝" mandates that you need to do everything possible to honor them and lift them up.

There are even popular expressions and idioms in Chinese literature such as "不孝之子，天地不容," which means, "For a son without '孝,' there is no space/tolerance for him in heaven or earth." This means that if you do not have "孝," you are such an epic scumbag you don't even deserve to have ever existed; both the heaven and the earth are so disgusted by your existence they are literally spitting you out of their presence.

Some sources translate the character "孝" to mean "Filial Piety" – "a virtue of respect for one's parents and ancestors." Yet, having grown up with this term I feel it goes a long way beyond the word "respect." When I was little and just started to comprehend the world, I remember reading or listening to the thrilling and sometimes gruesome stories of the well-known children of "孝" in Ancient China. These children would fight tigers to protect their parents, warm up their parents' mattresses before bedtime, or cut off their own flesh in order to feed their hungry parents. In one story, a sixty year old man of "孝" pretends to play on the ground in a humorous way in order to entertain his eighty-year-old parents. (Note: regardless of the tactics to educate such Epic Meaning & Calling, "孝" is truly a great virtue that is slowly being lost in a globalized "flat world" of instant gratification and self-centeredness).

Other examples of "孝" in the *24 Paragons of Filial Piety*[45] include:

- a man sells himself into slavery to pay for his father's funeral
- a man tastes his sick father's stool to understand the health of his father
- a woman cooks part of her own liver to feed her mother
- an eight year old boy attracts mosquitoes to suck his blood so they won't bother his parents
- a father decides to bury his three year old son so he can afford to care for his own mother. While digging the hole, he finds treasure and doesn't have to kill his son.

While some of these actual stories are disturbing, it illustrates how important "孝" is as a value within the culture. Of course, parents aren't just hypocritically manipulating their children. The children who see their parents treat their grandparents poorly, regardless of whether these stories are told to them, will most likely not buy into the Epic Meaning of 孝. This is an important factor in using the motivation elicited through Core Drive 1 - it must feel authentic.

In Traditional Ancient Chinese Culture, when one's parents pass away, they need to dress in mourning attire, abstain from all

---

[45]Jujing, Guo. *The Twenty-four Paragons of Filial Piety*. Yuan Dynasty (1260–1368).

entertainment and sometimes meat, as well as exclude social relationships for three entire years to express his grief. This act is called "守孝", which literally means "guarding 孝" and was traditionally set to be three years because Confucius stated that it takes three years for us to leave our parents' arms; hence, it is proper to spend three years mourning for them. Of course, in today's modern society, much of the three-year mourning is lost and reduced to days or weeks as a symbolic gesture to honor one's parents.

And because of this culture of "孝," Asian children grow up feeling that they have to do a lot for their parents – they have to study hard, they have to get into a good school that their parents can be proud of, they have to support their parents throughout life, they should live with their parents to always be available and make sure everything is taken care of for their parents' life-long wellbeing. As an example, I have a close relative in his fifties who has left his wife and son in the United States for close to a decade now - so he could live with and take care of his aged mother in Taiwan; only visiting his immediate family a few times each year.

In contrast, in many Western societies where the concept of "孝" is not as prevalent, people still respect their parents immensely. However, once they form their own families, they generally become more disconnected and simply bring their children to grandpa and grandma once or twice a year, instead of constantly making life decisions that are tailored to their parents.

Even today, if my parents told me I don't have 孝 because of any behavior, it would crush me emotionally and motivate me towards almost anything to amend for it. Just because I understand the nature of the motivation does not mean I am exempt from it. It is something deeply ingrained within me and my values. In similar faith, my parents have never made that accusation towards me, because it would be one of the greatest insults a parent could give a child. It is that serious and tangible when it comes to this type of motivation.

Game Techniques within Epic Meaning & Calling

Now that you have the main concept of Core Drive 1: Epic Meaning & Calling, the question is how to implement it into your experiences. Below I introduce a few Game Techniques that, if designed correctly, can bring out the sense of Epic Meaning & Calling. Keep in mind, in my terminology, when I mention Game Techniques, I mean techniques that incorporate Game Elements (which includes Game Mechanics) to drive motivation.

You will also start to notice many "Game Technique numbers (#s)" that follow each Game Technique mentioned. These Game Technique #s are part of a scavenger hunt that originated from my website YukaiChou.com. My readers would try to collect all the numbers, which will one day result in some fascinating things that one can do with Octalysis down the road.

One key thing to remember is that the entire premise behind the Octalysis Design Framework is that one should not be too stuck on game mechanics, game techniques, or any outer appearances of a design. Rather, one should focus on the Core Drives and how it brings out motivation in an actionable manner. The Game Techniques, as well as the associated #s, are all just bells and whistles for great motivational design. If you do not focus on the Core Drives, it will simply have the *Shell* of an engaging game, not the *Essence*.

Narrative (Game Technique #10)

Most games start with a narrative that gives the player some context about **why** they should play the game. Many of them are related to saving the world, a princess, solving a case, or even just helping a dragon or crocodile take a bath. So why don't we use narrative to give people context in other things?

One of the more effective ways to instill Epic Meaning & Calling into your user base is through an engaging Narrative. This allows you to introduce a story that gives people context for a higher meaning through interacting with your company, product, or website.

Zamzee, a "wearable technology" company for children, uses narratives to instill epic fantasies into children to motivate them to exercise more. Through its online software interface, Zamzee gives kids fantasy quests, such as becoming a sorcerer's apprentice. In order to learn your first spell, you run up and down the stairs 15 times. Even though the action itself is disconnected from the narrative, just having them make-believe a magical meaning inspires the kids to exercise more because they are now motivated by their own imaginations. Zamzee shows that kids who participate in these imaginary missions move 59% more than kids who don't[46].

Humanity Hero (Game Technique #27)

If you can incorporate a world mission into your offerings, you can gain even more buy-in during the Onboarding process. One company that does an incredible job of instilling a sense of Humanity Hero is TOM's Shoes, which sends one pair of shoes to a child in a third-world country whenever you place an order with them[47]. The idea that you can help underprivileged kids every time you make a purchase is extremely motivating. Additionally, when customers wear the shoes, they let others know that they are helping the world, which is a form of Trophy Shelf (Game Technique #64) within Core Drive 5: Social Influence & Relatedness.

FreeRice is another example that utilizes the Humanity Hero technique. FreeRice.com is a website that donates 10 grains of rice for every correct answer to the educational questions posted on their

---

[46]Zamzee Blog. "New Research Shows Zamzee Increases Physical Activity by Almost 60%". 09/06/2012.

[47]Groden, Claire. Times. "TOMS Hits 10 Million Mark on Donated Shoes". 06/26/2013.

site. The funding comes from the ads and the number of page views they generate from those answering the questions. To date, FreeRice has donated 6100 metric TONS of rice, consisting of 93 billion grains of rice and enough to feed 10 million people.[48]

Often, if you can tie your system to a cause that many people care about, you can build an entire business on the goodwill of others.

Elitism (Game Technique #26)

Allowing your users or customers to form a prideful group based on ethnicity, beliefs, or common interests also makes them feel like they are part of a larger cause. Elitism instills group pride, which means each member tries to secure the pride of the group by taking specific actions. The group also attempts to frustrate its rivals, which can lead both groups upping their actions to beat the competition.

This is why University Rivalries are so engaging. When I was attending UCLA (University of California, Los Angeles), it was very difficult to not feel the strong rivalry against USC (University of Southern California). Starting from orientation as a Freshman (Onboarding), there is no lack of content and jokes that sets the scene of the USC rivalry. During sports seasons, this rivalry reaches its pinnacle, with both sides aggressively, sometimes violently, insulting each other. There are even T-Shirts printed with the text, "My 2 favorite teams are UCLA, and whoever is playing USC."

---

[48]Burbano, Jaime. Gamificators Blog. "Gamification for a Better World". 10/27/2013.

Both sides believe that this rivalry is bigger than themselves, and with this newly instilled sense of Elitism, they engage in many irrational activities because they "should" as a proud representative of that school.

Even though rivalries are engaging or even fun for students, who actually benefit the most from these rivalries? More often than not, it is the universities themselves. By creating an outside enemy that students "should hate with a passion," it creates more "school spirit" where students bond together and commit *Desired Actions* in frenzies. Tickets to games against USC sell out quickly, with everyone gearing up with UCLA merchandise and war paint. More importantly, students feel a stronger tie towards their Alma Mater, which means that later on in their careers, they are more prone to donate to their schools since that's what successful alumni "should" do.

Similar in effect to the concept of "孝," I too implicitly feel that I "should" donate to my Alma Mater. Not because of any personal gains, but for a purpose beyond my own selfish and family matters. In one of my speeches, an attendee asked me, "I would like to figure out how to add more alumni participation for our university. Academically, we rank really well, but for some reason, our alumni don't feel proud coming here and just see us as a stepping stone. They rarely participate or donate!" My response to him was, "Sounds like you need to add more *school spirit* to students while they are still attending. I'm guessing you don't have competitive athletic teams or big school rivalries?" "No, we don't! How did you know?"

Even a colleague of mine, Jerry Fuqua, chose to attend UCLA many years ago over having a full scholarship into Harvard and other Ivy League schools because he loved UCLA's basketball team. Another friend of mine who aced all his Calculus exams as a Freshman in High School also chose to attend the University of Kansas over other more prestigious school because he grew up being a fan of the KU Jayhawks. If you ever wondered if it was worth an educational institution's budget to support an expensive athletic team, now you at least see the justification.

Another great example of Elitism is demonstrated by the microlending platform Kiva.org, which allows developed countries to pseudo-donate their money to help third world country villagers start their small businesses and help sustain their families. To create a sense of Elitism, Kiva.org created groups and published statistics that allowed Christians and Atheists to compare their giving against each other, to see who contributes more money in helping third world countries.[49]

The Christians believed that, since the Bible tells them to love God and love one another beyond all things, they should demonstrate generosity to the world and help those in need. As a result they increased their contributions. The Atheists, on the other hand, wanted to prove that one does not need to believe in a god to simply be kind to fellow human beings, so they also increased their contributions. Again, both sides contributed more than they would have otherwise, simply because they felt they were doing it for a greater purpose than themselves - protecting their group's reputation. (Disclaimer: I am myself a person of Christian faith).

Beginner's Luck (Game Technique #23)

Beginner's Luck focuses on the *Calling* part in Epic Meaning & Calling. Calling makes people think they are uniquely destined to do something. With Beginner's Luck, people feel like they are one of the few chosen to take action—which makes them much more likely to take it. If a gamer, upon the first day of playing a game, randomly earns one of the most powerful swords in the game, one that even veteran players couldn't easily obtain, chances are he isn't going to quit on day one. He'll likely be using that powerful sword to kill monsters fanatically until the next hook in the game shows up.

The game designer would likely also add in Social Influence & Relatedness (Core Drive 5) by designing in Trophy Shelves (Game Technique #64), which are mechanisms that allow the user to implicitly show off what they are proud of. If the game designer also adds Scarcity & Impatience (Core Drive 6) through Moats (Game Technique #67) by telling the user he can only equip this sword once he defeats all the adversaries at a particularly difficult level,

---

[49]Lebo, Lauri. ReligionDispatches.org. University of Southern California."Atheists and Christians Compete to Give More". 1/19/2011.

the user now becomes obsessed and tries to figure out all sorts of ways to conquer that level.

Free Lunch (Game Technique #24)

Along the lines of the "Calling" theme, giving freebies (that are normally not free) to selected people in such a way that it binds them to a larger theme can make customers feel special and encourage them to take further action.

For example, Spoleto, a Brazilian restaurant chain with over 200 restaurants throughout Brazil, Spain, and Mexico, gave a literal free lunch to any female who told them she was beautiful, in celebration of International Women's Day.[50] This helped promote a positive message and made women feel special for that day. This will likely bring them back in the future too, as this venue is now associated with a positive memory that makes them feel unique.

Believability is Key

Even though Epic Meaning & Calling is powerful "beyond measure," it can also backfire and fail in epic proportions. As you use these concepts, keep in mind that you can really turn people off when you're appearing disingenuous in your efforts to create Epic Meaning and Calling.

For example, if a major gasoline company that was known to "profit from evil" tried to convince people to use their brand by saying, "pumping with us protects the planet." Customers would not only be unimpressed, they would likely feel insulted. Or if a certain fast food conglomerate that is known for cheap unhealthy foods (that happen to never decompose) runs a marketing campaign that says, "Eating our food protects your health and your family," people would likely see that as a manipulative slap in the face.

---

[50] AOTW. "Spoleto Restaurant: Beautiful women don't pay". Accessed 1/20/2015.

Even in fantasy make-believe settings like *Zombies Run*, where users are motivated to run more because they are trying to save their village from hypothetical zombies, you want to make sure the user is prepared to believe in the higher fantasy meaning in that context. Pretending that there are zombies in the room during large corporate board meetings in order to get everyone to stand up more often would likely not fare all that well. (So please don't tell your Board Directors that you did it because you read my book on Epic Meaning & Calling).

Once you have firmly established believability in your Epic Meaning & Calling, you will have a good chance of applying this Core Drive effectively to bring out the fun and selflessness out of people.

Core Drive 1: The Bigger Picture

Core Drive 1: Epic Meaning & Calling is the prime White Hat Core Drive within the Octalysis Framework, and is often very powerful in the Discovery and Onboarding Phases of a player's journey. It underlines the purpose behind the activity and strengthens all the other seven Core Drives when it is introduced correctly. In later chapters, we will also explore how some companies utilize Epic Meaning & Calling (among other White Hat Gamification Core Drives) to inspire their employees to work with more passion and stay in the organization, even when other companies offer them greater monetary incentives.

Core Drive 1: Epic Meaning & Calling's weakness lies in the difficulty of implementing believability, as well as the lack of urgency within the motivation. While people constantly aspire to become part of something bigger and would feel great if they actually took the actions, they will often procrastinate and delay those very actions. Thus, to create desirable behavior, the gamification designer needs the help of the other Core Drives within Octalysis.

To get the most out of the book, Choose only ONE of the below options to do right now:

Easy: Think of an example where Core Drive 1: Epic Meaning & Calling motivated you or others to take certain actions. Does it make people act more selflessly?

Medium: Identify a project you are working on. Think about whether there are ways to install Core Drive 1: Epic Meaning & Calling into the experience. Can you tie the experience into a bigger theme?

Share what you come up with on Twitter or your preferred social network with the hashtag #OctalysisBook and see what ideas other people have.

New Section Unlocked! - Get Inspired

Now that you are becoming familiar with the Octalysis Framework, check out my TEDx talk on how eight different world-changing products utilize each of the 8 Core Drives to make the world a better place. The TEDx talk can be accessed at http://yukaichou.com/tedx, or you can simply go on Google and search "Gamification Tedx."

Chapter 6: The Second Core Drive - Development & Accomplishment

Development & Accomplishment is the Second Core Drive of the Gamification Framework Octalysis. This is the Core Drive where people are driven by a sense of growth and a need to accomplish a targeted goal. It is what focuses us on a career path, generates our enthusiasm and commitment to learning a new skill, and ultimately motivates us by showing us how far we've come and how much we've grown.

Many people have memories of their kindergarten teachers giving them gold stars to emphasize good behavior. Even though these stickers don't become real prizes, children are often extremely intent on obtaining more stars and will focus on determining how best to gain them. That's a very straightforward demonstration on the effects of Development & Accomplishment and how easy it is to add them into an experience.

This is also the most common implementation of gamification we see in the market, as most of the PBLs – points, badges, and leaderboards – appeal heavily to this drive.

Development & Accomplishment in Games

Almost all games show you some type of progress towards the *Win-States*. A Win-State is often a scenario where the user has overcome some sort of challenge - that's the "win" in the Win-State. Games break down user challenges into stages to help the user feel like there is always progress.

Our brains have a natural desire to achieve goals and to experience growth in order to feel that real progress in life is being made. We need Win-States. Games can sustain long forty-hour or even four-thousand-hour player journeys because they use distinctive stages and boss-fights to recognize user accomplishment along the way.

To display that sense of accomplishment, some games show you points, others use levels, badges, stages, progress bars, better looking gear, victory animations... the list goes on. However, just because you *see* your progress through these elements does not necessarily mean you *feel* accomplished.

The key to Core Drive 2: Development & Accomplishment is to make sure users are proud of overcoming the challenges that are set out for them. Jane McGonigal, renowned game designer and Ph.D. in Performance Studies, defines games as "unnecessary obstacles that we volunteer to tackle." [51] (This is originally defined by the philosopher Bernard Suits).

McGonigal points out that challenges and limitations are what make a game fun. For example, if golf was just a game without any limitations, every player would just pick up the ball and put it into the hole to win. Everyone would score high, and every individual who has outgrown the "putting a round peg through a round hole" game will probably feel bored.

By adding unnecessary obstacles, such as requiring the use of a strange stick, certain distances, and landscape hazards, golf becomes fun because the player actually feels accomplished once such challenges are overcome. Gamification aims to integrate that feeling of Development & Accomplishment into everyday experiences within your product or service.

The First Gamification Site that I was Addicted to

One of the most popular blog posts on my website is a list of the "Top 10 eCommerce Gamification Examples that will Revolutionize Shopping." At the top of this list is eBay (full disclosure – I worked with eBay on a couple projects in 2013)[52].

eBay.com is an online auction site that was founded in 1995, fairly early in the World Wide Web era. It became one of the largest Dot Com boom successes, and as of today it is one of the leading tech

---

[51]Jane McGonigal. *Reality is Broken*. P22. Penguin Group. New York, NY. 2011.

[52]Chou, Yu-kai (Hey, that's me!). YukaiChou.com. "Top 10 eCommerce Gamification Examples that will Revolutionize Shopping". Posted 7/7/2013.

companies in Silicon Valley. It is also one of the earliest eCommerce companies that built gamification into its core DNA. If you plan to create a simple, generic eCommerce site, it's not necessarily intuitive to include a competitive bidding system or a scored buyer-seller feedback interface. Nor is it obvious to provide a "path to level up" through achievement symbols such as Yellow, Purple, and Golden Stars, as well as creating a Power Seller status system.

eBay was the platform that triggered the founding of my first business. Without eBay, it is very likely that I would not have become an entrepreneur, and as a result you would not have this book to read.

When I was about to enter UCLA as a Freshman, there was a local barbecue event where second year students shared their experience and tips with us "newbs." At that event, there was a drawing for two football tickets to the first game of the season. I was conveniently selected to be the student to draw a single name out of a box to win these two tickets. Call it Divine Will, fate, coincidence, or what have you; I drew my own name out of the box.

When I announced it was my own name, everyone was astonished, and the event organizer joked with a wink, "Congratulations! Just make sure you don't sell it on eBay! We'll check!"

At the time, I thought "What's eBay? I've heard about it before." I did some research about eBay, and shortly after I sold my two tickets through the platform (I hope the barbecue organizers don't read my book).

That one transaction was surprisingly thrilling and fun for me. When I received my first bid from an anonymous stranger on the Internet, I almost jumped for joy (cultural joke: but I did not get stuck). Shortly after, I became obsessively glued to the screen after another bidder joined in on the "war."

During the few days of the listing, it was the only thing on my mind. I continuously checked my listing, trying to see if people would outbid the last bidder. Of course, it was life-endingly depressing when no one had put in a new bid after my *fourth* three-minute check! By the way, this is what I now call a "Torture Break" (Game Technique #66), where a user must wait an interval of time regardless of their actions, a game technique to be explored under Core Drive 6: Scarcity & Impatience.

When I finally sold the two tickets for a few hundred dollars, I was ecstatic. I felt that I had just accomplished something great (for a person just graduating high school). I made my first money as a seller! I started to find other things to sell on eBay. During this time, I noticed that the final price of an eBay auction is usually determined by what part of the day the listing ends. This is because most people like to wait for the last few minutes to put their bids in and steal the deal.

In that frenzy, people quickly outbid each other before the time runs out. This effect is a combination of a Countdown Timer (Game Technique #65) and a Last Mile Drive (Game Technique #53), where users feel that they are so close to the goal that they rush to complete it. For the record, these mostly employ Black Hat techniques.

Observing this effect, I began a small business buying and selling TI-83 Calculators, which was often a high school and college math class requirement. I would start to buy all the TI-83s I could find that ended their listings at 2AM, when no one was bidding against me, typically for $40. I would then resell them with auctions ending late in the afternoon when everyone was bidding against each other, typically for $60. As opposed to the boring mathematical theories from economics class and the social intermingling within college parties, this was the game that I needed to master.

True to the gamified spirit, when I sold my tenth item on eBay, I received an email from eBay itself! It was a certificate sent from this person named "Meg," congratulating me as a valuable eBay seller and giving me a Yellow Star Certificate! I was so excited about this Achievement Symbol (Game Technique #2), that I printed it out and put it on my dorm room for many years. Even today, I think it is still sitting somewhere in a box at my parents' home.

Even though this was not the original certificate I received, it looked something like the image below.

Eventually I would sell a plethora of other items, including new electronic products such as digital cameras, iPods, GPS devices, and even some string quartet songs I wrote! In my second year of college, at the height of my eBay career, I received a 100% satisfaction rating with over 1,100 positive feedbacks. As a result, I was awarded a Red Star ranking.

"I overpaid for my product. Take that, suckas!"

Based on the above, it's easy to see how eBay uses Core Drive 2: Development & Accomplishment to make the experience more fun and addictive for the Seller. But what about the Buyer? What makes a buyer want to continuously buy on eBay?

From the buyer's perspective, the genius thing about eBay is that when a purchase is made, you aren't just buying something online like you do on other eCommerce platforms. No, instead of feeling that you are just acquiring some items in exchange for your money, you feel like you've actually **Won!**

Sure, after some adrenaline-filled bidding at the end, you may have ended up paying ten percent more than you otherwise would have, but you at least achieved victory over those eleven other bastards who were bidding against you!

"Take that suckas! It's mine!"

Instead of just paying your way to success, which anyone could do easily, you worked hard and actually achieved a Win-State! You feel accomplished, and the value of that happiness far exceeds the extra money you end up paying for the item. On eBay, you are not paying to purchase; you are paying to play.

This is similar to games where people spend money in order to beat difficult levels that they can't overcome. To be exact, people aren't buying *victories*. If, immediately after people pay the game studio, a message pops up and says, "Congratulations! You have won!", very few people would feel excited. Anyone could just pay money and get something. What gamers are paying for, is the feeling of being awesome. They pay to get powerful weapons or boosters that allow them to defeat a bunch of enemy monsters quickly, ultimately achieving dominating victory.

Another example that builds on the same principle is the General

Mills brand Betty Crocker cake mixes. When it first launched many decades ago, it was designed to be the easiest cake mix for stay-at-home-moms to make, where they just have to add water to the powdered mix and then stick it into the oven for delicious cakes to come out. Unfortunately, sales were fairly stagnant and the company eventually hired business psychologists to help determine why.

One of the hypotheses was that the cake mixes were so easy to make, customers didn't *feel* they were actually baking, and therefore did not have a sense of accomplishment or competence. Based on this concept, instead of making the process easier by removing steps, General Mills decided to *add* additional steps to the process. They decided to remove the conveniently powdered eggs from their Betty Crocker cake mixes and required the bakers to add in their own fresh eggs before putting them into the oven.

To many's surprise, the product immediately became a breakout success. By adding that extra step of throwing in an egg yourself, people *felt* that they were actually baking a delicious dessert to compliment a meal. This made them feel great about themselves and their contributions to the family.[53]. The philosophy of, "Games are unnecessary obstacles that we volunteer to tackle" can be seen clearly here, where adding a few extra steps increased Core Drive 2: Development & Accomplishment within the experience.

As a result of the gamified systems mentioned above, many claim that being on eBay is "addictive." It eventually transformed from a personal hobby to a Fortune 200 company that is worth over $70 Billion.[54]

[53] Marks, Susan. *Finding Betty Crocker: The Secret Life of America's First Lady of Food.* Fesler-Lampert Minnesota Heritage. p68. 03/19/2007.

[54] Fortune.com. Fortune 500 2014: eBay Inc.

What about Amazon?

After looking at eBay, you might ask, "What about Amazon? Aren't they even more successful? I don't see any gamification on their platform." It's true, founded in 1994, just a year before eBay, Amazon is now a Fortune 50 giant worth around $150 Billion, and they don't do "gamification."

Well, they don't do gamification as in integrating points, badges, narratives, avatars or paths to leveling up. However, they have spent a great amount of resources nailing down many techniques within Human-Focused Design and many of the 8 Core Drives, which are the backbone drivers of successful games.

If you recall from previous chapters, good Implicit Gamification is often invisible like a doorknob – you don't even notice it's there, but you do use it to open and close a door without thinking. Through Amazon's optimized design, we can see a few Core Drives being implemented with great effect.

First of all, the main Core Drive behind Amazon's business is Core Drive 4: Ownership & Possession. As mentioned in Chapter 3, the premise behind this Core Drive is that if you feel like you own something, you tend to want to improve it, protect it, and get more of it.

Amazon has worked hard to streamline this process of Ownership & Possession. It is an optimized engine that allows you to own and possess things quickly, accurately, and without hassle. It has established itself as the prime place to "get more stuff," and you know you are likely getting the cheapest bargain on the market. With Amazon, you know you can own more, faster.

Also, Amazon is constantly learning about your preferences and personalizing what you see to who you are, something I call the Alfred Effect (Game Technique #83). As it does so, the sense of Ownership & Possession grows even more as people now identify it as a unique "My Amazon" experience that no other eCommerce site can provide.

Don't fall behind your neighbors!

Accompanying the Alfred Effect is Amazon's Recommendation Engine, now infamous in the personalization industry. Amazon's recommendation engine, according to Amazon themselves, led to 30% of their sales[55]. That's a fairly significant factor for a company that is already making billions of dollars every month. In fact, JP Mangalindan, a writer for Fortune and CNN money, argues that a significant part of Amazon's 29% sales growth from the second fiscal quarter of 2011 to the second fiscal quarter of 2012 was attributed to the recommendation engine.[56]

And what does this recommendation engine look like?

"Customers Who Bought This Item Also Bought."

Amazon quickly realized that, by learning about what other people similar to you are buying, you have a much higher tendency to buy the same items too. Can you think about a Core Drive that pushes this behavior?

You may have guessed it (but I won't judge you if you haven't) - Core Drive 5: Social Influence & Relatedness. By knowing what other, similar people are buying, social proof and relatedness help

---

[55]Christopher Matthews. Time. "Future of Retail: How Companies Can Employ Big Data to Create a Better Shopping Experience". 08/31/2012.

[56]Mangalindan, JP. Fortune. "Amazon's Recommendation Secret". 07/30/2012.

consumers make decisions with greater confidence. This helps Amazon increase their sales and subsequent up-sells.

Of course, another "Social Influence & Relatedness" factor of Amazon that heavily contributed to its early success, was the millions of user reviews on books and other items.

"My friend Bob says the doctor is wrong – and he reads a lot about health."

Studies on Trust and Reputation in Peer-to-Peer Networks by researchers like Yao Wang and Julita Vassileva of the University of Saskatchewan, as well as Minaxi Gupta, Paul Judge, and Mostafa Ammar of the Georgia Institute of Technology found that the average consumer prefers and trusts reviews by peers over those by professional critics[57][58]. This is somewhat odd, because professional critics have made it their life mission to distinguish the good from the bad. For every published review, they would spend a significant amount of time collecting all the necessary information, going through the experience, just to write a well thought-out piece reflecting their depth of knowledge and commitment.

But when it comes down to it, consumers seem to prefer the thoughts and opinions of other consumers, who likely do not have the same level of sophistication and understanding with the product, let alone spent the same amount of time experiencing and reviewing the item in question. At the end of the day, we value the thoughts of people we can relate to, often more than the voice of authoritative experts.

---

[57]Yao Wang and Julita Vassileva. University of Saskatchewan. *Trust and reputation model in peer-to-peer networks.* 2003.

[58]Minaxi Gupta, Paul Judge, and Mostafa Ammar. Georgia Institute of Technology. *A Reputation System for Peer-to-Peer Networks.* 2003.

In Amazon's review interface, you see a statement such as, "4.6 out of 5 stars," followed by a "leaderboard" of reviews that expresses the voting sentiments of the community. For the top review, "400 of 445 people found the following review helpful." Coincidently, the review was given by "Book Shark," who is labeled a "Top 500 Reviewer."

Oh wait, there are also leaderboards, community voting, and status labeling on Amazon? If you thought Amazon does not use gamification, think again. While you are at it, try to remember what was the color of the last doorknob you held.

Never make Users Feel Dumb

I'd like to take a moment here to point out that though the focus of this chapter is on Core Drive 2: Development & Accomplishment, it is almost impossible to evaluate a good experience or product without considering the other seven Core Drives, as they intricately work together to create a unified and motivating experience. Even though the success on Amazon is seen through many other Core Drives, such as Scarcity & Impatience, as well as Empowerment of Creativity & Feedback, let's refocus back on the theme of Development and Accomplishment.

Beyond improving one's ranks and obtaining badges, a very important type of emotional accomplishment is to "feel smart." We all like to feel capable and competent, and feelings of being incompetent or powerless can create some of the most scarring moments of our lives.

A product that makes users feel stupid, no matter how great the technology, is often a failing product. From my experience, **if a user spends four seconds on an interface and can't figure out what to do, they feel stupid and will start to disengage emotionally**.

The Google Search Engine makes sure this doesn't happen. Before Google became "Google," Yahoo! was the quintessential "search engine." giant. However, Yahoo! saw itself as an online portal where people could discover new content instead of being a pure search engine.

Interestingly, when the Google Founders wanted to sell their search engine to Yahoo for a measly $1 million, Yahoo turned it down, even though they recognized Google to be a more efficient search engine that took people to their destinations faster. This was because it went against Yahoo's portal strategy of showing users many links to click on, leading to many more clickable links (a Core Drive 7: Unpredictability & Curiosity Core Drive play). And along the way, offering advertising links to click on.[59]

Consequently, when you go to Yahoo's homepage, you will see a great deal of content along with links. Even though it does drive many clicks and exploratory activities for many users, it can be a

---

[59]David Vise & Mark Malseed. *The Google Story*. p42. Random House, New York, New York. 2005.

bit daunting or even paralyzing for users who can't navigate and decide through so many choices. Google, on the other hand, focuses their strategy on the Development & Accomplishment Core Drive.

When you go on Google.com, you usually see only two things: Google's logo, and a search box. There is almost no chance for you to feel confused about what to do next. You type your inquiry in the search box. Even if you are not exactly sure what to search (a moment of feeling partially incompetent), the auto-fill function jumps right in to give you suggestions.

Google understood this key point very early on. According to the book The Google Story by David A. Vise and Mark Malseed, the company was so clearly focused on the strategy of having a clean homepage, that they turned down many great monetization opportunities which could be leveraged from their launch point; even till today.[60] It is said that an organization's strategy is not what they choose to do, but what they insist on not doing.

Unfortunately, the understanding and sophistication of making users feel smart from Google doesn't always spill into their other product lines. Google+ is a common example of how a great technology can make users feel dumb and lose traction.

Even though Google likes to tout how Google Plus' "active users" count makes it the second largest social network in the world, the average consumer understands that it is because they were some- how "tricked" into the Google+ interface while using YouTube or Gmail, something I call *brute force distribution* (no game technique here). Despite hundreds of millions of "active users," according to ComScore and Nelson, average Google+ usage time per user every month is less than 7 minutes. Compared to the 400 minutes per month from Facebook, it clearly isn't the place everyone is hanging out at.

---

[60]David Vise & Mark Malseed. *The Google Story.* p88. Random House, New York, New York. 2005.

Other web savvy users also continue to use Google+ because of alleged Search Engine Optimization advantages for marketing, which is credited to the brilliant work done by the search engine itself rather than the merits of the social platform.[61] After all, some people would even eat insects if it helps them increase their search rankings.

Despite being the "number two social network in the world," if you look at Google's own blog, with its user audience being the most biased towards Google products, you will often see way more tweets and Facebook Likes than Google +1's on each post. An unnamed Google employee once told me, "At Google, there's this joke, 'If you are organizing a party and you don't want anyone to know about it, share it on Google Plus.'"

Star of Bethlehem - Guiding Users Forward

If you have played the popular hit game Candy Crush, have you ever wondered why when you don't make a move for a few seconds, the game shows you a "Glowing Choice" (Game Technique #28) of a *possible* solution that is often not the optimal way to match the gems? In almost all cases, if you just blindly follow the *Glowing Choices*, you will end up losing the game. Why would they show me a solution that does not make me win? Is this a trap?

The truth is, Candy Crush understands that, feeling a sense of progress and ultimately losing is much better than feeling stuck and confused. If you play the game through and lose, your natural reaction is to start a new game; but if you get stuck and can't find three gems to match for a long period of time, you may just abandon the game altogether and start doing other things. Perhaps the expert

---

[61] Gareth Llewellyn. Quora.com: "Are Facebook and Twitter the best tools for social media marketing?". 5/14/2013.

consultant has already answered the email you just sent out - better check now!

Back to Amazon; Amazon makes people feel smart when they buy things. They do it in many different ways. First of all, Amazon tries to avoid the 4-Second Rule by making sure users always know what to do next.

On this screenshot of a product listing, most of the screen is white with black text, but graphically, the experience guides the user towards two Desired Actions. The first is the "Look Inside" button on the book, displayed in vibrant colors with a pointed arrow, similar to the *interactive onboarding tutorials* found within games. This is another example of a Glowing Choice, where a user is visually guided by obvious signs towards how to proceed.

The second Desired Action is the green zone on the right, with two time-tested orange action item buttons that serve as the real conversion metric for the business. Interestingly, the two orange buttons don't even have the same color, with the "Buy Now with 1-Click" showing a cursor index finger pressing a button within the button.

It is important to note that this Desired Action is the only part of the page that is visually "colorful," and the eyes automatically are guided to that direction. I call that a Desert Oasis (Game Technique #38), where visually nothing else is prominent besides the main Desired Action. The Desert Oasis looks green and juicy and it subconsciously suggests that there is a Win-State behind this option.

Finally, Amazon never forgets to show you a bogus List Price that is crossed out, a real selling price below it, and it tells you the amount and percentage of your savings if you didn't pay the bogus List Price. This again makes people feel like they are making the smart choice for getting a great deal. A misunderstanding of this concept led J.C. Penney to fire their former CEO Ron Johnson, widely known for pioneering the Apple Store, after a "Fair and Square" campaign of removing "fake" discount numbers, resulting in one of the biggest failures in retail history.[62]

The Premium Price of Smarty Pants

Bogus prices that make users *feel* smart are seen everywhere. In the Behavioral Economics Bestseller book *Predictably Irrational*, Dan Ariely describes a case where a group of MIT students are presented with a choice between paying $59.00 for a one-year subscription to the digital edition of the Economist magazine or to pay $125.00 for a one-year subscription to both the digital and print editions of the magazine. The majority of the students (68%) chose the digital version for $59.00.[63] Who wants to pay $66 more for physical copies of magazines when you can just read it digitally for half the price anyway?

However, when another $125.00 option to buy a one-year subscription for *just* the printed editions of the magazine was inserted in the middle of the above two options, it changed everything. Technically, this shouldn't do anything right? Why would anyone get a $125 subscription for printed editions of the magazine when they could get printed *and* digital editions for the same price at $125? And we already determined above that very few people wanted both

---

[62] Alexander Chernev. Harvard Business Review. "Can There Ever Be a Fair Price? Why Jcpenney's Strategy Backfired". 5/29/2012.

[63] Dan Ariely. *Predictably Irrational.* p2. Harper International. New York, NY. 2008.

editions for $125 anyway. How could adding an even less desirable option change user behavior?

But surprisingly, when showing these three options to new groups of MIT students, zero people chose the new print version only option as we might have expected (they are smart MIT students after all), but a overwhelming majority of the students (84%) suddenly wanted to order the digital *and* print subscriptions for $125, and only 16% of the students wanted the digital-only copy for $59.

If you were the Economist magazine, this means adding the useless option that no one wants will suddenly increase your total revenues by 44.6%! How does that make any sense? The secret lies in the fact that **people do not take actions that are necessarily the most economical, but actions that make them feel the smartest.**

I have personally seen rich women who spend dozens of hours clipping coupons so they could reduce a $20 item to $0.60. Do they need the extra savings? No. Is it the most economical use of their time? Probably not. But they do it because it makes them feel smart. They get to buy a $20 item with a dollar bill, and they even get change back! Similarly, in the case of the magazine, when a person sees that it takes $125 to get the print versions alone, but also $125 to get the print version *and* the digital version, it now feels like the digital version was obtained for *FREE*! By putting out a bait reference price, people now feel smarter getting the one that seemed like a no-brainer good deal. Sometimes feeling smart comes at a luxurious cost.

Limitations of eBay's Design

Because of the Glowing Choices, Personalized Recommendations, Peer Reviews, and Desert Oasis design elements mentioned above, Amazon users never feel confused about what to do next. You move quickly towards the Win-State, and especially if you made the "feel-smart" decision of purchasing Amazon Prime, your item will ship to your home within two days, with easy return and refund options.

eBay on the other hand, does not enjoy the same luxuries of making users feel smart. To start, eBay's interface is a bit more like Google+, where the user doesn't really know where to find what they want. With a variety of horizontal and vertical menus on the same screen, along with multiple dropdown menus, it's easy for a user to spend over four seconds before figuring out where they want to go.

Also, because of eBay's DNA of being a bidding marketplace, it does not have as much control over the experience of the users. When a user finally buys a product, eBay cannot guarantee the item will arrive within two days. In fact, eBay is at the mercy of the amateur sellers, who may not even ship the product out in a week. Even when the seller has shipped the item, they sometimes don't record it as shipped, let alone include a tracking number. During this time of waiting, the buyer has no idea whether the product was shipped or not, and when it will arrive. This definitely does not induce feelings of competency.

Luckily, when that dream item finally arrives, joy is reinstalled, and that delayed gratification fuels the drive to buy again on eBay. Unfortunately, when the item doesn't come in the form you dreamt it to be, therein lies the limitations of eBay. Especially as a used-item market, you may receive items that are in different conditions than described, damaged during shipment, or just plain out not what you paid for. And in the case of eBay, they can't just give you a return-refund. The seller who shadily sold you the product in the first place has to.

Sure, you have the option to leave negative feedback on eBay's reputation system, but for years there was a strange feedback stand-still phenomenon which paralyzed further activity. When there has been a bad experience, both sides refuse to leave the first negative feedback in fear of negative feedback retaliation. Even though I had a bad experience buying at eBay, I didn't want to give the seller a bad review because the seller could turn around and say I was a bad buyer, hurting my reputation. That stalemate is another bad feeling to go through, where the user feels unsettled and not feeling so smart about the purchasing decision (Note: this experience has been improved upon in recent years).

Sure, the user can take this bad experience up to eBay or even report fraud on Paypal (which is owned by eBay), but that process is grueling, with lots of waiting, frustration, and often poor communication. Letting users get stuck in bureaucracy (or be transferred back and forth on hold) is a sure way to make them feel helpless.

Imagine a game you play, where by working hard and reaching the Win-State, you have to wonder for a week when your reward will show up. When it does, it might actually show up as a penalty instead of a reward, and the only way to sort it out is to go through long steps of negotiation and bureaucracy. How often would you play this game? It becomes much easier to move on and never come back again. Perhaps this would make another great story in the users' daily complaining rituals too.

Of course, though I firmly believe that both Amazon and eBay can drastically improve their metrics even more with better gamification and Human-Focused Design, both companies are incredibly and intimidatingly successful. With billions of dollars in revenue, each company powerfully wields different Core Drives that make them successful, engaging, and even addictive.

Wait, that's not new!

Perhaps at this point, some people will say, "Making things easy for users and making them feel smart... that's not profound at all! That's what all Usability, User Interface, User Experience, and so-called User-Centered Design efforts already work on. How is Gamification or Human-Focused Design different?"

I believe the main difference between Human-Focused Design and the other fields mentioned is that they primarily focus on the "ease" of doing an activity instead of the motivation behind it. While usability focuses on making users complete their tasks more intuitively, assuming users already want to do that activity, Octalysis Gamification focuses on the motivation to do those tasks in the first place.

Even though most UX (User Experience) Experts also focus on the ease and flow of the experience, I have not seen many UX professionals try to improve motivation through a higher epic vision that users can believe in, nor withholding certain parts of the experience to create emotional scarcity. The focus is quite different.

In reality, Gamification is a combination of Game Design, Game Dynamics, Motivational Psychology, Behavioral Economics, UX/UI, Neurobiology, Technology Platforms, and Business Systems that drive an ROI. Interestingly, games have all of the above besides the last part: business systems that drive an ROI (or Return on Investment).

Gamification
=

Game Mechanics
+Motivational Psychology
+Behavioral Economics
+Technology Platforms
+Neurobiology
+UX/UI

Combined with
Business Systems
that generate ROI

Required to
make a great
game

+Business Systems

In order to make a great game, one needs to have great game dynamics, great UX/UI, have an understanding of Behavioral Economics through its virtual economy, motivational psychology and reward schedules, as well as the intricate relationships between hitting Win-States and dopamine firing. If any of these factors are off, the player simply abandons the game.

For this reason, when we study good gamification/game design, we will also inevitably bring up many concepts of creating behavior and great experiences in many other fields.

Game Techniques within Development & Accomplishment

You have learned more about the motivational and psychological nature of Core Drive 2: Development & Accomplishment. To make it more actionable, I've included some Game Techniques below that heavily utilize this Core Drive to engage users.

Progress Bars (Game Technique #4)

One of the simplest and best known examples of Development & Accomplishment is the LinkedIn Progress Bar. As the largest professional social network in the world, LinkedIn realized that its value is only as good as the information people choose to input into the system. But inputting one's profile and job history on LinkedIn is tedious, and users quickly drop out early in the onboarding process.

LinkedIn realizes that simply making the interface easier for users to maneuver was not enough. They needed to make the interface more motivating. As a result LinkedIn introduced a little Progress Bar (Game Technique #4) on the side of user profiles to show people how complete theirs were. Our brains hate it when incomplete things are dangled in front of our faces. When we see a progress bar that is taunting us as only being 70% of a human being, it gives us that extra push to finish the Desired Actions and achieve the Win-State of completeness.

The amazing thing is, this progress bar didn't take developers many hours to code, but improved LinkedIn's profile completeness by 20%, an impressive change considering how they have spent millions of dollars on achieving this same goal[64].

Progress Bars are seen in many places nowadays, and are often used in the Onboarding experience. It is one of the simplest gamification design techniques out there. Of course, if designed incorrectly, it would also fail to create meaningful engagement. A parody example called *Progress Wars* by Jakob Skjerning shows a meaningless game where every time you click a button, a progress bar fills up, allowing users to level up[65]. This is a great example of having game design

---

[64]Kevin Werbach. University of Pennsylvania. Coursera Gamification Course. 2012.
[65]Progress Wars Website: progresswars.com

techniques in a system without Core Drives powering them, leading to low engagement results.

The Rockstar Effect (Game Technique #92)

The Rockstar Effect is a gamification design technique where you make users feel like everyone is dying to interact with them. In essence, if you make people feel like they have *earned* their way in becoming a Rockstar, they will feel so much pride in it that they will continue to perform the Desired Actions of building up an even greater fanbase and sharing with others.

Twitter is a great example of utilizing the Rockstar Effect. Most people remember Twitter's innovation being the limitation of only 140 characters within a message (which is an interesting balance between Core Drive 6: Scarcity & Impatience combined with Core Drive 3: Empowerment of Creativity & Feedback), but few people remember that another one of Twitter's key innovations was the one-way follow.

Back in the day, social connections were mutual – either both sides agree to be friends, or no relationship existed. When Twitter was launched in 2006, it came with this new one-way follow system, allowing users to follow the message updates of people who are interesting, without these people following the users back. Because of the one-way nature of the relationship, many people saw getting many followers as a true achievement – meaning that everyone wanted to listen to your valuable opinions, even though you didn't give a rat's pancreas about their opinions.

People tried as hard as they could to "earn" followers – tweeting out witty comments, sharing valuable links, and retweeting others to gain attention. Some even pressured their non-tech friends to follow them just so they could look better on Twitter. This became a game for many, where the goal was to reach the highest amount of followers and retweets.

Then, at one point, influential people started to compete with each other to see who had more followers. At the beginning, the implicit comparing came between influencers in the tech world, such as Guy Kawasaki or Robert Scoble. This is a typical condition that many new tech companies go through - where bloggers and people in Silicon Valley love the platforms, but the mainstream population isn't yet aware of their existence.

However, because of the "Accomplishment" nature that is baked into Twitter's DNA, Twitter finally caught massive mainstream attention when celebrities like Ashton Kutcher joined the mix of "follower competitions" against other celebrities, and most notably, the official CNN Breaking News Twitter Channel.

In 2009, Ashton Kutcher, publicly challenged CNN Breaking News to see who could first reach 1 million Followers.[66] Both sides, not wanting to lose the competition, started promoting Twitter and their own Twitter profiles on all their media outlets, hoping to be the first to hit that "golden million." Ashton Kutcher's fans, who loved his movies but had no idea what Twitter was, also started to write blog posts and make Youtube videos telling everyone else to follow him.

---

[66] John D. Sutter. CNN. "Ashton Kutcher challenges CNN to Twitter popularity contest". 04/15/2009.

Towards the end, Ashton Kutcher did achieve his victory of reaching 1 million Followers on Twitter before CNN Breaking News. Again, because he considers this to be a true accomplishment, he brags with joy and pride with nine exclamation marks.

CNN Breaking News, on the other hand, behaves in a sportsmanlike manner, as a big company should. In the above screenshot, you can see that by the time Ashton Kutcher won, CNN Breaking News had 999,652 followers, mere hundreds away from winning. Instead of bitterly saying, "So close! We were only off by a few hundred," they gracefully announced to the world "Ashton Kutcher is first to reach 1 million followers in Twitter contest with CNN" with a "Congrats" on the tweet below.

This contest has turned out very positive for the brand names of both CNN and Ashton Kutcher, but the biggest beneficiary is Twitter, whom received millions of dollars worth of free press with an audience that was unfamiliar with their platform.

Achievement Symbols (Game Technique #2)

As discussed in Chapter 2, points and badges can ruin good gamification design as often so-called "gamification experts" slap them onto everything they see. However, they are useful tools to drive Development & Accomplishment and have their place in a gamified system.

Badges are what I call "Achievement Symbols" and can come in many forms – badges, stars, belts, hats, uniforms, trophies, medals, etc.. The important thing about Achievement Symbols, is that they must symbolize "achievement." If you go on a website and click a button, and then suddenly a popup springs out and says, "CONGRATULATIONS!!! You just earned your 'Clicked On My First Button Badge'! Click here to see other cool badges you can earn!" Are you going to be excited?

Probably not.

You may even think, "Well this is pretty lame...what else is there? A 'Scrolling Down Badge'? A 'Click on the About Us Page Badge'?" You're almost insulted.

But if through your creative skills you solved a unique problem that not everyone could solve, and as a result received a badge to symbolize that achievement, you feel proud and accomplished. Now the motivation is valid.

Achievement Symbols merely reflect achievement, but are not achievements by themselves. A similar example evolved from where badges came from – the military. If you join the military, and immediately get a badge on your chest, "Joined the Military Badge!" And on the next day, another badge gets pinned on your chest that says, "Survived My First Day Badge!" followed by "Made my First Friend Badge!" and "Made Five Friends Badge!" You probably won't feel accomplished and wear all these badges to your social gatherings. You are more likely to feel nonplused or even insulted. But if you performed acts of valor – you risked your life to save a fellow soldier, and as a result received a Medal of Honor on your chest, you are likely to truly feel proud and accomplished.

Keep in mind some of those "insulting badges" do work great for children, because as small children, these are actual feats and accomplishments. More often than not, making your first friend is not something you have a parade about when you are a grown person.

Therefore, when I work with clients on gamification, I never ask them, "Do you have badges?" I ask, "Do you make your users feel accomplished?" Having badges (or any game element in itself) does not mean users are motivated towards the Win-State. That's why we focus on the 8 Core Drives instead of game elements.

Status Points (Game Technique #1)

There are two types of *points* in a motivation system: Status Points, and Exchangeable Points. Status Points are for keeping score of progress. Internally, it allows the system to know how close players are towards the win-state. Externally, it gives players a feedback system for tracking their progress. As a great candidate for "Feed-back Mechanics" in the *Octalysis Strategy Dashboard* (discussed in more detail in Chapter 17), showing people their score and how it changes based on small improvements often motivates them towards the right direction.

Within Status Points, there are also smaller divisions of types. For example, Absolute Status Points (which measures the total amount of points earned during a journey) versus Marginal Status Points (which are points that are specifically set for a given challenge or one time period, and can be reset once that challenge or time period is over). Another example is that of the One-Way Status Points (points that can only go up) verses Two-Way Status Points (it can also go down as the user fails to achieve the Win-State).

How you craft the gain and loss of points, as well as meaning behind the points can significantly change the users' perception of your product. Done incorrectly, it can cause the user to devalue the entire experience and distrust your intentions as a systems designer.

A year prior to my advisory role as Behavioral Scientist to the Israel-based company *Captain Up*[67], I was looking for a good PBL platform to use for my own blog *yukaichou.com*.

I found Captain Up's gamification platform to be the most customizable and easiest to use out of my options during the time.

When I was designing my Points and Badges system using the Captain Up platform, the first thing I did was to change almost everything in the default settings. The default settings at the time rewarded a few points for watching a video and commenting on my blog posts, and a lot more for tweeting and sharing the post on Facebook. This design is generally sound, especially since I indeed get more value when my readers are sharing my content to others. However, I felt the default points/rewards economy was not optimized.

The first thing I changed, was to make commenting on my blog worth 100 points, and watching a video worth 40 points. Facebook Liking and Tweeting were only worth 25 and 10 points. After I made the changes on the platform, the supportive team members from Captain Up reached out to me to make sure I felt comfortable with their platform. They also asked, "Isn't 100 points way too much for just commenting?"

That's a very good question.

---

[67]CaptainUp Website: captainup.com

During the Discovery and Onboarding Phases of a Player's Journey (the initial two phases) the first thing you want to communicate to users is whether this is "a game worth playing?" With the rules you set, you are establishing an interaction with the user and communicating your values.

If you give people a bunch of points just to do marketing for you, or reward them with virtual items for every little stupid thing, users will feel like the game is shallow – this is not a game worth playing. Users have no interest in a game if they know the game designer is just trying to benefit themselves instead of caring about their community. For instance, if there are points, progress bars, and badges for "How much money you donated to the site owner," people will feel insulted by your lame attempt to use them for solely personal gains.

People know that sharing on Twitter/Facebook mostly benefits me, and so I don't want to tell them that my game is about sharing. When I state that commenting on my site is worth more than anything else, I'm expressing that I value interacting *with you* more than anything else. I want to communicate with you, and that is what I value. And if you don't want to talk to me, at least watch my videos so you can learn something! And of course, if you are willing to share my content with your friends and family, I would be very grateful too, but I'm not going to use that as a big carrot in my site.

This tells users that the key of this game is "engagement." I want you to be engaged, learn a lot, and participate in a community. This becomes a game worth playing.

When you design your Status Point systems, make sure it is based on something meaningful - something that the users themselves want to engage in. Or else, points just become meaningless counters meant to stress people out.

Leaderboards (Game Technique #3)

Leaderboards is a game element where you rank users based on a set of criteria that is influenced by the users' behaviors towards the Desired Actions. Even though Leaderboards are meant to motivate people and bring in status, if designed incorrectly, it often does the exact opposite.

If you use a site for a few hours and received 25 points, and then see on the Top 20 list that number 20 already has 25,000,000 points, that would likely discourage you from trying further.

This was an issue that *Foursquare*, a geolocation mobile app that gamified the check-in process, had many years ago. Often, a new user would check into a new coffee shop, and then realize that the "Mayor" there has already achieved 250 check-ins and increasing their total every day. "Fighting for the Mayorship" is probably not something the user would be interested in, because he knows the odds of developing progress and feeling accomplished are very low.

What users need is *Urgent Optimism*, another term coined by Jane McGonigal[68], where the user feels optimistic that they can accomplish the task, but also the urgency to act immediately. When you set-up a leaderboard, there are a couple variations that have shown to perform more effectively.

First, you always want to position the user in the middle of the leaderboard display, so all they see is the player ranked right above them, and the player ranked just below. It's not very motivating in seeing how high the Top 10 players are, but it's incredibly motivating when one sees someone who used to be below them suddenly excelling.

Another variation that has proved successful is to set up *Group Leaderboards* where the ranking is based on the combined efforts of a team. In this case, even though not everyone is competitive and

---

[68]Jane McGonigal. *Reality is Broken.* P69. Penguin Group. New York, NY. 2011.

needs to be at the top, most people don't want to be the laggard that drags the team down. As a result, everyone works harder because of Social Influence & Relatedness (Core Drive 5).

The next variation is to set up constantly refreshing leaderboards, where every week the data would refresh and the leaderboard will start tracking progress anew; hence no one falls too far behind and always has a renewed sense of hope, leading towards that Urgent Optimism. Finally, it's a good idea to implement micro-leaderboards, where only the users' friends or very similar people are compared. Instead of seeing yourself ranked 95,253 out of 1 million users, you see how you are top five among twenty-two friends.

The key way to effectively integrate a leaderboard is to ensure that the user can quickly recognize the action items that drives them to reach the win-state. If there's no chance of achievement, there is no action.

Core Drive 2: The Bigger Picture

Since Development & Accomplishment is the easiest Core Drive to design for, many companies focus on this Core Drive- sometimes almost exclusively. Consequently, many of the Gamification Platforms out there are specialized in appealing to this Core Drive too. However, if you do plan to implement these game elements into your product, make sure you do this carefully and elegantly. Always focus on how you want your users to feel, not what game elements you want to use.

Core Drive 2: Development & Accomplishment is often a natural result after good implementation of other Core Drives, such as Core Drive 3: Empowerment of Creativity & Feedback, Core Drive 4: Ownership & Possession, as well as Core Drive 6: Scarcity & Impatience. Often, it also leads to Core Drive 5: Social Influence &

Relatedness, where the user wants to share with their friends that sense of achievement and accomplishment. We will be learning a lot more about these Core Drives in the next few chapters.

To get the most out of the book, Choose only ONE of the below options to do right now:

Easy: Think of an example where Core Drive 2: Development & Accomplishment motivated you or others to take certain actions. Did it keep people engaged for longer?

Medium: Think of the last time you saw a points or achievement symbol system. Were the points or achievement symbols representing something meaningful? Or were they pointless? What would you change to make them represent a sense of true progress and accomplishment?

Hard: For your own project, create a Status Points and Achievement Symbol economy via spreadsheets. Define what the Desired Actions are, assign point values to these actions based on how meaningful they are to the user, and assign Achievement Symbols based on more creative factors beyond just "Woot! You did the action a hundred times!"

Share what you come up with on Twitter or your preferred social network with the hashtag #OctalysisBook and see what ideas other people have.

Investigate the Experience

In this chapter, I talked about how I completely revamped the Captain Up system on my blog to create a "game worth playing." Go to my blog at YukaiChou.com and experience the motivation design from the Captain Up widget on the right hand side. After playing with it, read up on the full blog about my design decisions at http://bit.ly/YukaiCup, or simply go on Google and search, "how yu-kai chou designed his blog."

There are still many things I would like to change and add into the gamified experience if I only had more time. Please feel empowered to come up with ways it can be improved and share your findings with me.

Chapter 7: The Third Core Drive - Empowerment of Creativity & Feedback

"The man whose whole life is spent in performing a few simple operations, of which the effects are perhaps always the same, or very nearly the same, has no occasion to exert his understanding or to exercise his invention in finding out expedients for removing difficulties which never occur. He naturally loses, therefore, the habit of such exertion, and generally becomes as stupid and ignorant as

it is possible for a human creature to become." - Adam Smith, The Wealth Of Nations

The third Core Drive of Octalysis Gamification is Empowerment of Creativity & Feedback, which really emphasizes on what most people refer to as "Play." Some of my fondest memories growing up are of when I got to play with Legos and engage in assembling, dismantling, and rebuilding basic structures in a practically infinite number of combinations. It gave me and millions of others around the world great joy and fulfillment simply because it allowed one to be creative and see immediate results. I could admire the outcome of my ideas, while ensuring that I could recalibrate my efforts over and over again in bringing my imagination to life. I believe that humans are by nature creative beings, and we yearn to learn, imagine, invent, and partake in creative processes where the journey in and of itself brings happiness.

The beauty of this Core Drive lies in its perennial ability to continually engage us at all moments in our lives. Recalling the structure of Octalysis, with the top-down Core Drives being White/Black Hat, and left-right Core Drives being Extrinsic/Intrinsic, you will notice that Core Drive 3: Empowerment of Creativity & Feedback resides in the upper right "golden corner." This implies that it is White Hat – meaning it has long-term positive emotions, as well as Right Brain – emphasizing Intrinsic Motivation. Unfortunately, this Core Drive is also possibly the hardest to implement correctly.

The Computer Game that Became a National Sport

In a large stadium, over 100,000 audience members sit earnestly in front of a stage. These players all paid a fine fee to be there and are excitedly waiting for their long time idols to compete with other pros in the league.

Two professional commentators are setting the scene, introducing the background and importance of this match in the overall context of the season, and what it would mean for each opposing player and their careers. They're speculating on the odds for each player based on their strengths, weaknesses, style of play, and possible innovations that will be revealed during this pivotal match, all while popping in a few jokes here and there.

Simultaneously, over a million people are watching the stage on TV and all over the Internet, with the logos of some of the biggest sponsors in the world prominently displayed.

This is a typical setting for any professional athletic sport. The only difference is, on the stage, below a few enormous screens, there are only two computer "workstations," each surrounded by soundproof glass. Seated in front of the workstations, two "star competitors," both around twenty years old, exercise their pre-match rituals before the crucial game.

This is a championship match within the "eSports" industry, a newly emerging field where people around the world watch full-time professional gamers compete against each other.[69]

This is an industry that was pioneered by Blizzard Entertainment's big-hit game: Starcraft. Starcraft is a real-time strategy (RTS) game launched in 1998[70]. Upon beginning an RTS game, players usually start off with a few workers that can mine resources. The resources can then be used to create more workers, erect buildings that have different functions, recruit combat units, research science and technology, and/or unlock certain powers, all for the purpose of defending against and defeating other players who are also building their dominions.

Users are constantly making quick decisions based on a scarcity of time and resources. Should they recruit more combat units and march into enemy territory, or invest in slow developing but dominant technologies at the risk of being run down by enemies who alternatively chose to train combat units in the meantime?

Each match in Starcraft (and for most RTS games) lasts around ten minutes to an hour, with each player starting from scratch with every round. This means nothing is accumulated from previous game efforts except for the players' skills.

Moreover, the "real-time" part of RTS games means that the faster you can make sound decisions and execute on them, the stronger player you can become. Good Starcraft players have the concept of APM – Actions Per Minute. This indicates the number of actions a player can execute every minute. Actions could be anything from ordering a soldier to guard a certain post, or selecting a building to initiate new scientific research.

For new Starcraft players, it is common to only have 10-20 APM, as it normally takes a few seconds to determine what is possible and decide on what to do. For more experienced hobbyists, this rate could rise to 50-60 APM, which is about one action every second.

---

[69]Matthew Jarvis. MCV. "eSports: Behind the next billion-dollar industry". 08/11/2014.

[70]Blizzard Entertainment. "StarCraft's 10-Year Anniversary: A Retrospective". 2008.

The mind-blowing thing about Starcraft (or most eSport games) is that the top professional players often have shocking APM numbers between 300-400! This means that every second, they are literally executing five to six actions throughout the game.

This is very important in an RTS game, for if every action you execute your opponent can execute two, you are bound to be outmaneuvered and "pwned," given that both players have similar judgments and strategies. In the documentary "The Hax Life," when asked how he trains to become better, a top Starcraft player answered that he would put heavy sandbags on his wrists when he practices so that in a real game, his uninhibited hands and fingers would move much faster[71].

In fact, Starcraft has become so popular in South Korea that for over a decade now, there have been dedicated TV Channels that broadcast Starcraft matches between professional players. The very best Starcraft players can make over $300,000 a year, especially with all the sponsorships from major brands. I know to all my rich readers this isn't much, but for a country like South Korea this is considered quite an achievement, especially for someone under 25 years old. Not only are the professional Starcraft players becoming famous, the top professional Starcraft commentators are also becoming quite well known.

Starcraft has also been wildly popular in the US. The University of California, Berkeley pioneered one of the first courses on Starcraft and its strategy, while many students at other academic institutions have incorporated the economic dynamics and decision strategies within Starcraft as key themes in their research papers and theses[72].

In 2009, 10 years after Starcraft was first released, students from Princeton University established the Collegiate Starleague, a seasonal intercollegiate league for competition between the member

---

[71]Chris Means. Gamezone.com. "Razer and team WeMadeFox presents 'The Hax Life'". 2011.

[72]Brian Crecente. Kotaku.com. "Competitive StarCraft Gets UC Berkeley Class". 01/28/09.

institutions. Over 100 North American universities and colleges participate, including Harvard, Yale, Cornell, MIT, and many more[73].

When Starcraft II was launched in 2010, the frenzy on Starcraft I had not diminished, with many players insisting that Starcraft I was still better. Of course, over a few years, most professional players transferred from Starcraft I to Starcraft II.

This actually is a great demonstration of how great Endgame design and the use of Core Drive 3: Empowerment of Creativity & Feedback can remove so-called "gamification fatigue."

Gamification Fatigue?

Every once in a while, attendees at my speaking engagements or workshops would ask, "Yu-kai, I want to add gamification to my company, but aren't most games short-lived? Wouldn't we be shooting ourselves in the foot if we implemented gamification?"

It's true, many fun games are played for two to eight months, but afterwards players move on to new games. However, it doesn't mean that gamifying your system would automatically result in the same situation due to two important reasons.

First, remember I mentioned earlier that there is generally no real *purpose* for playing a game; that is, most people never *have* to play a game. The instant a game is not fun, people will leave and play other games or go on Youtube/Facebook/email. As a result, after two to eight months, the game will often fail to engage people so they drop out. Hopefully the system that you are designing actually has a purpose to it, and so even if it becomes boring (which is probably the current state anyway), your users still have a reason to stay on.

The second reason is because most of these games have not been designed for continued motivation in the "Endgame", the fourth

---

[73]Patricia Cohen. New York Times. "Video Game Becomes Spectator Sport." 04/01/09.

and final phase of a player's journey. If the experience is no longer engaging in the endgame, you simply move on to other games.

Many well-designed games, like Starcraft, have managed to engage the interest of players for more than a decade. Other games like Poker, Golf, Chess, Mahjong, have all stood the test of time and are still popular after centuries of use. Now there are many ways to design an engaging Endgame, but the reason why so many of these games stand the test of time is largely due to their utilization of Core Drive 3: Empowerment of Creativity & Feedback.

In a study published by Queen Mary University of London and University College London in 2013, researched compared the effects of different games on the brain. After six to eight weeks, the study revealed that students who played Starcraft roughly an hour a day improved their memory, visual search and informational filtering abilities, as well as other cognitive skills (Trivia: I happen to be quoted in the Wall Street Journal article on this study).[74]

When a user can continuously tap into their creativity and derive an almost limitless number of possibilities, the game designer no longer needs to constantly create new content to make things engaging. The user's mind becomes the evergreen content that continuously absorbs their attention into the experience. That's the power of Core Drive 3: Empowerment of Creativity & Feedback in retaining users for the long haul.

Tic-Tac-Draw

Almost every culture has the game Tic-Tac-Toe, with some calling it by another name, such as Xs and Os[75]. Many of us enjoyed the game when we were younger because it was easy to initiate with

---

[74] Riva Gold. Wall Street Journal Blog. "'StarCraft' Gameplay Boosts Mental Flexibility, Says Study". 08/25/13.

[75] Jad Abumrad and Robert Krulwich. Radiolab Podcast. "Mapping Tic Tac Toe-dom". 09/06/2011.

just a pen and a piece of paper (or a stick with sand), and can be finished within half a minute.

However, as we grew older, the game became less interesting[76]. Why? Because at some point it became too easy. Most games end up in draws, and the only thrill is trying to see if you can trick a new opponent into making a careless move due to reckless/hasty actions (which is Core Drive 7: Unpredictability & Curiosity). With just a little bit of learned strategy, it became boring[77].

Because there is a limit on the Empowerment of Creativity and Feedback, Tic-Tac-Toe became a lot less engaging for users.

On the other hand, chess is a game that has been studied and played rigorously for centuries. Today there are still thrilling matches between some of the strongest players in the world that are exciting to watch.

When I was a freshman in high school, having recently moved to the United States, I realized my English skills were quite poor. (In fact, in the 11th grade I met a friend who hadn't seen me for 2 years that openly exclaimed, "Wow, you speak English now! That's crazy!"). Making up for my lack of communication skills, I often played chess with my American peers, as it was quite similar to the Chinese Chess I played in Taiwan. With a few friends and the sponsoring teacher, Mr. Richard Gill, we formed the Blue Valley High School Chess Club.

During this time, I was quite shy and could not imagine myself ever speaking in public. (In fact, for a long time, just seeing someone else speak on stage made my palms sweat.) My reputation in my high school, (besides being one of the few Asians there) was that I was "nice." Most people who study persuasive psychology will agree that having a reputation of "nice" was not very motivating in most scenarios. Descriptions such as "sincere," "passionate," or "radiant"

---

[76] Note: even though I came up with this example independently a few years ago, I later read that Raph Koster used this exact example too to discuss a similar point.

[77] Raph Koster. *A Theory of Fun*. 2nd Edition. p4. O'Reilly Media. Sebastopol, CA. 10/2013.

would be personalities that are similar but much more engaging for people.

Though I had yet to build up my confidence as an individual, by my 10th grade I was elected to be the Chess Club President. My speech to garner votes was literally, "My last name is the shortest to write down. Vote for me!" After unexpectedly winning the election (I guess people liked the humor), I suddenly felt a sense of responsibility – Epic Meaning & Calling! It was no longer just about me but about the greater good of the organization! At this point I committed to become a stronger chess player, so that I would be able to lead and coach our team to greater victory. For over two years, I absorbed myself in the openings, strategies, and variations of chess for four hours a day, trying to expand my understanding of positional play and establishing my style as a player.

In chess, there are a substantial number of opening variations, with possible lines of play exponentially expanding into far more variations than the total number of atoms in the observable universe (just after 4 moves each, there are over 288 billion possible positions).

In 1996, then World Chess Champion Garry Kasparov competed against IBM's specialized chess supercomputer *Deep Blue.* Deep Blue at the time could calculate 100 million positions per second. Both Deep Blue and Kasparov had approximately three hours each to think, with Deep Blue also calculating during Kasparov's moves. If you multiply 100 million positions a second for three hours, that's a whole lot of chess positions.

When the competition commenced, Kasparov lost the initial game, which seemed to surprise him. Subsequently, he comfortably won three games while tying two to win the match.[78]

In 1997, a rematch was called. IBM had a full team whose only role was to improve Deep Blue's chess playing skills. By then Deep Blue could examine 200 million positions a second, doubling the prior

---

[78]ChessBase.com Chess News. "Garry Kasparov begs to differ...". 04/12/2002.

year's capabilities. This match ended with Kasparov winning one game, drawing two, and losing two, resulting in his defeat.[79]

The second match stunned the chess world - for the first time ever a powerful computer could defeat the leading human in a game of chess. To me, this was rather odd. Intuitively-speaking, *of course* a computer could beat a strong human player. Isn't chess all about memorization and calculations? Computers could obviously "remember" and calculate substantially faster than humans with much better precision.

This was like being shocked that a motorized vehicle was starting to travel faster than a human runner, or that a human lost to a calculator in a multiplication contest. I thought that, instead of being amazed that computers were finally beating humans at chess, people should be amazed that humans stood a chance at all! How could a computer that is processing billions of positions and outcomes not see the loss coming and prevent it?

The reason why computers can't simply dominate human players, even today, is because chess is more than just calculations and memorization. *Chess requires creativity, intuition, and understanding.* Chess is so complex that the most powerful computers still can't completely figure out the game against human creativity and intuition.

Chess computers can calculate, but they cannot *understand.* Even though chess computers can figure out what a position can look like exactly fifteen moves later, unless there are obvious hints such as a checkmate or a significant loss in pieces, the computer does not know whether that position is "good" or "bad." A human, on the other hand, cannot tell exactly what the position will be like fifteen moves later but they have the intuitive understanding that, "My knight would be established on a very strong spot. What it will do, I'm not completely sure yet, but I know it will benefit me one

[79] Jonathan Schaeffer & Aske Plaat. University of Alberta & Vrije Universiteit. "Kasparov versus Deep Blue: The Re-match"ICCA Journal, vol. 20, no. 2, pp. 95-102. 1997.

way or another." It is this type of understanding and analysis that allows human players to triumph over strong computers from time to time.

Earlier when I mentioned that there are far more possible chess moves than atoms in the universe, the rightful skeptic may think that I'm just pulling numbers out of my spleen for exaggeration's sake. However, if you actually look into the numbers, a game of chess that is 40 moves long would have 10^{120} possible variations, which ends up being 10^{40} times the number of atoms in the known Universe. [80]

The reason I bring up these facts is to elicit the point that: because there are so many possible variations in chess, there is an abundance of strategies and styles of play. This variability is essential for creating a great gamified campaign utilizing Core Drive 3: Empowerment of Creativity & Feedback. Some chess players are fanatically aggressive, some are defensively positional; some like to slowly squeeze their opponents to death, while others strive for a winning endgame. You can almost tell who is playing the game based on the types of moves they make.

At UCLA, I once wrote a paper on how the style of each World Chess Champion reflects the historical events of their time. José Capablanca, the third World Chess Champion, lived during a golden period of peace in Cuba, and as a result played chess in a harmonious and elegant way, collecting little advantages that would eventually lead to a win. The next World Champion Alexander Alekhine lived during times of revolution in Russia, often escaping persecution and facing death. As a result, his style is known to be vigorously aggressive, ramming down the enemy king's protective forts with sacrifices. Mikhail Botvinnik, another world champion lived during the time of the Soviet Union's "Iron and Engineering" prowess. As a result his style was aggressively positional, similar to assembling a

---

[80] Andrew Breslin. *Andy Rants.* "The number of possible different games of chess." 10/12/2009.

tank and then trampling the enemy territory with irresistible force.

The great thing is, to be at the top of the chess world, you don't need to play in one, specific "best" way. You can create your own style of play through *meaningful choices* that reflect your personality and style. As long as you invest the rigorous work, maintain the commitment, and have passion for the game, you will have a chance of becoming a great chess player.

This capacity to allow players to express their unbounded creativity, see immediate feedback, and offer them meaningful choices to demonstrate different styles of play is what makes Core Drive 3: Empowerment of Creativity & Feedback so appealing to gamers, users, customers, and employees alike. **When you design a great gamified system, you want to make sure that there isn't one standard way to win. Instead, provide users with enough meaningful choices that they can utilize drastically different ways to better express their creativity, while still achieving the Win-State.**

As for my chess club, by the time I finished 11th grade, the Blue Valley High School had became the Kansas State Champion of Kansas for our division and successfully defended the position for five straight years. Beyond this, the club also finished strong in national tournaments. This experience also taught me how to be a leader and built my confidence when I had very little. I can't thank chess and the BVHS Chess Club enough for where I am today.

The General's Carrot in Education

When you design for Core Drive 3: Empowerment of Creativity & Feedback, it is important to create a setup where the user is given a goal, as well as a variety of tools and methodologies to strategize towards reaching that goal. Often your users are not motivated because they don't understand the purpose of the activity, do not clearly identify the goal of the activity, and/or lack meaningful tools to create expressive strategies to reach the goal.

In the past few decades, physical battle card games such as *Pokemon* or *Magic: the Gathering* have become a new phenomenon, gaining significant traction in many countries[81]. Similar to chess or *Starcraft*, there are many dedicated tournaments where players young and old, duke it out to become the champions at the games.

What's interesting about this phenomenon is that there is actually a great deal of information to memorize in order to play the game well. There are hundreds of cards, each having its own unique stats and numbers (such as hp, attack, etc.). Children who are good at these card games not only remember all the cards and stats, they even remember which cards counter which, and which other cards counter those in return.

If you run the numbers, that is actually more information to memorize than the contents on the periodic table. It's as though the child not only memorized every single element on the periodic table, but also the exact weight and placement of each element, as well as exactly how every element interacts with every other element.

That's pretty mind-blowing.

But if you ask the same brilliant child what's the fifth element on the periodic table, you will likely get a response along with the lines of, "Umm...Oxygen?" Why is that? Clearly the child did not suddenly transform from a genius into an idiot. This gaping difference is not a transition in intelligence but simply a change in motivation.

When the child is memorizing the periodic table, they do not see the purpose of doing so. It is only to pass a test, get a good grade, and please their parents. As a result, the child studies hard enough to pass the test, and forgets most of the subject matter thereafter. But in these card games, the child is learning the information in order to come up with awesome strategies, beat their friends, and

---

[81]XPRIZE Homepage: xprize.org

feel accomplished. Also, since they personally own many of these cards, they are anxious to study them, understand their strengths and weaknesses, and research what other cards are out there (an effect within Core Drive 4: Ownership & Possession).

If the *means* to that end is to memorize thousands and thousands of terms and stats, it becomes worth it, even fun. As designers, it is important to recognize that they understand the goal (beating their friends), build ownership and familiarity with their tools, and use their unique strategies and experience towards that.

Folding into the Crowd

One of the best examples of Empowerment & Creativity & Feedback is seen in the new trend of Crowdsourcing. Crowdsourcing is the activity of throwing a challenge or activity into the public and having the masses collaborate or competitively solve the problem.

Well known examples such as the *XPRIZE* allows individuals and teams to engineer new solutions in advanced technology such as aerodynamics and space travel to advance the human race; while Kaggle allows the brightest mathematical minds to solve predictive modeling and analytics problems[82].

A very popular example in the *serious game* space has been FoldIt introduced in Chapter 4. For many years, scientists have tried to decipher the crystal structure of an AIDS virus labelled as the Mason-Pfizer monkey virus (M-PMV), in order to advance their understanding of AIDS treatment and prevention. Unfortunately, after fifteen years of research, this problem remained unresolved[83].

Fortunately, in 2008, David Baker from the University of Washington launched the FoldIt project, where through an interactive game-

---

[82]Kaggle Homepage: kaggle.com

[83]Michael Coren & Fast Company. *Scientific American.* "Foldit Gamers Solve Riddle of HIV Enzyme within 3 Weeks". 09/20/2011.

play interface, players could modify various protein structures with objectives such as "maximizing the surface area of this protein."

Surprisingly, this problem, which had baffled researchers for over fifteen years, was solved in a mere ten days. By tapping the efforts of thousands of "players" around the world, a creative solution was revealed through their vigorous play.

To this day, Foldit continues to help biochemical researchers find cures to major diseases that plague humans, including HIV/AIDS, cancer, and Alzheimer's.

If you are able to utilize this sort of intrinsic motivation where people can leverage their creativity and receive quick feedback with either a product or within the workplace (especially if it is tied to Core Drive 1: Epic Meaning & Calling as in the case of FoldIt), you will likely unlock long-term user engagement and high productivity.

The Elysian Stairs to Health

You often hear that it is better to take the stairs instead of the escalator. However, in practice it is convenient to forget this bit of good advice and take the escalator anyway. To combat this, Volkswagen's viral campaign "The Fun Theory" (a database of videos that is now the staple of many gamification workshops) piloted a campaign called the *Piano Staircase* in Sweden.

For the Piano Staircase, engineers integrated movement-tracking hardware to detect activity on the staircase, which subsequently plays a piano note whenever a specific step is triggered. The staircase is also decorated as piano patterns to show which note is being played and to elicit the commuters' curiosity (Discovery Phase design is very important).

As people walked up and down the stairs, they started to hear notes playing. Soon, many commuters who heard others go up the stairs started taking the stairs too themselves to see if it would work for them. Eventually, some individuals attempted to play some simple tunes.

When you empower people by allowing them to easily play an instrument, you make the simple activity of walking more fun and engaging. During the pilot, the piano staircase led to an increase in commuters taking the stairs by 66%.[84]

From an Endgame design point of view, the staircase does have its limitations. The actual tunes people can play is fairly limited since jumping up and down staircases in producing a pleasing rhythm is rather challenging. Pedestrians could quickly lose interest after stepping through the same notes over and over. Once the initial surprise and novelty wears off, the repetitive tones may become boring. However, many people may still prefer this over a regular staircase, just to get some delightful feedback on each step.

This is an example of a Core Drive 3 implementation that focused well on the feedback it gave users, but it didn't provide them full

[84]Volskwagon. *TheFunTheory.com*. "Piano Staircase". 09/22/2009.

control to express wider ranges of their creativity.

Empowerment and Creativity in the Corporate Space

Core Drive 3: Empowerment of Creativity & Feedback also applies to the workplace and employee motivation.

Occasionally, my friends with corporate positions reach out to me about making the switch towards a career in entrepreneurship. More often than not, the reason they want to start their own companies is simply due to the frustration of not seeing feedback on their creative ideas in the corporate environment. Frequently, months will pass after they have proposed a plan or concept before there is any response or feedback through the corporation's bureaucratic channels. More often than not, the employee never hears back on that creative idea.

In a bureaucratic organization, though everyone likes to talk about innovation, innovation requires risk, and the corporate ladder trains people to be risk averse. If anything new is happening, it is only after authorization through many signatures - to the point where no one could claim full responsibility if things went wrong. Managers often push everyone to come up with innovative ideas, but when they actually hear something new, they immediately respond with, "Hmm, has any other company done that before?"

This is incredibly frustrating for those who have creative ideas which may positively impact the status quo, especially when their ideas are immediately shot down or the approval process is dragged out indefinitely. It is a sad scenario - as companies grow larger and more bureaucratic, they become less agile, less adaptive to changing business conditions. As a result, younger and more nimble companies adapt to changing business models more swiftly than their cumbersome counterparts and quickly take advantage of new opportunities. All too often many great companies from the past century eventually fall into extinction.

In the Motivational Psychology Bestseller *Drive*, Daniel Pink explains that allowing employees to have full *autonomy* over what they work on, how they work, who they work with, and when they work often becomes greater motivators than giving them a raise.[85] Convincingly, researchers from Cornell University studied 320 small businesses, half of which empowered employees to work through autonomy, while the other half had a top-down management structure. For the group of companies which gave their employees more control in using their own creative processes to perform their work, business growth was four times the rate of the other group, with only one third of the turnover rate.[86]

An example of a company who attempted to embed Empowerment of Creativity & Feedback into their workplace was Google. They implemented a program called *20% Time* – where one day in the week, employees can work on any project they would like, as long as the Intellectual Property belonged to Google.

Many employees who wanted to become an entrepreneur mostly did so because they had great ideas and wanted to see it become reality. But most of them still don't enjoy the risk and the hassle of starting a company. With *20% Time*, employees no longer felt a need to start their own companies because they could simply build their ideas in the safe and comfortable haven of Google.

As a result, some of the most successful product lines such as Gmail were spawned from an emphasis on this Core Drive of Creativity. Unfortunately, 20% Time was shut down as Google became larger and wanted to "put more wood behind fewer arrows."[87]

---

[85] Daniel Pink. *Drive.* p84. Penguin Group, New York, NY. 2009.

[86] Paul P. Baard, Edward L. Deci, Richard M. Ryan. *Journal of Applied Social Psychology.* p34."Intrinsic Need Satisfaction: A Motivational Basis of Performance and Well-Being in Two Work Settings". 2004.

[87] Christopher Mims. Quartz. "Google's "20% time," which brought you Gmail and AdSense, is now as good as dead". 08/16/2013.

Draw a Gun for Bad Endgame Design

While we talked about how Core Drive 3: Empowerment of Creativity & Feedback can often create Endgame Evergreen Content, if it is not thoughtfully designed for the Endgame, it may still fail in the long run.

For example, Draw Something (essentially Pictionary, where one side draws something with a pen and the other side guesses) was an extremely popular and fun mobile game for a short while in 2012. They amassed 35 million downloads within seven weeks of launch, and later that year was sold to Zynga for close to $200M.[88]

The game was fun because it allowed people to utilize their creativity in determining how to best draw a picture of the challenge word, so that the other person can understand and guess the correct answer. The game even monetized by having people unlock certain colors and drawing tools, so that they would have a richer variety of ways to express their creativity in helping the other person guess better (this is what I call a *booster*, which we will cover later in this chapter).

Furthermore, Draw Something brought in an addictive Social Influence & Relatedness element (Core Drive #5) that made people curious to see if their friends could guess the meaning of their drawings (which adds Core Drive 7: Unpredictability & Curiosity). All these elements contributed to the huge success of Draw Something during its time.

---

[88]Dashiell Bennett. Yahoo News. "The Decline and Fall of 'Draw Something'". 05/01/2012.

144

[89]IGN Drawsome Gallery: http://www.ign.com/wikis/draw-something/Drawsome_-Gallery

The Downfall of Draw Something

Despite tapping into these Core Drives, once Zynga purchased the exciting game, the numbers started to decline. Many users started to drop out as the game failed to provide fresh content and challenges that would give people a sense of continued improvement and novel conditions for further mastery.

Perhaps the Draw Something makers OMGPOP were too busy integrating with Zynga's team to add more words to the pool, for the same word challenges started to repeat again and again. The element of creativity became null as people drew the same picture over and over.

Here we see something that is not considered Evergreen Content – even though there are many ways to draw something. If the company does not add more word challenges for its players, the creativity aspect diminishes and the game becomes dull.

Another issue is, when you are juggling too many ongoing games at once (as the design makes it natural for you to play a new game after each match, as well as invite more friends to play new games), it may start to feel like a big burden to answer all of them instead of feeling excited about the actual gameplay. As we know, play should be voluntary, and once you feel like you are not in control of your gameplay, you fall into Black Hat motivation, leading to a long-term fallout of a player's engagement.

Finally, the game also lost its appeal because many users simply bypassed the creative elements and began to "game" the system by drawing the actual letters of the answer instead of a picture. As a result, many of the people who had really high scores were the ones who were cheating. People will exert their creativity in a multitude of ways, including coming up with ways to cheat a system.

In my client workshops, I often explore how having a system that is "gameable" is not necessarily bad and may even help their company if it is designed properly. However, if done incorrectly, it could seriously devalue the gameplay and clearly demoralize the experiences of those seeking to legitimately participate.

If you block users from expressing their creativity in ways that are beneficial for the ecosystem, they will ultimately use their creativity to find loopholes and gain the upper hand by playing "behind your back."

Game Techniques within Empowerment of Creativity & Feedback

You have learned more about the motivational and psychological nature of Core Drive 3: Empowerment of Creativity & Feedback. To make it more actionable, I've included some Game Techniques below that heavily utilize this Core Drive to engage users.

Boosters (Game Technique #31)

Have you ever played the game Super Mario and felt blissfully excited when you picked up a mushroom or flower that made you stronger? These are considered Boosters in a game, where a player obtains something to help them achieve the win-state effectively.

Different from simply leveling up or acquiring new skills, Boosters are usually limited to certain conditions. You can enjoy the brick-breaking and fire-throwing as long as you stay out of harms way. Once you get hit by an enemy, you return back to your "natural state" prior to the boosters.

Boosters such as obtaining a "jumping star" in Super Mario are limited by time, and temporarily give users the power of invincibility. For the next dozen seconds (I actually went on Youtube and counted the seconds just to write this), a player would rush as quickly as he can (sometimes falling into pits) as he enjoys the adrenaline rush of using his evanescent power (with a touch of Core Drive 6: Scarcity & Impatience).

That feeling of being empowered with new, but limited power-ups is exhilarating and is an extremely strong motivator towards the desired action. Very few people are willing to stop the game while the Star Invincibility effect is still active.

In games like Candy Crush, Boosters are also very powerful mechanics, especially for its monetization. A player can earn (or buy) a limited number of boosters that will help overcome some of the most difficult challenges at a specific stage; such as getting a Bubblegum Troll to defeat the menacing chocolates, or a Disco Ball-like Color Bomb to remove all candies of a certain color. Without different boosters and power-ups, the game would not be nearly as engaging as it is today.

Example of Boosters within Superbook.tv

One of my clients, Superbook.tv, runs an incredibly high-quality Computer Graphics (CG) animation series with millions of fans, both online and via international TV. Superbook.tv is part of the non-profit Christian Broadcast Network, and its goal is to teach children about stories in the Bible through vibrant graphics, modern relatedness (Core Drive 5), and quirky humor. It even has a funny red robot named Gizmo that says goofy things while performing mind-blowing tricks - such as having a robot pet parrot fly out of its chest when it was pretending to be a robot pirate.

On top of the high-quality movies, SuperBook.tv also has a website that aims to engage children to learn more about the back stories presented within the episodes. When I work with clients, I always first ask them to define five items within the Octalysis Strategy Dashboard that we will cover in Chapter 17: Business Metrics, Users, Desired Actions, Feedback Mechanics, and Incentives. While most of my clients define revenue growth or active users as their number one Business Metric, Superbook's Director of Creative

Media Gregory Flick stated that, "Our number one Business Metric is to get kids more engaged with the Bible."

To attract children's attention, Superbook's strategy is to implement a variety of fun games on their website that kids can enjoy playing. These games provide opportunities to accumulate "SuperPoints" that can later be redeemed for merchandise, gift cards, and other rewards.

While the children are enjoying their games, some of them will start to explore other content on the site, including the "Episode Guides." These guides explain much of the back stories of each episode, such as the historical setting of the time, characters, and other interesting trivia.

The ultimate goal is to use the Episode Guide to direct children towards the Bible App, where they can interact with the Bible more. This is a very clear funneling strategy: Play Games –> Explore Episode Guide –> Interact with Bible App.

Turning the Funnel Around

The disadvantage of funneling strategies, is that the bottom of the funnel is often only a tiny fraction of the top. Many Kids will play the games, and *maybe* some of them will notice the Episodes Guides, but only a few of those kids will try out the Bible App. It would be nice if part of the *game* is to go into the Episode Guides and the Bible App, as opposed to simply being a curious discover.

A potential solution to this issue is to embed Boosters within both the Episode Guides and Bible App. Let's say, by completing Bible-related challenges within the Episodes Guides (which requires utilizing the Bible App to do well on), a child can increase their "Knowledge Score" that will serve as a multiplier towards Super-Points when they are playing the fun games on the site.

After they win a game with the boosters on, it would show them a "Knowledge Score Multiplier" next to their points, allowing them to earn SuperPoints much faster than other kids. Of course, for Scarcity & Impatience sake, it should also display "Knowledge Score Multiplier: 0%" if the child does not have these boosters yet, just to make them yearn for it.

What's interesting here is that instead of playing games and *maybe* going to the episode guides and possibly going into the Bible App; it is now strategic for the child to *first* go to the Episode Guide, maximize their Knowledge Scores, and then go back to play the games. Now the child's own creative strategy process motivates them to engage with the Bible App before playing games, and the "funnel model" before has been turned upside down in favor of their top Business Metrics.

Milestone Unlock (Game Technique #19)

One of the most successful design techniques within games is something I call the Milestone Unlock. When people play games, they often set an internal stop time in the form of a milestone – "Let me beat this boss and then I'm done." "I'm close to leveling up. Once I level up I'll go to bed."

What the Milestone Unlock does is open up an exciting possibility that wasn't there before that milestone was reached.

In some RPGs (Role Playing Games), whenever you level up, you learn a new set of skills. These skills are awesome and generally help you vanquish monsters faster and with more style. Consequently, they would have made your earlier gameplay a lot easier.

Once players level up (their "stop-time milestone"), they naturally want to see what these new skills are like. They will want to test them out a bit, then test them out on stronger enemies, enjoy how powerful they are, and then realize they are so close to the next milestone that they might as well get there before stopping.

This is when people plan to stop playing at 11PM but end up playing till 4AM in the morning.

Milestone Unlocks in Plants vs Zombies

Plants vs. Zombies is a dynamic "tower-defense" game geared towards forming a creative strategy to utilize resources and "plants" to solve puzzles of zombie attacks. In the spirit of Core Drive 3, the game embodies an aspect of allowing people to incorporate their creativity to come up with various solutions towards solving the same problem. Interestingly, this is the only "fighting" game and the only "zombies" game that both my mother and my wife got very into.

In terms of Game Techniques, Plants vs Zombies utilizes Milestone Unlocks to the extreme. When you complete each level, you will usually unlock a new Plant to help you defend against Zombies. Not by coincidence, that new plant is often the exact plant that directly counters the toughest zombie in the stage you just defeated, and would have made your life a lot easier if you had it earlier!

Of course, this is usually not the time to stop playing. If you didn't start the next stage and try out these new found powers, you would be laying in bed, thinking about it all night long!

Poison Picker/Choice Perception (Game Technique #89)

Many studies[90] have shown that people like something more when they are given a choice, compared to simply having one option. This holds true even if the multiple options are not as appealing compared to the single choice. Any parent with a two year old will recognize the influence of choice perception.

---

[90] Sheena S. Iyengar & Mark R. Lepper. Columbia University & Stanford University. "When Choice is Demotivating: Can One Desire Too Much of a Good Thing?". 12/2000.

"Do you want to eat your vegetables before or after your chicken?"

When children turn two years old, they quickly discover that they possess a special power called "Free Will." And once they discover this power, they start to exercise it with great fluency.

*"Which one do you want?"

"…"

"Do you want A?"

"NO!"

"Okay. Do you want B then?"

"NO!"

"Well, you have to make a choice. A or B?"

"NO!"

"So you don't want anything. I'll take them away okay?"

"NO!"*

Negotiating with children is serious parenting work. You have to make the child think that whatever happens, it's a result of their own decision and not someone else's suggestion. (Interestingly, this aspect of us does not change as we grow older.) When the child does not know what they want, it's the toughest because they can't make a choice on their own. But they still hate it if they went along with someone else's suggestion.

When I was little, my mother would have me learn to play the piano. It was very frustrating for me, and many times I would cry out in anger. After two years of piano, my mother saw how much misery it caused me, and told me, "Okay, if you hate it so much, you don't have to play the piano anymore. But you have to play an instrument. What would you like to play?" At the time I saw a popular singer in Taiwan named Lee-Hom Wang play the violin on-stage at a large concert, and it made an impression on me. I therefore told my mother that I wanted to play the violin.

After I switched from playing the piano to the violin, things didn't necessarily become easier. But because I made a choice to play the violin, I sucked it up and played with a much better attitude. After all, if I also hated playing the violin, it would mean my previous choice was "wrong." And people hate being wrong! When I would start to whine and complain, my mother would ask me, "So you hate playing the violin then?" I would immediately shoot back with, "No! Who said I hate playing the violin? I LOVE playing the violin! I just need...more practice."

What a win for the parent!

The key to the Choice Perception is that the choice itself is not necessarily meaningful, but merely makes a person feel like they are empowered to choose between different paths and options. In my case, I was still forced to play an instrument – I did not have the choice to stop learning – but because I felt that I could choose which instrument to play, I felt empowered.

When I say the choice is not meaningful, it could mean that either the user is presented with a good option and a bad option, inviting the user to naturally choose the better one (again, often the user will feel happier with this situation, rather than being forced to take the better option); or it could mean that all the options are too limiting and therefore undifferentiated from one another.

Jesse Schell, in his book *The Art of Game Design - A Book of Lenses*, introduces two Lenses: The Lens of Freedom and the Lens of Indirect Control[91]. Schell describes that, *"we don't always have to give the player true freedom - we only have to give the player the feeling of freedom. [...] if a clever designer can make a player feel free, when really the player has very few choices, or even no choice at all, then suddenly we have the best of both worlds - the player has the wonderful feeling of freedom, and the designer has managed to economically create an experience with an ideal interest curve and*

---

[91]Jesse Schell. *The Art of Game Design: A Book of Lenses.* p284-292. CRC Press. Boca Raton. 2008.

an ideal set of events."

According to Schell, this can be accomplished by 1) Adding constraints to player choices, 2) Incentivizing players to take certain choices that actually meets the player goals, 3) Create an Interface that guides the user towards the Desired Actions, 4) Adding visual designs to attract the player's sight, 5) Provide social guidance (often through computer generated characters in the game), and 6) Music control that affects player behaviors.

Choice Perception influences our decisions in many other significant ways, such as wasting time and energy keeping meaningless doors or options open, even though they were formerly written off as bad options, simply to maintain a perception of having a choice.[92]

Obviously, since Choice Perception suggests a lack of meaningful choices, it often is not ideal in an implementation as it does not truly bring out the creativity of the user. You could also offend users if too many options are blatantly meaningless. However, for many businesses, it is easier on the designer to implement choice perceptions into its systems than to actually create Meaningful Choices.

Plant Picker/Meaningful Choices (Game Technique #11)

Beyond choices that allow people to feel like they are empowered, there are choices that are truly meaningful and demonstrates preferences that are not obviously superior over others. I refer to these techniques as "Plant Pickers" because, just like deciding what to plant in a garden, it is often a preference on style and strategy, something that fuels Core Drive 3.

If you create a gamified environment with a hundred players, and *all* hundred of these players reach the Win-State in the exact

---

[92]Dan Ariely. *Predictably Irrational.* p188. Harper Perennial. New York, NY. 2010.

same way (such as "do action A, get points, do action B, get badges, do action C, win!"), there are no meaningful choices present. (Often times this could be seen if the gamified system has a no-brainer *dominant strategy*[93], which falls under Choice Perception.) If thirty players play the game one way, thirty play it another way, and the last forty play it yet another way, then you have some level of Meaningful Choices. If all hundred players play the game differently, then you have a great amount of *meaningful choices.*

If you tell a hundred kids to sit there and play with a set of Lego, it is statistically impossible for any two children to build the same thing in the exact same order (outside of copying each other, of course). That level of meaningful choices and play is the ultimate state of Core Drive 3: Empowerment of Creativity & Feedback.

Plants vs Zombies Strategy

I mentioned above how the Milestone Unlock is such a huge component in Plants vs Zombies good game design. Another aspect of its success is the Plant Picker. When you start a stage in Plants vs Zombies, you are faced with a challenge – a wave of zombies, each with different strengths and capabilities. You, as the player, have a limited number of plants you can "pre-pick" before a game to defend against those zombies. There are sun-resources that allow you to sow a plant, and there are a limited number of squares that you can place them in.

To defeat a level in Plants vs Zombies, there are a variety of ways and strategies that each work extraordinarily well, among many ways that don't work at all. A player can choose to power up their economy first with many sun-gathering plants and fewer defense plants; lay out the field with basic pea-shooters; save up to use more powerful plants that do massive damage; completely focus on

[93]Jesse Schell. *The Art of Game Design: A Book of Lenses.* p180. CRC Press. Boca Raton. 2008.

explosives and traps; or use stinky onions to herd all the zombies into one lane before wiping them all out with penetrating attacks.

Often, one would defeat a level with one strategy, just to replay it again to test out another new strategic idea that the player conceived. The process of being able to select many options, each with its unique strengths and weaknesses, and resulting in a variety of style and creativity-based strategies, is the core essence of the Plant Picker technique.

Unfortunately, when Plants vs Zombies 2 was first launched, it completely forgot about its original design roots and turned Plant Pickers into Poison Pickers, with some plants being overpowered, while having others being completely useless in the early phases.

Farmville Art

I believe that Farmville is actually not a "fun" game to play, because it does not use many intrinsic motivators, though it still creates a compelling and mind-numbing machine that brilliantly utilizes all the black hat game mechanics to bring out our Core Drives.

Generally, during the Endgame Phase, carrying out your daily grind is not fun. However, some players have created their own endgame in Farmville that I think is positive and fun for the right reasons – it allows everyone to creatively express themselves through their Farms.

After Farmville players have participated in the game long enough, having unlocked all sorts of plants and colors, some of them even become Farmville Artists to express their creativity . Many create amazingly beautiful pieces of art through the digital pixels of Farmville. Of course, using an actual drawing technology like *Microsoft Paint* might still be more efficient, but hey, the canvas is your farm!

Because there are so many things you can do with your crops, this element of Farmville can be considered an Evergreen Mechanic.

Users can continuously stay engaged without adding any additional content, just like paint and a paintbrush can be Evergreen material. The tricky thing here is that players must quickly plant the art and then take a screenshot, for within a few hours the plants will all wither and die.

Here are some pretty noteworthy pieces of art:

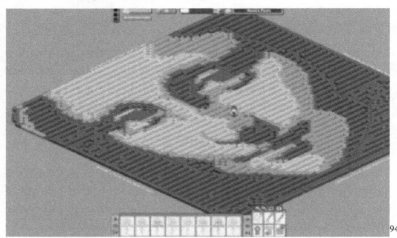

94

95

---

[94] Kevin Johnson. Wikia Farmville. URL: http://farmville.wikia.com/wiki/File:Farmville-mona-lisa-by-kevin-johnson-300x186.png

[95] Jenny Ng. Games.com Blog. "FarmVille Pic of the Day: Embrace of Swan Lake at Liveloula46's farm." 03/01/2012.

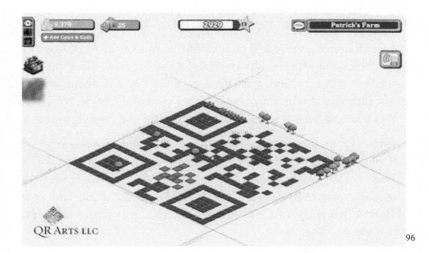

QR ARTS LLC

96

Basic Components; Infinite Combos

Meaningful Choices make games like Lego, Chess, or even Minecraft[97] fun. Your choices create a tangible difference in your gameplay, and it shapes how the experience evolves over time. Often, there are only a few building blocks to select from, but based on the context, challenges, and constraints, these building blocks come into play in varying ways for different scenarios.

In the book *A Theory of Fun for Game Design*, game designer Raph Koster introduces a hypothetical game with a single hammer that can only do one thing, which likely results in a dull experience. Koster compares it to the game of Tic-Tac-Toe, which also does not require a meaningful range of abilities and strategy. In comparison, checkers players can start to learn the importance of forcing other players into disadvantageous jumps. "Most games unfold abilities over time, until at a high level you have many possible stratagems

---

[96] Amy-Mae Elliott. Mashable.com. "15 Beautiful and Creative QR Code". 11/7/23.

[97] Wikipedia Entry "Minecraft": http://en.wikipedia.org/wiki/Minecraft

to choose from."[98]

Game designer Jesse Schell points out that one of the most exciting and interesting ways to add Meaningful Choices is to allow players to choose between playing it safe, and go for a small reward, or take a big risk, and try for a big reward. This type of dynamic, which he coins *triangularity*, is seen in many successful and engaging games.

Ultimately, there are no one-size-fits-all solutions to implementing Meaningful Choices in your experience. If there were, it would be a paradox. You have to decide and carefully design which challenges the user must resolve, what plants the users can pick, and how different plants options will reshape the user experience into new inspiring lush forests.

Core Drive 3: The Bigger Picture

Core Drive 3: Empowerment of Creativity & Feedback is a great Core Drive on many different levels. It taps into our innate desire to create, by providing us the tools and power to direct our own gameplay and giving us the ability to affect the environment around us through our own imaginations.

Unfortunately, Core Drive 3 is often the most difficult to implement into a product design, primarily because it requires so much attention from an already attention-deficit society. In an age of information overload, people have shorter attention spans in order to filter out all the worthless content they are bombarded with on a daily basis. So unless you design your experience with finesse, people will likely shy away from committing the time and energy needed to invest their creativity into something. That is why Core Drive 3 is more commonly seen effective in the Scaffolding and

---

[98]Raph Koster. *A Theory of Fun*. 2nd Edition. p122. O'Reilly Media. Sebastopol, CA. 10/2013.

Endgame Phases, as opposed to the Discovery and Onboarding Phases.

Once you are able to unlock the power of Core Drive 3: Empowerment of Creativity & Feedback, it often creates a rush of other Core Drives, such as Development & Accomplishment, Social Influence & Relatedness through collaborative play, as well as Unpredictability & Curiosity. When effectively implemented, this Core Drive becomes a key evergreen engine that can be the difference between a short-lived flower and a timeless Redwood.

To get the most out of the book, Choose only ONE of the below options to do right now:

Easy: Think of an example where Core Drive 3: Empowerment of Creativity motivated you or others to take certain actions. Did it keep people engaged for longer?

Medium: Think of the last time you were engaged in an activity that really drew you in. Did it involve a lot of creativity, strategy, or meaningful choices? If yes, describe the process in which these elements were brought out. If not, think of ways to add these components into the experience. Would that make the activity even more engaging?

Medium: For your own project, think of ways you can implement Milestone Unlocks into the experience, while rewarding the users with Boosters once they hit the milestone. Are the Boosters something that users will see in a favorable light because it allows them to do what they desire to do, but more efficiently? Or is it something that users will perceive as a controlling tool to make what *you* want more efficient without caring about their own interests?

Share what you come up with on Twitter or your preferred social network with the hashtag #OctalysisBook and see what ideas other people have.

Get Your Feet Wet

Now that you are diving into the fascinating world of Octalysis Gamification and motivation, try out the Octalysis Tool on my website. Play with the Core Drive sliders, add short notes on each Core Drive to help understand each better, and read the automatically generated Octalysis Insights to better understand the strength and weaknesses of the design. Use this as a creative process and see the insights as feedback for your analysis. The Octalysis Tool can be accessed for free at YukaiChou.com/octalysis-tool.

Chapter 8: The Fourth Core Drive - Ownership & Possession

Ownership & Possession is the fourth Core Drive in Octalysis Gamification. It represents the motivation that is driven by our feelings of owning something, and consequently the desire to improve, protect, and obtain more of it.

This Core Drive involves many elements such as virtual goods and virtual currencies, but it is also the primary drive that compels us to collect stamps or accumulate wealth. On a more abstract level, Core Drive 4 is connected to our investment of time or resources into customizing something to our own liking. This can also be found in a system that constantly learns about your preferences in order to mold an experience that uniquely fits you.

Ownership & Possession is positioned to the far left of the Octalysis Framework, and therefore represents the Core Drive that exhibits the strongest influence on the Left Brain (again, this is not scientifically geographical but more symbolic) relating to analytical thinking. Here, decisions are mostly based on logic and analysis, reinforced by the desire for possession as the primary motivating factor.

For example, in Farmville, you are constantly striving to increase the value of your assets by developing your land, establishing higher crop yields, and improving the quantity and quality of your livestock. You can further develop your property's infrastructure and dwellings – establishing that country manor on your dream estate.

Because of this, you find yourself constantly investing more time and energy in expanding your farm. Accumulating more cows, plants, and fruits as well as purchasing stables to house your horses or grooming services to make them look "prettier."

Wait, it's mine? Hold on, I do care then!

Our brains form a natural association with the things that we own. Pretend for a moment that you generally prefer most drinks to beer (for many readers, this exercise would be a very difficult one). If we were at a party and I gave you a bottle of beer, you may respond, "Oh that's okay. I'm not a big fan of beer." I then respond with, "Nah, just take it! I'll put it here next to you."

At this point, you may still not care about this bottle of beer. You may even abandon it when you stand up and leave. But at that moment, if someone walks by, picks up the beer and begins to drink it, you will likely feel the urge to say, "Hey! What are you doing?" They may respond with, "What's the big deal? You're not drinking it anyway!" There's a good chance you would still be unhappy. "Still, you should have asked before taking it."

Once you feel a sense of ownership over something, its status elevates and it begins to motivate your behavior differently. If a beer you didn't care about could provoke your displeasure towards someone, imagine how much more you would be influenced if it was something you deeply cared about.

A friend of mine named Chris Robino once explained to me that he was never any good at math until he started running his own business and added a dollar sign to the numbers. The math suddenly became very engaging, and he quickly mastered everything he needed to know.

With his new sense of mastery over money, he quickly built his business into a successful and lucrative consulting firm. Chris jokingly said, "Once the numbers started to represent my own money, I instantly became a genius."

Similar to the beer example, the nature of the motivation and engagement completely shifted when his mind realized that these boring numbers were now a representation of what he owned and cared about.

Stamps of Sanity

One of the most common manifestations of the Ownership & Possession Core Drive is the desire to collect things, such as stamps or baseball cards. Many of us have had the experience of collecting certain items, where the items themselves have relatively low practical functionality but are only meaningful because they represented a piece in a larger set.

Initially, some readers might feel that Core Drive 4 only entails the actions of accumulating more possessions, but it also provides emotional comfort to those who simply dwell upon those possessions. This is like the owners of expensive cars or paintings who spend hours admiring and enjoying their prized possessions without needing to do anything with them. Some people even hide their paintings so no one can steal them, while still enjoying the utility by just *knowing* that the paintings are in the safe.

In Malcolm Gladwell's book *David and Goliath*, Gladwell describes a physician at a children's hospital in the 1950's who was treating young patients that were very ill from childhood leukemia and were bleeding constantly. Gladwell writes:

The kids bled from everywhere - through their stool, urine - that's the worst part. They paint the ceiling. They bleed from out of their ears, from their skin. There was blood on everything. The nurses would come to work in the morning in their white uniforms and go home covered in blood. [...] The Children would bleed internally, into their livers and spleens, putting them in extraordinary pain. They would turn over in their beds and get terrible bruises. Even a nosebleed was a potential fatal event."[99]

In those day, there was a ninety percent fatality rate where the children would bleed to death within six weeks. Working in such demoralizing environments, you could imagine that most doctors didn't last very long. Gladwell describes how, after returning from a emotionally crushing day at work, all this particular physician wanted to do was to quietly sit in front of his stamp collection each night.

This struck me as very odd. This man is watching children die in his hands on a daily basis, and the one thing that makes him feel better

---

[99] Malcolm Gladwell. *David and Goliath*. P144. Hachette Book Group. New York, NY. 2013.

is a set of stamps? Also, it seems that he would simply sit in front of the stamps for a nontrivial period of time each evening. What was he actually thinking as he sat there? Was he just looking at them, as if he had forgotten which stamps he owned, or just feeling good about them?

This is the power of Ownership & Possession - it not only has the ability to engage, it has the ability to comfort and instill a sense of well-being. You see the same phenomenon with baseball cards, pens, and even impressive looking books that no one reads neatly placed on a shelf (hopefully my book doesn't become one of those). People just like to display them and marvel at the collection for hours, while seemingly "having fun" in the process.

How Stoned Can You Be

A fascinating example on the feeling of ownership is seen on Yap, a small island in the Caroline Islands of the Western Pacific Ocean. Besides sounding cheerful and carefree, the "Yapese" are known for using a currency called *Rai*.[100]

Rai functions like most currencies, except they are often large, circular stone disks carved out of limestone from aragonite and calcite crystals. The issue with some Rai being very large, is that it is almost impossible to carry them around, let alone pass them on to others. In fact, some Rai are so large that it is generally impractical to move them at all and are therefore left in the wild. As a result, when the Yapese buy something with Rai, they simply leave an oral history that the ownership of the Rai is now transferred to another person.

---

[100]Eric Guinther. WonderMondo.com. "STONE MONEY OF YAP IN GACHPAR VILLAGE". Accessed 02/22/2015

Image of a Rai Stone by Eric Guinther

In the most extreme case, there was a famous Rai stone that fell off a ship during transportation and sunk to the bottom of the ocean. Even though no one has seen it for over a century, the Yapese assume it is still there, so the rightful owner of the Rai stone in the ocean could still exchange that ownership for other goods. That's pretty wild, with some pun intended.

What if I told you that a large piece of stone somewhere in the world is in my possession, and I will trade it to you for a million dollars. However, you won't be able to move it and it will have to be left in its original place, just like the owner before me did. what would you think of the arrangement?

You may think I'm stoned or crazy, and elect your preferred method of interacting with such people. (Popular options include: laughing at me, yelling at me, looking at me strangely, pretending to take me seriously just to entertain yourself, pretending to take me seriously just to be polite - all reactions I've received when I talked about gamification between 2003 - 2008).

However, that's what we actually see in modern, developed societies regularly. If a businessman told you that he owns a famous building or monument in Chicago, and will pass the ownership rights to you if you paid him $100 million, suddenly it's not as crazy - beyond the fact that you may not have the money handy.

You may not have even seen the property - it's not strictly required for the purchase, especially if it is already well known - nor will you be able to move it anywhere, but now it is considered a legitimate business transaction that anyone will take seriously. Of course, in order to make sure you can prove the transfer of ownership, you in this case would prefer to have this agreement on paper instead of memorized orally. Such is the strange nature of ownership.

Ownership is often a feeling or agreement, but it can also take the form of an idea. I own the Octalysis Framework, and many people who want to borrow or license it ask for permission because they recognize and respect this ownership. My ownership of Octalysis will stay intact until I agree that the ownership should be transferred to someone else. Once I agree and sign it over to someone else, *poof*, my ownership of the idea or methodology instantly disappears.

The Perfect Pet

Another interesting example of the unique aspect of Core Drive 4: Ownership and Possession is the Pet Rock.[101] The Pet Rock was a strange and popular product executed by Californian advertising freelancer Gary Dahl in 1975. Upon hearing his friends complain about their pets, he conceptualized the perfect pet that would not need to be fed, bathed, groomed, toilet-trained, walked, and would

---

[101] Mortal Journey. "Pet Rocks (1970's). 12/20/2010.

not become disobedient, get sick, or even die. The perfect pet was
the rock.

For a short period, the Pet Rock became a popular sensation. It came
in a box with holes (just in case it needed to breathe), and provided
some with soft straw for its comfort. There was also an owner's
manual with instructions on how to give commands such as "sit"
and "stay," as well as proper hand gestures to get the Pet Rock to
"roll over," "jump," and "attack."

Finally, there was something that people could love, hold, and
cherish, without dealing with all the physical hassles and emotional
difficulties of a biological pet.

To write this book, I purchased an original 1975 Pet Rock on eBay for $14.75 plus taxes and shipping.

Though the craze was short-lived, between 1975 and 1976, over 1.5 million Pet Rocks were sold. As of today, many of them are still playing "sit, stay" on a daily basis, though I imagine most are strays by now. The love didn't last.

Of course, Gary Dahl was less concerned about whether the Pet Rocks were loved, because he walked away with millions of dollars. His only regret may be that the Internet wasn't around during the 70s to make the Pet Rocks even more viral.

When people feel like they have ownership of something, they naturally want to care for and protect it. Unfortunately, the Pet Rock provided no Core Drive 3: Empowerment of Creativity & Feedback. As a result, people moved on to other conceptual pets that actually could provide some feedback mechanics.

The First Virtual Pet Game

When I was in fifth grade, it was my third year back in Taiwan after living in South Africa for six years. Those years were very difficult for me, both academically and socially. My level of Chinese was significantly behind all my peers, and my grades were very poor.

Back then, there would be Chinese quizzes where each time you wrote a character incorrectly, you needed to write a full column of the same character as punishment and practice. Most of my classmates only had to write two or three columns of "punishment practice" after each quiz, but I often had to write three to four pages of them. I remember when I was in third grade, I would be writing these penalty characters until 3AM in the morning with my mother next to me, with constant tears on my face. To my knowledge, this was not typical for most third graders.

To add to the difficulty, I was always the odd one out because I came from a different culture. I didn't really fit in, and other children would make fun of me. It was during this period that I started to pay close attention to what different types of people in different environments thought and felt. I also spent a great deal of time trying to understand how I could get people to accept me as their peer or perhaps, even respect me one day. Though painful, it may have helped me become more resilient and initiated my intellectual curiosity towards human motivation - which later manifested itself into the 8 Core Drives.

While I was working so hard to be "cool" among my classmates, I realized that almost all of them had become crazed with this new thing called Tamagotchi, where kids would carry this tiny egg-like device with a little digital display. Inside the display, you started off with an egg. Once you have set the time and selected a name, the egg quickly turns into a small baby ball that you have to nurture and raise. There are a few simple options to feed the baby, play with it, discipline it, clean up its boo-boos, and give it medicine when it is ill.

Under weeks of tender care, the little baby grows into a larger "animal" that responds to all your loving activities. In some versions, the pet lays an egg before it passes away, so you can start to play the game all over again without feeling that you failed. Back then as I was trying to fit in and be accepted, I really wanted one of these. Luckily, a classmate and I discovered a little abandoned pet in the boy's restroom. We had great sympathy over the poor little thing, so we decided to raise it as our own.

For a few months, we took turns taking care of the little thing, deciding what to feed the animal on a regular basis when it cried out, and took it for walks in its electronic world. Though the activity itself was rather tedious and not necessarily "challenging" nor "unpredictable," we fought over who should take care of the little pet because we felt like it was our own. In that sense, it was enjoyable for us to do these chores, even "fun."

Eventually, the animal grew into a brachiosaurus. It was actually an eDinosaur! Interestingly, for this particular device, what type of dinosaur it became was determined by what food you chose to feed it. If you fed it more vegetables, it would become a brachiosaurus; if you fed it more meat, it would become a Tyrannosaurus Rex. I was sad to discovered this too late, as I would have really wanted a T-Rex. (Can you identify what Core Drive this game mechanic appeals to?)

Many years later, I learned that Tamagotchi was a huge craze that swept Japan and the western world. Launching in 1996 in Japan, it was an early effort to create a toy/game that targeted girls who didn't care about the fighting games of the time. The appeal of Tamagotchi obviously went well beyond its target audience.

It swept the world and was even banned in many schools because kids had to take their Tamagotchi to school to feed, as a lapse of 12 hours not caring for your pet would result in its death - appealing to the *Scarcity* and *Avoidance* Core Drives. Australia banned it as well due to some slot machine mini-games designed within. The government decided that it incorrectly taught children to become gamblers (this is the *Unpredictability* Core Drive). The Black Hat Game Design did its work.

Over the years, there were 76 million Tamagotchi's sold worldwide. It became one of the earliest precursors of popular social games where the key objective is to care for an animal, a property, or a business.

It looks like this ingrained sense of Ownership & Possession, along with some added benefits of novelty (Core Drive 7: Unpredictability & Curiosity), made products like Pet Rocks, Tamagotchi, and later on Facebook games like *Farmville* or *Pet Society*[102] such big successes worldwide.

The Endowment Effect

There is quite a bit of scientific research on how our psychology changes when we believe we own something. Much of it is summed up in what Academics call the *Endowment Effect*.

---

[102]Ben Parr. Mashable.com. "Pet Society Sells 90 Million Virtual Goods Per Day". 12/7/2010.

In his book *Thinking: Fast and Slow*, Economics Nobel Prize Laureate Daniel Kahneman describes how a certain well-respected academic and wine lover becomes very reluctant to sell a bottle of wine from his collection for $100, but would also not pay more than $35 for a wine of similar quality.

This made little economic sense because the same or similar wine should hold the same value in a person's mind. The purchasing price and selling price should be roughly the same, deducting transaction costs. This illustrates that when a person starts to own something, they immediately place more value on that item relative to others who don't own it.

Researchers Dan Ariely and Ziv Carmon took this concept further by testing it on Duke University students who were avid basketball fans and would go through a demanding process to obtain tickets for Duke basketball games.[103] After a semester of camping in small tents and checking in regularly whenever an air horn sounded, students who camped in front of the line were only given a lottery number towards obtaining the actual tickets. After the lottery results were announced, some students became ticket holders, while others did not.

The Researchers called up the students who were winners in the lottery and asked them what would be an acceptable price that they would sell their tickets for. Concurrently, the non-winners were contacted and asked how much they would be willing to pay in order to get a ticket. It turned out, the non-winning students (who gave the exact same amount of sweat and labor towards it) were willing to pay $170 for a ticket on average. On the other hand, can you guess what the average ticket owner was willing to sell it for?

The average ticket owner, whose only merit was that they were lucky enough to win the lottery, demanded $2,400 on average for their tickets. That is *fourteen times* more than the average buyer

---

[103] Ziv Carmon and Dan Ariely. *Journal of Consumer Research. "Focusing on the Forgone: How Value Can Appear So Different to Buyers and Sellers". 2000.

price. Clearly, the value of these tickets in the students' minds went through drastic changes the moment they became owners.

In a more lab-like example, Researcher Jack Knetsch asked two classes to fill out some questionnaires while promising a reward - prominently displayed in front of the students for the entire duration of the session. One group was promised an expensive pen, while the other group was promised a bar of swiss chocolate. After both sides had earned their rewards, they were allowed to trade their rewards with the other group. Only 10% of the participants wanted to trade, showing that most of them valued their own rewards simply because they already had ownership.[104]

James Heyman, Yesim Orhun, and Dan Ariely further showed that the Endowment Effect is also realized when we simply imagine ourselves owning something. They found within auction sites, the longer people remained the top bidder (having imagined themselves as the official owner for longer), the more aggressively they would bid when someone offered a counter bid[105]. The envisioned ownership actually motivates people to fight for their divine rights to that item they don't yet own.

This is why advertisers often try to get consumers to imagine themselves owning the promoted products by asking consumers to think about what they would do with those products. Also, *trial promotions* and "money-back guarantees" work the same way by letting consumers own the product first without any friction. Since we now know that the value of something becomes much greater after it is in our possession, consumers often feel reluctant to return that product and get their money back afterwards.

---

[104]Daniel Kahneman. "Thinking, Fast and Slow." P297. Farrar, Straus and Giroux. New York, NY. 2013.

[105]James Heyman, Yesim Orhun, and Dan Ariely. *Journal of Interactive Marketing*."Auction Fever: The Effect of Opponents and Quasi-Endowment on Product Valuations". 2004.

For Sale Not For Use

One caveat to the Endowment Effect is, if the person owns something as a token "for exchange," they will not feel attached to the item in a biased manner. If a merchant owns hundreds of shoes in the hopes of exchanging them for money, he obviously does not feel that sense of attachment when someone buys the product. Similarly, when consumers part ways with their money to buy these shoes, they also are not pulled back by the Endowment Effect (unless they are already in financial difficulty)[106].

Interestingly, when Economist John List studied trading behaviors at Baseball Card Conventions, he noticed that novice traders were heavily influenced by the Endowment Effect, inappropriately valuing their own cards much higher than what the market would bear. However, as they became more experienced traders, they started to see the baseball cards as tradable goods, resulting in the Endowment Effect gradually diminishing[107]. This is why we often make more rational, and hence consistent, decisions when we are simply reminded to "think like a trader."[108]

Identity, Consistency, and Commitments

Another interesting effect of Core Drive 4: Ownership & Possession is that it also drives us to value our own identities and become more consistent towards our past. After all, there are rarely things we hold more closely than our values, characters, and past commit-

---

[106] Daniel Kahneman. "Thinking, Fast and Slow." P294. Farrar, Straus and Giroux. New York, NY. 2013.

[107] John A. List, "Quarterly Journal of Economics 118. "Does Marketing Experience Eliminate Market Anomalies?". P46-71. 2003.

[108] Daniel Kahneman. "Thinking, Fast and Slow." P339. Farrar, Straus and Giroux. New York, NY. 2013.

ments[109].

In fact, science has shown that the longer we live, the more attached we become to our existing beliefs, preferences, methodologies, and even our own names.[110]

A surprising study conducted by social psychologist Brett Pelham revealed that people are much more likely to choose careers that sound similar to their own names[111]. To test this idea, Pelham looked up names that sounded like the word "dentist," such as Dennis. According to the census data, the name Dennis was the 40th most common male first name in the U.S., while Jerry and Walter were the 39th and 41st, respectively.

Pelham then searched the national directory of the American Dental Association for dentists that have these three first names. It turns out, 257 dentists were named Walter, while 270 dentists were named Jerry - fairly consistent with the statistical base rate. However, there were 482 dentists named Dennis, which is close to eighty percent higher than the normal base rate of other names. This indicates that, if you happen to be named Dennis, you have an eighty percent higher chance of becoming a dentist compared to if you were named something different.

Similarly, Pelham found that names starting with "Geo" such as "George" or "Geoffrey" are disproportionately more likely to become researchers in the geosciences. Hardware store owners are eighty percent more likely to have names that start with the letter "H" than the letter "R," while roofers are seventy percent more likely

---

[109]Robert Cialdini. *Influence: Science and Practice.* 5th Edition. P64. Pearson Education. Boston, MA.

[110]Stephanie Brown, Terrilee Asher and Robert Cialdini. *Journal of Research in Personality*, 39:517-33. "Evidence of a positive relationship between age and preference for consistency". 2005.

[111]Brett Pelham, Matthew Mirenberg, and John Jones. *Journal of Personality and Social Psychology, 82:469-87. "Why Susie sells seashells by the seashore: Implicit egotism and major life decisions". 2002.

to have names with the letter "R" than the letter H."[112]

Moreover, people tend to move to places that are similar to their own names too. People who move to Florida are disproportionately more likely to be named Florence, while people who move to Louisiana are skewed towards being named Louise. Mr. Washington is also much more likely to live on Washington Street than Mr. Jefferson. On that note, I'm glad that I have never considered a career in the medical profession, or else I might have ended up becoming a Urologist!

Though no one would recognize or admit that their names play any role in determining these important life choices, our attachment to our own identities become so strong that anything connected to that identity becomes desirable to us. Studies have even shown that we prefer brands and even spouses that remind us of our own names[113][114]. It has to be good because, well, it reminds me of *me*!

Consistency: Valuing Who We Were

Stemming from the attachment to our own identities is the need to behave consistently with our past actions. Dan Ariely describes this as *self-herding*, where we believe something is good (or bad) on the basis of our previous behavior.[115]. Often we buy certain items and brands just because we bought them in the past and we would like to stay consistent with our own choices, even though the particular product or brand may no longer be the best for our current needs.

---

[112]Noah Goldstein, Steve Martin, and Robert Cialdini. *Yes! 50 Scientifically Proven Ways to Be Persuasive.* P129. Simon & Schuster. New York, NY. 2010.

[113]John Jones, Brett Pelham, Mauricio Carvallo, and Matthew Mirenberg. Journal of Personality and Social Psychology, 87:665-83. "How do I love thee? Let me count the Js: Implicit egotism and interpersonal attraction". 2004.

[114]Miguel Brendl, Amitava Chattopadyay, Brett Pelham, and Mauricio Carvallo. *Journal of Consumer Research, 32:405-15. "Name letter branding: Valence transfer when product specific needs are active". 2005.

[115]Dan Ariely. Predictably Irrational. P39. Harper Perennial. New York, NY. 2010.

In fact, studies have shown that people instantly become much more confident in certain racehorses the moment they place a bet on the horse.[116] This is like a person estimating that a horse has a 30% chance of winning (which is pretty good given how many horses there are on a track) prior to making a bet, and then suddenly believing that the horse has a 60% chance of winning after placing the bet. This is because the horse suddenly transformed from "a good bet" to "my bet," and we learned from the Endowment Effect that once something becomes our own, we immediate place a much higher value on it.

Our need to be consistent with our past can also cause us to do unreasonable things for others. In 1966, psychologists Jonathan Freedman and Scott Fraser did an experiment where they went door-to-door to ask California residents whether they would agree to have a big public-service billboard erected on their front lawns.

The researchers showed a picture of a beautiful house almost completely obscured by a six-by-three feet, and poorly lettered billboard that read "DRIVE CAREFULLY," and asked if residents would agree to have it installed. Understandably, only 17 percent of the residents complied.

However, there was one particular group of residents that reacted to the offer positively, with 76 percent of them agreeing to the installation[117]. Why did this particular group respond so favorably? It turns out that two weeks prior to this intrusive offer, another "volunteer worker" went to those residents and asked if they would display a harmless three-inch-square sign that read "BE A SAFE DRIVER" in their windows. Since the request was fairly trivial, nearly everyone agreed to it.

What the residents didn't expect, was that this small act of public service would cause them to start believing they were publicly

---

[116] Robert Knox and James Inkster. *Journal of Experimental Social Psychology, 9, 551-562. "Postdecisional dissonance at post time". 1968.

[117] Jonathan Freedman and Scott Fraser. *Journal of personality and Social Psychology, 4, 195-203.* "Compliance without pressure: The foot-in-the-door technique". 1966.

conscious people who cared about drivers in the neighborhood. As a result, when the imposing request came two weeks later, in order to be consistent with their publicly conscious self-images, they were inclined to accept such offers with less hesitation. Of course, there were elements of Core Drive 1: Epic Meaning & Calling involved too, but as you can see in the control group experiments, the Epic Meaning & Calling alone was not enough to motivate people to give up their beautiful home views.

What's astonishing is that even with a third group of residents, whom two weeks prior were only asked to sign a petition that favored "keeping California beautiful," compliance rate of the "DRIVE CAREFULLY" billboard still increased to 50% - despite the petition had nothing to do with safe driving. This suggests that the compliance has less to do with the effects of *repetition priming*[118], but more to do with that sense of ownership towards being a publicly responsible person.

A reader of Robert Cialdini's book *Influence* once wrote that when his insurance sales staff started to ask, "I was wondering if you would tell me exactly why you've chosen to purchase your insurance with [our company.]" as opposed to simply setting up a physical appointment to sign the paperwork, sales immediately rose from 9% to 19%[119]. This worked because as people recited their reasoning for taking an appointment, they were convincing themselves of certain values that they should stay consistent with and follow through on.

---

[118]*Repetition priming* refers to the effect when our brains believe something is desirable simply because it was repeated to us many times in the past, hence cognitively easy to process.

[119]Robert Cialdini. *Influence: Science and Practice*. 5th Edition. P62. Pearson Education. Boston, MA. 08/08/2008.

Commitments: The Power of Writing Something Down

Our need for consistency becomes even stronger when we create a commitment, especially when we write it down. Social Psychologists Morton Deutsch and Harold Gerard once did an experiment where they asked groups of students to estimate the length of lines that were shown.

One group of students only had to think of an estimate in their heads, while another group had to write it down on a Magic Writing Pad but would erase it before anyone could see it. A third group would not only write down their estimates, but would publicly announce their figures.

Afterwards, the researchers gave new misleading information that suggested the students' initial estimates were incorrect, and gave them a chance to change their answers. Interestingly, the students who just made mental notes of their initial judgement were the least loyal to the judgements and changed their answers quickly, based on the new information.

The students who wrote their estimates down without anyone seeing were far more reluctant to change their answers when the new contradictory information was presented. Of course, with a little help from Core Drive 5: Social Influence & Relatedness, which we will cover in the next chapter, the group that publicly shared their estimates were the most stubborn in changing their answers; insisting that they were correct all along[120].

This level of consistency to commitments is why car salespeople often try to pin you down by saying, "I can't promise anything until a dreadful plea with my manager, but if I could get you this price,

---

[120]Morton Deutsch and Harold Gerard. *Journal of Abnormal and Social Psychology*, 51, 629-636. "A study of normative and informational social influences upon individual judgement. 1955.

you will buy the car today, correct?[121]" Once you commit to this and he sure enough returns with the quoted price, you will feel a great need to stay consistent with your earlier commitment, despite having full right to say "no."

In a similar manner, a restaurant owner once shared that after he switched from using "Please call if you have to cancel" to "Will you please call if you have to cancel?" during reservation calls, the no-show rate dropped from 30 percent to 10 percent. This is because when people answer "yes" to the question (and most people would feel like a jackal if they said "no" to such a reasonable request), they emotionally feel more committed in taking more responsibility for their reservations.[122]

Often, asking users to fill out their own forms increases commitment towards a behavior. When door-to-door salespeople started to ask their new customers to fill out the sales form instead of doing it for them, fewer people took advantage of the "cooling-off" laws where they could regret and return the product after being persuaded by Black Hat motivation techniques. Based on this, hospitals would likely also decrease cancelation rates if they asked their patients to fill out the next-appointment sheets instead of doing it for them[123].

This is also why companies like Procter & Gamble and General Foods often run contests where people write "25-, 50-, or 100-words or less" testimonials for them, starting with, "I like the product because...". As people describe enthusiastically how amazing these products are, they start to own up to their statements and see the products more favorably. Of course, they also start to see themselves as, "People who like the company product prizes so much that they

[121]Robert Cialdini. *Influence: Science and Practice*. 5th Edition. P60. Pearson Education. Boston, MA. 08/08/2008.

[122]Noah Goldstein, Steve Martin, and Robert Cialdini. *Yes! 50 Scientifically Proven Ways to Be Persuasive*. P74. Simon & Schuster. New York, NY. 2010.

[123]Robert Cialdini. *Influence: Science and Practice*. 5th Edition. P70. Pearson Education. Boston, MA. 08/08/2008.

are willing to participate in a testimonial contest."

This type of ownership over your identity, past decisions, and commitments can be one of the more subtle elements of motivation within Core Drive 4: Ownership & Possession. After all, you already know that you are heavily motivated by making more money, collecting stamps, or protecting your expensive assets; but you likely will not recognize it when your decisions were simply based on what your name is and what you ate last week.

Game Techniques within Ownership & Possession

You have learned more about the motivational and psychological nature of Core Drive 4: Ownership & Possession. To make it more actionable, I've included some Game Techniques below that heavily utilize this Core Drive to engage users.

Build-From-Scratch (Game Technique #43)

When you create a product or service, it is often desirable for your users to increase their vested ownership in the process of its creation. This is why it is useful to have them involved in the development process early on – to "build from scratch."

Building from scratch means that instead of giving them the entire setup – giving them the fully furnished house and the developed avatar from the beginning, you want them to start off decorating the house from scratch. Pick and place the beds in the house for themselves, choose a hair color and style for their avatars, and select their preferred fashion statement. When people are building something from scratch, they feel like, "I own this. This is my thing."

But if you start off by giving them a perfectly enchanting character or a fully decorated home, they may not become as involved otherwise. Even if you tell them, "Hey, you can redecorate or add things to it," people will likely feel less ownership and be less engaged.

Studies[124] indicate that people feel more attached to their cheap IKEA furniture even compared to their expensive high-end furniture, primarily because they spent more time building the IKEA furniture with their own hands. That feeling of personal ownership also motivates them to talk about their IKEA furniture more often with friends. The same can be said of small carpentry projects like building a garden box, bench, or birdhouse.

In fact, behavioral scientists Dan Ariely and Mike Norton started to term this phenomenon "Ikea effect."[125]

One thing to note, if the Build-From-Scratch technique distracts people away from the First Major Win-State (where users first exclaim, "Wow! This is awesome!"), then it is not a good design. Either you should give users the option to Build-From-Scratch with some quick template options that will allow them to move forward quickly and customize later, or you want to ensure that the Build-From-Scratch Technique itself is a First Major Win-State that users will feel excited about.

Collection Sets (Game Technique #16)

One of the most powerful and effective ways to utilize Core Drive 4: Ownership and Possession is through Collection Sets. Say you give people a few items, characters, or badges, and you tell them that this is part of a collection set that follows a certain theme. This creates a desire in them to collect all the elements and complete the set.

[124]Michael Norton, Daniel Mochon, and Dan Ariely. "The IKEA effect: When labor leads to love". Journal of Consumer Psychology 22 (3): 453–460.

[125]Dan Ariely. Predictably Irrational. P175. Harper Perennial. New York, NY. 2010.

Now it's Personal, My Deer

An excellent example of a Collection Set is in the game *Geomon* by Loki Studio, a game company I advised from 2010 to 2012 (they were later acquired by Yahoo! and unfortunately the game was discontinued).

Geomon was a monster capture and training game, similar to Pokemon, except the monsters you could catch relied on your physical location as determined by your mobile device. For instance, if a player were on the beach, they could capture sea Geomons, while a player hiking in the mountains could capture mountain Geomons.

In the game, there's the theme of the *Four-Season Deer*, with four unique creators to capture. There's a Spring Plant Deer, a Summer Fire Deer, a Fall Wind Deer, and a Winter Ice Deer.

If a player by chance captured two or three of these four deer, they immediately felt compelled to capture the entire set. After all, it is rather awkward to only have two of the Four Season Deer. The problem was that a player could only capture a particular deer during the actual calendar season. This meant that players would have to wait three to six months to complete the set. In the gaming world, that is a torturously long period!

As a result, many players became obsessed with trading off rare and high valued pets in order to obtain the missing deer - some would even spend real money to obtain them. What is surprising is that these Four Season Deer aren't even that powerful - most players would never use them in a real battle. People simply wanted them because...well, they had to.

The mind-blowing thing about this level of ownership is that people felt extremely attached to the Geomons that they had captured and trained during the game. When the game announced that it was shutting down, players (mostly consisting of students) banded together and raised $700,000 to see if they could keep the game going. That was quite an impressive figure, mainly motivated by Core Drive 4: Ownership & Possession as well as Core Drive 8: Loss & Avoidance. In fact, in higher-level Octalysis studies, you will see that building Core Drive 4 often reinforces the power of Core Drive 8, and that the Endowment Effect connects directly to our irrational sense of Loss Aversion).

Monopolizing Billions

Another great example of Collection Sets is seen in McDonald's Monopoly Game[126]. McDonald's wants people to buy more fast food from them - the Desired Action, so it created the McDonald's Monopoly game where every time you hit the Win-State of "buying more burgers and fries" you will get a piece of property on the Monopoly Board.

Once you accumulate all the properties, McDonald's will give you great cash prizes and rewards. Now, like most of these collection games, there will be a few pieces that are extremely rare, and as a result, people are willing to spend real money to acquire these properties. That's somewhat odd, because people are not even paying real money in exchange for the reward. They are paying real money in exchange for a "part" of the reward, which by itself is technically worth nothing. But because people are so desperate in completing a set that is almost finished, they are highly motivated to complete it as a strong Endgame play.

---

[126] McDonald's Monopoly Website: http://winners.playatmcd.com

What makes Collection Sets so effective is that often a company cannot give out tangible rewards to every user, but every user expects some type of reward when they performed the Desired Actions and hit the Win-States. By giving users a piece of the reward instead of the full reward, every user feels that they are making progress towards the ultimate win-prize while the company maintains control of its budget. When you give users rewards, don't just give them physical items directly, for those generally have less motivational longevity. More often, giving them collection pieces will result in longer-term engagement.

One thing to note is that, when a user expects a full reward either due to your own advertising or because of what your competitors are advertising, giving them a Collection Set piece can sometimes backfire and end up insulting that user. Always be mindful that gamification is not a cookie cutter solution; it always relies on thoughtful design based on context and the profile of the players within your system.

Exchangeable Points (Game Technique #75)

As mentioned in Chapter 6, there are two main types of points that a gamified system can grant its users. The first type consists of Status Points (Game Technique #1), through which users can increase and keep track of their scores in order to see how well they're doing. Status Points for the most part can only go up as the user hits more Win-States and it cannot be traded for other valuables. This appeals more to Core Drive #2: Development & Accomplishment.

The second type is represented by Exchangeable Points, where users can utilize their accumulated points in a strategic and scarce manner to obtain other valuables. Exchangeable Points can have various types of uses. There are points that can only be redeemed within the game economy for valuables, or points that can be traded with other players in the same system. Some exchangeable points allow users to trade with people outside of the gamified system where they were originally earned in. Each of these types of points has pros and cons, and many good gamified systems (as well as games) have a combination of the above to ensure their economy maintains its value for its users. Many companies think that just giving users Exchangeable Points, which can be redeemed for rewards will make their system motivating. After all, now there is an in-system "economy!"

What companies don't always realize is that it is very difficult to run an effective economy. You have to carefully consider the correct labor-to-time-to-tradability-to-reward ratios while constantly adjusting the balance to ensure that people continue valuing your points and currency system. If the system no longer rewards the appropriate labor with the commensurate perceived value, then the economy loses its legitimacy.

The Federal Reserve Bank or Central Bank of any country knows that an economy is extremely sensitive and requires finesse. They understand that a change in interest rates by a modest 3% may result in substantial, even drastic behavioral changes with consumers, banks, insurance companies, real estate developers, and businesses. This complexity must be respected when attempting to introduce a market economy for tradable points. A company which believes that just having an economy will naturally lead to engagement with its users is relying on a very dangerous assumption.

Without writing a separate book on this subject (after all, this book is titled "*beyond* points, badges, and leaderboards"), one of the key points to pay close attention to is the scarcity control of the economy. This means that users should never feel like the exchangeable currency or goods are excessively abundant. This is often controlled by the true scarcity of *time* where labor in the system is balanced against the resulting rewards. We will dive more into this topic in Chapter 10 on Core drive 6: Scarcity & Impatience.

Monitor Attachment (Game Technique #42)

Monitor Attachment is a game technique that allows people to develop more ownership towards something, such that they are constantly monitoring or paying attention to it.

When users are monitoring the state of something, they naturally want that state to continually improve. If you are constantly looking at the progression of some numbers, you automatically grow more engaged with the success and growth of these numbers. This was definitely a driving force behind why I cared so much about my Tamagotchi. By being its steward, the Monitor Effect increased over time and it became my sole responsibility to keep the little dinosaur fed, healthy, and safe.

This can also be identified in the relationship developed over time with a favorite local coffee shop. You become friendly with the staff, learn the entire menu, and have your "favorite spot" where you go to regularly at set times. You build familiarity with the shop, which in turn makes you feel like you partially "own" the place as a committed community member and customer.

This tendency of liking something we feel familiar with is described in famed Psychologist Robert Zajonc's paper on "Attitudinal Effects of Mere Exposure[127]. Because our subconscious minds are bad at differentiating between things that are safe, comfortable, desirable, truthful, easy, or familiar, when we feel like something is familiar, our brain automatically associates it with something that is safe and desirable. Cognitive ease plays a substantial part towards what we decide to care about and spend time doing.

Google Analytics brings Gamification

Building on Monitor Attachment, often a very good way to get users engaged is to constantly show them stats, charts, and graphics of

---

[127]Robert Zajonc, *Journal of Personality and Social Psychology 9: 1-27. "Attitudinal Effects of Mere Exposure". 1968.

things they care about. As an example, I personally believe that the biggest motivator that fuels the blogosphere is not any blogging platform, but Google Analytics[128].

The early days of a blogger are lonely and discouraging. You spend hours upon hours pouring out your heart and insights, feeling that you are contributing your uniqueness and value to the world; but you also know that barely anyone will read your posts. You may share it with your friends on Facebook, and some might click the "Like" button. However, you also know that it would have been more time efficient to just call these people up and tell them about the same insights, one by one.

During this time it is very easy to give up and decide to do other things with one's life. However, what often keeps a blogger going is the Google Analytics dashboard and the constant staring towards it to see whether the visitor numbers increased from three people to four. Google Analytics allows any blogger to see how many visitors were on their blog, how long each person stayed, and what posts they read, all without paying a single dollar.

Because of this simple tool, many bloggers log into Google Analytics over a dozen times a day, monitoring the barely existing activities for their blogs, and paying attention to any possible changes (incorporating Core Drive 7: Unpredictability & Curiosity). When one spends a lot of time monitoring the outcome of something, they will likely develop new ways to improve those outcomes, developing into even more engaged activities within Empowerment of Creativity & Feedback (Core Drive 3).

People started to see how providing many links to other posts and other sites increased traffic by a modest amount; they saw how writing catchy and controversial titles attracted more click-throughs; and they saw how posting at certain times of the day generated more traffic. The Monitor Attachment opened up a whole

---

[128]Google Analytics platform website: google.com/analytics

new world of White Hat Motivation, despite the blogger being nowhere close to "popular."

If you could design your experience where users are constantly monitoring the progressive output of something (even if the numbers are going down at times), you have a good shot at absorbing the user into much deeper levels of ownership and engagement.

The Alfred Effect (Game Technique #83)

The Alfred Effect is when users feel that a product or service is so personalized to their own needs that they cannot imagine using another service.

As we march towards a fast-food world of more convenient and off-the-shelf options, people start to long for a deeper experience that is uniquely their own. That's why some wealthy people would spend ten times more to customize a product to uniquely fit their style and preferences.

Through Big Data, we are now able to provide users that sense of personalization by tailoring options based on what smart systems collect on users preferences and habits.

In a game, the system is constantly learning about the user and customizing the experience based on past behavior. A game would know, "This player is on level 3; he has learned these four skills, but not these six, picked up these three items, defeated these monsters, talked to these two characters, but not these other three characters. As a result, this door does not open."

A game remembers almost everything a player does in the game and modifies the experience accordingly. Gamers take this level of personalization for granted: if at level 3, the game forgot some details of what the player did in level 1, the player would often become furious and quit the game.

In the real world, most sites just give you the same static experience, no matter what you do. Some more advanced sites present different experiences based on region or gender, but most provide a very shallow experience. But when a user feels like a system has been fully customized to fit their needs, even if another service out there offered better technologies, functions, or prices, the user has a strong tendency to stay with this system because it now uniquely understands them.

These days, some of the biggest sites are implementing the Alfred Effect into their experiences, though most are still not ideal. Sites like Amazon are known to understand your preferences based on all your activities and recommend different products to you[129], while Google Search now shows personalized search results based on your search and browsing history[130]. Facebook also shows content that you or your friends would most likely care about[131], while Netflix can predict which movies you will enjoy better than your friends can[132].

Beyond automatic system customization, some people have spent time adjusting their Operating Systems or Browsers manually to suit their needs and preferences. Others have their own systems of customized Dropbox Folders in place that perfectly fits their workflow needs - picture switching to an entirely different file management platform from the one you currently have; a difficult prospect I'm sure. Even a person's workstation is often customized to meet their needs and habits, creating more engagement and attachment.

One great example is seen in the navigation app *Waze*. Beyond all

---

[129] Amazon Recommendation Customization Help Page: http://www.yukaichou.com/AmazonRecommendation

[130] Danny Sullivan. Search Engine Land."Google Now Personalizes Everyones Search Results". 12/04/2009.

[131] Mario Aguilar. Gizmodo. "Facebook now shows you personalized trending topics in your News Feeds". 01/16/2014.

[132] Anthony Ha. TechCrunch."Netflix's Neil Hunt Says Personalized Recommendations Will Replace The Navigation Grid". 05/19/2014.

the saved addresses and historical destination data (which strongly contributes to the Alfred Effect), with sufficient usage, it will remember your favorite spots based on context. If you open Waze at 6PM, it would immediately know that 6PM is return home time and ask you if you want to go home; if you open it at 8PM, it may remember that 8PM on Wednesday nights is gym time, and ask you if you would like to go to the gym. Personalized and customized experiences like these create strong attachment towards an experience.

Core Drive 4: The Bigger Picture

Core Drive 4: Ownership & Possession is a powerful motivator that can attract us to do many irrational things but could also give us great emotional comfort and a sense of well-being. Often it is a central focus that works closely with many of the other Core Drives.

When working with Core Drive 6: Scarcity & Impatience, people continually become drawn in by a carrot. When paired with Core Drive 8: Loss & Avoidance, people do everything they can to secure what they have obtained. When matched with Core Drive 7: Unpredictability & Curiosity, people become obsessed with the outcome and whether they would gain the precious good. Of course, the successful accumulation of goods leads to Core Drive 2: Development & Accomplishment, and when the sense of ownership sparks the need to become better and innovate, Core Drive 3: Empowerment of Creativity & Feedback comes in play.

Here you can see how all the 8 Core Drives work together in dynamic flows, each supporting the other and creating a spectrum of higher motivation. However, you must also be wary of designs where Core Drives sabotage each other. As one of the more Extrinsically Motivating Core Drives, if improperly design, it could make people act more selfishly, remove intellectual curiosity, and destroy any hopes of higher creativity. We will explore this in more depth in Chapter 13: Left Brain vs Right Brain Core Drives.

To get the most out of the book, Choose only ONE of the below options to do right now:

Easy: Think about something you collected or had a unique sense of ownership with. Did you feel that it was "fun" to spend time with it, even though from an outsider's perspective it could look like you weren't doing anything with it?

Easy: Think about something that has the Alfred Effect in your life. How did they implement it, and when did you recognize that effect was in place? Could it be designed to let users become aware of it sooner?

Medium Think about how you can introduce a Collection Set into a project that you are currently working on which will motivate users towards the Desired Actions. What kind of theme(s) can the collection set use? Do you want each piece to be given as an Earned Lunch whenever the user commits the Desired Actions, or have it as a Mystery Box where the pieces come out randomly after the Desired Actions?

Share what you come up with on Twitter or your preferred social network with the hashtag #OctalysisBook and see what ideas other people have.

Start Collecting

I'm sure you have noticed all the Game Technique hash numbers (#s) that follow each game technique within the different chapters. This actually started off as collection set designed for my blog audience to collect all the game technique numbers that are populated within my blog, videos, workshops, and other content such as this book. Later on, those who have a fairly complete set of game techniques #s will be able to use it as a guide sheet to study some of my most advanced content. Content such as Game Technique Combos where we determine what Game Techniques work best with each other to create various motivational effects, as well as the order in which they go, along with other fascinating things.

This is completely voluntary and only for those who really want to dig deep into my content and be able to wield the power of Octalysis one day. Of course, even if you don't plan to dig that deep, such a list of game techniques would become a useful cheat sheet in referring what is available in your arsenal whenever you are designing a project.

Chapter 9: The Fifth Core Drive - Social Influence & Relatedness

Social Influence and Relatedness is the fifth core drive within Octalysis Gamification and involves activities inspired by what other people think, do, or say. This Core Drive is the engine behind many themes such as mentorship, competition, envy, group quests, social treasure, and companionship.

Core Drive 5: Social Influence & Relatedness is a Right Brain

Core Drive that bases its success off our desires to connect and compare with one another. With the proliferation of new social media tools and platforms, more and more companies are working on optimizing Core Drive 5 during the Discovery and Onboarding Process.

Almost every consumer app these days urges you to "Invite Your Friends" upon joining their service. However, just because the social platform is there to spread a message does not necessarily mean there is engaging, share-worthy content. There are many pitfalls as Social Influence & Relatedness is a double-edged sword and needs to be wielded carefully.

When utilized properly, it can serve as one of the strongest and long-lasting motivations for people to become connected and engaged to your experience.

The Mentor that Stole My Life

In 2012, I was doing research on some games that didn't have great graphics, but were very successful from the prospective of engagement and monetization (yes, part of my work is to research and play games, among other grueling activities such as talking about games, traveling the world, and coming up with random comments while filming my videos).

During this time, a game called *Parallel Kingdom* popped up on my radar[133].

---

[133]Parallel Kingdom Website: parallelkingdom.com

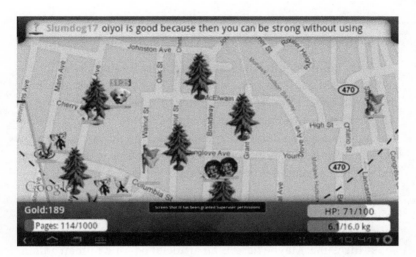

Parallel Kingdom is a mobile location based MMORPG (Massively Multiplayer Online Role-Playing Game) that allows players to access and grow in a virtual world laid out on top of the real world, based on the player's GPS location. The game has fairly unrefined and unimpressive graphics, but monetizes handsomely and makes millions of dollars as a small team.

When I started doing preliminary research on the game, I initially planned to spend no more than two hours to learn about its game mechanics design and how it could engage players so well. After that, I would return to focusing on my other work.

The initial stage of the Onboarding experience was so-so, with basic tutorials and explanations on the backstory of the game. I saw that the game was interesting because players get to build a kingdom on top of their actual home locations on a virtual map that reflected the real world (which ties in some Core Drive 4: Ownership & Possession and Core Drive 7: Unpredictability & Curiosity). The interface wasn't very intuitive and there were many instances where I felt I needed to make decisions without having enough information.

Like the majority of first-time users on any site, within thirty minutes I felt that I learned enough of what the game was about, and planned to leave the system. I was behind on my work anyway.

But forty minutes into the game (probably enough time for the game to determine that I was a serious player), I received a message that said, "Hey, [User X] has been assigned to be your mentor. He will contact you the next time he signs-in." The message in itself was interesting. By indicating the mentor could not talk to me immediately, it was more convincing that he was an actual player, and not just a computer or a company employee.

That built up some curiosity and anticipation (Core Drive 7: Unpredictability & Curiosity and Core Drive 6: Scarcity & Impatience). I wanted to know who this user was and what he would have to say about the game. Maybe he was an artificial bot or a human admin? If he were an actual player, perhaps I could learn more about the Scaffolding and Endgame Phases from him.

When my "mentor" logged in some twenty minutes later, he requested to teleport to my location. I granted him permission. He showed up, and quickly started to share some tips about how I should think about my "career development" in the game – what skills would be useful to learn, what viable trades and professions to pursue in the game, and the best items to collect.

He also started giving me gear - items he knew I needed to become more powerful such as swords, shields, helmets, boots etc. The default sword I had only gave me +2 damage, but the new sword he gave me (which was his old gear that he no longer needed) had +7 damage. That's a significant boost to anything I could find on my own. With this new, more powerful gear, I was anxious to go back to the dungeons (or levels) that I was struggling at earlier and show those monsters my new powers. I wasn't going to quit the game until I could demonstrated my new powers and could feel accomplished.

At that point, a thought crossed my mind. This mentor had given me all these amazing items that I couldn't get on my own; at least not within the first few hours of gameplay. If I took his items and then quit the game, I would be wasting all these "valuables," and he would likely be very disappointed about it. Morally or responsibly, I couldn't quit the game...not until a little bit later anyway.

At that point, he asked me to follow him into some lower level dungeons. I listened. Wow. The monsters in those dungeons were tough, even for my new gear! I tried to fight them as skillfully as I could, but I still came close to dying several times. My mentor then started attacking the monsters, and with each blow he would wipe out a batch of them. It seemed so easy and effortless for him. At that point, a subconscious feeling crept into my mind.

"I wish I could be like that one day."

This is an interesting thought because I didn't really care about the game at that point. But when we see someone else effortlessly complete something that we struggle hard against, our brains automatically develop a feeling of envy. How people deal with that envy may be different – some become inspired with "I want to be like that one day!", whereas others enter into denial, "Well, I can never do that, but the whole thing is stupid anyway." This game had cleverly designed for the former.

When you design an environment where people are prone to be envious of others, you want to make sure there is a realistic path for them to follow to in achieving what they are envious about. Otherwise you will simply generate user denial and disengagement. We will explore this theme more in Chapter Ten on Core Drive 6: Scarcity & Impatience.

After following my mentor for a couple hours to conquer a few dungeons, another thought began to hit me. "Man...this guy is a high level player. He should be fighting in the high level dungeons. He gains nothing here and is just wasting his time. He is investing in me! Of course I can't quit now. I would be the biggest disappoint-ment ever!"

As a result, instead of quitting, I joined his Kingdom, became a valid member on his team, and helped the Kingdom collect resources such as lumber, fruits, stones, and equipment. Instead of playing the intended two hours, I ended up playing the game for two months before I forced myself to quit in order to start researching other games. Sadly, when I did quit, one of the members in the Kingdom did become fairly upset with me because he spent a good amount of time helping my character grow, in the hope that I would become a strong force within the Kingdom. At the time, I felt quite horrible being such a big letdown.

This is the power of Mentorship, one of the Game Techniques in Core Drive 5: Social Influence & Relatedness that we will cover in this chapter.

How many times have you tried to withdraw from a volunteer group, team, church, or even a relationship, but had an extremely hard time because you didn't want to upset other people?

We derive some of our most joyful experiences when we are with friends and family, and experience stress and anxiety when these relationships aren't going well. We are innate social animals, and naturally endowed with a sense of empathy. We are influenced by what other people feel and think about us.

Understanding the dynamics of Social Influence & Relatedness is something every good Octalysis Gamifier should become familiar with.

We're all Pinocchios at Heart

In 1972, the *Keep America Beautiful Organization* created an advertising campaign with the theme, "People Start Pollution. People can stop it." It was considered to be one of the most moving and effective public service announcements of all time. The ad campaign featured a Native American reacting to the widespread corruption of the environment, and shedding a single but powerful tear.

Many years later, the organization wanted to revisit the same theme, so they created a new pollution prevention campaign with a poster of the same Native American shedding that single but powerful tear with the slogan, "Back by Popular Neglect."

Unfortunately, this time around the ad campaign was not only ineffective, it may have backfired and caused even more people to pollute the environment.[135] Can you tell why?

Let me give you another example and see if you can hone in on what's wrong with these campaigns. For many years, the Petrified Forest National Park in Arizona suffered heavy losses due to the vandalizing and theft of their petrified wood. They wanted to come up with a message that would decrease such theft.

As a result, they put up a sign that read, *"Your heritage is being vandalized every day by theft losses of petrified wood of 14 tons a year, mostly a small piece at a time."*

This message seems to make sense, as it tells people how serious

---

[134]"The Crying Indian," from Keep America Beautiful by Advertising Council: http://www.yukaichou.com/KeepAmericaBeautiful

[135]Noah Goldstein, Steve Martin, and Robert Cialdini. *Yes! 50 Scientifically Proven Ways to Be Persuasive.* P20. Simon & Schuster. New York, NY. 2010.

these little transgressions can be, hoping to appeal to people's Core Drive 1: Epic Meaning & Calling as well as some Core Drive 4: Ownership & Possession.

However, when the sign was posted, both theft and vandalism increased. *Why?*

Here we learn that, just because one attempts to appeal to various Core Drives does not mean it will be done elegantly and effectively (This is why we study games to learn how they successfully do it). But more so, it's because this message created an Anti-Core Drive, or the motivation to *not* do the Desired Action. Both messages imply, "It is the crushing *norm* that people pollute, steal, and vandalize. Please don't be like them."

While there are some people in the world that go out of their way to be different, unique, or weird (I may fit that bill a little bit), most people benchmark themselves with what everyone else is doing. The updated slogan for the *Keep America Beautiful* campaign, "Back by Popular Neglect" told people that, "Hey, it's actually popular to pollute." Though their message was that you shouldn't do it, it actually encouraged people to be more like the norm.

Don't believe me? A group of Behavioral Psychologists did further investigations to prove this concept[136] . The researchers decided to do a split test at the same National Park in Arizona with two different signs and a control test to see how behavior changes based on three different messages. They also threw many "easy-to-steal" petrified wood pieces along the way to measure how many were stolen. The signs were as follows:

Sign #1 — Social Norm: "Many past visitors have removed the petrified wood from the park, destroying the natural state of the Petrified Forest." (A picture of park visitors taking pieces of wood accompanied this.)

---

[136] Noah Goldstein, Steve Martin, and Robert Cialdini. *Yes! 50 Scientifically Proven Ways to Be Persuasive.* P22. Simon & Schuster. New York, NY. 2010.

Sign #2 — No Social Norm: "Please don't remove the petrified wood from the park, in order to preserve the natural state of the Petrified Forest." (This sign showed a lone visitor stealing a piece of wood with the universal "No" symbol, a red circle with a diagonal line).

The final condition was having no sign at all to serve as the control test for the study.

Stunningly, they found that having no sign at all led to a 3% theft rate while having Sign #1 (Social Norm) led to a 7.9% theft rate. This meant that, the Social Norm sign increased theft by 160% compared to having no sign at all! The sign that says "Everyone steals and hurts the environment" not only failed to deter theft, it literally *promoted* theft.

On the other hand, Sign #2 (No Social Norm) performed as expected and lowered the theft rate to 1.67%.

What do we see here? What we perceive as the *social norm* greatly influences our decisions and behavior, often more so than personal gains or even moral standards. In the extreme, this "social norm override" can explain many of the devastating acts performed done by Nazi soldiers, who may have otherwise been decent people had they lived in another country at the time[137]; or mass suicide attempts by the Peoples Temple Agricultural Project[138]).

The famous fictional puppet Pinocchio had a dream – to be a normal boy just like everyone else. Perhaps we all have a little bit of Pinocchio inside of us.

The Average Person is Above Average

There have been numerous studies on how "social norming" affects our behaviors. Often, when we see how other people are perform-

---

[137] The famous Stanford Prison Experiment suggests that anyone could potentially behave like a Nazi in given circumstances:http://www.yukaichou.com/StanfordPrison

[138] The mass suicide project known as Jonestown: http://www.yukaichou.com/Jonestown

ing, we begin to compare ourselves to the norm and start to adjust accordingly. Our social standing among our peers turns out to be a strong motivator for us regardless of whether we think others recognize our standings or not.

Interestingly, when researchers study how people perceive themselves relative to others, the majority consider themselves to be "above average" at almost anything you ask them about. This of course, is statistically impossible.

In a survey of faculty at the University of Nebraska, 68% of the faculties rated themselves in the top 25% percentile for their teaching abilities.[139] Similarly, a survey done on Stanford MBA students showed that 87% of them believed their academic performances to be above the medium. [140] Even among high school students, a survey attached to the SAT Exams in 1976 revealed that 85% of the students believed they had better social skills than the average, while 70% believed themselves to be above the medium in being leaders. In fact, 25% of the students rated themselves as the top 1% when it came to social skills[141]. Many times, when you show all these people who are "above average" that they are in fact not so above average, that is when they decide to change their behaviors.

One notable study on the power of social proofing involved hotel bathrooms messages that urged guests to reuse their towels for environmental reasons[142]. Among other variations, a social proof message in the hotel bathroom read, "Join Your Fellow Guests in Helping to Save the Environment" and noted that 75% of guests participated in the towel-reuse program.

It turned out that people who saw that 75% of other guests reused

---

[139] Patricia Cross. *New Directions for Higher Education*. 17: 1–15. "Not can but will college teachers be improved?". 1977.

[140] Ezra Zuckerman. *Stanford GSB Reporter*. April 24, P14–5. "It's Academic." 2000.

[141] " Suls, J.; K. Lemos, H.L. Stewart (2002). "Self-esteem, construal, and comparisons with the self, friends and peers". Journal of Personality and Social Psychology (American Psychological Association) 82 (2): 252–261

[142] Noah Goldstein, Steve Martin, and Robert Cialdini. *Yes! 50 Scientifically Proven Ways to Be Persuasive*. P16. Simon & Schuster. New York, NY. 2010.

their towels (establishing a "social norm") became 25% more likely to reuse their own towels. Interestingly, an alternative sign that was specific to the guest's room was tested, saying, "nearly 75% of guests who stayed in *this* room reused their towels." This created even better results because the "relatedness" principle indicates that the more you can relate to a group, the more likely you will comply with its social norm.

There is also an interesting combination of both Core Drive 1: Epic Meaning & Calling and Core Drive 5: Social Influence & Relatedness in this behavior.

Core Drive 5 is apparent – when you believe the social norm is to recycle towels, you have a stronger tendency to do so, especially when there is high *relatedness*. However, there is also an odd sense of Epic Meaning & Calling that's called into action. No one will notice, regardless of whether you recycle your towels or not, so why should that social influence affect you? This ties back to the Elitism Theme of Epic Meaning & Calling. Because you feel that you are part of a larger group, you need to behave like people who are in that group – it's a cause beyond yourself, even if your group will never find out what you have done. The action, or inaction, calls your integrity into question.

Of course, if the hotel tells you that your picture and your towel-recycling behaviors will be broadcasted to everyone who has stayed in your room and recycled their towels in the past (assuming there are no privacy concerns), then there will suddenly be an even higher level of Social Influence & Relatedness towards the Desired Action (mostly in a Black Hat way, which we will cover on Chapter 14).

To further reinforce this concept, consider another study that was done to examine social conformity, featuring public-service messages that were hung on the doorknobs of several hundred homes in San Marcos, California. The messages all encouraged residents to use fans instead of air condit ioning, but used different reasoning and motivations for doing so.

Some messages told residents that they could save $54 a month on their utility bill. Others messages explained that 262 pounds of greenhouse gases per month would be saved from being released into the environment. The third message informed people that it was their social responsibility to protect the environment by switching to fans. A fourth message informed the residents that 77% of their neighbors already used fans instead of air conditioning and that it was "your community's popular choice!" By now, you can likely guess which one was the winner. Compared to the three other messages that utilized weaker forms of Core Drive 4 and Core Drive 1, the strong Core Drive 5 message on "everyone like you is doing it" emerged as the winner by a long shot, with residents reducing their energy consumption by 10% compared with the control group. All other groups reduced consumption by less than 3%.[143]. As the research suggests, simply informing your users on how their fellow "elite" users are behaving is a simple way to significantly boost the Desired Actions towards that activity.

Social Influence vs. Epic Meaning within a Team

An interesting dynamic between Core Drive 1: Epic Meaning & Calling and Core Drive 5: Social Influence & Relatedness can further be seen in team relationships and leadership practices.

Within a group, the leader is often motivated by Epic Meaning & Calling. They are typically the one with the long-term vision for the group and understands how it plays out with each individual on their team. For that vision to succeed, they are often willing to sacrifice their own well-being in order to fulfill that higher meaning which they are passionate about.

---

[143] Stephanie Simon. *The Wall Street Journal.* "The Secret to Turning Consumers Green". 10/18/2010.

The team members of the group, however, are often motivated by Social Influence & Relatedness. They are performing the tasks because their team leader wants them to, and they don't want to be thought of as slackers - an element of Loss & Avoidance). They don't necessarily believe in the higher meaning and vision to the extent that it drives their behavior, but if the leader is compelling or charismatic, they will commit to the Desired Actions toward that vision.

Generally, the leader's goal is to motivate each teammate to feel driven by Epic Meaning & Calling. The leader is successful if everyone becomes passionate about the higher meaning of the project or company mission and is willing to make some personal sacrifices to successfully push their shared agenda forward.

On the other hand, if the leader loses that Epic Meaning & Calling and becomes solely motivated by Social Influence & Relatedness, the team will start to crumble from within. Now the leader is no longer motivated by the higher vision of the group, but only working to please their teammates. They have now become an insecure leader, and an insecure leader is an ineffective leader.

When you are leading a team, never lose sight of that Epic Meaning & Calling. Of course, you always want to pay close attention to the feelings and motivations of each teammate, as well as the Core Drives that motivate them. However, if making them feel good becomes the priority you think about day in and day out, then you may end up with a happy group that goes nowhere and fails in the end. The opposite is true too: neglect your teams' well-being and you'll have a sad group that's burnt out and struggling to fulfill the mission.

Corporate Competition as an Oxymoron

Alongside this theme of leadership is the concept of competition in the workplace. When potential clients reach out to me for internal gamification support, many of them ask me about competition in the workplace and how to properly implement it to improve workplace productivity and office dynamics.

Almost every company I talk with assumes that competition always makes things fun and is critical for a robust office culture. Unfortunately, while competition in the workplace can be very useful in different scenarios, it can often backfire and demoralize team morale in the long run.

The problem of competition in the workplace is that it is easy to measure the temporary surge in activities, especially among the top 10 percentile that usually drive a major portion of the measured metrics. However, it is more difficult to follow the gradually decreasing motivation among the other 90% of employees, as well as the anti-collaborative stress that competition generates in the workplace.

Many competitive workplaces create an unhealthy environment where employees put self-interest above corporate and even customer interests. Instead of working towards a win for the company and a win for the customer, the individual simply focuses on beating the internal competition and coming out ahead of their colleagues.

Even though competition in general creates an adrenaline rush and adds a sense of urgency to an effort, most human beings do not like to be in a constant state of competition. When our ancestors were focused on surviving in the wild, this adrenaline rush was meant to be used in short bursts for survival purposes, not as a prolonged condition.

Mario Herger, a colleague and one of the leading experts in gamified competition in the workplace, points out that competition is often contrary to the essential meaning of the corporation. Corporations are formed to bring people together and pool their different strengths in a collaborative way[144]. The fundamental design of an effective corporation taps into its collective talent to build something greater than its individual parts.

If members of a basketball team were competing against each other instead of their opponents in an important match, they would play more selfishly, avoid passing the ball, and try to feature themselves as the star player. In fact, in both professional and collegiate basketball, besides standard stats such as 2-Point Shots, 3-Points Shots, Rebounds and other personal performance metrics, there is an important stat called *Assists*. Assists represents the amount of passes to teammates that immediately led to a score.

Studies have shown that most successful offensive teams have a high percentage of assists associated with their scoring efforts. This is because assists lead to higher quality shots, which in turn, result in higher shooting percentages and greater success on the floor. In fact, it has been shown that NBA teams with higher assist numbers win about 72% of their games[145]. Under the premise that whatever is measured will be improved, emphasizing on *assists* will lead to more collaborate play and teamwork, even if the player is still driven by a self-interest to succeed.

When we implement competition in the workplace, we need to thoughtfully analyze the risks as well as the benefits, in determining whether there might be any significant and long-term harm to the employees and ultimately the enterprise.

Adding competition-driven stress to the daily challenges that employees face can often increase the probability of burnout and skewed performance. Employees may become more motivated to

---

[144]Mario Herger. *Enterprise Gamification*. P195. EGC Media. San Bernardino, CA. 07/24/2014.

[145]Tom Lyons. Strauss, Factor, Laing & Lyons. "What Wins Basketball Games Review of 'Basketball on Paper: Rules and Tools for Performance Analysis' By Dean Oliver". 2005. Accessed 04/01/2015.

make each other fail and even look for new opportunities elsewhere. In my own experiences, when people around me constantly talk about quitting their jobs, more often than not it is because of dysfunctional people dynamics between their bosses and/or coworkers, and not because the tasks themselves are too difficult.

One well-known example of a dysfunctional workplace competition was GE's "Rank-and-Yank" system, where the bottom 10% of the organization's employees were fired on a regular basis. Another was Microsoft's "Stack Racking" system, where an employee's expectations for promotion were based on how they were ranked among their peers.

A personal friend of mine who worked at GE many years ago stated, "The Rank-and-Yank system there made sure that everyone hired people weaker than themselves so they were never in danger of being yanked. When we interviewed a brilliant candidate, we made sure they never got the job because it would put ourselves in jeopardy or potentially result in a smaller bonus."

A Vanity Fair article by Kurt Eichenwald cites that "Every current and former Microsoft employee I interviewed — every one — cited stack ranking as the most destructive process inside of Microsoft.[146]" Peter Cohan from Forbes stated that, "[Stack Ranking] directed [Microsoft employees] to prevent their peers from getting outstanding performance reviews and brag about their accomplishments to each member of the management committee that determined their relative ranking.[147]"

As you can see, workplace competition can be extremely destructive to company morale, especially during weak and uncertain economic conditions where people are preoccupied with getting laid off. On the other hand, collaborative team dynamics are much

---

[146] *Vanity Fair.* "Microsoft's Downfall: Inside the Executive E-mails and Cannibalistic Culture That Felled a Tech Giant". 07/03/2012.

[147] Peter Cohan. Forbes. "Why Stack Ranking Worked Better at GE Than Microsoft". 7/13/2012.

more common in start up companies because employees often get paid with equity. In that case, employees only "win" if the entire company stays competitive against the industry giants that are stagnant and competing internally. It's a collaborative Group Quest as opposed to an individualized Leaderboard which compels the employee's motivation to fulfill their company's mission and create subsequent equity value.

So how to implement competition correctly?

Mario Herger suggests to consider the following when designing competition into the workplace.[148]

When competition works:

- In situations where players aim to achieve mastery of the task
- In gain-oriented scenarios and mindsets where players focus on becoming the winner
- When contestants reach their Individual Zone of Optimal Functioning (IZOF), which means their anxiety and arousal level reaches a heightened degree of focus[149].
- When players care about the welfare of the team
- When players are primed to overcome obstacles, and not what they will do after reaching the goal
- With situational anger to confrontations
- When there is an even matchup and players feel that they actually have a chance
- When players care about the competitors (competing against your friends instead of every stranger in the world)

Competition does not work:

---

[148]Mario Herger. *Enterprise Gamification*. P200-201. EGC Media. San Bernardino, CA. 07/24/2014.

[149]Yuri Hanin. *European Yearbook of Sport Psychology, 1, 29-72*. "Emotions and athletic performance: Individual zones of optimal functioning model".1997.

- In learning-focused environments
- In prevention-oriented situations and attitudes where players focus on not being the loser
- When teams are too harmonious and competition becomes awkward
- When creativity is required
- When the competition is regarded as skewed and there is little chance to win

Though game mechanics and elements can be used to motivate employees and promote the behaviors that the company wants to see, each competitive initiative should be well thought out and designed with considerable finesse. Arbitrary use of game elements modeled on competition may be useful for short-term sales campaigns, but may be disruptive and anti-productive in the long term.

Instead of taking the zero-sum approach to motivate the best performers, we should consider strategies which bring individual strengths together and produce effective cooperation. In the long run, this formula will generally outperform the individualistic paradigm of workplace motivation.

Cooperative play can help preserve and improve a positive corporate culture, as well as support and encourage the development of talent and skills. At the same time, it increases competitive strength where it really matters – outside in the marketplace.

Game Techniques within Social Influence & Relatedness

You have learned more about the motivational and psychological nature of Core Drive 5: Social Influence & Relatedness. To make it more actionable, I've included some Game Techniques below that heavily utilize this Core Drive to engage users.

Mentorship (Game Technique #61)

At the beginning of the chapter, I shared how powerful mentorship could be in a game setting such as Parallel Kingdom, but it is also a consistently effective tool in every medium of activity that requires sustained motivation.

American universities are well known for their student social groups consisting of highly active fraternities and sororities. Many fraternities have rather long and involved initiation rituals for their new members. During the rigorous process of joining a fraternity, a "Big Bro/Little Bro" system is employed where an experienced member in the organization will be matched up with a new potential member going through a semester-long training process known as "pledging."

The Big Bro is there to serve as a mentor,not only providing directional guidance, but also emotional support to make sure the time-consuming process of pledging becomes more bearable. This practice has endured for over a century and shown to improve the Onboarding experience of members joining the organization.

Having a mentor helps employees better connect with the culture and environment in the workplace. This can effectively increase overall work satisfaction and lower turnover rates.

Unfortunately, most organizations require individuals to become proactive in finding their own mentors, making it difficult for them to find a good match. That is why it is beneficial for companies to create a systemized mentorship program that works to match their employees based on compatibilities. I would even recommend starting the mentorship relationship as early as the interview process, where the interviewer doesn't just grind the interviewees but seeks to help them improve.

Saying things like, "If you manage to get an offer here, I will be your mentor and help develop your potential" would make your company much more attractive, whether the interviewee is hired or not. Furthermore, this would likely increase your acceptance rates from prospects receiving offers as potential employees, as they would feel that your company would take care of them from the very start. This would go a long way in accelerating their transition into the office culture and environment.

The other benefit for Mentorship is that it also helps veteran players stay engaged during the Endgame Phase. In the Four Experience Phases of a Player's Journey, we learn that the Endgame is the most neglected and one of the hardest phases to optimize. Good mentorship design in the Endgame also makes veterans feel as if they've worked hard enough to prove their status and demonstrate their skills through mentorship with a new employee. (We will cover how to design for the Endgame in more detail in Chapter 20).

While the benefits of utilizing Mentorship within an organization are apparent, how can one utilize Mentorship to motivate people who are outside of the organization?

Mentorship Design within Customer Support

Mentorship can be an amazing way to super-charge a consumer-facing website, such as eCommerce marketplaces and the associated online communities.

One of the observations I have made while consulting for eCommerce companies is that most online community support calls are often not about technical problems or bugs, but rather focus on "how do I do this?" questions. Normally, the customer support agent will patiently walk users through a very simple training process to answer these questions. The sequence might start with something like, "Now click on 'Settings' on the right top. Great! Now scroll down until you see 'Privacy.'"

This model is not very effective because:

1. Users are not exactly enthralled when talking to "customer service" operators because they believe these reps do not really empathize with their problems or understand their needs. This is even more so when the rep appears to be from another country (lack of *Relatedness*).
2. Costs for customer service can run very high, especially when the majority of the costs are on solving these "how-to" interface problems.
3. Newbies to the site don't feel emotionally engaged with the platform nor the user community. They also aren't motivated to behave well as stewards of the community.
4. The veterans of the website do not feel the fulfillment of reaching higher status and may start to feel emotionally unengaged.

The solution? Have the veterans support the newbies! What if each time a veteran logs onto the website, there is a little overlay widget where they can move a slider that says, "I am available for mentorship." This enables them to become available to answer questions from newbies through an on-site chat interface.

In this case, whenever a new seller on an eCommerce marketplace has a question, they have the option to connect to a veteran seller - one who has "been there, done that," and can help mentor the newbies reach their aspirational sales goals. The veteran mentor can provide useful information such as, "To adjust your privacy, you want to go to the bottom of settings. Oh also, make sure whenever you sell something, you upload at least four images. Those usually sell the best. I nearly doubled my ratings when I figured that one out."

Of course, if the veteran expert can't answer the questions, the newbie can immediately click a button that says, "Talk to an actual customer rep." But people in general would love to have the opportunity to converse with experienced mentors who can not only help solve their interface problems, but also serve as great exemplars who they can aspire to become.

Needless to say, this is what the eCommerce company would love also, as each new seller who skipped the boring tutorials can now learn how to become great sellers in an engaging fashion.

At the end of every month, the eCommerce site could then calculate how many "mentorship hours" the veteran had accumulated, and apply that to some type of fee discount or free shipping credit for them. Since successful veterans typically sell in large volumes, these benefits would become attractive incentives. As mentioned in Chapter 7, when you can give users "boosters" as rewards to help enhance their core activities, that is the most ideal. Boosters, such as white screens for better photo-taking, or shipping services that deliver items directly from the seller's home, act to further increase engagement towards the Desired Actions.

This is still economically efficient for the eCommerce site because compared to the massive costs of expensive support teams, fee discounts or free shipping plans would be considered negligible. That way, the veterans get their status perks and bonuses, the newbies get their questions answered and feels like they are part of a larger community, and the site saves a massive amount in support costs while having more engaged and professional sellers on their platform. What a fantastic win-win-win situation.

Brag Buttons (Game Technique #57) and Trophy Shelves (Game Technique #64)

Bragging is when a person explicitly and vocally expresses their accomplishments and achievements, whereas a Trophy Shelf allows a person to implicitly show off what they have accomplished without really saying it.

Intuitively encouraging users to brag about and show off their achievements comes in handy when it comes to recruiting new players and keeping veteran players active, but the two techniques are appropriate for different scenarios.

A Brag Button is a Desired Action that users can take in order to broadcast what they feel accomplished about - driven by Core Drive 2: Development & Accomplishment. In other words, Brag Buttons are little action tools and mechanisms for users to broadcast how awesome they are. Take the game Temple Run for example. Whenever a game is over, there is a quick and easy way for users to tap a button and share a screenshot of their high scores on Facebook, Instagram, and Twitter.

 As the game gained in popularity, people were competing with those who were scoring in the millions and high-scoring users were proud to post their scores for everyone to see.

These days, many games and websites encourage users to share more with their friends on every single interface. Most of these Brag

Buttons are ignored though, because they're not fueled by strong Core Drive 2 motivation (the dynamics and relationships between each Core Drive and how they power each other will be studied in higher level Octalysis). You want to implement the Brag Buttons at the Major Win-States when users actually feel awesome about what they have just completed.

A Trophy Shelf, on the other hand, is an obvious display that exhibits the achievements of the user. In other words, the user simply has to put up the Shelf, and further promotion, everyone who comes by will see and acknowledge these great achievements.

Trophy Shelves are seen when you walk into someone's office, and on their walls you see all types of awards, certificates, and credentials. These professionals don't necessarily want to brag about how they graduated *cum laude* from Stanford University and have a Level 4 Octalysis Certificate to everyone all the time, but by having it on their walls, they implicitly show it.

In that sense, adding the Ph.D title after one's own name in their bio is usually considered a Trophy Shelf. However, once they verbally introduce themselves as "John Doe, Ph.D," they've pressed that Brag Button.

In gaming, Trophy Shelves can often be seen as crowns, badges, or avatars. In many games, some avatar gear or items can only be obtained after reaching difficult or exclusive milestones, such as beating a certain boss, inviting 100 friends to the game, or simply having been with the game since it launched. This allows everyone to clearly see that this user has achieved a lot without the person annoyingly bringing it up all the time.

Keep in mind that there needs to be some level of Relatedness when someone brags about or shows off something. When there is a mutual understanding of the difficult work required to reach a certain level, people are more likely to brag about or show off their scores because they know others recognize how hard it was to obtain the scores.

Temple Run does a great job gaining new users through utilizing the mechanism of Brag Buttons. This helped them become one of the most successful mobile games of all time with over a billion downloads throughout the franchise's history[150]. Not bad for a monotonous game of constantly running forward.

Unfortunately, the interface for Temple Run 2 dimmed down the option of the Brag Button, which I believe would result in slightly lower frequency of someone sharing their scores based on the Glowing Choice and Dessert Oasis game techniques we discussed in Chapter 6.

Group Quests (Game Technique #22)

Another Game Technique that draws power from Core Drive 5: Social Influence & Relatedness is the Group Quest. Group Quests are very effective in collaborative play as well as viral marketing because it requires group participation before any individual can achieve the Win-State.

A successful game that utilizes this is World of Warcraft (WoW), another hugely successful and addictive game produced by Blizzard Entertainment[151]. In WoW, there are many quests that are so challenging that it requires an entire team of forty max-leveled players to work collaboratively, each specialized in their own responsibilities, before they have a chance of fulfilling the quest. In well-designed instances, even though the 40-player requirement is not imposed by the program, the users simply find it difficult to succeed if they only have 39 players.

This motivated many players to group together into clans and guilds to orchestrate raids on a regularly basis. Because of this, people were

---

[150]Dean Takahashi. *VentureBeat*. "Imangi's Temple Run sprints into virtual reality on the Samsung Gear". 2014/12/23.

[151]World of Warcraft Website: http://us.battle.net/wow

encouraged to login regularly and not drop out due to the social pressure.

Farmville by Zynga is another game that has Group Quests. These quests require users to invite a group of farming friends to produce a certain yield of crops within 24 hours. The game forces you to not only invite your friends to join, but to participate with you, which is more powerful than a spammy "I just started playing this game. Click on this link!"

Group Quests have been experienced in games for decades, but only more recently have they been adopted into the business world. In late 2008, the newborn startup Groupon realized that businesses and consumers would be highly motivated if they were offered Group Quests that ensured consumers would get dramatic discounts provided that enough of them signed up for the discount[152].

They promoted 60%-off discounts if "over 200 people buy this deal." In essence, if enough people in the group takes the Desired Action towards the Win State, only then could each group individual obtain the discount. Naturally, people who wanted the tremendous discount invited their friends to "go in on this together," making the company a huge success at the time.

Through later on Groupon failed to realize the full potential that late investors hoped it would obtain due to operational issues, during 2013 it still generated $2.57 Billion in revenue with $1.48 Billion in profits just off the Group Quest game technique[153]. Similar Group Quest models such as Kickstarter and Indiegogo have also become very popular services that crowdsource funds to support the development of innovative projects that cannot raise money from institutional investors.

There are so many of these fascinating concepts within games that we are just beginning to extract into the real world. If we

---

[152] Groupon Website: groupon.com

[153] Market Watch. Stock Profile: Groupon. Accessed 1/18/2015.

just understood these techniques and applied them effectively to meaningful projects, we might even create the next billion dollar business.

Social Treasures (Game Technique #63)

Social Treasures are gifts or rewards that can only be given to you by friends or other players.

Back in the days of Farmville, there were certain types of virtual goods that were not obtainable through regular channels, including purchasing with real money. The only way to obtain these items was to have friends click on the "Give to Friend" button and have them sent to you, without your friends losing anything in the process. As a result of this type of design, when people wanted these unique Social Treasure items, they just gave one to each other, ensuring a win-win situation.

This of course, pushed people to get their friends to join the game, so they could get more opportunities to obtain these *Social Treasures*.

Soon, people were requesting items from their friends on Facebook non-stop, badgering friends to give them various items all the time. Though it became a nuisance, even an annoyance for many Facebook users, it effectively attracted more users to the game and massively advertised the game across millions of pages.

I remember there was a time around 2007 where people kept posting on my Facebook wall and requesting that I give them a *Goat* in Farmville. After receiving a few of those, I became annoyed and simply responded with, "I don't play Farmville," thinking that it would effectively stop these people from asking again. Unfortunately, the response I received was, "Hey! That's okay, just create a Farmville account, and I can give you a Goat too!" It was striking to me that these people assumed I would also value a goat so much that I would be motivated to create a Farmville account.

Social Treasures are commonly found these days in games such as *Candy Crush*, to obtain more lives or with *Angry Birds Epic* where you can obtain more "rerolls" for its reward slot/dice machine.

In the real world, the most common form of a Social Treasure is a *vote*. Other than your own vote, you cannot (legally) get yourself more votes in an election or poll, even if you were ready and able to spend money. The only way for you to obtain more votes is if other people give them to you.

There are many "popularity contests" conducted by companies that utilize Social Influence by having people compete to get the most votes on their submissions. To obtain more votes from their social network, applicants will blast their friends with links to the submissions which directly promote the company to thousands of people.

Social Prods (Game Technique #62)

Another game technique that is often seen within Core Drive 5 is the Social Prod. A Social Prod is an action of minimal effort to create a social interaction, often a simple click of a button. Good examples are Facebook Pokes/Likes and Google's +1s.

In the early days, Facebook provided a small "Poke" button that didn't do anything other than notify the user that someone had "poked" them. At first, it seems pretty pointless. I just got poked? What does that mean? The advantage of a Social Prod is that the user does not need to spend time thinking about something witty to say, or worry about sounding stupid when they just want to have a quick, basic interaction.

When you get poked, you don't know what it means either but you don't worry about it. You just poke back. Now both of you will feel like you have interacted socially without having to spend notable effort.

A less obvious example of a Social Prod is the Linkedin Endorsement. The professional social network generally does very well with Left Brain (Extrinsic Tendency) Core Drives such as Core Drive 4: Ownership & Possession - as your profile represents your life/career, and Core Drive 2: Development & Accomplishment - as these are real achievements you've accomplished.

However, for many years LinkedIn wasn't able to successfully implement many Right Brain (Intrinsic Tendency) Core Drives to keep users frequently engaged on LinkedIn. Most people just create profiles and then leave it sitting there for months. Some engage in exclusive community or professional forums but generally these are only utilized by a relatively small number of LinkedIn users.

This is why in the past few years, LinkedIn has been focusing on Core Drive 5: Social Influence & Relatedness, by showing you how much you have in common with certain people, recommendations, and endorsements.

LinkedIn Recommendations are actually considered Social Treasures, as they are true valuables that only other people can give you. Unfortunately, they take time and work to generate, and so the growth rate of Recommendations haven't picked up over the years.

Endorsements on the other hand, are Social Prods – they are designed to be fairly meaningless but easy to execute. Early on in the design, there were even buttons that allowed you to endorse people in batches of four, allowing you to quickly endorse dozens of people without even thinking about who they were.

Does Michael have these skills or expertise?   ✕

Analytics ✕   Social Media ✕   Social Media Marketing ✕   SaaS ✕

Start-ups ✕   Type another area of expertise...

Endorse   **Skip**   What is this?

However, most people have no idea whether or not this individual is good at all the activities listed. But if you just want to endorse one specific skill that you actually want to acknowledge, you cannot simply select that skill. You have to click on the "x"s to slowly cancel out the other ones listed before you can endorse the one you know about. Most people would rather not do that much work, and as a result simply click the "Endorse All" button.

This reveals that *by design*, LinkedIn does not want endorsements to be meaningful. It's designed to be easy, thoughtless, and abundant.

And as a result, people start to endorse each other left and right. This leads to LinkedIn sending users multiple e-mails each day notifying them that they've just been endorsed by a friend, which prods them to feel the reciprocal urge and go on LinkedIn to endorse their friends in return.

Though these endorsements mean very little from a career stand-point, by allowing users to aimlessly endorse each other, there is finally *something to do* on Linkedin.

Conformity Anchor (Game Technique #58)

Earlier we learned about the power of Social Norming. A game design technique I call *Conformity Anchors* implements this effect into products or experiences by displaying how close users are to the social norm through Feedback Mechanics.

The SaaS (Software-as-a-Service) company Opower, which supplies services to public utilities, is a great example of using Conformity Anchors. Opower's mission is to reduce our collective energy consumption. Their model is inspired by Robert Cialdini whom we have mentioned a few times in this book and is one of the leading experts on Core Drives 4 and 5, as well as the upcoming Core Drive 6: Scarcity & Impatience.

Opower has discovered that, the best way to motivate households to consume less energy is to show them a chart comparing them to their neighbors.

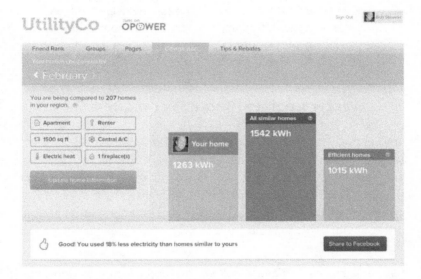

With this interface, Opower reportedly reduced 2.6 terawatt hours of electricity through 16 million households worldwide between 2007 and 2013, the equivalent of $300 Million[154]. They were personally endorsed by President Barrack Obama, named a Technology Pioneer at the prestigious World Economic Forum, and placed on

---

[154] oPower.com Press Release. "Opower Wins WWF Green Game-Changes Innovation of the Year Award". 07/04/2013.

the CNBC Disruptor 50 List[155].

When oPower applied the Conformity Anchors to the utility billing process, one unexpected observation emerged. The top energy savers actually started to consume more energy because they felt they could relax a bit and be more like the norm.

As a result, the company started to apply smiley faces to those who were above average, and two smiley faces to those who were at the top, in an effort to reinforce Core Drive 2: Development & Accomplishment. This has reportedly reduced the effects of negative social norming, where users on the top decide to fall closer towards the average. Of course, there's much more that Opower can do to add the other Core Drives into the process and motivate behavior, but so far the smiley faces seem to do their jobs :-).

Water Coolers (Game Technique #55)

Another way to reinforce Social Influence and Conformity Anchors in your system is by establishing Water Coolers. In American corporate office culture, the water cooler is often the place where people take a small break from work and chat about a variety of non-work related topics. Much of the conversations focus around office gossip or complaints, and actively gets employees to bond with one another.

One example of a Water Cooler is adding a forum to your site. Forums are very helpful for getting a community to bond and share ideas with each other. For this purpose, it also provides an environment to broadcast a *social norm*, while also connecting veterans to newbies for Mentorship opportunities.

When I first started playing the game Geomon, I was skeptical about buying virtual goods with real money. Without paying, I could only

---

[155]Wikipedia Entry: "oPower": http://en.wikipedia.org/wiki/Opower. Accessed 1/18/2015.

capture 10 monsters. After that, when I wanted to capture more monsters, I would have to "evaporate" an old one. That scarcity design (Core Drive #6) tempted me to spend some money, but I held on and painfully continued to play without committing any cash.

However, when I visited the game's forum I found many people talking about how they were spending their purchased gold coins as if that was common practice. After that, I was influenced by the social norm established in the forum and had no problem spending a few dollars to unlock a few slots required to capture more monsters.

Surprisingly, two years after the game had ceased operation, I discovered that the Geomon forums was still active with some loyalists still sharing about the fun old days with each other.

In the *Battle Camp*[156], another mobile game where you train monsters and team with other players to fight bosses, spending is even more established as a social norm than Geomon. Players who spend money are referred to as "Coiners" and many troops would post messages such as, "We only accept coiners." In response, people would plead, "I'm not a coiner, but I'm literally on every hour that I'm not sleeping. Please let me join your troop!" It is not uncommon for regular coiners to spend $50-$100 a week on Battle Camp.

One thing to take note of is that when you introduce a forum-like Water Cooler into your system, it could easily become plagued by constant inactivity. Generally forums are not very good at creating a community, but are good at mingling within an already-established community. If people visit a new forum and see that it's relatively empty, it reinforces a negative social proof. As we have learned in this chapter, this is a big sin which will only demotivate people towards the Desired Actions.

It's important to first create a strong community that already has a lot to discuss and then introduce the Water Cooler to unleash the social energy. Otherwise, you will end up having an office with a

---

[156] Battle Camp Website: pennypop.com/

water cooler but no employees in it.

Core Drive 5: The Bigger Picture

Social Influence & Relatedness is one of the best studied and prac-ticed Right Brain Core Drives in gamification, with Development & Accomplishment being the well-studied counterpart Left Brain Core Drive.

Most people recognize spending time with friends as an intrinsically fun activity. Social Influence & Relatedness adds more fun to Core Drive 3: Empowerment of Creativity & Feedback as well as Core Drive 7: Unpredictability & Curiosity. It makes Core Drive 1: Epic Meaning & Calling more meaningful and Core Drive 2: Develop-ment & Accomplishment feel more like an accomplishment. Also, it gives people a benchmark on how they are doing with Core Drive 4: Ownership & Possession, as well as creates envy when others have what they don't have (Core Drive 6: Scarcity & Impatience).

However, there is such a thing as oversaturation: where many platforms abuse the mechanics for mass friend-spamming, losing the original social purpose of fun and collaboration. If your friends all feel like everything you do is for Left-Brain self-gain purposes, you will begin to lose their trust and be treated like a network marketer who is simply cashing out friends for money.

To get the most out of the book, Choose only ONE of the below options to do right now:

Easy: Think of a time when you had a mentor. Did your behavior change because of the mentor? If you haven't never had a mentor before, come up with a plan to obtain one.

Easy: Think about a Social Treasure you received, or a Social Treasure that you were asked to give. Was it designed to encourage applicants to spread the name of a brand or project?

Medium: Think about another example that heavily utilized Conformity Anchors to change behavior. How was it utilized and can it be improved?

Hard: Think about how you can implement a Group Quest into the project you are doing right now that will motivate users towards the Desired Actions. Does it have a theme? Could it utilize collection sets and boosters to become even more engaging?

Share what you come up with on Twitter or your preferred social network with the hashtag #OctalysisBook and see what ideas other people have.

Join the Movement:

If you have read up to this point, you have become a great candidate to join our Facebook Group of Octalysis Enthusiasts called "Octalysis Explorers[157]." Go on Facebook and search for this group, then request an invitation to join and see what other learners such as yourself are doing with Octalysis. Many thanks to Mike Finney for starting and orchestrating this group.

---

[157] Octalysis Explorers Facebook Group: https://www.facebook.com/groups/octalysis

Chapter 10: The Sixth Core Drive: Scarcity & Impatience

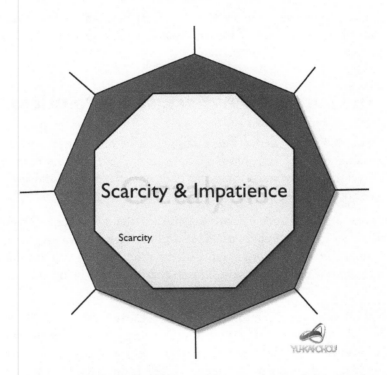

Scarcity and Impatience is the sixth core drive of the Octalysis Framework. It is the drive that motivates us simply because we are either unable to have something immediately, or because there is great difficulty in obtaining it.

We have a natural tendency to want things we can't have. If a bowl of grapes were sitting on the table, you may not care about them;

but if they were on a shelf just beyond your reach, you would likely be thinking about those grapes: "Are they sweet? Can I have them? When can I have them?"

Personally, Core Drive 6 was the last Core Drive I learned about and is the one that intrigues me the most, particularly because this core drive can feel completely unintuitive, irrational, and emotionally difficult to utilize.

In this chapter we'll explore this Black Hat/Left Brain Core Drive, understand its powers, and learn about some game techniques that harness it for behavioral change.

The Lure of being Exclusively Pointless

South Park, a popular American animated sitcom created by Trey Parker and Matt Stone, has many lessons to teach us about human behavior (once you get past the potty-mouth cursing and gory scenes).

In one of the episodes, "Cartmanland"[158], the controversial main character Eric Cartman inherits $1 million from his deceased grandmother. He decides to use most of the funds to buy a struggling theme park just to entertain himself there without being stuck in lines.

Instead of trying to improve the business, Cartman makes a full 38-second TV commercial to show how amazingly fun "Cartmanland" is and emphasizes that no one besides himself can enjoy it. "So much fun in Cartmanland, but you can't come!" is the catchy slogan.

After realizing he needs more money to hire a security guard to keep his friends out, Cartman starts to accept two customers a day to pay for the security costs. He soon realizes that he needs to pay

---

[158]Wikipedia Entry "Cartmanland": http://en.wikipedia.org/wiki/Cartmanland. Accessed 1/19/2015.

for other things such as maintenance, utilities, and other operational services, so he begins to open the park up to three, four, tens, and then hundreds of people each day.

Since people all saw how inaccessible Cartmanland was for them, when they learned that it was accepting more people, they rushed to get in.

Eventually, everyone wanted to go to Cartmanland and it went from being a near-bankrupt theme park to one of the most popular parks in the region. Experts within the episode even called the "You Can't Come!" campaign a brilliant marketing ploy by the genius millionaire Eric Cartman.

Unfortunately, with more people in his precious park, Cartman became miserable and eventually sold it back to the original owner. Subsequently, he lost his money due to tax mismanagement, which is typical of Cartman.

What you see here is a classic example of scarcity through exclusivity. Though this is an exaggerated example, in this chapter you will see how our brains have a natural tendency to pursue things just because they are exclusive.

On the other side of popular media, in the movie Up in the Air[159], protagonist Ryan Bingham, played by George Clooney, is a corporate "downsizer" that flies all over the place to help companies lay off employees. In a conversation with the young and ambitious status-quo disruptor Natalie Keene, played by Anna Kendrick, Bingham gives us a lesson about the value of scarcity, status, rewards, and exclusivity, as he explains about his obsession with accumulating airline miles.

Ryan Bingham: I don't spend a nickel, if I can help it, unless it somehow profits my mileage account.

Natalie Keener: So, what are you saving up for? Hawaii? South of France?

---

[159] Up in the Air Official Website: theupintheairmovie.com

Ryan Bingham: It's not like that. The miles are the goal.

Natalie Keener: That's it? You're saving just to save?

Ryan Bingham: Let's just say that I have a number in mind and I haven't hit it yet.

Natalie Keener: That's a little abstract. What's the target?

Ryan Bingham: I'd rather not...

Natalie Keener: Is it a secret target?

Ryan Bingham: It's ten million miles.

Natalie Keener: Okay. Isn't ten million just a number?

Ryan Bingham: Pi's just a number.

Natalie Keener: Well, we all need a hobby. No, I- I- I don't mean to belittle your collection. I get it. It sounds cool.

Ryan Bingham: I'd be the seventh person to do it. More people have walked on the moon.

Natalie Keener: Do they throw you a parade?

Ryan Bingham: You get lifetime executive status. You get to meet the chief pilot, Maynard Finch.

Natalie Keener: Wow.

Ryan Bingham: And they put your name on the side of a plane.

Natalie Keener: Men get such hard-ons from putting their names on things. You guys don't grow up. It's like you need to pee on everything.

Beyond the collection, status, and achievement (Core Drives 4, 5, and 2), one thing that was very important for Ryan was that "I'd be the seventh person to do it. More people have walked on the moon." This shows that because it's something that he (along with billions of others) couldn't get right now, he valued obtaining it more. It was simply more appealing because of how exclusive it was.

The Value of Rare Pixels

In the previously mentioned game *Geomon*, gamers try to capture monsters in order to battle each other. The game is similar to Pokemon, but influenced by the environment where the gamers are physically located based on their phone GPS, such as being next to a river or a desert.

In *Geomon*, there are certain monsters that can only be found in very limited or special situations. Because some of these monsters are extremely rare, people are willing to spend real money in order to obtain them.

One such example is the Mozzy, a blazing fox made of fire.

The Mozzy can only be caught on hot days and close to an office run by the Mozilla Organization - creators of the Mozilla Firefox browser. This means, for a game that has players throughout the world, it is extremely difficult, sometimes impossible for the average person to capture a Mozzy. In the forums, people sometimes say, "This summer my parents are taking me to San Francisco. I'm going to rent a car and drive down to Mountain View. Maybe I'll catch a Mozzy. So excited!"

This drive is further illustrated with the live comments made by Geomon players, through in-game chat, during game play. In the following screenshot I randomly took while playing, notice how desperate users are in obtaining a Mozzy. Emphasized with all caps – "I'LL DO ANYTHING FOR A MOZZY."

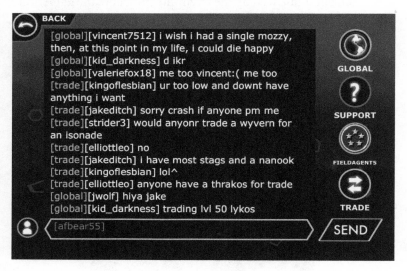

Though it seems rather extreme, the desperate plea above is surpassed by the following conversation below:

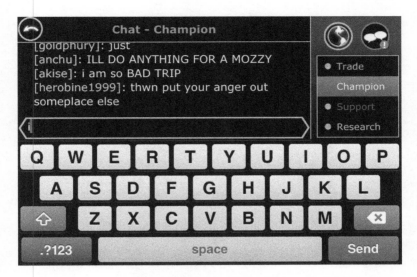

Here, you see "Vincent7512" claim (adjusted for capitalization), "I wish I had a single Mozzy, then, at this point in my life, I could die happy."

Now you would expect that when someone says this, others would respond with, "Come on... get a life! It's just a game!" But no. Three lines down, you see "Valeriefox18" echo the same sentiment, "me too vincent :(me too."

Here is a community of players who are so desperate about getting Mozzys that instead of playing the game more, they hang out on the chat board just to mope about it and feel "connected" to one another (CD5 Relatedness). Pretty extreme right?

Another example of this within Geomon is the *Laurelix*, the magnificent golden phoenix.

In order to catch a Laurelix, you need to be at a location that has an extremely high temperature, possibly over 110 Fahrenheit or 40 Celsius. The result of this design was, at one point there were only 3 players in the entire world that owned a Laurelix. As you might imagine, everyone wanted one too. Once the game studio even received a call from the mother of a player, saying, "My son has been sick for two whole weeks, and he said nothing could cheer him up unless he had a Laruelix. I don't know what that is, but he said you had it. I'm willing to pay $20 for a Laurelix. Can you give that to my son?"

Interestingly, the Mozzy and Lauralix are not the most powerful geomons in the game – there are plenty of geomons that are more powerful than they are. But because these two are so difficult to obtain, their perceived value increased immensely, helping the company better monetize their game.

What's amazing is that when something is this scarce, it has a tremendous amount of stickiness to it also. As an advisor for the company, I played the game for a while (okay, more than a while), facilitated the online communities, and helped the company redesign and rebalance their entire ability skill trees and combat systems. After that, I became a passive advisor, quit the game, and moved on to my "other work."

For an entire seven months, I haven't been playing, nor thinking about the game (except when meeting the CEO and advising them on management and monetization strategies). But one day I was traveling for work and found myself at a place that was excruciatingly hot, to the point where I felt like I was burning if directly exposed to the sun.

At that moment, instead of shouting or complaining about it, the first thing that came to my mind and mouth was, "I wonder if I could catch a Laurelix here..." This of course confused my client who was giving me a tour of his great country.

Even though, again, I didn't care about playing the game anymore and haven't played for over half a year, because a Laurelix was so scarce, I naturally thought that, "Well, when I *can* capture one, I probably *should* capture it!"

The Leftovers aren't all that's Left Over

Most of us would like to believe that we make purchasing decisions based on the price and quality of a good. A purchase is seen as a very rational exchange of money for an item that we desire. If the price were greater than the "utility," or happiness that we derive from the valuable, then we don't make the purchase.

However, psychological studies have shown again and again that this is only partially true. We buy things not because of their actual value, but rather based on their *perceived* value, which means many times our purchases aren't very rational.

In 1975, researchers Worchel, Lee, and Adewole conducted an experiment to test the desirability of cookies in different cookie jars[160]. The experiment featured two cookie jars, one with ten cookies in it, and the other with only two. Though the cookies were exactly the same, the experiment revealed that people valued the cookies more when only two were available in the jar. They valued those cookies more, mainly for two reasons: 1) Social Proof – everyone else seems to prefer those cookies for some reason, and 2) Scarcity- people felt that the cookies were running out.

In a second experiment conducted by the team, subjects watched as the number of cookies in the "ten-cookie" jar were reduced to two cookies, while the other group saw the "two-cookie" jar get filled up to ten cookies. In this case, people started to value the former more and devalue the latter. When people saw that there was now an abundance in the first jar which earlier had only two cookies, they valued these even less than those from the "ten-cookie" jar of the first experiment where there were ten cookies to begin with.

Here we see that, when there is a *perceived abundance*, motivation starts to dwindle. The odd thing is, our perception is often influenced by relative changes instead of absolute values. People with $10 million would perceive their wealth differently (and feel differently) if they only had $1 million the year before, versus if they had $1 billion the year before.

Persuasively Inconvenient

As illustrated in the examples above, our brains intuitively seek things that are scarce, unavailable, or fading in availability.

Oren Klaff is a professional sales pitcher and fundraiser who claims to close deals through a systematic method which he calls *neuroeconomics*, a craft that combines both neuroscience and economics. By

---

[160] Stephen Worchel, Jerry Lee, and Akanbi Adewole. Journal of Personality and Social Psychology, Vol 32(5),906-914. "Effects of supply and demand on ratings of object value". 11/1975.

digging deep into our psychology and appealing to what he calls the "croc" brain, the method utilizes various Core Drives such as Social Influence & Relatedness, Scarcity & Impatience, as well as the upcoming Core Drive 7: Unpredictability & Curiosity and Core Drive 8: Loss & Avoidance.[161]

In his book Pitch Anything[162], Klaff explains the concept of *Prizing*, and how it ties into three fundamental behaviors of our "croc" brains:

1. We chase that which moves away from us
2. We want what we cannot have
3. We only place value on things that are difficult to obtain

His work suggests that, instead of ABS – Always Be Selling, salespeople should practice ABL – Always Be Leaving. If you are always leaving the discussions, it means that you are not desperate, are highly sought after, and not dependent on this deal. You are the Prize. Klaff claims that, when you correctly do this, money will flow in.

Through his methods, Klaff has raised over $450 million and claims to continue so at a rate of $2 million a week.

It is oddly true that as we place limitations on something, it becomes more valuable in our minds. In Yes! 50 Scientifically Proven Ways to Be Persuasive, the authors share how Colleen Szot revolutionized her infomercials by simply changing the call-to-action line from "Operators are waiting, please call now," to, "If operators are busy, please call again.[163]"

---

[161]The discerning Octalyst may identify that there is a heavy focus of Black Hat Core Drives here. We will return to why sales and closing deals mostly appeals to Black Hat Core Drives, while workplace motivation mostly appeals to White Hat Core Drives in Chapter 14.

[162]Oren Klaff. *Pitch Anything*. P64. 1 edition. McGraw-Hill. 02/16/2011.

[163]Noah Goldstein, Steve Martin, and Robert Cialdini. *Yes! 50 Scientifically Proven Ways to Be Persuasive*. P9. Simon & Schuster. New York, NY. 2010.

Why would this be? In the first case, viewers can imagine operators sitting around, waiting to answer calls and take orders for products that may be of marginal value. In the second case viewers will perceive that the operators are struggling to answer a flood of calls just to keep up with the demand on orders. Even though this message suggests an inconvenience to buy a product, the perceived scarcity alone is enough to motivated people to call quickly before the product potentially runs out.

My father is a diplomat for Taiwan, and sometimes he would talk to a colleague who was deployed to a former communist country in Eastern Europe. I once heard the colleague say, "If you see a line on the street, don't even waste time finding out what they are in line for. Just get in line. It must be something essential like soap or toilet paper. It doesn't matter if you have money. If there is no toilet paper in the region, your money is useless." Here, the *sheer inconvenience* driven by scarcity and social proof can compel a comparably wealthy person to stand in line for hours.

In Pitch Anything, Oren Klaff also brings up another example where BMW released a special-edition M3 that required the buyer to sign a contract promising to keep it clean and take care of the special paint. Without this promise in writing, they won't even allow you to purchase the car! In this case, BMW is inflating its value so that the buyer will believe it is a special and exclusive privilege to drive the car. Maybe that's why the hard-to-get strategy in dating culture is so prevalent. Through Core Drive 6: Scarcity & Impatience, you can keep your prospective partner on their toes.

Curves are better than Cups in Economics

When I was studying Economics at UCLA, the one fundamental lesson that my professors regularly talked about was the Supply and Demand curve. It basically explains that if the price of an item drops, the demand will increase. If the item becomes completely free, the curve will indicate the maximum number of buyers that will acquire it.

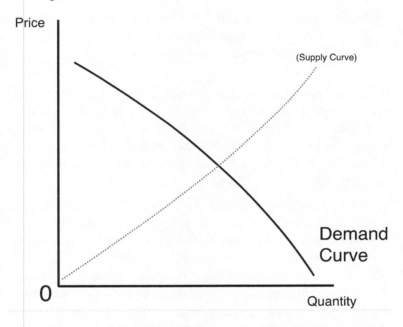

However, if you study behavioral psychology, gamification, and/or Human-Focused Design, you will find that there is another side to the story. As it turns out, Scarcity is another driving force of consumer behavior. In economic theory, scarcity is well understood, but only in the sense of objective limits matched against the consumer's *utility* derived from a purchase.

This is different from the Scarcity we are discussing in this chapter, which is related to *Perceived Scarcity* instead of Objective Scarcity. Sometimes objective scarcity is present without a person ever feeling or knowing it. At other times there is a sense of perceived scarcity without a true limit being present.

The difference here is that neo-classical economic theory starts off with three key assumptions[164]:

1. Consumers behave rationally
2. Consumers have full and relevant information
3. Consumers try to maximize their utility (or happiness derived from economic consumables)

But in the real world, the first two assumptions almost never hold true - people are often irrational and never have perfect information. Sometimes they react to pricing in another, more surprising way: the more expensive something is, the higher the value (utility) is placed on it. This leads to increased demand. As a result, sales may actually increase with pricing.

Normally, if an item were free (the extreme right of the demand curve), everyone who would want this product would obtain it for free. Say hypothetically, 100 people want this product for free. But in certain scenarios, if the product is unusually expensive, people who previously didn't care might suddenly desire it. Now sales may exceed 150 items! Because of this scarcity effect, a modified demand curve in some products might produce a C-Shape instead of a diagonal line moving down to the right.

---

[164]E. Roy Weintraub. *The Concise Encyclopedia Of Economics*. Neoclassical Economics. 2007.

Economic <u>Demand Curve</u> with Behavioral Scarcity

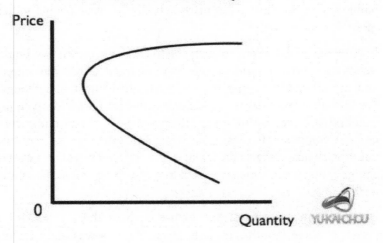

Scarcity works because people perceive something to be more valuable if it is more expensive or less attainable. Because people don't have "perfect information," they generally do not fully know their utility for a certain good. Therefore, they rely on cues - such as how expensive or limited something is - to determine its value. If everyone wants it, it must be good! This goes hand-in-hand with the last chapter on Core Drive 5: Social Influence & Relatedness.

Of course, at some point, the C-Curve needs to curl back towards the left (zero in quantity) as the item becomes exceedingly expensive beyond anyone's wealth, producing a reverse S-Shape on the graph. Objective Scarcity (of money) ultimately still wins over Perceived Scarcity at large extremes.

"This guy's not expensive enough."

I've personally seen numerous examples, both first and second hand, where increasing the price actually allowed people to sell more.

In 2013, one of my clients was trying to choose between two Public Relations service providers, one who charged $8,000 per month and the other $10,000 per month. I informed him that I thought the $8,000/mo provider would deliver better services. However, my client remained doubtful, feeling that the $10,000/mo provider must be more competent to charge that price. I told him that just because one service provider has the audacity (I used a more vulgar term) to charge more doesn't mean he is better. But my client still couldn't decide.

Ultimately my client decided to use both of the services for a period of three months. Though expensive, this was great for me personally because it allowed me to gather valuable data on their actual performances and draw comparisons. After the period was up, it was clear that the $8,000/mo provider was exceptional, while the provider at $10,000 per month proved to be very disappointing. My client fired the $10K guy and retained the $8K guy after that.

What's odd is that if the weaker service provider recognized that he was less suitable for the project and only charged $6000 instead of $10,000, he might not have been given a second thought. His aggressive pricing strategy yielded him a new opportunity and $30,000 more! Of course the ultimate lesson here should be to focus on creating strong value for your client- so you don't lose your job after 3 months.

On another occasion, I had a client that needed a Cost Per Click (CPC) campaign audit. I contacted a friend from Eastern Europe who was the best in the industry. Since I had done some favors for him in the past, I was able to persuade him to help my client with a free audit, for which he normally would have charged thousands for.

Though my client was excited about the arrangement, he hesitated and moved very slowly. I pressed my client on this and he said, "What worries me is the free price ... is he really as good as you say he is?" He had perceived that my friend's service was not really valuable because it was offered for free. That's why it might have been more advantageous to charge a smaller fee such as $500 for the audit, instead of providing it pro bono.

"I Don't Feel Good When My Pocket Is Too Full After A Purchase"

This situation doesn't just happen with high-end services. In the book Influence: Science and Practice, Robert Cialdini also describes a story of a friend who ran an Indian jewelry store in Arizona that tried to sell some high quality turquoise pieces during the peak tourist season[165].

Despite her constant efforts to promote, cross-sell, and emphasize these pieces to shop visitors, no one seemed interested in purchasing them. Finally, the night prior to an out-of-town buying trip, the owner concluded that she needed to lower the prices and make the pieces more attractive to her customers. As a result, she left a note for her head salesperson with instructions to reduce the prices by "x$\frac{1}{2}$."

However, the salesperson misunderstood the note, and mistakenly doubled the price instead. Upon returning a few days later, the owner was pleasantly surprised to learn that all the pieces had been sold. Doubling the price on each item had actually allowed her to sell more because their perceived value had increased.

---

[165]Robert Cialdini. *Influence: Science and Practice*. 5th Edition. P2. Pearson Education. Boston, MA. 08/08/2008.

Since you don't *do* anything with jewelry other than show it off to others (or yourself), the value is usually based on perception as opposed to functionality. You may quickly dismiss the value of an ugly and cracked pottery piece on the shelf, until someone told you that it was made 1,200 years ago for a historically significant event. The pottery itself did not functionally or aesthetically become more valuable, but its *perceived value* immediately went up due to the principles of scarcity.

Up to this point, you may have observed that the high-price principle within Core Drive 6 works powerfully for luxury items that serve little functional purpose such as jewelry, or expensive services that provide essential expertise. Surprisingly, it also works with everyday functional items.

Just a week prior to writing this chapter, upon realizing my knee pains were getting worse, I decided to visit a sports utility store. I wanted pick up some knee braces for hiking or when I'm walking up and down the stairs during phone meetings. When I entered the store, I saw that there were two types of braces, one for $24.99 one another for $49.99.

I thought to myself, "Well, my knees are very important to me. I better not spare a few extra bucks and end up with busted knees down the road." As an extension to this thought, I reached out for a pair of $49.99 braces and bought them.

It didn't occur to me until writing this chapter and searching for examples, that I automatically assumed that the more expensive knee braces were better than the cheaper ones. I didn't even bother to carefully read the product descriptions. If you were to ask me how the $49.99 one was better than the $24.99 one, I wouldn't be able to give you an answer. I would likely say something along the lines of, "Well, the $49.99 one is more expensive, so I'm sure it offers better protection for my knees or feels more comfortable. Probably both."

This was very powerful because, in my head, I was not thinking about the actual differences between the two knee braces. I was simply thinking whether I wanted to, "save money and get lower quality," or "not skimp and invest in quality goods for my long-term health."

Daniel Kahneman, author of *Thinking: Fast and Slow*, refers to our brain's neocortex as our "System 2," which broadly controls our conscious thinking[166]). Since the processing capabilities of our brain's neocortex are limited, we regularly rely on mental shortcuts, known as heuristics, without noticing them. In this situation, the mental shortcut was that "expensive equals quality" when it may not have necessarily been the case.

Another mental shortcut can be, "The Expert said it with confidence - I will assume it to be true without looking too deeply into it." Sometimes people let pass some obvious blunders and oversights simply because the authoritative expert or scientist said so. They let their "System 2" become lazy and simply become motivated by Core Drive 5: Social Influence & Relatedness.

Perhaps I am alone in my silliness and financial irresponsibility in buying knee braces simply because they were more expensive. But the chances are, at some point in your life you have also taken mental shortcuts based on assumptions that may not always hold true. Perhaps you have purchased a bottle of wine or detergents based on very little information other than the price, and disdained some selections simply because the merchant labeled it at a low price.

---

[166]Daniel Kahneman. "Thinking, Fast and Slow." P41. Farrar, Straus and Giroux. New York, NY. 2013.

Game Techniques within Scarcity & Impatience

You have learned more about the motivational and psychological nature of Core Drive 6: Scarcity & Impatience. To make it more actionable, I've included some Game Techniques below that heavily utilize this Core Drive to engage users.

Dangling (Game Technique #44) and Anchored Juxtaposition (Game Technique #69)

Many social and mobile games utilize game design techniques within Core Drive 6: Scarcity & Impatience to heavily monetize on their users. One of the more popular combinations among games are what I call Anchored Juxtaposition (Game Technique #69) and Dangling (Game Technique #44).

For instance, when you go on Farmville, you initially may think, "This game is somewhat fun, but I would never pay real money for a stupid game like this." Then Farmville deploys their Dangling techniques and regularly shows you an appealing mansion that you want but can't have. The first few times, you just dismiss it, as you inherently know it wouldn't be resource-efficient to get it. But eventually you start to develop some desire for the mansion that's constantly being dangled there.

With some curiosity now compelling you, a little research shows that the game requires 20 more hours of play before you can afford to get the mansion. Wow, that's a lot of farming! But then, you see that you could just spend $5.00 and get that mansion immediately. "$5 to save 20 hours of my time? That's a no-brainer!" Now the user is no longer paying $5 to buy some pixels on their screen. They are spending $5 to save their time, which becomes a phenomenal deal. Can you see how game design can influence people's sense of value by alternating between time and money?

The humorous part about this phenomenon is that most of these games can be played for free, and yet people are spending money, just so they could play *less* of the game. In this sense, it is hard to determine if the game itself is truly considered "enjoyable" or "fun." As opposed to Core Drive 3: Empowerment of Creativity & Feedback, this Black Hat Left Brain Core Drive is more about being persuasive and obsessive, but users don't necessarily enjoy the process.

An important factor to consider when using the Dangling technique is the pathway to obtaining the reward. You have to allow the user to know that it's very challenging to get the reward, but not impossible. If it is perceived as impossible, then people turn on their Core Drive 8: Loss & Avoidance modes and go into self-denial. "It's probably for losers anyway."

For example, if the banner of an exclusive club is dangled in front of you, but you find out that the prerequisite to join is that you must be a Prince or Princess through royal blood, you might not even look at what the organization does. Instead, you may think, "Who cares about a bunch of stuck up, spoiled brats." Because there is no chance of qualifying, it activates Core Drive 8 as an Anti Core Drive – the drive to not execute the Desired Action.

However, if the banner said, "Joining Prerequisite: Prince/Princess by royal blood, OR individuals who have previously ran a marathon." Now you are motivated, and might even ponder the effort required to run a marathon. As long as there is a realistic *chance* to get in, the Scarcity through exclusivity is enough to engage you. Interestingly, at this point you still haven't even determined what the organization actually does! Without any information on its actual function, the human-focused motivation of scarcity is compelling enough for you to consider running a marathon.

This leads to a game technique I call *Anchored Juxtaposition*. With this technique, you place two options side by side: one that costs money, the other requiring a great amount of effort in accomplishing the Desired Actions which will benefit the system.

For example, a site could give you two options for obtaining a certain reward: a) Pay $20 right now, or b) complete a ridiculous number of Desired Actions. The Desired Actions could be in the form of "Invite your friends," 'Upload photos," and/or "stay on the site for 30 days in a row."

In this scenario, you will find that many users will irrationally choose to complete the Desired Actions. You'll see users slaving away for dozens, even hundreds of hours, just so they can save the $20 to reach their goal. At one point, many of them will realize that it's a lot of time and work. At that moment, the $20 investment becomes more appealing and they end up purchasing it anyway. Now your users have done both: paid you money, and committed a great deal of Desired Actions.

It is worth remembering that rewards can be physical, emotional, or intellectual. Rewards don't have to be financial nor do they need to come in the form of badges - people hardly pay for those. In fact, based on Core Drive 3: Empowerment of Creativity & Feedback principles, the most effective rewards are often Boosters that allow the user to go back into the ecosystem and play more effectively, creating a streamlined activity loop in the process.

With Anchored Juxtapositions, you *must* have two options for the user. If you simply put a price on the reward and say, "Pay now, or go away," many users will go back into a Core Drive 8 denial mode and think, "I'm never gonna pay those greedy bastards a single dollar!" - and then leave. Conversely, if you just put on your site, "Hey! Please do all these Desired Actions, such as invite your friends and complete your profile!" users won't be motivated to take the actions because they clearly recognize it as being beneficial for the system, but not for themselves.

Only when you put those two options together - hence Juxtaposition, do people become more open to both options, and often commit to doing both consecutively as time goes by. But does this work in the real world, outside of games? You bet.

Dropbox is a File Hosting Service based in San Francisco that has obtained extraordinary popularity and success. When you first sign-up to Dropbox, it tells you that you could either a) pay to get a lot of storage space, or b) invite your friends to get more space. In the beginning, most people started with inviting their friends.

Refer friends to Dropbox		16 GB
Spread the love to your friends, family, and coworkers		500 MB per friend
Get started with Dropbox		250 MB
Take a tour of the basics of Dropbox		
Connect your Facebook account		125 MB
Share folders with your friends and family in a snap		
Connect your Twitter account		125 MB
Invite your friends to Dropbox with a tweet		
Follow Dropbox on Twitter		125 MB
Stay up to date with the latest Dropbox tweets		
Tell us why you love Dropbox		125 MB
We'd love to hear your feedback		

Eventually, many of those users who are completing the Desired Actions decide that inviting/harassing their friends is a lot of work, but they still need a lot of storage space, so they end up becoming paying users (just like I did). Again, because of the Anchored Juxtaposition, users commit both the Desired Action, and pay for the full product.

Dropbox's viral design, along with a great seamless product design, accelerated the company's growth to a point where it reportedly raised over $300 million, with a valuation of around $10 billion and revenues above $200 million in 2013. Not too shabby for a company that didn't exist seven years prior to that.

Magnetic Caps (Game Technique#68)

Magnetic Caps are limitations placed on how many times a user can commit certain Desired Actions, which then stimulates more motivation to commit them.

When I consult with my clients, I often remind them that they should rarely create a feeling of abundance. The feeling of abundance does not motivate our brains. Scarcity, on the other hand, is incredibly motivating towards our actions. Even if the user committed the ultimate Desired Action by paying a lot of money, a persuasive system designer should only give people a temporary sense of abundance. After a few weeks or months, the feeling of scarcity should crawl back again with new targets for the user to obtain - perhaps after they have used up all of their virtual currencies and needing to purchase their next batch.

A great system designer should always control the flow of scarcity, and make sure everyone in the system is still striving for a goal that is difficult, but not impossible, to attain. Failure to do so would cause a gratifying system to implode with users abandoning it for better grounds.

This plugs nicely into Mihaly Csikszentmihalyi's Flow Theory[167], where the difficulty of the challenge must increase along with the skill set of the user. Too much challenge leads to anxiety. Too little challenge leads to boredom.

---

[167] Wikipedia Entry, "Mihaly Csikszentmihalyi": http://en.wikipedia.org/wiki/Mihaly_-Csikszentmihalyi. Accessed 1/20/2015.

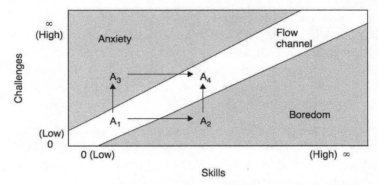

The Flow. After Mihaly Csikszentmihalyi, *The Flow (1990)*, p. 74

There have been many interesting studies showing that by simply placing a limit on something, people's interest in it will increase. If you introduce a feature that can be used as much as people want, often few will actually use it. But once you place a use limit on the feature, more often than not, you will find people enthusiastically taking advantage of the opportunity.

In Brian Wansink's book Mindless Eating: Why We Eat More Than We Think, he describes that when a grocery store just displays a promotional sign that says, "No Limit Per Person," people often just buy a few of the promoted item[168]. However, if the sign were to say, "Limit 12 Per Person," people will start to buy more – in fact, 30% - 105% more, depending on other variables. That's another odd characteristic of scarcity: by drawing limits, we're drawn *towards* the limit.

This means that you should place a limit on an activity if you want

---

[168]Brian Wansink. *Mindless Eating: Why We Eat More Than We Think*. Bantam. 10/17/2006.

to increase a certain behavior. Of course, you don't necessarily want the Magnetic Cap to limit the activity so much that you lose more than you gain. The best way to set a limit is to first find the current "upper bound" of the desired metric, and use that as the cap to create a *perceived* sense of scarcity but doesn't necessarily limit the behavior. A behavior designer could speculate "Even though we want users to select an unlimited number of hobbies, 90% of our users choose fewer than five hobbies on our website." In this case, it would be appropriate to set a limit at five or six hobbies instead of having no limits.

What about the 10% of users who go beyond six hobbies - the "power users", you ask? Aren't they important? Yes they are (and if you asked that question, it means you have been thinking about user motivation and experience phases, which is great). This is when you let the power users unlock more capabilities and have the limit rise as they continue to prove their commitment, as described with the Evolved UI technique below. Again, you still want to let these power users to confront a Magnetic Cap at the top, so that they always feel a sense of Scarcity, but not have it truly limit their activities.

Appointment Dynamics (Game Technique #21)

Another way to reinforce this Core Drive is to harness the *scarcity of time*. The best known game technique that leverages this is the Appointment Dynamic. Popularized by Seth Priebatsch's TEDx Boston talk on The Game Layer on Top of the World[169], Appointment Dynamics utilize a formerly declared, or recurring schedule where users have to take the Desired Actions to effectively reach the Win-State.

One of the most common examples are Happy Hours, where by hitting the Win-State of showing up at the right time, people get to

---

[169] Seth Priebatsch. TEDx Boston. "Game Layer on top of our world". 07/2010.

enjoy the reward of 50% off appetizers and beer. People expect the schedule and plan accordingly.

Appointment Dynamics are powerful because they form a trigger built around time. Many products don't have recurring usage because they lack a trigger to remind the person to come back. According to Nir Eyal, author of Hooked[170], External Triggers often come in the form of reminder emails, pop-up messages, or people telling you to do something.

On the other hand, Internal Triggers are built within your natural response system for certain experiences. For instance, when you see something beautiful, it triggers the desire to open Instagram. Facebook's trigger, on the other hand, is boredom.

A friend once told me how one day he was using Facebook and suddenly felt bored. Surprisingly, He instinctively opened a new tab on his browser and typed in "Facebook.com." Once the website loaded, he was shocked, "Oh my. I was already on Facebook. Why did I open Facebook again?" Again, this is the power of an Internal Trigger that connects to a feeling as common as boredom - for instance, what do you do when you are waiting in line?

With Appointment Dynamics, the trigger is time. My garbage truck comes every Tuesday morning, so on Monday nights, I automatically have an internal alarm clock reminding myself to take out the garbage. If the garbage truck comes out every day, I may procrastinate until my garbage overflows before taking it out.

One extremely innovative example (and I rarely call things "innovative") of a company utilizing the Appointment Dynamic is a large Korean shopping center named eMart. The company realized that their traffic and sales are usually great during most hours of the day, but during lunch time, foot traffic and sales drops significantly. To motivate people to show up during lunch time (Desired Action), they mustered up the principles of Core Drive 6:

---

[170] Nir Eyal. *Hooked*. Kindle Version v 1.0. Chapter 2: Trigger. 2014.

Scarcity & Impatience and a bit of Core Drive 7: Unpredictability & Curiosity. They ended up launching a campaign called "Sunny Sale" and built an odd-looking statue in front of their stores.

On its own, this statue looks fairly abstract and doesn't seem to resemble anything. During noon time, however, the magic starts to happen. When the sun reaches its greatest height at noon, the shadow of this statue suddenly transforms into a perfect QR Code where people can scan with their mobile phones and see unique content.

Isn't that cool? Because the QR Code can only be scanned within a limited window between 12PM to 1PM, people are now rushing to get there in time. Honestly, at that point, it doesn't matter what the QR Code is about – the scarcity and intrigue (stemming from Core Drive 7: Unpredictability & Curiosity) is enough to get people to show up. In the case of eMart, the QR code links to a coupon that consumers can redeem immediately for a purchase online.

This tactic reportedly improved eMart's noon time sales by 25%. Not bad when you are already the largest player in the industry.

Torture Breaks (Game Technique #66)

By now you may have noticed that another kind of game technique of Core Drive 6: Scarcity & Impatience can utilize "Impatience", which means not allowing people to do something *immediately*. In the old days, most console games tried to get users to stay on as long as possible. If a player were "glued to the screen" for five hours straight, it would be a big win for the game. Nowadays, social mobile games do something completely different.

Many social mobile games don't let you play for very long. The game will let you play for thirty minutes, and then tell you "Stop! You can't play anymore. You need to come back 8 hours later - because you have to wait for your crops to grow / you need to wait for your energy to recharge / you need to heal up."

For some parents who don't understand Core Drive 6, this design makes them very happy. "That's great! These game designers are so responsible – now my son's play time will be limited!" But in fact, what they don't recognize is that the game is implementing what I call *Torture Breaks* to drive obsessive behavior.

A Torture Break is a sudden and often triggered pause to the Desired Actions. Whereas the Appointment Dynamic is more based on absolute times that people look forward to (Every Monday morning the garbage truck will come; on July 4th when you open the app, you will get a huge bonus), Torture Breaks are often unexpected hard stops in the user's path toward the Desired Action. It often comes with a relative timestamp based on when the break is triggered, such as "Return 5 hours from now."

My differentiation between the two Game Techniques may differ somewhat from Priebatsch's definition. Though they often work hand in hand together (sometimes after a Torture Break is triggered, an Appointment Dynamic follows), it is important to note the difference so you can plan your gamified systems accurately.

In the example of social mobile games, because the player was forced to stop playing, they will likely continue to think about the game all day long. Often, they will log back in after three hours, five hours, six hours, just to check if they are finally able to play - even though their brain knows as a fact that the allotted eight hours haven't passed yet.

If the player was allowed to play for as long as they wanted – say three hours, they would likely become satisfied, stop playing, and not think about the game for a day or two. Therefore, an omniscient game designer would perhaps allow them to play for two hours and fifty-nine minutes, and then trigger the Torture Break. At this point, they will be obsessively trying to figure out how to play that final one minute. Sometimes the game may even provide another option – "pay $1 to remove the Torture Break immediately!"

Another game, *Candy Crush*, which by many metrics is considered to be one of the most successful games in the world, making approximately $3 million per day[171], incorporates the Torture Break very well. After losing a life, the game pauses and forces you to wait 25 minutes before you can gain another life and proceed to the next level.

---

[171] MarketWatch. "Candy Crush Maker Reports Lower Revenue Earnings". 11/06/2014.

This draws players to constantly think about those slow-passing 25 minute intervals, and makes it difficult to plan other activities while being occupied by the obsession.

Of course, the game also gives you two options: ask your friends to give you a life (Social Treasure), or pay right now (Anchored Juxtaposition). See how all these game techniques work together to become a holistic motivational system towards Desired Actions?

Accidental Fails sometimes become a Blessing

Another good example of the Torture Break is the "Fail Whale" in the early years of Twitter. The Twitter site was often down in 2007. Though this frustrated many users, they waited more eagerly for the service to return, while talking about it on Facebook.

When the site was down, users would only see a "404 Error Page" displaying the iconic Fail Whale – a large whale being pulled out of the water by many struggling birds.

Twitter's combination of "limitations" – you can't go over 140 characters, can't tweet over X times a day, can't access the site 60% of the time – compelled many to spend countless hours on Twitter, even though there truthfully wasn't much to do there in those early days.

I've seen other cases where people were planning to retire from playing a game, but then encountered issues due to massive server problems. Instead of quitting, they checked the app every day to see whether they could play it or not. Even though they planned to quit, they needed to quit on their own terms. When these players were prevented from playing because they "couldn't," their desire to play actually increased.

What made the situation worse was that players would occasionally be able to play the game, only to experience another crash. If it were down indefinitely, people would lose interest. But by "sometimes working," the game would take on an addictive appeal. Remember, for Core Drive 6 to work, users have to perceive that obtaining the goal is possible, or else they fall into a Self-Denial Mode driven by Core Drive 8: Loss & Avoidance.

This is also similar to some relationships I've witnessed, where one person wants to break up with the other, plans the breakup for months, and suddenly gets dumped by the other person. Even though the person wanted to break up from the start, when they gets dumped, they may become obsessed with wanting to get back together with the other person. They want the separation to be on their terms. But when forced to separate, it becomes a Torture Break that makes them yearn for a reconciliation.

This behavior is much like people pulling on a slot machine lever, hoping for, but not necessarily expecting, good results. The same effect happened with Twitter, where users became obsessed with checking the site each minute to see if the service had been reestablished, subsequently becoming delighted when it ultimately returned.

Evolved UI (Game Technique #37)

One of the techniques that I often recommended to my clients, but have faced resistance on, is the Evolved UI - short for "Evolved User Interface". The problem with most user interfaces is that they're too complex during the Onboarding stage, while too basic for the Endgame.

In the popular gaming phenomenon World of Warcraft, if you monitor the top-level players, their interface could make you dizzy. There may be close to a dozen little windows open, all with different stats, options, and icons. It displays a plethora of information about how your teammates are doing, how the boss is doing, where everyone is, and your own resources. So much information that you can barely see the animation of your own character fighting! It truly is one of the most complex user interfaces around.

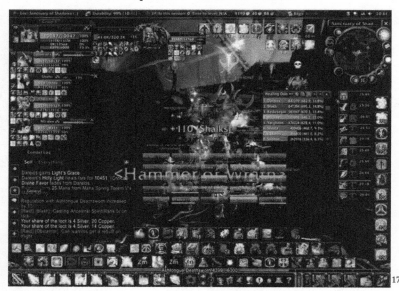
[172]

However, World of Warcraft, along with many other well-designed games, never starts off with this level of complexity. At the beginning they only provide a few options, buttons, and icons. But as you reach more Win-States, you unlock more options, skills, and capabilities. With the help of effective Step-by-step On-boarding Tutorials, Narratives, and Glowing Choices, a beginner never gets confused about what to do at the start.

Based on the concept of Decision Paralysis, if you give users twenty amazing features at the beginning, they feel flustered and don't use a single one. But if you give them only two or three of those features (not just one, since our Core Drive 3 loves choice), and have them slowly unlock more, then they begin to enjoy and love the complexity.

---

[172]Image by Shamus from http://www.shamusyoung.com/twentysidedtale/?p=8660.

However, the Evolved UI concept is very difficult for a company to implement emotionally, because it feels weird to withhold great features and functionalities from the user. For the designer though, it is important to acknowledge that withholding options can drive more behavior towards the Desired Action. Just because it makes users *feel* uncomfortable doesn't mean it's necessarily bad for you, nor for the user.

One company that did implement the Evolved UI concept was Sony, calling it *Evolution UI*[173](in fact, I modified my game technique name to fit Sony's, just to avoid semantic ambiguity within the industry).

Though the Android smartphone system developed by Google was very powerful, Sony realized that it had a high learning curve that could fluster beginning users. To address the situation, they launched the Evolution UI, which presented a very limited set of core options during the Onboarding process.

---

[173]Daniel Cooper. Engadget. "Sony's Evolution UI tries to make learning Android fun". 04/30/2014.

Once users have shown that they have mastered the basic UI, such as opening 5 apps, they unlock an achievement, which in turn unleashes new features. In this way, the difficulty of the user experience never surpasses the skill sets of the user, following the principles of Mihaly Csikszentmihalyi's Flow Theory mentioned earlier.

So what's the consequence of having an UI that is too complex at the beginning? *Google Plus*. As mentioned earlier, even with a lot of great features and functions, Google Plus did not have sticky traction because of the learning curve it required. Most mainstream users feel confused when they are accidentally pushed onto Google Plus when using Youtube or Gmail; and thus quickly leave the platform.

Gmail, on the other hand, implements a small version of Evolved UI, which manifested itself in the form of *Gmail Labs*. In Gmail, users are provided a basic set of features and functionalities by default. But there are many cool features that they can be unlocked through the "Labs" tab under Gmail Settings, opening up complex but helpful features once the user feels ready.

Great! So now what?

Of course, understanding Scarcity & Impatience doesn't mean that startups should shut down their servers on purpose, or set up fake and corny limitations in their systems. Some users may become obsessed, but you could likely turn away many others who quickly jump into denial mode and never come back.

The most obvious application for start-ups based on Core Drive 6 principles is to launch with a confident pricing strategy. Instead of just offering everything for free or making them easily available, a more premium pricing model or well-structured exclusivity design can increase the confidence of users/buyers resulting in increased conversion rates.

Of course, if you price an item beyond your target market's capability to afford, this would obviously backfire. But more often than not, when customers don't buy your product, it's not because they can't afford it, it's because the perceived value they have for your product is not worth the cost. Sometimes that cost is in the form of time, energy investment, or reputation in their organizations.

Beyond pricing, you may want to create a sense of exclusivity for each step during the Discovery and Onboarding stages. A design, where the service makes them feel that it's uniquely for them and that they are only qualifying for access - similar to Facebook's early marketing strategy.

Every step of the way, you want to show users what they may want but can't have - just yet. Scarcity only exists as a motivator when people know the reward actually exists, so *when in doubt, Dangle about* (but don't say you learned that from my book during court). For actions that lead to rewards and investments, consider using more restrictive options. Placing a cap on how many actions a person can take (or investments that they can make) will cause them to desire the actions more.

By increasing perceived value, customers and users are more likely to stay engaged and take greater interest in your venture. This will help insure you from giving out all your hard-earned work for close to nothing.

Core Drive 6: The Bigger Picture

Scarcity and Impatience is considered a Black Hat Core Drive, but if used correctly, it can be very powerful in driving motivation. Often, Core Drive 6 is a first source of generating Core Drive 3: Empowerment of Creativity & Feedback in the system. Overcoming scarcity can cause a higher sense of Core Drive 2: Development & Accomplishment.

When fused with Core Drive 7: Unpredictability and Curiosity, Core Drive 6 becomes a great engine to drive online consumer action. Finally, working alongside Core Drive 8: Loss & Avoidance, Scarcity and Impatience becomes a powerful force that not only pushes for action, but pushes for action with extremely strong urgency.

To get the most out of the book, Choose only ONE of the below options to do right now:

Easy: Think about a time where you wanted something, mostly because it was exclusive, or because you felt you were uniquely qualified. Try to describe the nature of that feeling from Scarcity & Impatience.

Medium: Think about a time when a company attempted to implement a corny form of Scarcity, and it backfired because it caused people to go into denial. What could the company do to actually implement principles of Scarcity correctly?

Hard: Think about how you can implement combinations of Dangling, Torture Breaks, Evolved UI, and Anchored Juxtaposition into one of your own projects. Does it automatically increase the desire for other Core Drives? Or does it hamper it? Does it drive long-term engagement, or short-term obsession?

Share what you come up with on Twitter or your preferred social network with the hashtag #OctalysisBook and check out what ideas other people have.

Share your Knowledge!

Beyond sharing my own research and interests, I regularly have guest bloggers posting their research on gamification, motivational psychology, behavioral design and much more on my blog Yukai-Chou.com[174]. If you have interesting knowledge to share through your own experiences and research, consider sending a message through the site and offer a guest piece to promote your work. I've done all this work so you could learn a little bit from me. I would love to get the opportunity to learn from you too!

---

[174] My Blog: YukaiChou.com

Chapter 11: The Seventh Core Drive - Unpredictability & Curiosity

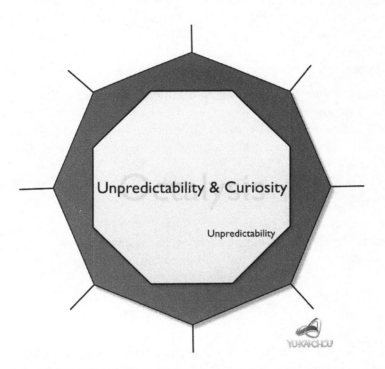

Unpredictability & Curiosity is the seventh Core Drive in the Octalysis Gamification Framework and is the main force behind our infatuation with experiences that are uncertain and involve chance. As mentioned in earlier chapters, our intellectual consciousness is inherently lazy, and if the tasks at hand do not demand immediate attention, the neocortex delegates the mental legwork to our subconscious mind, or "System 1" according to Economics Nobel Prize winner and psychologist Daniel Kahneman[175].

The intellectual consciousness only wants to be disturbed when it is absolutely necessary, such as when a threat is present or when the brain encounters new information it hasn't processed before.

Indeed, Oren Klaff, author of Pitch Anything, states that during meetings, people pay attention to what you say until they can fit you into a pattern that they have previously recognized[176]. Once they fit you into a recognized pattern, they immediately zone out. Therefore, it is important to give a pitch that continuously serves unexpected and unpredictable information to keep people engaged.

Coupled with this is our natural curiosity to explore. Exploring the unknown, though dangerous, helped our ancestors adapt to changing environments and discover new resources to survive and thrive. Jesse Schell, game designer and author of Art of Game Design: A book of Lenses, even goes as far as defining the word "fun" as "pleasure with surprises.[177]" Why is the "surprise" element so important in *fun*?

In this chapter, we will explore how this Core Drive of Unpredictability & Curiosity motivates our behavior and how a system designer can effectively incorporate this into their experiences.

And, Now it's Fun

If I told you to play a game, where you continuously press a button and every ten times you press it, you give me $5 - would you play it? The rational reader would not only reject this offer but would feel utterly insulted that I tried to dupe them into playing in the

---

[175] Daniel Kahneman. "Thinking, Fast and Slow." P20. Farrar, Straus and Giroux. New York, NY. 2013.

[176] Oren Klaff. *Pitch Anything*. 1 Edition. McGraw-Hill. 02/16/2011.

[177] Jesse Schell. *The Art of Game Design*. P26. CRC Press. Boca Rato, FL. 2008.

first place. Now what if the terms change, and I told you that out of a hundred people, two people who play this game would win $10 back? You may ponder for a moment, but still reject it. The offer is not as insulting as before though, just not economically attractive.

But what if I told you that every time you press the button, you may periodically win some money back, and there is an extremely small but possible chance of winning $10,000?

I can't exactly predict what my smart rational readers would do in this case, but I do know that every single day millions of people throughout the world play the game I mentioned above. More commonly known as slot machine gambling, players are consistently losing money every time they pull a lever or press a button, but are engaged, even addicted, to the unpredictable chance of winning a lot of money back. With the *right* risk/reward incentive, the game suddenly becomes so much fun!

Studies have shown that we are more engaged in an experience when there is the possibility of winning than when we know our odds for certain[178]. If we *know* we will receive a reward, our excitement only reflects the emotional value of the reward itself.

However, when we only have a chance to gain the reward our brains are more engaged by the thrill of whether we will win or not.

The Core Drive in a Skinner Box

There's a substantial amount of research on how the unknown and the unpredictable intrigues and engages our minds. One of the most notable motivational design case studies that explored this phenomenon is the Skinner Box[179].

---

[178] Max Seidman. Most Dangerous Game Design. "The Psychology of Rewards in Games". Access 01/25/2015.

[179] Image from http://www.mostdangerousgamedesign.com/2013/08/the-psychology-of-rewards-in-games.html

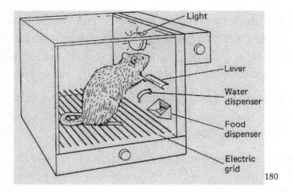

The Skinner Box was an experiment conducted by the scientist B. F. Skinner, who placed rodents and pigeons in a box with an installed lever. In the first phase, whenever the animal pressed the lever (the *Desired Action*), a portion of food was released. As long as the animal continuously pressed the lever, food would continue to be dispensed.

The end result is that when the animal was no longer hungry, it would stop pressing the lever. This makes a lot of sense - the animal is no longer hungry and does not need food anymore.

The second phase, however, introduced unpredictability into the test mechanics. When the animal pressed the lever, there was no guarantee that food would be dispensed as before. Sometimes food came out, sometimes nothing came out, and sometimes even two pieces of food came out.

Skinner observed that with these mechanics in place, the animal would constantly press the lever, regardless of whether it was hungry or not. The system was simply "messing" with its brain: *"Will it come out? Will it come out? Will it come out?"*

Here we see that satisfying our burning curiosity is intrinsically motivating to our primitive brain, sometimes more so than the

---

[180] Image from http://www.mostdangerousgamedesign.com/2013/08/the-psychology-of-rewards-in-games.html

extrinsic reward of food. Have you ever seen a person so addicted to gambling that he forgot that he was tired, hungry, or even thirsty?

I often hear critiques of how the Points, Badges, and Leaderboards in gamification simply turns the world into a large Skinner Box, where people are manipulated to mindlessly doing meaningless tasks. I feel the more profound lesson from the Skinner Box is not that Points and Badges motivate people, but that unpredictable results stemming from Core Drive 7 can drive obsessive behavior.

Sweepstakes and Raffles

In Chapter 5 on Epic Meaning & Calling, I mentioned how I started my first business because of a small raffle held at a UCLA barbecue. Raffles are fairly popular because they add an element of "fun" to an event, as people are drawn by the possibility of winning a prize. Most of the time, the "Desired Action" is for people to stay until the end of the event, and therefore the results of the raffle is announced towards the end of the schedule. Though primarily driven by Core Drive 7, these events draw power from Core Drive 4: Ownership & Possession (the desire to win a prize), and a bit of CD8: Loss & Avoidance (if I leave too early, I'll lose my chance to win...).

As you remember when I first recounted my story, upon drawing my own name out of the hat, I was also hit by a strong sense of *Calling* (from Core Drive 1), feeling that I was destined to start my own business. My perceived *calling* compelled me to be persistent in the face of some dark days and difficult challenges throughout my entrepreneurial career. Many times, on the brink of failure, I felt like giving up. But because I believed that I was meant to walk this path, I pressed on and became more convinced that I could persevere in the startup world as a young entrepreneur. As you can see, being "lucky" in a scenario of chance can install a higher sense of mission and purpose. The same goes for the effects of Beginner's Luck (Game

Technique #23), where people who are extremely lucky the first time they do something feel that they are somehow destined to do it.

As you can see, the power of the raffle is more than the value of any individual reward. Beyond the prize itself (which is extrinsic in nature, stemming from Core Drive 4), the intrinsic motivation behind the "will I be lucky?" thought plays an important role in ensuring people remain engaged with the process.

On a larger scale, many companies that utilize social media marketing are now successfully deploying techniques such as sweepstakes to engage users with their brand and message. Often, these companies will give out a quest where those who commit the Desired Actions will have a chance to win some promotional prize. Sweepstakes can vary quite a bit. The Desired Actions can be as simple as "liking" the company website on Facebook. An example of such a campaign is Macy's marketing campaign where "liking" their Facebook profile gave fans a chance to win $500-$1,000 in gift cards[181].

The Desired Actions can also be something more complex, such as Kelloggs' "The Great Eggo Waffle Off!" challenge, where entrants submitted their best waffle recipes for a chance to win $5,000[182]. They also utilized Core Drive 5: Social Influence & Relatedness by incorporating the Social Treasure game technique into their sweepstakes. The odds of an entrant winning the competition could be based entirely, or at least partially affected, on the community voting. In that way, an added Desired Action of "promoting our brand to all your friends!" comes into effect. This works great for a challenge like The Great Eggo Waffle Off since users are sending images of guilty-pleasure waffles to their friends, asking them to vote up their submissions. Eye candy works like a charm.

Some Sweepstakes are theme-based, tying in some Core Drive 4:

---

[181]Krista Bunskoek. Wishpond Blog. "10 Amazing Examples of Branded Facebook Contests Done Right. Access 1/25/2014.

[182]PR Newswire. Press Release: "Eggo Sparks Kitchen Creativity With Eight Weeks Of Waffle Wednesdays". 09/10/2013.

Ownership & Possession or even Core Drive 1: Epic Meaning & Calling. Dove applies a theme-based sweepstake that is visually appealing to users. In their "Real Beauty Should Be Shared" contest, Dove asked their fans to share why their friend "represents Real Beauty."[183] Instead of receiving monetary prizes, the winners got to be the new "Faces of Dove" at various stores in the huge local Shoppers Drug Mart Canadian retail chain.

---

[183]Jennifer Powell. Business2Community.com. "The Art of Crafting Engaging Social Media Contests". 1/13/2014.

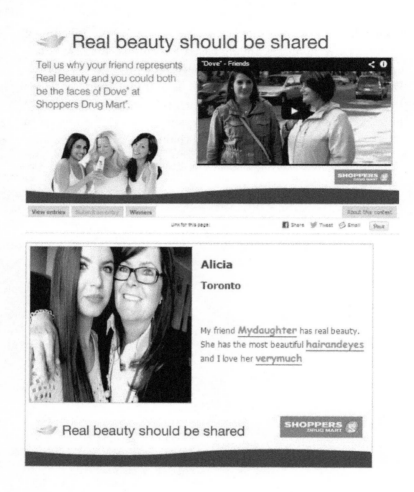

This was a great design, because the campaign involved photos of beautiful/confident women that attracted attention. It promoted a cause that contestants' friends could all get behind and support them on, with a prize that appealed to status while giving users a higher sense of ownership.

Another less-effective example of a theme-based sweepstake is the *Father's Day Clock Giveaway* launched by Tires Plus, which used an essay contest asking contestants to write about who they thought qualified as the best dad. Then participants voted for their favorite dad to determine who would ultimately take home a Michelin Man clock[184]. The good part about the sweepstake's design was that its theme fit Tires Plus' target demographic - guys who like cars.

The slight design flaw in its implementation was that the Desired Action required significant effort. Although they used the same gamification techniques as Dove, the writing and reading of essays is a Desired Action that requires a lot of time and non-car-related effort - just for a simple extrinsic prize. Core Drive 8: Loss & Avoidance prevented many people from participating. This is known as an Anti Core Drive in my framework, which we will cover in more detail with Chapter 16.

Some brands decide to double down on Core Drive 7: Unpredictability & Curiosity by making everything about the sweepstakes unpredictable. Coca-Cola is one of those brands that has been at the forefront of developing creative and innovative product promotions.

You can often see that Coca-Cola commercials attempt to turn simple acts of drinking carbonated sugar water into a Core Drive 1: Epic meaning and Calling experience through using magical kingdoms, promoting happiness, and friendly polar bears.

The company launched an especially appealing sweepstakes contest for teenagers in Hong Kong. Users are offered a free app called "Chok." During each evening, a television commercial will run, asking fans to open the app and shake their phones to catch virtual bottle caps and earn mobile games, discounts, and sweepstakes entries[185].

This prompted users to enthusiastically shake their phones in front of the television screen, hoping for prizes that may or may not pop

---

[184]Krista Bunskoek. Wishpond Blog. "10 Amazing Examples of Branded Facebook Contests Done Right. Access 1/25/2014.

[185]Branding Magazine. "'Chok' With Coca-Cola". 12/12/2011.

out. Because the time of the activity, whether one will win or not, and what the winner will get are all unknown, there's a strong sense of excitement.

Even in the campaign's Discovery Phase (where users first decide to try out a product or experience, which works hand-in-hand through marketing and so-called *growth hacking*), if you are watching TV with a group and you see someone suddenly shake their phone when a commercial comes on, your curiosity will surely be piqued and perhaps compel you to join.

Coca Cola strategically aligned this campaign with its brand strategy and Chok received 380,000 downloads from Hong Kong users alone within a month of launch. The beverage conglomerate claimed this campaign was their most successful marketing effort in Hong Kong for 35 years.

A Lucky Day with Lucky Diem

When I'm not under confidentiality agreements, I love promoting my clients and the work they are doing. Some of my clients work in marketing and hustle to implement good gamification design to significantly improve key marketing metrics for a variety of businesses. One example is the New York Based company LuckyDiem.

LuckyDiem takes brand promotion marketing to a whole new level by utilizing Unpredictability and Curiosity in concert with other Core Drives. Using a series of game devices such as slots, trivia questions, and wheels of fortune, LuckyDiem's mobile platform allows any brand to engage their customers and turn their target market into loyal evangelists. Sound like a marketing cliché? The numbers below tell a compelling story.

On one project, LuckyDiem worked with La Quinta Inns and Suites – an international hotel chain consisting of over 700 properties and franchises – to supercharge their loyalty program through a new gamified campaign called Play & Stay. In a publicly available case study, La Quinta sent out emails to 83,600 potential customers on their email list, promoting the *Play & Stay* game. Out of the total number of email recipients, 2000 people signed up to the Lucky-Diem promotions program, which is a 2.4% email conversion rate. These were fairly average email marketing numbers. No additional promotional effort was conducted afterward.

The amazing thing is, within a three-month period, those 2000 users eventually led to 10,700 new referral signups, representing a K-Factor[186] of 5.3K (or a viral coefficient of 530%). 34% of these users returned every single day and spent an average of 3.75 minutes on the game, creating 23,000 unique user invites, 10,000 new Facebook Likes and 4,500 new Twitter Followers for La Quinta. More importantly, these users turned into customers. 14.1% of the users ended up becoming paying customers, with LuckyDiem's platform generating 1,784 new bookings for La Quinta, leading to a 712% sales lift against the control group. That's a tremendous win for any established chain or company that is already extremely successful in their own right.

How did Lucky Diem do it?

LuckyDiem first launched with a general slot machine game that most people are very familiar with. Users click the big Spin Button and get a chance of winning points or collectables (remember from Core Drive 2 principles that this button is called a Desert Oasis – a large Win-State action that visually attracts the user to interact with it).

---

[186]In viral marketing, the K-factor can be used to describe the growth rate of a product based on how many users invite other users. The formula is $k = i * c$, where i is the number of invites sent by each customer, and c is the percent conversion of each invite. A K-factor of over 1 indicates viral growth.

Play & Stay!

La Quinta Returns points will be deposited into your La Quinta Returns account within 24 hours*. See below for details. Winnings while playing as a guest can be saved only once.

To play, users needed virtual tokens, which is a good utilization of Core Drive 6: Scarcity & Impatience. Tokens are recharged regularly, with an additional wheel of fortune game that can generate more tokens once the initial supply runs out.

Bonus Wheel

Congratulations you have the chance to win
more tokens and more spins!

In addition, there are "instant grand prizes" such as big as "10 Free Nights" that can be won with every spin. The small chance of winning the grand prize did not deter people very much, as the hope of winning a major prize was enough to make the experience fun and addicting. Because the prize was so enticing, people were highly motivated to continue playing, while being assured that their general La Quinta points were accumulating as they played - a combination of Core Drive 2 and Core Drive 4. These techniques are called Lotteries and Rolling Rewards, which we'll discuss later in the chapter.

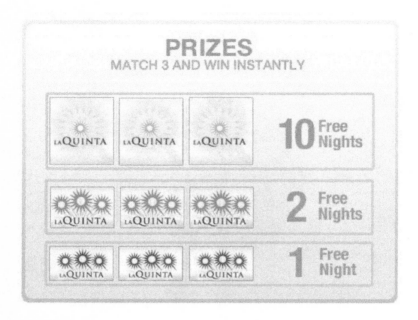

Finally, the reward was dangled in front of the players, including an image of the reward as well as a large action button to redeem it.

If you have been studying my work, you will know that much of the above is merely the "shell" of a game. Though a fantastic success story, if you simply copied their game devices and mechanics for your own project, you may not experience the same success. The depth of the work is embedded within months of planning, hard-gathered research, and many hours of interface design and balance tweaking.

In the end, thoughtful design and implementation created a wonderful and engaging user experience that drove strong results for La Quinta. Ariana Arghandewal, a writer for FrugalTravelGuy.com, wrote about La Quinta's Play & Stay game in an article:

"Warning: This game is extremely addictive. [...] You can win La [Quinta] points, additional spins, tokens that essentially increase your spins, free nights, and more. I initially dismissed this, as I don't anticipate staying at a La Quinta anytime soon, but this game is highly addictive and I've already earned 3,000 points by playing it for the past two days."[187]

As you can see, even when a person thinks that she doesn't necessarily care about the prizes, the Human-Focused Design motivated her to play for a lot longer than she intended. As we see from the numbers above, many users like her ended up becoming paying customers.

Most of my clients like to keep the work I do for them confidential. So when I get an opportunity to obtain a public quote with fantastic metrics that are not inflated, I quickly jump on that opportunity (remember the Brag Button game technique?):

"Yu-kai's Insights were instrumental in helping LuckyDiem supercharge our client La Quinta's bookings per user by 206% and incremental revenue per user by $157 (132% Lift) against the control group. Being able to achieve a viral coefficient of 530%, I would recommend any business to work with Yu-kai and learn his Octalysis Framework." - Andrew Landis, Founder & CEO of LuckyDiem

In 2015, Lucky Diem decided to use these powerful game design techniques to focus on helping brick-and-mortar businesses engage

---

[187] Ariana Arghandewal. "Are You Playing the LaQuinta Play & Stay Game?". 12/13/2013.

and retain customers. Soon we will see whether the company can translate the proven model to a new market correctly.

Suspense and Mystery in a Blender

Many companies also use Core Drive 7 to promote their brands by adding suspense and mystery to their marketing campaign. One classic example is Blendtec's *Will It Blend?* campaign. Blendtec is one of those power blenders that sell for a whooping $300-$400 - about the price of an iPad Mini. Not cheap by any means, but since the value it promises is long-term health and love for your family, people will purchase it if they believe it is notably better than other blenders.

With some very creative marketing, Blendtec's Founder Tom Dickson decided to launch a video series on YouTube called *Will It Blend?* In a long series of videos, the CEO dressed up in a lab coat as an scientist and throws novels, golf balls, broomsticks, and highly valued products such as the latest iPhone or iPad into the blender. Before blending the items, Dickson would ask the famous question, "Will it blend?"

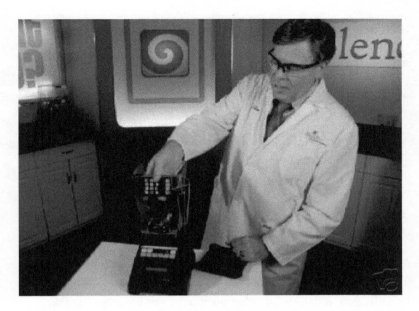

Needless to say, this generated a great deal of suspense and curiosity as people watched to see if he would go so far as to destroy a brand-new iPhone. After a visually interesting and noisy display, the iPhone, sure enough, turned into a pile of black dust. These videos were so entertaining and engaging that they were eventually watched by millions.

Having that many viewers is great, but the question remains: did this create a high return on investment (ROI)? Even though the millions of viewers watched the videos for pure entertainment, when they eventually thought about getting a blender, the first name that came to mind was Blendtec: "Well, a Blendtec blender can shred golf balls into dust. I'm sure my vegetables wouldn't be that bad."

As an added bonus, the company became the natural recommendation too when friends and family's mentioned that they needed a new blender. According to a case study released a couple years after the campaign, Blendtec's revenue shot up by 700%[188].

As of 2014, the Blendtec videos had over 242 million viewers on their Youtube channel - close to the population of the United States. Not bad for a blender.

Faking your Way to Virality

Another good marketing example that utilizes Core Drive 7 is Adobe's *Real or Fake* campaign. In 2008, Adobe wanted consumers to understand the power of their Adobe *Photoshop* and *Illustrator* products. With the new Facebook platform seen as a potential marketing tool for reaching college students, a campaign was created on Adobe's Student Facebook Page called *Real or Fake*. Each week five bizarre looking images were posted and college students were challenged to determine whether the images were real or fake.

---

[188]Christian Briggs. SociaLens. "BlendTec Will It Blend? Viral Video Case Study". 01/2009.

The participating users were extremely motivated by the mystery of whether these photos were actually real or "photoshopped." The motivation to participate was also heavily driven by Core Drive 3: Empowerment of Creativity & Feedback. "This can't be real. It has to be fake. But it looks so real... even the shadow and textures are perfect. I need to find out."

As a result, this drove students to revisit the page and regularly participate in the challenges. The beauty of this design was that even if the students got the answer wrong, it only demonstrated how powerful Adobe's Photoshop and Illustrator programs were.

At the end of the one-month campaign, most users were impressed by Adobe's products. According to Elisa Haidt, then Senior Marketing Manager of Adobe, the game was played 14,000 times (keep in mind that Facebook was still a young platform with a much smaller reach than today), with 22% of the users checking out the product tutorials, 6% sharing it with their friends, and 6% clicking the "Buy Now" button.[189]

Now imagine if the element of suspense and mystery was removed and Adobe simply created a campaign that said, "Check out the amazing photos we created with Adobe products!" I'm quite certain that they would not have had nearly the success of their gamified marketing effort.

Google's Curious Second Button

Another interesting example that utilizes suspense is Google's "I'm Feeling Lucky Button." Generally, searches on Google.com lead users to a results page that Google curates to best fit what they deem as most relevant to the keywords entered - alongside some ads that pay Google very well. The user will usually look through the top 3 to 10 search results and find the one that seems to be the most appropriate.

However, on the front page there's a button that was originally designed to directly bypass all of that. It's called the "I'm Feeling Lucky" button which took users directly to the website of the top search result.

---

[189] Adam Kleinberg. iMedia Connection. "Case study: A Facebook campaign that connected". 05/29/2009.

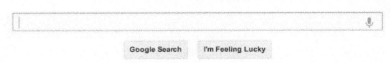

This is very interesting because Google guards its front page design very, very carefully. As told by The Google Story[190], Google decided as a young company that they did not want to clutter their front page like Yahoo.com. They were adamant about keeping ads off their front page, despite the tremendous amount of additional revenue it would bring. They maintained this discipline throughout the years, keeping their homepage clean by only including Google's logo, a text box, and a search function. In the earlier days of the Web, when sites were still loading very slowly over dial-up connections, the simple page strategy paid off like a charm.

But here's what's unique about the "I'm Feeling Lucky" button: Though Google ensures that ads would never be shown on their front page, they make a lot of money every day on ads that are embedded in their search results pages. The "I'm Feeling Lucky" feature bypasses the search results page, which is where Google makes the majority of its ad revenue from. As early as 2007, Tom Chavez from Rapt estimated that Google was losing $110 million a year due to people using the "I'm Feeling Lucky" button.[191]

So why would Google place a silly feature like this on their homepage that costs them significant revenue?

There are a few reasons why: On one hand, if you believe in

[190]David Vise & Mark Malseed. *The Google Story*. p94. Random House, New York, New York. 2005.

[191]Nicholas Carlson. Gawker. ""I'm feeling lucky" button costs Google $110 million per year". 11/20/2007.

Google's search engine intelligence, you will use this button regularly and know that it'll get you to your destination faster. On the other hand, this button provides a great internal feedback mechanism that incentivizes Google to continue optimizing their search engine algorithms so that more people would choose to click the button. After all, prior to Google, search engines performed rather poorly, even when they brought up 30 results on a page. Google wanted to boast of its ability in finding *THE* right search result for their users.

From the perspective of user motivation, this button creates a playful and unpredictable experience that drives more engagement with Google. Note that the button was named "I'm Feeling Lucky" instead of "One-Click Search." The latter would set up incorrect expectations and lead users to think that the technology was terrible if it didn't perfectly capture the search query.

Google's playful culture was also famously demonstrated by their periodic logo changes. Major holidays, historic dates, or notable current events are periodically represented by logo doodles, which inspires a lot of Core Drive 7 among their users. The first doodle was created in 1998 to mark the first full company trip to the week-long Burning Man festival.

The doodles and the I'm Feeling Lucky Button have remained intact within the company culture despite their transformation into something "more corporate-like" in the early 2010's.

More recently, Google changed the "I'm Feeling Lucky" button so that, true to Core Drive 7 principles, when users moused-over it, a slot machine mechanism is revealed, featuring different search options. Selecting "I'm Feeling Wonderful" led you to Google's World Wonders Project, highlighting cultural sites from around the world. The "I'm Feeling Trendy" option led to their Hot Searches pages, which showed you what was trending on Google. "I'm Feeling Stellar" displayed images of the Orion Nebula. This feature allowed Google fans to satisfy their curiosity by exploring the Google universe and other features. Mashable Journalist Sam Laird writes:

"Fair warning, though — you might get hooked and it's a major temptation for procrastination. But the Doodle-y pastime isn't just addictive. It's smart, too. Think about it: What better way to pimp the vast array of services, tools and pure randomness Google offers its online users? I wasn't super familiar with the World Wonders Project, for example — but may well go back for some enlightening entertainment later."[192]

Using the Octalysis Framework, we can see that despite Google's weak Core Drive 5: Social Influence & Relatedness efforts throughout their products, they have demonstrated a keen interest in bringing out Core Drive 7: Unpredictability & Curiosity in their user experiences.

Woot! Creates Midnight Cinderella's

In an earlier chapter, we talked about how eBay and Amazon are great examples of gamified eCommerce sites. Another lesser known website that heavily integrated gamification is Woot.com. Woot! uses an interesting combination of Core Drive 6: Scarcity and Impatience and Core Drive 7: Unpredictability & Curiosity to create a compelling experience for their users.

[192] Sam Laird. Mashable. "Google's 'I'm Feeling Lucky' Button Has a Cool New Trick". 8/24/2012.

Before daily deal sites became popular, Woot! would display one interesting product every day at a great price for users to buy. The enticing nature of Woot! is that you never know what the product is going to be beforehand and there is always a limit on the number people could purchase. Each day a new product would be introduced at exactly midnight, with the previous deal being removed. Because of that, Woot!'s users were continuously curious about what the next cool product would be and would often check-in daily to see what was the new item on sale.

As you can see from the mechanics, there are also heavy effects from Core Drive 6: Scarcity & Impatience. Often, when you logged in at 4pm in the afternoon, especially in the early days of Woot!, the item would have already been sold out. You then login at 11am the next day, and the new item is still sold out; 8am sometimes yielded no success either. As their eagerness to get the next item continually increased, users would constantly return to the website. Eventually, the website's default mechanics indirectly trained users to login every day (the Desired Action) at 11:59pm and refresh the page until the new item popped up. Buying the new product at the displayed price *became the reward* for hitting the site's win-state.

Consistent with the chapter's theme, Woot.com's most coveted item was something called the "Bag of Crap." This was literally a bag of random items that they would send users in the mail. The bags usually included past demo products that didn't make the cut, as well as humorous items. There are actually blog posts talking about the best strategies to get the Bag of Crap, as it is quite difficult to obtain. Below is a snippet of some important tips from the blogger "BiomedGirl" to help you get your Bag of Crap[193]:

Make a Woot.com account and always sign in BEFORE the antici-pated Bag of Crap. You will waste precious time if you have to sign in to your account after you finally get the page to load. On a similar note, make sure all your account information is correct when you

---

[193]BiomedGirl Blog. "Woot and the Bag of Crap: How I got one". 04/01/2011.

sign in as well. This includes shipping and billing addresses, and the credit card info. Another good idea is to either memorize the security code on the card or have it copied to your clipboard so you can paste it in when the time comes. **Furious F5 (refreshing) Method.** *This is the most common method for the attempted Bag grab, because it involves no frills. You guesstimate when the coveted Bag of Crap will appear based on the tips above, then open your browser to the Woot! website and refresh the page continuously until you see the Bag of Crap appear. You can tell if the Bag is the item up for grabs when the page seems to refuse to load. At this point I usually have a couple tabs/windows open and watch them until one loads. As soon as you see the 'I want one!' button appear, click and wait for the next page. You will have to confirm your account information (which you should have already done) and type in your security code, then click 'this info is correct', then the final page you click 'buy it' and hope it goes through.*

As you can see, there even appears to be a lot of Core Drive 3: Empowerment of Creativity & Feedback in playing this game. When things are fun and unpredictable, even a bag of crap becomes extremely valuable.

Game Techniques within Unpredictability & Curiosity

You have learned more about the motivational and psychological nature of Core Drive 7: Unpredictability & Curiosity, but to make it more actionable, I've included some Game Techniques below that heavily utilize this Core Drive to engage users.

Glowing Choice (Game Technique #28)

In Chapter 6, we briefly talked about how the Glowing Choice game technique makes users feel smart and competent during the

Onboarding Phase. Of course, the Glowing Choice game technique also leads players in the right direction by appealing to their Curiosity.

Most players don't enjoy reading huge manuals or watching long videos before beginning a game; players would rather have the option to jump right in and test things out. This is where the Glowing Choice comes into play. In many role-playing games, the user is thrown into a massive virtual world with a plethora of things to do and places to explore. However, the player is never confused about what they are supposed to do, because often a specific computer character is highlighted with a glowing exclamation point that prompts the player to engage with them.

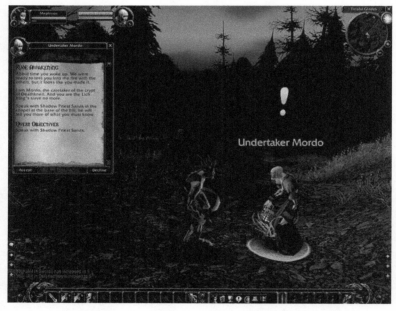

Glowing Choice Screenshot of World of Warcraft

Once engaged, the character will reveal the following quest or the next clue to help the player move forward in the game. The player now knows the next Desired Action and never feels directionless.

In contrast to the Desert Oasis game technique mentioned in Chapter 6 where the designer highlights a Desired Action by clearing out everything surrounding it, the Glowing Choice technique is about applying an overlay item that shines like a bright star in the midst of a complex environment. You can apply this method with apps by placing a strong emphasis on a key feature that represents the Desired Action that users need to be guided towards. Many apps do this by having a question mark on top of the key feature, or an arrow that points directly to what they want their potential customers to focus on. I always tell my clients, *"Never allow your users to accidentally stumble upon a bad experience."* If users cannot figure out what to do within 4 seconds, they will become disengaged. If a user clicks on any button or tab and reaches a dead end, they are penalized for executing the Desired Action.

The key to good design is to ensure that users don't need to think about committing the Desired Actions. In fact, users should have to think hard and *decide* not to take the Desired Action if they don't want to. If there were a huge animated arrow indicating that you should click on a certain button within an app, the user can still choose not to, but their brain has to work harder to avoid it. Once your customer clicks on the question mark or the arrow, the question mark should disappear. The players can then click on the next highlighted feature to find out what it does and why it helps them.

Mystery Boxes/Random Rewards (Game Technique #72)

One of the more common ways to utilize Core Drive 7: Unpredictability & Curiosity is through reward structures. Instead of giving users Fixed-Actions Rewards where the steps to obtain them are known - such as the "Earned Lunch" Game Technique in Core Drive 4: Ownership & Possession - you can build unpredictability into the experience by altering the context of how the reward is given by the nature of the reward itself.

In games, there is "loot" or "drops," which are random rewards that appear once the player achieves a Win-State such as opening a treasure box or defeating an enemy. Often, this unpredictable process is what drives players in the Endgame Phase. I call this technique Mystery Boxes (more gameful) or Random Rewards (more technical).

With random rewards, the participant receives an unknown reward by completing a required action. Using this technique recreates the excitement that children have on Christmas Eve. They see the gifts under the tree and know that they won't find out what the gifts are until a given time has passed. The anticipation of getting the gift, even though they have no idea what's in the boxes, is part of what makes the experience so exciting.

One example of this technique can be found at holiday parties in the form of the White Elephant gift exchange[194]. Also known as the "Gift Swap," this game provides an add-on mechanism for distributing inexpensive or undesirable gifts (often from previous holiday seasons) among participants.

The exchange starts with each participant providing a wrapped gift for the gift pool, and then drawing (unpredictability in itself) a number to determine the order in which they will select a gift. The first person selects and unwraps a gift from the pool.

The next participant can then either select from the pool of un-opened gifts or "steal" the opened gift from the first participant, who then has to reselect a replacement gift from the pool.
The subsequent participant repeats the process, having the option to select from the pool or "steal" either gift from the previous players. This goes on until the last player selects the last gift or steals from one of the others, which causes the individual whose gift is stolen to

---

[194]Wikipedia Entry, "White Elephant Gift Exchange": http://www.yukaichou.com/WhiteElephant

open the last gift. Again, in this case, everyone knows that once they complete the game, a reward will be earned, but what the reward is can only be determined at the end. White Elephant is actually a really fun game, which I personally enjoy greatly. It incorporates almost every single Core Drive in Octalysis. You should try it out with family friends when you have a chance.

A second example of Random Rewards can be seen with a company that is literally called Mystery Box Shop[195]. Customers join the service through subscription with a monthly fee. Similar to Woot's "Bag of Crap," at the first of each month a package containing 5 to 10 "fabulous curiosities," is shipped out to the customer. The contents of each package follow the theme for that month. Recent themes include "Never Grow Up," "Hallowawesome," "Another World," and "Old School." Promising to be cool, curious, odd, or even bizarre, each Mystery Box provides an element of curiosity. Consisting of a mixture of clothing, toys, gadgets, snacks, electronics, and who knows what, each delivery is like opening the presents on your birthday. It keeps customers coming back for more.

Easter Eggs/Sudden Rewards (Game Technique #30)

Different from Mystery Boxes, Easter Eggs (or Sudden Rewards) are surprises that are given out without the user acknowledging it beforehand. In other words, where Mystery Boxes are unexpected rewards based on a certain *expected* trigger, Easter Eggs are rewards based on *unexpected* triggers.

Our brains are drawn to the element of surprise, and because these rewards are so unexpected the added feelings of excitement and good fortune make the experience extremely exciting. Sudden rewards incentivize customers to keep coming back in the hopes

---

[195] Mystery Box Shop Website: http://www.mysteryboxshop.com

that they can inadvertently feel the same bliss again. In this case, ignorance of the rewards *does* lead to bliss.

Easter Eggs are effective in two ways: They get great word-of-mouth exposure because everybody loves to share something exciting and unexpected that happened to them. Upon telling their friends about the good fortune, their friends may also become excited about the experience too.

Easter Eggs also create speculation on what caused the trigger in the first place. If the Easter Egg seemed to be random, participants will wonder how they can replicate the experience in order to "game" the system. They will start to develop theories about how they won, and will commit to the assumed Desired Actions over and over again to either prove or disprove these theories.

A good example of an Easter Egg is the *Chase Picks Up The Tab* program[196]. Chase wanted their customers to swipe more with their debit cards since the company would have have better margins compared to their credit card counterparts. As a result, in the *Chase Picks Up The Tab* program, whenever a Chase customer swipes their Chase debit cards (the Desired Action), there is a very small chance the customer will get a text from Chase that says (paraphrased), "Chase just picked up the tab! Your $5 will be credited back to your account. Have a nice day." Though the rewarded dollar amount is not great, it compels consumers to regularly swipe with their Chase cards in preference to other cards to see if they can repeat their success and "win" again. Often, users will also tell their friends about their win, which may compel the friends to sign-up for this "game" too to see if they can also win.

Another great example of an Easter Egg was implemented by the previous version of Foursquare (a pioneering app in the gamification space, which has recently pivoted)[197]. Foursquare (now

---

[196] Bob Brooks. PrudmentMoney.com. "Chase Picks Up The Tab By Sticking It To The Retailer". Accessed 1/25/2015.

[197] Harrison Weber. Venture Beat. "How a Relaunch Saved Foursquare from Certain Death". 08/10/2014.

Swarm) allows users to "check-in" at different locations they visit, share where they are with their friends, and earn badges based on impressive check-in patterns. Top check-in users of a location earn the status of "Mayor," who besides bragging rights, may even gain a location-specific reward such as free drinks or snacks (some design flaws present but this is beyond the scope of this chapter).

Mario Herger, author of *Enterprise Gamification*, had an interesting experience with Foursquare's Easter Eggs a few years back. In fall 2011, he was a moderate Foursquare user. On the day of Steve Jobs passing, many people flooded the Apple Store in Palo Alto to lay down flowers and leave commemorative messages on the walls. Mario was at the Apple store and decided to check-in on Foursquare. Unexpectedly, he unlocked a new badge that was titled "Jobs" with the subtext, "Here's to the crazy ones. #ThankYouSteve"

..ıll AT&T 4G 13:17 ✈ ✳ 100 % ▱

←

Jobs

Here's to the crazy ones. ⧉ #ThankYouSteve

Unlocked at **Apple Store, Palo Alto**
8:28 nachm. on Oktober 6, 2011

As far as we know, this is a badge that can only be earned in a few places, in a very narrow window of time. As you may expect, this was a huge surprise for Mario (not detracting from the somber event of Steve Job's passing) that motivated him to check-in on Foursquare at more places and further compelled him to often talk about this experience to the point where I am now sharing it in this book.

Lottery/Rolling Rewards (Game Techniques #74)

Another type of reward context that is fueled by Core Drive 7: Unpredictability & Curiosity is the Rolling Reward, or sometimes called the "Lottery." The key idea of rolling rewards is the rule that somebody has to win during each period. Therefore, as long as the user "stays in the game," the chances of you winning increase linearly.

In smaller group settings, Rolling Reward designs are seen in forms such as "Employee of the Week" where employees work hard, hoping that one day they will be the one that earns that status and recognition. (Note: Mario Herger in his book, Enterprise Gamification, suggests that Employee-of-the-Week programs won't work in countries and cultures that frown upon individual recognition[198]).

Another form of Rolling Rewards is when an employer or big client states, "After this project, one of you will receive a free two week vacation to Maui!" In fact, at most workplaces, the thought of being promoted one day is in itself a Rolling Reward – someone has to become the new Vice President: I hope it will be me.

On a larger scale where there are a great number of participants, Rolling Reward programs have low barriers to entry and the rewards are substantial (think state or national lotteries), but there's a very slim chance to win, regardless of how long you spend playing the "game". Yes, individuals can increase their odds of winning by performing more of the Desired Action, such as purchasing additional tickets, or collecting additional entries. But again, the larger the program, the more daunting the odds.

The reason why lotteries work so well is because our brains are incredibly bad at distinguishing small percentages. We can't con-

---

[198]Mario Herger. *Enterprise Gamification.* P94. EGC Media. San Bernardino, CA. 07/24/2014.

ceptually understand the difference between "one in ten million" and "one in a hundred million." We just register both odds as "a very small chance" without really comprehending that you could be winning the "one in ten million" prize ten times before you can win the "one in a hundred million" prize once!

Robert Williams, a professor who studies lotteries at the University of Lethbridge states, "we have nothing in our evolutionary history that prepares us or primes us, no intellectual architecture, to try and grasp the remoteness of those odds.[199]" As a result, as long as there is some chance, people are willing to invest small amounts of money to obtain a gigantic reward.

Rolling rewards work on a number of levels. For starters, because they have moderately low barriers to entry, they can easily attract a large number of participants. Furthermore, if a participant actually wins, they may easily become a fan for life. This is simply because they feel that they were chosen to win, which draws power from Core Drive 1: Epic Meaning & Calling.

Taiwan's Government Gamifies Tax Collection

Taiwan is my home country and as I became more knowledgeable in gamification, I continue to be more impressed with the level of gamification that is implemented in its society and culture - without these innovations actually being called gamification. Beyond all the point-collecting and little reward structures from small businesses and public transportation everywhere, one of the things I have been most impressed with is how the Taiwanese government uses gamification (specifically Rolling Rewards) to ensure tax compliance from small businesses.

Tax evasion is very common in many countries, where businesses prefer to take cash over credit cards so they could report less on their earnings. Most countries use the penalizing Core Drive 8:

---

[199] Adam Piore. Nautilus. "Why we keep playing the lottery". 08/01/2013.

Loss & Avoidance by cracking down and punishing companies that are caught for evading taxes. However, besides a chronic lack of complete enforcement, it is also extremely costly to investigate all the businesses that are suspected of tax evasion.

As early as 1951, the Taiwanese government sought to address this problem by doing two things. First, it unified all receipt and invoicing platforms into a central system, which meant that all businesses which gave out receipts would automatically send the unique receipt numbers and invoice amounts to the government for tax reporting. (In fact, in Taiwan most people don't need to hire accountants to do their taxes - the government can directly tell you how much you owe them or how much they should return to you).

But the second step is where we see true innovation. The Taiwanese government turned each receipt and invoice number into a lottery ticket for citizens to play. For every odd-numbered month, citizens can see if their receipt numbers match the winning prize. The first place would win the equivalent of $62,000 - about five years of salary for an average new college graduate, while the second place would win $6,200, with subordinate prizes scaling all the way down to $7.

Because of this "Uniform Invoice Lottery" system, consumers are now demanding receipts and invoices from businesses, preventing the businesses from evading taxes by exchanging cash under the table (or purchasing with Bitcoins). In addition, consumers are more likely to spend more since each time they make a purchase they can become a winner, boosting the economy in the process.

Even my grandmother has won many of the small $7 and $31 awards over the past two decades, just by doing what she already does – buying groceries and essentials.

As a result of the Uniform Invoice Lottery, the Finance Ministry collected 75% more in tax revenue in 1951 compared to 1950. Great

ROI, especially for government efforts[200]. The program was so successful, they increased the top prize to over $330,000 in 2011, hoping to get more consumers to demand their receipts.

In 2006, the Taiwanese government also started to transition these unified invoices into e-invoices, reducing the involved processing costs by $250 million and saving 80,000 trees every year[201].

We should see more of our governments implementing innovative solutions by motivating and engaging its constituency instead of just clamping down harder or making punishments for infractions more severe.

Core Drive 7: The Bigger Picture

Core Drive 7: Unpredictability & Curiosity is a powerful Black Hat Core Drive that is intrinsically thrilling. For any engagement design, it is productive to ask yourself, "Is there any way to add a little bit of randomness and chance to the process?" By using techniques that are designed for curiosity and unpredictability, companies can drive their customers to engage with their product and retain these customers much longer into the Endgame Phase.

Working with White Hat Core Drives, Core Drive 7 is a great way to inspire Epic Meaning & Calling, stir up Empowerment of Creativity & Feedback, and improve the value of Ownership & Possession. Working with other Black Hat Core Drives, Unpredictability & Curiosity matched with Scarcity & Impatience, creates obsessive and addictive behaviors, while substantially amplifying the negative emotions of fear and worry when matched with Core Drive 8: Loss & Avoidance.

---

[200] Seok Hwai, Lee. Straits Times. p. B1. "Odds of a jackpot hit just got better". 08/06/2010.

[201] Taipei Times. "Electronic receipts set to begin a trial run at select stores". 12/19/2010.

To get the most out of the book, Choose only ONE of the below options to do right now:

Easy: Think about your favorite TV-series (if you have one) that you are constantly glued to. Once you watched it through once, would you go back and watch it again alone? What happens to your motivation when Unpredictability diminishes?

Medium: Unpredictability magnifies our emotions towards both gain (Core Drive 4) and Loss (Core Drive 8). Think about a scenario where unpredictability was attached to a gain and it made the entire experience more playful and exciting compared to a guaranteed chance of gain. Then, think about a scenario where it is tied to a loss and how it paralyzed activity more-so than if the loss had a sure chance of incurring. Can you see how unpredictability can make any event more emotional engaging through a Black Hat Intrinsic way?

Hard: In your own project, try to design a Group Quest Mystery Box combo, where if the entire group commits various Desired Actions, a surprise reward will be given to everyone. Evaluate the pros and cons of that compared to just giving a Group Fix-Action Reward, where everyone already knows exactly what the reward is if they did the Desired Actions (Earned Lunch).

Share what you come up with on Twitter or your preferred social network with the hashtag #OctalysisBook and check out what ideas other people have.

Explore Octalysis Content in Unpredictable Ways

One of the creations I have on the Internet is a video tutorial series called *Beginner's Guide to Gamification*. It is basically a combination of the Octalysis and gamification knowledge that you are reading from this book, footage from all my travels across the globe (U.S., India, China, Denmark, Kingdom of Bahrain, U.K., Germany, Hawaii and more), and a bunch of goofy activities that I do just to prevent viewers from leaving these videos prematurely. Some of the things I do in these videos are so outrageous that I still feel embarrassed to show people. It may serve as an interesting way for you to review the contents learned from this book in an more entertaining way. The video series can be accessed on my website at http://www.yukaichou.com/video-guide[202].

---

[202] YukaiChou.com/Video-Guide

Chapter 12: The Eighth Core Drive - Loss & Avoidance

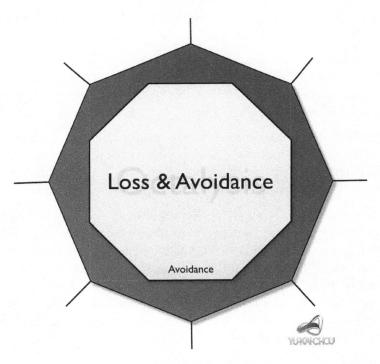

Loss and Avoidance is the eighth and final core drive in my Octalysis Framework. It motivates through the fear of losing something or having undesirable events transpire.

A concept within many popular games is to stay alive in order to advance to the next round. Depending on the game's design, dying or injuring your character means that you're now forced to start over or lose something significant - be it coins, money, the number of lives you have, or other setbacks that make it more difficult to reach the Win-State.

This aversion towards loss is obviously not limited to games. There are many situations in the real world where we act based on fear of losing something that represents our investment of time, effort, money, or other resources. To preserve our ego and sense of self, Core Drive 8: Loss & Avoidance sometimes manifests itself through our refusal to give up and admit that everything we have done up to this point has been rendered useless.

Even new opportunities that are perceived as fading away can exhibit a form of Loss & Avoidance. If people do not act immediately on this temporary opportunity, they feel like they are losing the chance to act forever.

A common example can be seen in the coupons that arrive regularly in the mail. Let's say you receive a coupon that gives you a 10% discount to a popular chain store that you have no interest in visiting, and the coupon is labeled to expire on February 12th.

Your brain may be absolutely certain that, if you let the coupon expire, the very next month you will receive the exact same coupon that expires on March 12th. But you might get an annoying feeling that you are somehow losing something if you don't use the coupon before the expiration date. Rationally it shouldn't matter, but you are compelled to think about the offer a little more. As a result, you become a bit more likely to go to the store for a discount that you may not truly care about.

Cropping your Losses

Many social games effectively employ Core Drive 8: Loss and Avoidance to motivate players towards taking the Desired Actions. In the now familiar example of Farmville, if we look at the early part of their onboarding stage, we can see that avoidance design was already integrated into the system, inducing users to "log in" multiple times each day.

The first few minutes of Farmville seems very positive as the player spends time creating their avatar and starts working on their farm with an initial pool of free *Farm Cash*. However, Farmville soon demands that each player maintain their crops and livestock through routine farming chores - mostly in the form of coming back and clicking on the crops and livestock to harvest their products.

If you don't return to reap your harvest within a given number of hours, as determined by the crops' profiles (you can choose which crop to plant, which plays into Core Drive 3: Empowerment of Creativity & Feedback), you will lose your invested hard work and be shown demoralizing images of crops withering and dying. This mildly depressing incident upsets the user, compelling them to log back in frequently to keep their crops alive. The player becomes proactively involved in avoiding this negative outcome.

When players lose their crops, it not only costs them Farm Cash to replace but also their time, as they have to replant and maintain new crops again. Each time you see the discouraging images of dead crops, you are hit with the triple whammy of having lost your time, effort, and resources.

Many years ago I was astonished at how effective this design could be, as my technology abhorrent mother suddenly became obsessed with playing Farmville. Back then, my mother was the type of person who thinks that technology is a source of evil that is polluting society and crippling authentic relationships; she still barely checks her email.

But in 2009, due to her close friend's enthusiastic recommendation

- a nice example of Core Drive 5: Social Influence & Relatedness, my mother signed up on Facebook and started to play Farmville. The beginning of the Onboarding phase was smooth and fun, as she used the game to relax her mind and connect with her friends.

However, after a few months of playing, my mother would sometimes wake up at 5:00am in the morning simply to harvest her crops and prevent them from withering. It became so bad that when my mother needed to travel out of town, she would call up my cousin and ask if he could log into her Facebook account and help manage her farm. She needed to make sure her crops didn't die. (Though she also used to ask me, being a son that was lacking in "孝" as discussed in Chapter 5, I eventually deferred the responsibility so I could focus on my "other" important work).

At the time, this blew my mind. I initially thought the reason for most people to play games was because they had too many responsibilities in the real world and needed to immerse themselves into a fantasy world to escape those responsibilities. However, here you have a brand new set of virtual responsibilities that add on even more stress and anxiety to daily life. It didn't make any sense.

Of course, today I understand the nature and power of Black Hat Motivation. For a period of time, Farmville was able to successfully increase its Daily Active Users Metrics and lower short-term turnover with this type of Loss & Avoidance design. That is, until users hit a "Black Hat Rebound," where they eventually burn out and find the courage to pursue freedom outside of Farmville.

Affection Held Hostage

In early 2014, I was invited to the global conglomerate *Huawei* in Shenzhen, China to do a few workshops on gamification. During this trip, I had an assigned tour guide that took me to the beautiful *Tea Stream Valley* for a full day trip. (You can see much of this trip, including my camel ride and a jaw-dropping lion dance performance, in my video series - *The Beginner's Guide to Gamification*.) Between all that excitement, the educational part of my trip came towards the end.

As I was leaving Tea Stream Valley, I saw people soliciting for pencil drawn portraits. My tour guide was using the restroom, so I decided to check them out and see if they were any good - that's the power of Core Drive 7: Curiosity. They saw me approach and asked if I wanted a portrait which I politely turned down.

I was about to leave, when I saw another artist drawing a portrait based on an iPhone photo for another customer. I asked (in Mandarin of course), "Oh, so if I give you a mobile photo, you can draw it too?" He responded, "Of course! Do you want one?"

I decided that this would be a great way for me to bring something back for my wife to show that I was thinking about her during my long trip away from home. Instead of just buying something expensive on the shelf at an airport, a hand-drawn portrait of her would be more personal and more endearing. It would show her that I actually spent time to have something unique and custom-made for her.

I asked the artist, "So how much for one?" He told me it was about the equivalent of $50 USD. I thought, "Wow, that's extremely expensive, even by U.S. standards." Instead of negotiating with him, which I generally dislike doing because it requires too much emotional energy, I decided to use the walk-away tactic in Core Drive 6: Scarcity & Impatience.

"Sorry, that's way too expensive for me." As I started walking away, he rushed to say, "What if I could do it for $35?" I felt happy that my scarcity tactic was working, but $35 was still too expensive so I said, "Naw, like I said, it's way too much." Of course, I wasn't bluffing. I truly did not intend to buy anything at that point.

He then said, "Okay...I can do it for $25. Since the day's about to end, I'll just do you a favor and wrap up with this one." At this point, even though it still wasn't very cheap (for comparison, a 90-minute massage in Shenzhen was only $25), I thought I haggled well by cutting his original asking price down by 50% - feeling a sense of Core Drive 2. He also just used a Core Drive 5: Social Influence & Relatedness tactic of "I like you, so I'll do you a favor," so I thought I might as well agree to do it. I'm on a fun trip anyway.

After working for twenty minutes, he was almost done with the portrait. It was alright. It wasn't great but you could tell that it looked like my wife.(That was my main goal - I didn't want her thinking that I was having another woman drawn!)

As he was wrapping up, he asked, "Would you like to add a transparent protective layer to the drawing? It will protect the pencil lead from being smudged." I said, "Sure, sounds good!" He gave me a concerned look and said, "It's going to cost more though." Slightly surprised, I asked, "How much more?" He told me nonchalantly that for the protective layer, it was going to cost me $15 extra.

I then realized his sneaky tactic and felt fairly annoyed. I responded in an emotionally disturbed tone, "Then forget about it. I'm not going to pay $15 just for that layer."

Then, with a very concerned and considerate facial expression, he explained, "But if you don't add the protective layer, the pencil lead will definitely smudge in your luggage bag and ruin the whole drawing. Look how easily the pencil lead falls off." He then proceeded to use his thumb to rub a corner of the portrait, and indeed a layer of graphite came off onto his thumb. "It would be such a shame if this nice drawing got destroyed!"

What would you do in this situation?

As you can imagine, it was a very uncomfortable situation to be in. Nevertheless, it was also a very compelling educational experience. The power of Core Drive 8: Loss & Avoidance had taken over my behavior and I ended up paying him $40 for a rather mediocre drawing. And if you recall, just a few minutes earlier I turned down the same drawing for $35!

I walked away, reminding myself repeatedly, "I'm not buying his drawing skills for $40. I'm buying my wife's happiness for $40. It's totally worth it."

A couple of very important observations in persuasive design should be made from this interaction.

I was highly compelled to take the Desired Action. I ended up paying $40 for 20 minutes of the artist's work, even if I rationally understood that the price wasn't fair nor its delivery honest. The "artist" made his money. In addition, I felt extremely uncomfortable after taking the Desired Action, and from that point on, would never be strongly inclined to purchase something from street vendors in China again.

This is very important to understand. Utilizing this Black Hat Core Drive is extraordinarily powerful in getting someone to take the Desired Action, but in the long run, it demoralizes the user's experience and creates burnout which can lead to high turnover. Once they commit the Desired Actions, people don't want to ever put themselves in the same situation again.

In the situation above, where the artist is only making money from one-off tourists, this tactic only harms other street vendors in China so it may be worth it. At least, until a few years later when all tourists know to avoid buying anything from sleazy street vendors - unfortunately, including the honest ones. However, in your own experience design, I'm guessing you would like your users to commit more Desired Actions subsequent to the first Desired Action, as they enter into the Scaffolding and Endgame Phases.

As a result, when we utilize design elements in an experience that appeal to Core Drive 8: Loss & Avoidance, it should only be at critical bumps where you really need the user to take the Desired Action. This should be followed by a series of White Hat Core

Drives to encourage and balance the motivations of the user. We will explore this theme further in Chapter 14 on White Hat versus Black Hat Motivation.

This is the beauty of the Octalysis Framework (from my point of view). We not only can use it to understand how to engineer and design for motivation, but we can understand and optimize for the nature of that motivation to make sure it fulfills both our short-term goals and long-term goals.

And if you must know: upon returning to California, my wife recognized herself in the portrait and was extremely touched by the gesture. I also felt extremely accomplished (Core Drive 2) because she was so happy and because my plan worked like a charm.

Perhaps the $40 was worth it after all.

"Why don't you take all my money?" in Poker

The same type of Core Drive 8 behavior happens frequently in psychological wagering games such as poker[203]. Consider the following situation in which many Texas Hold'em Poker players often find themselves:

At the beginning of a match, you may start off with a very strong hand, or set of cards. In order to avoid scarring off other players, you increase the bet by a small amount, so that anyone who has *some* hope of improving their hand in the current match stays. As more community cards (center cards that everyone can use and "share" to build their hands) are flipped, your hand remains strong and everyone continues to call your small bet by adding little increments to the pot. This often means that the players are not confident with

---

[203]Not everyone knows the rules of poker, but hopefully the text within is descriptive enough. For the full rules of Texas Hold'em Poker, visit: http://www.yukaichou.com/PokerRules

their own cards, but they don't want to fold (give up) yet in the hope of getting a better hand, so they keep putting in the minimum amount of money to stay in the round.

You continue to feel very good about your hand, especially compared to your opponents. Finally, when the last center card is turned over and there is nothing more to see or hope for, you feel like it is time to reap your winnings. But knowing that everyone else likely has weaker hands, you still don't want to scare the entire table off. So you decide to put 40% of your chips in and see if anyone will challenge you with the same amount. You hope to get someone with a semi-decent hand to think that perhaps you are bluffing and bet against you.

With such a show of strength, most people fold because they are aware that you truly have a strong hand and they only have mediocre ones. But one individual suddenly goes "All-In" and pushes all his chips into the center.

This is a difficult moment for a poker player. You have already demonstrated full confidence and strength in your hand. Even if the other player also believed he had a great hand, he could simply match your bet instead of raising it. That way he could control the amount just in case your hand turns out to be stronger than his.

But by going "All-In," this person is demonstrating that he is so confident in beating your high hand, that he doesn't care what you might have. In poker, the worse hand a player can get is not the smallest hand at the table but the second largest hand. When you *know* you have a small hand, you simply fold and only lose a few chips. But when you *believe* you have the biggest hand at the table but ultimately don't, you are at risk of losing all your chips.

In this scenario, you quickly do some calculations in your head and conclude that there are three possible hands that, though extremely unlikely, this other person could have to beat you with. Maybe he's just bluffing? You become nervous and start to think about how he played his hand in the last few moves. Your rational brain becomes fully convinced that this person is not bluffing and has your hand beat. **You've lost.**

If you were a computer, your calculations would quickly recognize that losing 40% of your money is better than losing more than 40% of your money. And so you would fold your hand and acquiesce the loss.

However, the human mind thinks differently. In this moment, we tend to focus our eyes on the money laying on the table. We start feeling the pain of losing 40% of our chips and then start to have second thoughts: "What if he has a smaller hand? What if he is bluffing? What if he actually has a small hand, but he thinks it's big?"

We forget that our rational brain has already determined that this person is not bluffing and has our hand beat. It's our emotional brain that's doing the thinking now. You also don't want to look like a loser in front of others (Core Drive 5) after confidently raising your bets and suddenly bowing out upon the first challenge you face. *Pride is an expensive thing to possess.*

Finally, Core Drive 7: Unpredictability & Curiosity kicks in to elevate another aspect of Loss & Avoidance. If you fold now, you will never know if the person had a better hand (In poker, a player does not need to reveal their hand if their challenge isn't met by an equal or higher bet). You might live the rest of your life wondering if he actually had your hand beat or not, and that's a terrible thing to live through!

As a result, you ultimately make the irrational decision: you push in all your money, simply because you don't want to give up on the 40% you already committed. Through this, you choose to meet your opponent's challenge and reveal both of the hands to see whose is bigger.

Finally, as you already know in your heart, the person reveals that he actually does have a better hand than you. Instead of losing 40%

of your money, you have lost it all.

This is why in poker, the term "Tough Muck" refers to the situation where players fold a very strong hand after betting a lot of money. Any player can win money when they truly have the best hand, but only true professionals know how to execute tough mucks when they need to.

The Good Chasing the Bad

The same phenomenon happens in investing too. Say you are wealthy and invested a billion dollars into a biotechnology company called LOSR. After many years, they are running out of money but have yet to reach any conclusive findings. They tell you they are very close, and just need another $400 million to make that major breakthrough.

Now if you had just become knowledgeable about this company, you might conclude that based on the traction you have seen, the executive team is completely incompetent and you wouldn't even invest $20 in them. Why throw money down the drain?

As in the poker example, our inability to cope with sunk costs pushes us to take irrational actions – putting in good money to chase after bad money. You end up reluctantly putting the extra $400 million into LOSR in order to save the $1 billion you've already sunk into it.

Sure, there might be a slim chance that the company does end up making a major breakthrough, in which case the world will think you are brilliant and insightful. However, you made the investment not because of clever wit, but simply because of your fear and attachment to what was already lost.

The financially rational decision here is to cut your losses and invest your $400 million into other, more promising opportunities. (Unless, of course, you are investing for non-financial reasons - such as preventing the epic tragedy of mad scientists experimenting on themselves due to lack of funding, and becoming super-villains that destroy civilization).

True to the nature of Black Hat motivation, you are strongly compelled to take the Desired Action, but do not necessarily feel comfortable with the behavior.

Zombies Make you Skinnier

Even though large doses of Black Hat motivation demoralizes us, a little bit of Black Hat can add the thrill and excitement to an experience. Mild forms of countdown timers, small penalties, or even playful fear tactics can further engage users towards the experience.

A good example of "playful" Loss and Avoidance can be seen with the mobile app Zombies, Run! This app immerses the user in a fictional apocalyptic setting where zombies have taken over the world. The user assumes the role of "Runner 5" in a little town called "Abel." Sometimes, Abel town runs out of resources, and "Runner 5" must go out into the wilderness to accomplish missions and save the town.

Donning a pair of headphones and listening to a series of narrations while physically running in the real world, the user is motivated to run because they "don't want to get eaten by zombies." In strategic parts of the run, the "Abel town radio station" will motivate the user to sprint for certain periods of time, simply because they see fast-moving zombies right behind the user through their imagination binoculars.

Whereas Nike+ makes users run primarily because of a feeling of Accomplishment (Core Drive 2), Zombies, Run! makes users run because they do not want to be eaten by zombies.

Often when I run my quarterly online workshops on Octalysis Gamification, many people bring up Zombies, Run! as the app that fully engaged them to get back into running. I myself have been quite impressed with how well it drives regular and repetitive workouts for users.

Of course, to be an engaging experience, Zombies, Run! uses a variety of both White Hat and Black Hat core drives beyond Loss & Avoidance to motivate the users. The game's backstory has Runner 5 setting out on a mission to help save his stranded community from the zombies, which introduces Core Drive 1: Epic Meaning & Calling into the narrative. Every mission achievement plays strongly to Core Drive 2: Development & Accomplishment. The resources he "collects" while running (the feedback mechanic is just the audio from the earphones telling you that you have picked up a battery case) can be used to rebuild your character's community, which harnesses Core Drive 4: Ownership & Possession.

Finally, Core Drive 7: Unpredictability & Curiosity is driven through the plot. So if the user wants to find out why another in-plot companion runner suddenly started coughing heavily without reason, they will have to run more to find out whether the companion runner is infected by Zombies.

Flipping other Core Drives Off

Core Drive 8: Loss & Avoidance complements many of the other Core Drives for an interesting reason: often it manifests as the reversal of the other Core Drives. You don't want something bigger than yourself to fall apart (Core Drive 1), hence you act; or you don't want to look like a loser in front of your friends (Core Drive 5), hence you make a purchase.

Some may argue that this doesn't constitute a separate Core Drive. As an example, critics might point out that people are driven back to Farmville because they want to feel a sense of accomplishment or ownership and that the loss of either feeling is simply the removal of these drives. However, from a design standpoint, it is important to consider Loss & Avoidance as its own Core Drive.

This is because gaining something and preventing a loss is incredibly different from the standpoint of motivation. Studies[204][205][206] have shown over and over that we are much more likely to change our behavior to avoid a loss than to make a gain. It forces us to act differently and plays by different mental rules. In fact, Nobel Prize winner Daniel Kahneman indicates that on average, we are twice as loss-averse compared to seeking a gain[207]. This means that we have a tendency to only take on a risk if we believed the potential gain would be double the potential loss if the risk were realized.

Through using the Octalysis Framework, this differentiation improves behavioral design by specifically identifying opportunities to integrate proactive loss-avoidance mechanics that generate a more subtle set of motivational dynamics.

Ultimate Loss vs Executable Loss

Core Drive 8: Loss & Avoidance can be a tricky Core Drive to manage. If done improperly it can demoralize the user and lead to churn.

One important thing to keep in mind is that Loss & Avoidance is motivational in a proportional manner. The way users respond to

---

[204] Daniel Kahneman and Amos Tversky. *Econometrica*, 47:263-91.* "Prospect Theory: an analysis of decision under risk". 1979.

[205] Richard Thaler, and Cass Sunstein. *Nudge: Improving Decisions about Health, Wealth, and Happiness.* New Haven, CT: Yale University Press. 02/24/2009.

[206] Gary Belsky and Thomas Gilovich. *Why Smart People Make Big Money Mistakes - and How to Correct Them.* Simon & Schuster, New York. 01/12/2010.

[207] Daniel Kahneman. *Thinking, Fast and Slow.* P284. Farrar, Straus and Giroux. New York, NY. 2013.

Loss & Avoidance is generally proportional to how much they have already invested into the experience.

If users have played a game or used a product for ten hours, they will feel a more substantial loss than if they had invested only ten minutes. Starting over after losing is definitely more impactful on a player that's invested a few days into the game and is on level 37, as opposed to a player who just started and is on level 2.

The key strategy here is that the experience designer should dangle the threat of a large setback (the Ultimate Loss), but should only implement (if at all) small marginal setbacks (the Executable Loss) to emotionally train the user in taking the Ultimate Loss more seriously. The Executable Loss reinforces the avoidance.

As a general rule from my own experience, the Executable Loss should never be greater than 30% of what the user has already invested in time and/or resources, and ideally never more than 15%. Generally a small loss of 2-5% is enough to motivate users to take the activities seriously. If the users lose over 30% of what they have originally invested, the odds of them feeling demoralized and quitting become extremely high.

Since it benefits no one if the user actually suffers heavy losses, it's best to utilize the "ultimate loss" as a form of expectation management, with the system creating "grace systems" that the users appreciate but do not abuse.

For instance, in the workplace the manager may make it clear that performances below a certain level will result in being let go. So everyone becomes motivated, in a sure but limited sense, to avoid the dreadful loss. This Core Drive 8 manager may even exercise small loss-events ranging from pep talks, moving people off important assignments, to publicly scolding them (hint: generally a terrible idea). All to make sure the employees emotionally acknowledge this sense of loss, and are motivated to work harder.

However, when an employee has failed the performance goal and fully expects to be let go, the manager may execute another option. Knowing full well that turnover and retraining new talent is the least preferable outcome, the manager can tell the employee that the organization appreciates his effort and hard work, and that they will give him another chance to hit the target.

As you can see, the Ultimate Loss here is not actually implemented, but instead wielded as a black hat motivational tool. After this, the employee may appreciate the second chance and become more motivated to do the work. This then becomes an example of Core Drive 8: Loss & Avoidance setting up for Core Drive 5: Social Influence & Relatedness, where the employee potentially starts to work harder because of a new sense of gratefulness towards the manager.

Expectations have everything to do with happiness and motivation. A hungry teenager in a poor country will have an extremely difficult time understanding why a perfectionist student in a developed country would be depressed for three weeks simply because she received a "B" in school. On the other hand, a student who expects to fail the class celebrates for a week when they obtain a B.

Similarly, a billionaire who lost a lot of money and became a millionaire might end up committing suicide[208], while the average person who end up with a million dollars would become ecstatic. From my own observations, our happiness is almost exclusively determined by our expectations matched against our circumstances. Based on that, the easiest way to become happy may be to adjust our expectations and appreciate what we do have, instead of becoming upset because of the things we don't. Even many marriages fail because of unrealistic expectations for each other, leading to built up bitterness over the years that plagues the soul.

When it comes to interactions with people, it's always easier to start off stern and then become lenient, rather than being nice

---

[208] An example would be the German billionaire Adolf Merckle who committed suicide after his wealth dropped from £8.5 billion to £6 billion.

and then executing harsh punishment later. The dynamic between Core Drive 8 and Core Drive 5 often determines the relationship between landlord/tenants, teacher/students, employer/employees, and government/citizens.

Of course, if the employee starts to take the second (or third, fourth etc.) chance for granted, then it is crucial to maintain the credibility of the Loss & Avoidance system and let the employee go. If the ones breaking the rules aren't facing any real consequences, it demoralizes the experiences of those that are performing their parts, and overall motivation plummets.

With that said, one thing to always remember is that this same slacking employee may shine like a star if the manager actually implemented more White Hat motivation. Motivational designs such as providing more autonomy, feedback, and meaning, as opposed to pure punishment systems. However, since the scope of this chapter is to explore the nature and effects of utilizing Core Drive 8: Loss & Avoidance, we focus mainly on the uses and effects of that Core Drive.

A Caveat: Avoiding the Avoidance

One caveat in using Core Drive 8: Loss & Avoidance is that the user must know *exactly* what they should do to prevent the undesirable event from happening. As mentioned in Chapter 10 on Scarcity & Impatience, if a loss-focused message is simply there by itself, but it is not intuitively obvious what the user needs to do, it often backfires - the Core Drive 8 becomes an Anti Core Drive and the user goes into denial mode. The brain irrationally concludes, "Since I don't know how to deal with it, it's probably not that big of a problem anyway." *Status Quo Sloth*, which we will learn about later in this chapter, then dominates over the motivation towards loss-prevention.

A study done by health researchers Howard Leventhal, Robert Singer, and Susan Jones asked students to read pamphlets that describe the dangers of tetanus infection[209]. There were three groups of students in the experiment: the first group received the warning pamphlet, but without clear steps to prevent tetanus infections. The second group received the warning pamphlet along with a specific plan towards arranging a tetanus injection (a *trigger* towards the Desired Actions). The last group received the specific plan towards arranging a tetanus injection, but did not receive the high-fear warning pamphlet.

As you might expect, only the group that received *both* the high-fear warning pamphlet *and* the plan towards the remedy became highly motivated to take on the Desired Action. As mentioned in Core Drive 2: Development & Accomplishment, we only want to act if it makes us feel smart. If the user feels confused (hence stupid) when thinking about what to do regarding this potential threat, they would rather just dismiss it altogether instead of feeling incompetent over it.

As cleverly put by Noah Goldstein, Steve Martin, and Robert Cialdini, perhaps President Franklin Roosevelt's famous quote[210] should be amended into, "the only thing we have to fear is fear *by* itself"[211].

Game Techniques in Loss and Avoidance

You have learned more about the motivational and psychological nature of Core Drive 8: Loss & Avoidance, but to make it more

---

[209]Howard Leventhal, Robert Singer, and Susan Jones. *Journal of Personality and Social Psychology*, 2:20-29. "Effects of fear and specificity of recommendation upon attitudes and behavior". 1965.

[210]The original quote is: "The only thing we have to fear is fear itself."

[211]Noah Goldstein, Steve Martin, and Robert Cialdini. *Yes! 50 Scientifically Proven Ways to Be Persuasive*. P44. Simon & Schuster. New York, NY. 2010.

actionable, I've included some Game Techniques below that heavily utilize this Core Drive to engage users.

Rightful Heritage (Game Technique #46)

A common game technique that utilizes Core Drive 8: Loss & Avoidance is something I call the *Rightful Heritage*. This is when a system first makes a user believe something rightfully belongs to them (remember expectations matter a lot?), and then makes them feel like it will be taken away if they don't commit the Desired Action.

The Rightful Heritage game technique can sometimes be implemented in a simple word change. Have you ever been on a website, where you click around before you stumble upon the conversion page ("sign-up" or "purchase"), and then see some offer that reads, "Purchase now and instantly get a 20% discount!" or "Sign-up now to receive 3000 free credits"? Often, we dismiss these offers as gimmicky, and a poor appeal to Core Drive 4: Ownership & Possession, so we ignore them.

However, some sites integrate game techniques into the experience by harnessing our loss aversion tendencies. Imagine as you click around a website, there is a little popup widget that says, "Great! Your actions have earned you 500 credits!" As you click on more places, it will continue to say, "Great! Your actions have earned you 1500 credits!" Finally, when you get onto the landing page, the text reads, "You now have 3000 credits. Sign-up to save your credits for later!"

Even though this is the exact same result as "Sign-up now to receive 3000 free credits," the experience design makes signing up feel more compelling. Previously, the hassle of signing up did not justify the 3000 credits, but now it feels like you have "earned" these credits from your "hard work" of clicking around the site and the idea of losing what you have rightfully obtained feels absurd. As a result, there is a much higher chance of you signing up.

For eCommerce sites, imagine if a little widget showed you messages like, "Thanks for visiting our site during work hours. You have earned a 5% discount code. Click here to get the code." As you dismiss the small 5% discount and continue to browse, the message says, "Thanks for comparing prices on our site! You have earned a 10% discount code! Click here to get the code" and then followed by, "Thanks for checking out our awesome user reviews. You have earned a 15% discount code. Click here to get the code." Finally, a flashy message reads, "You have earned the maximum discount of 20%! Click here to get the code."

At this point, you may feel like your "hard work" of browsing around an eCommerce site has earned you a discount code. Even if you didn't want to make a purchase, you'd feel justified in getting the code anyway. Once you obtained the 20% discount code, another push of Loss & Avoidance emerges, similar to the expiring mail coupon mentioned previously. You now feel like you would be losing something if you don't use this coupon before the code expires. As a result, the odds of you making a purchase in order to use the discount code now increases.

In the startup world, companies often give their employees a comfortable amount of equity in the form of stock options, but with a couple of caveats. The first is a "vesting schedule," where employees obtain the entire package only if they stay with the company for a specified period - typically 4 years in length, obtaining 1/48 of the promised equity each month.

The other caveat is the "cliff", a period (often one year) after which employees begin to realize their vested options. Thus, if an employee leaves after 3 months, they get nothing. After staying for a year, they will immediately get ¼ of their entire equity package, and then start accumulating 1/48 every month from that point on. The purpose of the cliff is to make sure there isn't a plethora of ex-employees who own equity when they have barely contributed to the company.)

Because of this design, I have seen many employees who wanted to leave a company, stay much longer than intended because they didn't want to lose the months vested that they had deservedly accrued. Of course, if the company isn't able to turn around their motivation to leave (hint: probably because of a bad boss) by installing more White Hat elements such as purpose, autonomy and mastery, the employee will leave immediately after the cliff is reached.

Ironically, most companies don't give employees their deserved raises or promotions *until* they too are motivated by Core Drive 8: Loss & Avoidance, when the employee has already accepted an offer from another company. Based on sound motivational design, companies should actually reward their employees when they execute the Desired Actions of performing well; not when the employees perform undesirable actions of asking for more money or finding other offers. If you only reward people when they do undesirable actions, you simply encourage them (and all their coworkers) to do more of these actions.[212]

The Rightful Heritage game design technique can be very useful in many scenarios to motivate users in taking action. Similar to how some siblings fighting guilefully against each other over a large inheritance - which they have done little to deserve; when people feel like something is their rightful heritage, they often fight for that inheritance to the very end[213].

---

[212] An interesting side story: many years ago, my wife worked at a large financial institution. After continuously exceeding her targets, she asked her manager if she could get a raise. The manager nonchalantly said, "Come back if you can prove that other companies are willing to pay you more." Feeling unappreciated, my wife quickly found an offer that was 40% higher than her pay at the time, and as you might expect, never went back to that manager.

[213] Douglas McIntyre. DailyFinance.com. "The 10 Most Infamous Family Inheritance Feuds". 06/06/2011.

Evanescent Opportunities (Game Technique #86) and Countdown Timers (Game Technique #65)

An Evanescent Opportunity is an opportunity that will disappear if the user does not take the Desired Action immediately. One of the biggest sensations in the game *Diablo III* is a little monster called a *Treasure Goblin*. The Treasure Goblin is an enemy creature that appears randomly, but runs away when being attacked instead of attacking the player. With a significant amount of Hit Points (HP, health, or life), players will all rush to attack the Treasure Goblin as it runs away. Defeating the Treasure Goblin will sometimes (but not often) result in great treasures. However, if the Treasure Goblin is not defeated within a certain time frame, it will jump into a portal and disappear.

When a Treasure Goblin is spotted, players often ignore other monsters that are attacking them and solely pursue the goblin for the chance of obtaining its treasure. Some Youtube game broadcasters have been known to say things like, "I'm just going to show you how to defeat this boss, so right now I'm going to ignore all these monsters to get to the boss as soon as possible...OH LOOK, A TREASURE GOBLIN! Come on, don't run away! Argh, these monsters are in my way. No, don't go that way! Ah! I got killed... I blame the monsters for this." Even in a live performance, the Evanescent Opportunity steals the show.

In the real world, every limited-time offer that forces you to decide whether to buy the product or lose the offer forever uses this Game Technique. Used car salespeople love to tell you, "Look, I just had the biggest argument with my boss about how if you got the car at a deal like this today, you would be so happy that you would become a lifetime loyal customer. That finally convinced him! I couldn't believe it! Now, of course there's no real pressure for you to actually become a lifetime customer, but you have to take the deal today. If you walk away, I guarantee you my boss will quickly come to his right senses again and change his mind."

You snicker because you know the tactics car salespeople use and automatically put up a mental guard against them. But what about charity fundraisers? "We just got a generous donor that said for every dollar we collect in the next hour, he will match it! Your donation dollar will serve double the impact!"

Evanescent Opportunities motivate us to act quickly for fear of losing a great deal. Matching well with this technique is the simple feedback mechanic called the *Countdown Timer*.

A Countdown Timer is a visual display that communicates the passage of time towards a tangible event. Sometimes the Countdown Timer is to introduce the start of a great opportunity, while at other times it's to signify the end of the opportunity.

Earlier we mentioned that actually applying an Ultimate Loss to the user benefits no one, and that the Executable Loss is simply to make users take the Ultimate Loss more seriously. The smaller loss is meant to reinforce avoidance of the significant loss. However, if the user is not aware of the loss, the entire motivational factor is squandered.

Countdown Timers ensure that users recognize the presence of the Evanescent Opportunity better than a simple expiration date because the user constantly sees the window of opportunity narrowing, establishing a sense of urgency in the process. Intuitively for this purpose, Countdown Timers should display the smallest time interval that is appropriate (more often that not – seconds), instead of showing longer intervals such as weeks or months.

Status Quo Sloth (Game Technique #85) and the FOMO Punch (Game Technique #84)

Sometimes Core Drive 8: Loss & Avoidance comes in the form of simply not wanting to change your behavior. I call this lazy tendency of behavioral inertia *Status Quo Sloth.*

Every once in a while, a startup entrepreneur will tell me, "Hey Yu-kai, there's absolutely no reason why a customer wouldn't use our product. We save them time, we save them money, and we make their lives better!" On lucky occasions, even the customer himself would say, "Yeah, there's no reason why I wouldn't use your product. It saves me time, it saves me money, and it makes my life better. I'll definitely sign up tomorrow!"

For those who are experienced in launching new and innovative products, you might recognize that the key phrase here is "I'll definitely sign up tomorrow." More often than not, the true meaning of "tomorrow" is "never." Not because the person isn't being genuine, but due to the fact that with so many distractions in life, there simply won't be enough motivation to perform the Desired Action.

As experience designers, our goal is to build Status Quo Sloth into the Endgame phases of our products by developing highly engaging activity loops that allow the user to turn Desired Actions into habits.

Nir Eyal, an expert in building habit-forming products, developed the *Hook Model* to describe a cycle of *Triggers, Actions, Rewards, and Investments* that eventually attract users into performing daily activities without exerting any mental effort[214]. In fact, once an activity becomes a habit, users actually need to *spend* consistent mental and emotional energy before they can remove themselves from the habit permanently.

This Hook Model focuses on creating internal and external *triggers* that remind the user to take the *Desired Actions* on a daily basis. After the user commits the Desired Action, a variable (and often emotional) *reward* is provided, finally prompting the user to input an *investment*, where the user will build value for themselves when they return again via the next trigger. Investments are things like adding a photo, tagging friends, customizing folders, where the

---

[214]Nir Eyal. *Hooked.* Kindle Version v 1.0. 2014.

user builds value into this process (aligning with Core Drive 4: Ownership & Possession).

If done correctly, users begin to feel motivated by Status Quo Sloth, which means they may even work harder to *prevent* a change in behavior.

On the other hand, in order to counter the Status Quo Sloth that is working against you, something I call the "FOMO Punch" might be implemented. FOMO stands for "Fear of Missing Out" and it's trick is to apply Core Drive 8: Loss & Avoidance against itself.

In life, we fear losing what we have, but we also fear losing what we could have had. This fear of regret, when prompted correctly, can penetrate through the behavioral inertia of Status Quo Sloth and trigger the Desired Action.

When Steve Jobs wanted to recruit Pepsi executive John Sculley into Apple as the new CEO, he famously said, "Do you want to spend the rest of your life selling sugar water, or do you want a chance to change the world?"

Boom! That was a powerful FOMO Punch that prompted Sculley to think he would miss out on the opportunity of a lifetime if he "wasted" the rest of his career at Pepsi. He later remembers, "I just gulped because I knew I would wonder for the rest of my life what I would have missed."[215] (Ironically, Sculley's lasting legacy would likely be known as the guy who fired Steve Jobs and ran Apple into the ground - just for Steve Jobs to return and resurrect).

As the context suggests, FOMO Punches can be very effective in the Discovery Phase of an experience when users are trying out a new experience. In contrast, the Status Quo Sloth technique plays a bigger role in the Endgame phase when the designer wants to keep the veterans in the system.

---

[215] Jay Elliot and William Simon. *The Steve Jobs Way.* P90-91. Vanguard Press. 03/08/2011.

FOMO Punches in Action

Companies often ask me if their internal gamification systems should be mandatory for their employees. We generally know that play *must* be voluntary[216]. If one is forced to do something, even if it was a game, it is no longer considered "play."

In that sense, gamified systems should be voluntary by nature, and therefore the Discovery Phase design becomes important in order to entice the employee into playing. Since employees must commit the work related Desired Actions regardless of whether there are gamified systems or not, they might try out the system if it offered the feelings of competency, social appreciation, and autonomy they naturally crave.

However, because of Status Quo Sloth, the employee often does not want to change their behaviors to try something new. That's when the FOMO Punch can come in. Management can communicate how they are missing out on opportunities to achieve mastery, improve company recognition, and have more fun.

Another example of the FOMO Punch is the "Postcode Lottery" in the Netherlands. Each week, the Postcode Lottery awards a "Street Prize" to one random postal code (similar to a zip code but with a much smaller number of households). Everyone who played the lottery within that code will win the equivalent of around $12,500. Of course, the ones living in that postcode that did not buy lottery tickets get nothing except the agony of watching their neighbors celebrate the win.

In 2003 a study showed that the Postcode Lottery was more successful than other lottery programs because the Dutch residents were afraid of their neighbors winning without them[217]. Since we are more likely to change our behavior based on loss-prevention

---

[216] Johan Huizinga. *Homo Ludens; A Study of the Play-Element in Culture.* Beacon Press, Boston, MA. 1955.

[217] Adam Piore. Nautil.us. "Why We Keep Playing the Lottery". 08/01/2013.

than gain-anticipation, people bought tickets because they feared a situation where their neighbors win the prize and host a big neighborhood party - then nudging them with, "Too bad you didn't participate in this one buddy. Want me to buy you a beer?"

"The brain is very sensitive to loss — even low-probability losses," explains Giorgio Coricelli, an associate professor of economics and psychology at the University of Southern California. "So if you frame something as a loss, biologically there is a compulsion to avoid it. We have an aversion to it."[218]

With Core Drives 4, 5, 6, 7, and 8 all built into the design, it's no wonder the Postcode Lottery became such a huge success.

The Sunk Cost Prison (Game Technique #50)

Perhaps the most powerful and sometimes treacherous mechanism within Core Drive 8: Loss & Avoidance is what I call the Sunk Cost Prison. This occurs when you invest so much time into something, that even when it's no longer enjoyable, you continue to commit the Desired Actions because you don't want to feel the loss of giving up on everything.

Imagine a scenario where you played a game for a long time and it begins to become boring and meaningless. You ask yourself why you keep playing it, but subconsciously you realize that if you do quit the game, you will feel the pain of losing all the time, points, currencies, status, and customizations that you've invested. Quitting will result in that ugly sensation of admitting that you truly wasted hundreds of hours that ended up becoming nothing.

As a result, in order to avoid that depressing feeling of loss and emptiness, you instead convince yourself to use that powerful pristine sword to kill even more monsters, or tap into the two

---

[218] Adam Piore. Nautil.us. "Why We Keep Playing the Lottery". 08/01/2013.](http://nautil.us/issue/4/the-unlikely/why-we-keep-playing-the-lottery)

million coins you've earned with all your labor in an attempt to feel awesome again. Eventually you invest even more hours into the game and build up even more things to lose. You become trapped in a deadly spiral, and it can become quite depressing.

From a design standpoint, if you make sure the user is accumulating – and knows that they are accumulating – things that will be gone and wasted if they leave your system, it will be very difficult for the user to leave during the Endgame.

Sunk Cost Prisons, though powerful, adhere to the Black Hat principles of making users feel uncomfortable. As such, they should always be accompanied by White Hat Core Drives, (such as allowing users to recognize that they are actually helping the world and they shouldn't give up the impact accumulated to that point). These technique should only be employed when the user has a quick urge to leave the system, such as being attracted to Black Hat Techniques used by other companies. (for instance, a special "limited" promotion that the user *must* sign up for.)

Facebook is an excellent example of a social media website that perfectly portrays the Sunk Cost Prison. I have many personal friends I physically hang out with but do not have their phone numbers nor email. The only way for me to contact these people is through Facebook.

If I were to suddenly deactivate my Facebook account, I would feel that all the connections with these personal friends would be lost. On top of that, I spent many years feeding my Facebook account with photos, conversations, and posts. All of which would be difficult to access or share if I retired the account.

To add both salt and insult to the injury, I wouldn't be able to access and use all the virtual goods and currencies accumulated from the Facebook games I played. Facebook was smart in designing a product that people used so frequently and invested so much into that they would have a difficult time leaving – a sunk cost prison indeed.

On the other hand, even though Google's search engine is extremely popular, it doesn't really build up things to lose if you quit using it. It just happens that it is the best search engine in the market (in my unwavering opinion), so everyone wants to use it whenever possible.

But it just takes one change of mind, "hmm, today I think I'm going to search on Bing instead of Google," for Google to lose that user. If one day, somehow everyone is convinced that another search engine is better, Google could lose all of its traction overnight - though so far it looks like this is not likely in the near future.

Of course, Google is combatting that by introducing the Alfred Effect from Core Drive 4 through more personalized search results – Google understands **You**, and so if you stop using Google, you will lose all the customized results and experiences that no other search engine can provide you. This is not as strong as Facebook's "we have all your friends hostage," but it's a step in the right direction.

When you design your experience, you should think regularly about what makes users reluctant to let go and therefore stay in your system for longer.

Core Drive 8: The Big Picture

Core Drive 8: Loss & Avoidance is a powerful motivator that is bluntly utilized by all sorts of organizations and systems. Core Drive 8 generates Black Hat results such as a high sense of urgency and obsession. However, in the long-run this puts the user in a state of discomfort.

In many cases, Core Drive 8: Loss & Avoidance works hand-in-hand with Core Drive 6: Scarcity & Impatience because exclusivity and limited offers often come packaged with the anticipated fear of losing that exclusivity or having that offer fade away. These two Core Drives don't necessarily have to coexist though. For instance, the Core Drive 6 game technique of Anchored Juxtaposition (where you provide users two options for completing a Desired Action, a combination of Core Drive 6 and 3) does not draw much strength from Loss & Avoidance.

Matched with Core Drive 7: Unpredictability & Curiosity, the emotional fear of Core Drive 8 becomes magnified and even more crippling. Interestingly, Daniel Kahneman's insightful *Fourfold Pattern* shows that, in low probability *loss* events, we become risk-averse to prevent that small risk from happening. However, in high probability loss events where we are forced to choose a certain (100%) loss, or a 90% chance to lose $200 and a 10% chance to lose nothing, we become risk-seeking and choose the route where we can foresee a glimmer of hope[219]. After all, fear is what motivates us to stay alive, but hope is what many of us ultimately live for.

To get the most out of the book, Choose only ONE of the below options to do right now:

Easy: Think about any activities that you are currently engaged in that are no longer enjoyable or meaningful, but you continue to do it because of Core Drive 8: Loss & Avoidance. How does that make you feel, and what would it take for you to stop that behavior?

Medium: Think about a product that you still enjoy using, but are likely trapped in a Sunk Cost Prison, should you one day like to quit. Is much of your personal data such as photos or the fruits of your labor, stored in the service? Are important contacts or relationships siloed within the platform? Are important organizational data and insights recorded in the system and essentially impossible to export? Think carefully about how the companies carefully built the Sunk Cost Prison while you still enjoyed their services, and how you can possibly escape it when you would like to switch.

---

[219]Daniel Kahneman. "Thinking, Fast and Slow." P317. Farrar, Straus and Giroux. New York, NY. 2013.

Hard: Evanescent Opportunities, Countdown Timers, and FOMO Punches often work together to counter Status Quo Sloth and Sunk Cost Prisons. Can you devise a combination of these three game techniques in an optimal manner that can get people to leave their previous habitual comfort zones and give your project a try? After you grab the users into your experience, how would you add White Hat game techniques to make them enjoy it and feel empowered?

Share what you come up with on Twitter or your preferred social network with the hashtag #OctalysisBook and check out what ideas other people have.

Don't miss out! Watch Yu-kai research popular games on Twitch.tv

Remember I said the only way to fully understand how a game uses the 8 Core Drives to motivate us towards obsessive behavior is to actually play the game? I'm sure there are plenty of games out there that you hear are popular but seems too complex to try it out yourself. Starting in 2015, I began broadcasting my game design research for top-hit games on Twitch.tv. I showcase myself playing through these popular games while making comments on their game design and how they use various game techniques to entice me to come back every day and spend more money buying virtual goods.

I started out with Blizzard's new card-battling computer game *Hearthstone*, and plan to eventually move on to games like Minecraft, League of Legends, and others. I do this for my own research, but if you go to my channel http://twitch.tv/fdlink, you may be able to catch me broadcasting actual gameplay research. I also announce when I plan to live stream on my Twitter account at http://www.twitter.com/yukaichou so that's another place to experience a FOMO Punch.

Okay, time for me to do another research session. I'll see you during game-streaming.

Chapter 13: Left Brain vs Right Brain Core Drives

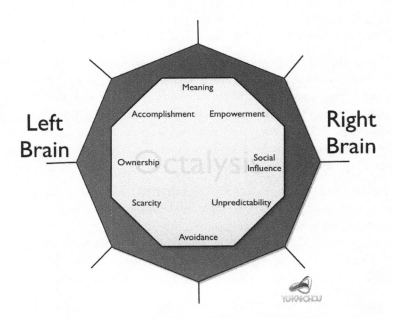

Using Octalysis in the Real World

Now that we have completed our journey through the 8 Core Drives, it is worth remembering that these Core Drives drive every action we take, whether it's inside or outside a game. If none of the 8 Core Drives are present, there is no motivation, and therefore no action takes place (that is, with the exception of the hidden ninth Core Drive: Sensation).

You may have noticed that I always include a specific number with each Core Drive, and in some instances, I've only mentioned the Core Drive number without the full title. After reading this book and continuing on your journey to understand and implement Octalysis Gamification, you will find that knowing these Core Drive numbers will become extremely helpful.

When I work with my team of Octalysis designers on a client project, I often say things like, "Over here you can clearly see a Core Drive 6 design, which enforces Core Drive 3, which in turn promotes Core Drive 2, and ultimately leads to Core Drive 5.[220]"

If you are not familiar with the Core Drive numbers, you would naturally have difficulty keeping up with the conversation. The 8 Core Drives are designed to be "mutually exclusive and collectively exhaustive" (also known as MECE[221]). Unfortunately, the full name of each Core Drive is a mouth full. By using their numbers, you can save time and effort in a long conversation and instead focus on creating valuable solutions.

For me, the Octalysis Framework has been incredibly useful because it not only provides a visual understanding of the intricacies of motivation, but also its nature: the placement of each Core Drive on the octagon shape provides visual cues that helps the designer determine if they have a long-term or short-term effect, or whether these experiences are intrinsically or extrinsically designed.

The Octalysis Framework also enables us to predict how motivation can evolve over subsequent phases and helps us identify the weaknesses of a design which can be addressed and improved upon.

---

[220] This is an actual example of a designed experience. For those hardcore Octalysis Learners out there, see if you can envision how these effects might take place from a specific set of events

[221] Arnaud Chevallier. Powerful-Problem-Solving.com. "Be MECE (mutually exclusive and collectively exhaustive)". 07/02/2010.

Left Brain vs. Right Brain Core Drives

A key aspect of the Octalysis Framework is the difference between *Left Brain and Right Brain Core Drives.*

The Left Brain Core Drives involve tendencies related to logic, ownership, and analytical thought. They are expressed in the following three Core Drives:

- Core Drive 2: Development & Accomplishment
- Core Drive 4: Ownership & Possession
- Core Drive 6: Scarcity & Impatience

The Right Brain Core Drives are characterized by creativity, sociality, and curiosity and as illustrated by the following:

- Core Drive 3: Empowerment of Creativity & Feedback
- Core Drive 5: Social Influence & Relatedness
- Core Drive 7: Unpredictability & Curiosity

(Note: there will be several points later in this chapter where you may find the need to refer back to the reference above.)

Again, it is worth noting that the terminology of "Left Brain Core Drives" and "Right Brain Core Drives" does not necessarily mean that they are physically located on the left side or right side of our brains. These references are merely symbolic in that some of the Core Drives are influenced more by the "logical brain," while other Core Drives are influenced more by the "emotional brain."

There have been past instances where some individuals tried to attack my work, pinpointing how the "left brain vs. right brain" model has been debunked and therefore is no longer scientifically valid. From my perspective, this is simply an issue of semantics, for I could very well name the emotional Core Drives, "Rainbow Core

Drives" and the logical Core Drives, "Stone Core Drives" - which would actually give a nice, game-like ring to them.

However, the current terminology is ideal for design purposes, as the "left/right brain" terminology is popularly understood in the social sciences. Therefore I designed the Left Brain Core Drives to be conveniently located on the left side of the octagon and the Right Brain Core Drives to be situated to the right. I'm a designer by trade, so even though I don't see anything wrong with the Left/Right Brain terminology to begin with, I prefer tools that are useful over ones that are simply "semantically accurate."

I believe that my intended goal to organize these Core Drives into intuitive patterns within a visually clear diagram was successful. This allows me and my students to follow complex motivational and behavioral design principles in an approachable manner. In turn, this enables us to design experiences that ensure long-term metrics are sustained.

Conveniently, the Left/Right Brain framework structure also allows us to differentiate and design for the differences between extrinsic and intrinsic motivation.

Extrinsic vs Intrinsic Motivation

The grouping of Left Brain and Right Brain Core Drives with correlated to what many motivational theorists understand as Extrinsic Motivation and Intrinsic Motivation.

Extrinsic Motivation is motivation that is derived from a goal, purpose, or reward. The task itself is not necessarily interesting or appealing, but because of the goal or reward, people become driven and motivated to complete the task. More often than not, people go to work everyday not because they actually love doing the work, but because they want to make a living, advance their careers, and be recognized for higher achievements.

For example, let's say you have a terrible job. Your job is to dig feces out of the ground for hours everyday. It's labor intensive, smells horrible, and you hate the job with a passion. But then someone shows up and says, "I'll give you $10,000 for every single piece of dung you dig out."

All of a sudden, you become excited and extremely motivated to dig, thinking, "Wow! This is easy money! Hahaha!" You're now engaged, joyful, and motivated with the job. Morale is high, and you start working much faster than you did before.

However, it is important to remember that the *task* itself is still not fun. You are motivated because the extrinsic reward is extremely appealing, and it creates the illusion that you enjoy the activity. Once the extrinsic reward is gone, you will go back to hating the task - and possibly more so than before, as we will see soon.

Intrinsic Motivation, on the other hand, is simply the motivation you get by inherently enjoying the task itself. These are things you would even *pay* money to do because you enjoy doing them so much. For instance, you don't need to reach any target to enjoy utilizing your creativity; you don't need a physical reward to enjoy hanging out with your friends; and you don't need any compensation to be absorbed by the suspense of unpredictability.

In fact, when you go to a casino, you have the opposite of a reward. Most people know that they are "statistically screwed" by the casino – that's how the casinos make so much money. But they still come out saying, "I lost $200, but I had so much fun!" Why? Because, throughout those five hours, they were constantly thinking, "Maybe I'll win this time!"

They are spending $200 to buy the intrinsic joy of "possibly" winning. If the unpredictability is removed and people know with absolute certainty that they will get $40 after pressing those buttons for five hours, they will no longer think it is fun. In fact, it would become very similar to the dreadful *work* of laboring in a factory.

Left Brain Core Drives are by nature goal-oriented, while Right Brain Core Drives are experience-oriented. Extrinsic Motivation focuses on results, while Intrinsic Motivation focuses on the process.

Slight Semantic Differences with the Self-Determination Theory

Intrinsic Motivation versus Extrinsic Motivation is a popular topic within the gamification space and was heavily popularized by Daniel Pink's book Drive[222]. The book explores how instead of being motivated by money (Core Drive 4: Ownership & Possession) and punishment (Core Drive 8: Loss & Avoidance), people are motivated more by *Purpose*, *Autonomy*, and *Mastery*.

While I believe Drive, as well as the Self-Determination Theory it advocates, are fantastic, I should point out that my terminology differs slightly from Pink on what Intrinsic Motivation consists of.

When a basketball player practices by shooting hoops a thousand times a day, their motivation is to achieve Mastery, something that is characterized as Intrinsic Motivation within Pink's theories[223]. However, within the Octalysis Framework, the activity itself is still monotonous and boring. It is only motivating because the athlete has a goal - an extrinsic motivation. That said, we will look at how Self- Determination Theory connects with White Hat Motivation within my framework in the next chapter.

Here is the test I usually apply to determine if something is extrinsically or intrinsically motivated: if the goal or objective were removed, would the person still be motivated to take the Desired Action or not?

In other words, at the end of the day, if the basketball player knows

---

[222]Daniel Pink. *Drive*. Penguin Group, New York, NY. 2009.

[223]Daniel Pink. *Drive*. Pages 107 - 128. Penguin Group, New York, NY. 2009.

that whatever they do, they will lose all "progress" and everything obtained or accumulated, would they still choose to shoot hoops?

Social hangouts and creative activities, such as solving fun puzzles, will pass the test for intrinsic motivation. However, accumulating goods, earning points, or even progressing towards mastery would likely not. What would you spend time doing if you knew the world was surely going to end tomorrow? It would be unlikely that you will decide to practice shooting basketball hoops - though you may decide to play a game of basketball with those you love and care about.

Again, these are simply differences in terminology and grouping, not a fundamental difference in beliefs about what motivates people. Daniel Pink only differentiates between Intrinsic and Extrinsic motivation, while I classify using the extra dimension of White Hat versus Black Hat motivation (you will soon see that Mastery falls into the White Hat camp of motivation). Hence our categorization and language differ slightly, while our overall beliefs in the nature and effectiveness of these drives do not.

In a similar fashion, Michael Wu, Chief Scientist of the engagement platform Lithium, differentiates between Intrinsic/Extrinsic Motivation and Intrinsic/Extrinsic Rewards[224].

Motivation is what drives us to do any action, and Rewards are what we obtain once we perform the Desired Action.

A person may receive Intrinsic *Rewards* after performing a certain task, such as gaining the appreciation of others or feeling a sense of accomplishment. However, since Intrinsic *Motivation* is derived from the activity itself without concern for the future outcome, if a person does something for any reward, including any Intrinsic Reward, it is not based on Intrinsic Motivation.

This is slightly tricky to comprehend, but along the lines of Michael

---

[224] Michael Wu. *Lithium Science of Social Blog.* "Intrinsic vs. Extrinsic Rewards (and Their Differences from Motivations)" 2/18/2014.

Wu's concepts, Core Drive 2: Development & Accomplishment may utilize Intrinsic Rewards, but ultimately does not focus on Intrinsic Motivation. The Left Brain Core Drives are result (goal) focused, while the Right Brain Core Drives are process (journey) focused. Core Drive 2 focuses on progress and achievements, and as a result is based on Extrinsic Motivation in my framework.

Motivation Traps in Gamification Campaigns

Most gamification campaigns typically employ loyalty programs, badges, progress bars, and prize rewards, which focus on Left Brain Core Drives. This is because it is much easier to add an extrinsic reward to a desired activity than to actually make the activity intrinsically fun or enjoyable.

However, there are many motivational traps which result from using too many Extrinsic Motivation techniques at the expense of Intrinsic Motivation[225].

Let's pretend for a moment that I love to draw and drew very often without any compensation. Research has shown that one of the best ways for you to make me stop drawing is to first *pay* me to do it and then stop paying me after a certain time period[226].

In fact, from my own experience, I believe that a more effective way is for you to pay me successively less until you reached a very insulting amount - say $0.02 per drawing. At that point, I would feel insulted and no longer have any desire to continue drawing, even though I happily drew for free prior to meeting you. This is because the Intrinsic Motivation of drawing for joy through Core Drive 3:

---

[225]Deward L. Deci. *Journal of Personality and Social Psychology* 18: 114. "Effects of Externally Mediated Rewards on Intrinsic Motivation." 1971.

[226]Mark Lepper, David Greene, and Robert Nisbett. *Journal of Personality and Social Psychology* 28, no. 1. P129-137. "Undermining Children's Intrinsic Interest with Extrinsic Rewards: A Test of the 'Overjustification' Hypothesis". 1973.

Empowerment of Creativity & Feedback, has now been shifted to an Extrinsic Motivation of drawing for money through Core Drive 4: Ownership & Possession.

As the pay decreased, drawing simply became less worthy of my time. Technically this is referred to as an "Overjustification Effect" - I become primarily engaged with the reward which subsequently eradicates and replaces the intrinsic motivation I originally had in the first place.

What's worse, if you still paid an acceptable amount for my drawings, say $20, more often than not, I would become incentivized to render the quickest, unrefined drawings possible in order to maximize the amount of money I would make. In essence, as long as I still get paid, I would have less focus on the *quality* of the work compared to the *completion* of the work. In fact, many studies have shown that Extrinsic Motivation, such as paying people money to perform a task, actually lowers the creative capability to perform the task.

Dan Ariely, author of *Predictably Irrational*, demonstrated in his experiments that people who were paid the most (5 months pay) for performing some relatively quick tasks performed far worse than people who were paid much less (only one day or two weeks pay for doing the same tasks)[227].

When people are thinking about the money, it distracts their focus from performance. Even the London School of Economics, after many experiments, concluded that, "'We find that financial incentives may indeed reduce intrinsic motivation and diminish ethical or other reasons for complying with workplace social norms such as fairness. As a consequence, the provision of incentives can result in a negative impact on overall performance."[228]

---

[227]Dan Ariely, Uri Gneezy, George Lowenstein, and Nina Mazar. *Federal Reserve Bank of Boston Working Paper* No. 05/-11. "Large Stakes and Big Mistakes". 07/23/2005.

[228]Bernd Irlenbusch. *London School of Economics and Political Science.* "LSE: When Performance-Related Pay Backfires." 06/25/2009.

This is because when we are doing something for Extrinsic Motivators, our eyes are set on the goal, and we try to use the quickest and most effortless path possible to reach it. As a consequence, we often give up our abilities to be creative, think expansively, and refine our work.

Daniel Pink states that, "Rewards, by their very nature, narrow our focus. That's helpful when there's a clear path to a solution. They help us stare ahead and race faster. But 'if-then' motivators are terrible for challenges like the [creative] candle problem."

Of course, in routine and mundane tasks that don't require any creativity and hold little Intrinsic Motivation to begin with, Extrinsic Motivation does often increase performance and results because of the goal-driven focus it generates. Dan Ariely points out in his New York Times article, "What's the Value of a Big Bonus"[229], "As long as the task involved only mechanical skill, bonuses worked as they would be expected: the higher the pay, the better the performance," but if the task required any "rudimentary cognitive skill," a larger reward "led to poorer performance" within his experiments.

The Problem with Educational Systems

The negative shift from Intrinsic Motivation to Extrinsic Motivation is a big issue within our educational systems.

I hold a firm belief that we as a species are endowed with an innate desire to learn, often driven by Core Drive 7: Unpredictability & Curiosity - a Right Brain Core Drive, and Core Drive 3: Empowerment of Creativity & Feedback - the Right Brain desire to use that knowledge in different ways. However, when it comes to school and training, that intrinsic motivation to learn quickly shifts into the extrinsic desire to obtain good grades, appease parents and teachers, gain respect from classmates, and secure prestigious,

---

[229]Dan Ariely. *New York Times*. "What's the Value of a Big Bonus". 11/20/2008.

career-requisite diplomas. All of which are powered by Left Brain Core Drives such as Core Drive 2 and 4.)

Because of this, students often stop caring about the learning itself and do the minimum amount of work to achieve those extrinsic results (which sometimes involves copying each others' home work or cheating on tests). They may even forget why they are learning the material in the first place.

In early 2014, I had a research interview with a high school senior student on a variety of games. He was an overachieving student who was finishing high school two years earlier than his peers. He knew just about everything there was to know concerning the elite universities he was applying to. Over the course of our conversation, he stated (paraphrasing of course), "Well, Stanford is great at these things, but I'm not sure about this. Harvard is okay on this subject matter, but they have an amazing program that could help my future."

Then, somewhere in the conversation, I mentioned that math is a very useful subject to prepare for one's career. To my surprise, this teenager who was polite and enthusiastic the entire time suddenly responded in an almost disdainful way:

"Come on Yu-kai. When do people *ever* use advanced math after graduating from school?"

I felt I had to justify myself: "I'm serious. Math is really useful. If you want to be a scientist, you need to use a lot of advanced math."

His eyes widened up. "Really?"

"Yeah, of course. You need math to calculate sound waves, gravity, satellite positioning information and such. Also, you need math if you want to become an engineer, economist, or even an accountant. How else would you tell the President that the economy would dry up if he doesn't bail out certain banks for nine billion dollars, or calculate how many days it takes for an asteroid the size of Texas to hit earth?" I said.

He exclaimed, "Wow, I never thought about that, but it makes a lot of sense!"

So here is a teenager who is doing everything he is *supposed* to do – get good grades, get good SAT scores, participate in extracurricular activities, write strong essays on his college applications, and research the schools he wants to attend. And yet, he does not know why he is studying math beyond the goals of getting into a good college and perhaps securing a good job.

It was eye-opening for me to see how bad the impact of goal-oriented education was on our learning. I can say this from my own experience: many students who neglect school and get in trouble all the time aren't like that because they are stupid or dislike learning. They just don't see the purpose of learning the subjects that are taught in class.

All too often, this tendency is even present at the college level. I do a fair amount of work with universities to improve their educational methodologies. I often ask professors about the students that attend their office hours. If humans were so passionate about learning, you would expect that these students should be thrilled that there's a professor who is brilliant, has spent decades researching a subject, and is dedicating their time just to transfer that knowledge to them!

With this in mind, every student should be excited about the opportunity to visit every single office hour and pick the professors' brains. (For some reason, I've always felt this phrase to be rather gory in a Hannibal Lecter kind of way).

As it turns out, the majority of their students that actually show up are only there when they have problems with their grades. Either they are approaching the professor because they are about to fail the course, or because they feel the professor incorrectly graded their tests and want to get their points back.

As a result of this extrinsic focus, students often forget what they learned immediately after their exams.

When I was a student, I once told a few friends, "Did you know that, since most people forget 80% of what they have learned after the test, if you simply remember 80% instead of forget 80%, you are immediately four times better than everyone else? That's not just a 20% or 30% improvement. It's a 400% improvement! What else can you do to quickly become four times better than others in the same major?"

To my surprise, my friends responded, "Wow, that's true Yu-kai! But... what's the point? We've already finished the test." At the time, I wasn't sure how to respond to a statement like that, but I'm guessing the most appropriate response would have been, "You're wrong. You still have to remember it for the Final Exam!"

You can see that Extrinsic Motivation design and goals has clearly taken its toll on our desire to learn and curiously explore subject matters that benefit our society.

Pay to Not Play

Remember when I mentioned that Core Drive 3: Empowerment of Creativity & Feedback is the golden Core Drive, where people use their creativity and "play"? Often, if you can establish a strong Core Drive 3 element in your experience, it becomes an evergreen mechanic that continuously engages the mind of users without needing to add more content.

Unfortunately, there are many examples where Core Drive 4: Ownership & Possession (in the form of financial rewards) overtake Core Drive 3: Empowerment of Creativity & Feedback.

There are studies that illustrate how our creative problem solving skills diminish when we are offered financial rewards. One of the more famous and effective demonstrations is the "Candle Problem" quoted earlier.

Many of my readers may have seen the Candle Problem in other literature, but if you have not (and thank you for choosing my book over the other literature first!), first take a look at the image below:

Karl Duncker was the notable psychologist who created the Candle Problem in the 1930s. The goal of the problem was to figure out how to attach a lit candle to a wall using only the tools given, so that the melting wax would not drip on the table.

Later in the 1960s, a psychologist named Sam Glucksberg divided participants into two groups to solve this problem. One group was promised $5 to $20 if they could solve the problem quickly - not bad for a few minutes of work. The other group was simply told that he was simply having them establish the norms for how long it typically took people to solve the problem.

[230] *Creativity Development and Innovation for SMEs* "Exercise 6: The Candle Problem". http://icreate-project.eu/index.php?t=245

I'll demonstrate the solution to the problem soon, but the originally findings were quite astonishing. It turns out that the people who were offered money to solve the problem took on average, three and a half minutes longer than those who weren't offered money.[231]

Getting paid resulted in the Left Brain Core Drive 4: Ownership & Possession overtaking the Right Brain Core Drive 3: Empowerment of Creativity & Feedback, in producing inferior results.

Before I present the solution, here's another image of the same problem, just in another setting.

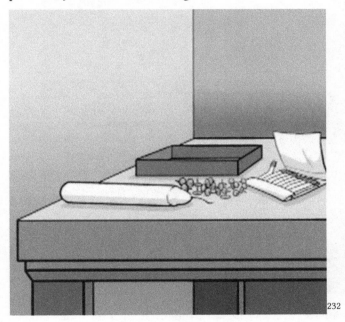

232

Remember that we talked about how Extrinsic Rewards enhance focus and increase performance towards straightforward tasks that require less creativity? If the problem is described using the Illustra-

[231]Sam Glucksberg. Journal of Experimental Psychology 63. P36-41."The Influence of Strength of Drive on Functional Fixedness and Perceptual Recognition". 1962.

[232]*Creativity Development and Innovation for SMEs*"Exercise 6: The Candle Problem". http://icreate-project.eu/index.php?t=245

tion above, the solution becomes more obvious. With this version, the people who were offered rewards did solve the problem slightly faster than those who weren't.

If you haven't solved the problem yet, don't worry - since you are in a "book reading" mode and less likely to be intensively focused on problem-solving. The solution is below:

[233]

As you can see, the way to solve the problem is to think "outside the box" and actually use the unassuming box itself.

When a person is trying to solve the problem for free, the activity resembles play. The mind searches for new, creative ways to do things. This makes the right solution easier to find because the mind

---

[233] *Creativity Development and Innovation for SMEs* "Exercise 6: The Candle Problem". http://icreate-project.eu/index.php?t=245

is flexible and dynamic.

In contrast, when a person is offered a reward, the situation immediately becomes one devoid of play. Unless clear, simple directions are laid out for the person, performance will actually decrease because the mind is fixated on completing the assignment.

How Market Settings Reverse Social Settings

Giving people financial rewards through Core Drive 4: Ownership & Possession doesn't simply reduce our intellectual curiosity (Core Drive 7) and our creative problem-solving skills (Core Drive 3), it also shifts the focus away from our social brain (Core Drive 5) to our economical brain. Depending on the actual goals of the gamification designer, this could become detrimental to the intended outcome.

In *Predictably Irrational*, Dan Ariely makes it clear that these aren't just two different ways of thinking; they are completely different behavioral modes that make us act differently in everything we do. Ariely defines these differences as *Social Norms versus Market Norms* to show the significant contrast between these paradigms[234].

For example, Ariely demonstrated that people were often very willing to perform mundane tasks, leave candy for others, perform free legal work, teach martial arts, solve difficult puzzles, move large pieces of furniture, and work on open source projects, all without any material reward[235]. This was because their brains were following a social norm mode, "I will do them a favor as we appreciate each other. We take care of each other when we can."

But once we offer money for the service, the brain immediately shifts into a market mode norm. If we offer as little as 1¢ for

---

[234]Dan Ariely. Predictably Irrational. P76. Harper Perennial. New York, NY. 2010.
[235]Ibid. P78-82.

the service, people will feel insulted with the amount of money and not only refuse to perform the activity, but question the social relationship itself. The social ties weaken and break, with everything boiling down to: "Are you paying me my worth to do this for you?"

Suppose you were willing to do me a favor for free because you genuinely take pleasure in helping me improve my situation. But then I asked you, "Can you do this for me? I can pay you $5." You are not likely to think that you are getting the pleasure of helping me out as initially intended, *and* making an extra $5 bonus on top of it. Our brains are either using the Social Norms, or the Market Norms. Once I offer to pay you, you begin to think, "My time is worth much more than $5. This is insulting."

Ariely adds another hypothetical scenario to drive this point home[236]: what would happen if you offer to pay your mother-in-law a few hundred dollars for hosting a great Thanksgiving meal and a wonderful evening? Immediately, you transition the situation from Social Norms to Market Norms, and it is not difficult to predict that she would respond quite poorly to this generous offer.

After conducting a few experiments, Ariely found that when the price of delicious Lindt chocolate truffles shifts from 10¢ to 5¢ to 1¢, demand from university students increased by 240 percent and then by 400 percent, which fits well into traditional economic models.

However, when the price went from 1¢ to free, instead of a massive increase in demand, as basic economic theory would predict, the number of truffles taken (without cost) by each student was immediately reduced to one. In the end this led to an overall decrease in demand by 50 percent.

When the price was shifted from 1¢ to free, our brains shifted from the Market Norm of "This is a great deal! I must get more!" to the Social Norm of, "I don't want to be a jerk and take too many. What

[236]Dan Ariely. Predictably Irrational. P75. Harper Perennial. New York, NY. 2010.

if it runs out and other people don't get to have any?"

In the Octalysis Framework, this is a perfect example of Left Brain Core Drive 4: Ownership & Possession shifting to Right Brain Core Drive 5: Social Influence & Relatedness. When you incentivize people with money, they lose some of their social altruism and generosity, which means that they are not selflessly collaborating and sharing useful information with one another as much as they would otherwise. They become more like rational economic calculators and tend to work more only when the pay justifies it. (Assuming of course, that there aren't much stronger Right Brain Core Drive forces within the environment.)

An interesting caveat is that when you offer gifts instead of cash, experiments reveal that the rules of Social Norms still apply. Your mother-in-law would unlikely become offended if you brought a nice wine as a gift for the Thanksgiving Dinner. This is because "Gifting" (or Social Treasures) is still mostly in the realm of Core Drive 5: Social Influence & Relatedness, so the interaction is still intrinsic in nature.

However, the moment you mention the dollar amount of the gift, the Social Norm shifts to a Market Norm once again. In another experiment by Dan Ariely, simply mentioning something along the lines of, "Can you help with something? I'll give you this 50¢ chocolate bar," caused applicants to immediately switched to their Market Norm mode and interpreted the statement as an insult.[237]

But when the experimenter simply said, "Can you help with something? I'll give you this chocolate bar," many people were eager to help because they were still operating within the Social Norm.

Exploring this further, let's look at a dating scenario. When you buy gifts for your date, once you make statements such as, "I would be happy to buy you this $80 steak!" or even "I've spent quite a bit of money on our dates now. Perhaps we should take this to

---

[237]Dan Ariely. Predictably Irrational. P81. Harper Perennial. New York, NY. 2010.

the next level?" the situation shifts dramatically. The person might become offended, because you have transitioned the Social Norm to a Market Norm. You likely won't accomplish the goals you intend, since the potential partner will likely prefer to treat your relationship as a "social" one instead of a "market exchange" one. Here again, when applying a Left Brain Core Drive technique, the Right Brain Core Drive becomes diminished.

Of course, our brains are quite easy to fool. A clever device that bypasses this gifting inconvenience is known as the *gift card*. Though in reality it functions like cash, since the value is stored on a card and can only be used at a certain place, people treat it as a gift. Sometimes they even include the receipt so that the recipients can even return the gift card for cash! However, since it is still a *gift*, not a real payment, people accept it without shifting to Market Norms - unless you say, "Here is a gift card that is worth $50. I would like you to have it."

The Chinese and some Asian cultures also disguise their cash gifts with "red envelopes." Though it is still just pure cash, the envelope represents good luck, and therefore it is received as a Social Treasure. But once the person takes the cash out from the envelope and gives it to another, the exchange becomes a Market Norm, and is therefore insulting again. After all, people don't like to be treated as beggars. Better put a red envelope around it or invest in a gift card.

The Advantages of Extrinsic Motivation Design

Obviously designing for Extrinsic Motivation is not all negative. Besides enhancing a person's focus on completing monotonous routine tasks, it also generates initial interest and desire for the activity.

Often, without there being extrinsic motivation during the Discovery Phase (before people first try out the experience), people do not find a compelling reason to engage with the experience in the first place. Promoting, "You will get a $100 gift card if you sign-up," usually sounds more appealing than "You will utilize your creativity and be in a fun state of unpredictability with your friends!" (Though both actually utilize Core Drive 6: Scarcity & Impatience.)

When people consider themselves "too busy," they won't justify spending time to try out your experience. But when you offer them an extrinsic reward to try out the experience, they will at least test it out, assuming of course that the reward is not an insult to the value of the user's time investment.

Rewarding users $2 for trying a new search engine for an entire month is pretty weak, while paying people $3 to spend weeks going to stores, taking pictures, and sharing them with their friends is also a path to failure. It is better to not give them a reward at all!

And of course, as we have seen earlier, if people continuously justify doing something for high extrinsic rewards, their intrinsic motivation dwindles as the Overjustification Effect settles in.

Therefore, as Michael Wu of Lithium points out, it is better to attract people into an experience using Extrinsic Rewards (gift cards, money, merchandise, discounts), then transition their interest through Intrinsic Rewards (recognition, status, access), and finally use Intrinsic Motivation to ensure their long term engagement. Through this process, users will start to enjoy the activity so much that they will focus on relishing the experience itself without thinking about what can be gained from the experience.

How to Make an Experience More Intrinsic

Since this book is entitled *Actionable Gamification*, we want to make sure you have a set of steps and tools to help you develop your own projects. The ultimate question that this chapter seeks to answer is: "How do I make my users more motivated intrinsically?"

Well, we've noted earlier that Intrinsic Motivation is often derived from Right Brain Core Drives, which relate to Core Drive 3, 5, and 7. Therefore, the actionable way to add Intrinsic Motivation into an experience is to think about how to implement those Core Drives into the experience.

1. Making the experience more Social

One of the common Right Brain Core Drives that the business world has been using in recent years is Core Drive 5: Social Influence & Relatedness. Many companies are seeking ways to make things more social by incorporating social media, and constantly spamming their users to spam their friends.

Of course, there are better and worse ways to make your experience more social. The first principle to note is that users are intrinsically interested in inviting their friends to an experience only if they are first sold on its value. Often this happens during the First Major Win-State, which is a term referring to the moment when the user first says, "Wow! This is awesome!"

Many companies make the gigantic mistake of asking users to invite all their Facebook friends at the beginning of the Onboarding Stage, which happens right after the user signs up. The users don't even know whether they will like the experience themselves, let alone risk their friendships by spamming others. In fact, this prompting interface actually delays the First Major Win-State, which could be detrimental to the entire experience.

The experience designer needs to identify exactly where that First Major Win-State is, and count exactly how many minutes it takes for the users to get there - because every second before that you will be seeing dropout. Once the user hits the first major Win-State, that's the best time to ask them to invite their friends or rate the product. (We will reiterate these important points on First Major Win-States in our chapter discussing the Experience Phases of a Player's Journey.)

Besides finding the right time to prompt friend-invites, it is important to determine the right type of message. I've seen many companies require their users to share a default text such as, "I just used Company A, the leader in B space, to solve all my problems! Sign-up right now for a 30% discount!" This is a message that is obviously not genuine, and will lead to users feeling like they are being baited to share crappy promotional messages.

Rather, it is better to have something less informative, but more believable, such as, "I've been reading Yu-kai's book on gamification. It's worth checking out! #OctalysisBook." A default tweet like this (which still allows the user to modify it anyway they wish), produces a social message that their friends will more likely recognize as a true endorsement.

With that all said, none of the above is actually making the *experience* itself more social. It is much better to foster collaborative play within the Desired Action, where users can help each other out, socialize, and grow together.

When you design for Intrinsic Motivation, you want to create environments that foster socializing, even with areas that are non-critical to the Desired Actions (such as the Water Cooler game technique). Also, consider adding in more Group Quests where users can work together, utilize their unique strengths, and accomplish tasks together. This often makes an experience more intrinsically motivating and enjoyable.

2. Add more Unpredictability into the Experience

Another way to add Intrinsic Motivation into the experience is to utilize Core Drive 7: Unpredictability & Curiosity. If every result is expected and the experience predictable, much of the fun and excitement will fade. Adding some unpredictability, though Black Hat in nature, increases the thrill to the experience and prevents the user from losing interest and dropping out.

When you design your experience, ask yourself if there is a way to build controlled randomness into the experience? If the user performs the Desired Action again and again, does the result have to be exactly the same each time? Or can some things be altered from time to time, even if they are just trivial things like alternating feedback dialogue or randomly generated tips.

Unpredictability matched with Core Drive 8: Loss & Avoidance will often make an undesirable event even more stressful, and sometimes more motivating in a Black Hat way; but unpredictability accompanying Core Drive 2: Development & Accomplishment or Core Drive 4: Ownership & Possession increases the excitement of the experience.

If you implement a variable reward, either in the form of a Mystery Box (users expect a reward but don't know what it will be) or an Easter Egg (users don't expect a reward at all), you will likely build positive anticipation and unpredictability. In the book Hooked, Nir Eyal confirms that, "Variable rewards are one of the most powerful tools companies implement to hook users"[238]

---

[238]Nir Eyal. *Hooked.* Kindle Version v 1.0. 2014.

Obtaining a reward is in and of itself extrinsic. However, when you make the reward variable, you add a layer of intrinsic excitement, much like how the animal in the Skinner Box continues to press the lever to get more food, even though it is no longer hungry.

Do be cautious though, since Core Drive 7: Unpredictability & Curiosity is by nature a Right Brain and Black Hat Core Drive, it may unsettle some users who feel uncomfortable because they are not in control of their own destinies. If I told an employee, "Work hard for a year, and you may or may not get a surprising reward!" I may have made the year more intrinsically "interesting" because of the suspense and guess work. However, it may also cause the employee to leave my company because of how uncomfortable it feels when a person is exposed to long-term Black Hat motivators.

Before you snicker for too long, it is worth noting that this is also what most companies implicitly communicate to their employees regarding their raises and promotions: work hard for a few years, and perhaps you will receive some type of promotion! Is it a wonder then that companies complain about their employees lacking loyalty and joining a competitor as soon as they are offered an immediate and higher compensation package? Once you are exposed to Black Hat Motivation *and* have received your Extrinsic Reward, there is often a very high chance you will leave the game for more "empowering" environments.

Like anything, there's a right way to design something, and a wrong way to design something. Ideally, if you use variable rewards, you should make sure the action to obtain them is relatively short and easy, such as pulling the lever on a slot machine or refreshing your Facebook home feed.

If I told you, "Can you please bring me my crystal ball that's lying on the couch? There's a chance I might give you a surprising reward when you do." Since the Desired Action is fast, my variable reward offer sounds intriguing, especially compared to just stating what the reward will be. If I asked you to get my crystal ball from the other side of town, the intrigue factor would be diminished and you would be less inclined to take this protracted action for me. Of course, if you consider me of high status and want to gain my liking, Core Drive 5: Social Influence & Relatedness might still be a motivating factor for you to take the Desired Action.

If you must drag out the Desired Action, it would be advisable to make sure all of the variable rewards are appealing to the users, and that the user knows that up front. If I promised my employees a free vacation either to Italy, France, or Denmark if they worked hard for a year, that likely would be much more appealing than being completely vague with what the reward might be. In this case, there is sufficient information for the employees to get excited about the reward. Perhaps they would even stay in the company for longer in anticipation of finding out which of the vacation options are finally offered.

3. Add more Meaningful Choices and Feedback

Since I mentioned that adding unpredictability into your experience utilizes Black Hat Core Drives, you may wonder about how to make an experience more intrinsic through White Hat methods. I've mentioned a few times that Core Drive 3: Empowerment of Creativity & Feedback sits at the top right of the Octalysis Framework, representing the "golden corner" of being both White Hat and intrinsic in nature. It is the Core Drive where the process becomes "play" and generates evergreen mechanics that keep a user engaged. Unfortunately, it is also the most difficult Core Drive to implement well.

In your own experience design, you want to make sure that users are able to make as many Meaningful Choices as possible to reflect their style, preference, and strategy (recall that this is done with the "Plant Picker" Game Technique).

If a hundred users go through your experience and all hundred take the exact same actions to achieve the Win-State, there are no meaningful choices present for the user to express their creativity. If thirty of those hundred take one path, another thirty take a second path, and the last forty take a third path to reach the Win-State, a greater feeling of having meaningful choices will be present.

If all hundred users played the game differently and still ended up reaching the Win-State, your experience will have been successful in generating an optimal meaningful choice design.

If you asked a hundred children to build something great with a box of Legos, it is almost statistically impossible that any two will build the same thing (outside of kids copying each other) in the exact same order. There is a high sense of Core Drive 3: Empowerment of Creativity & Feedback with this type of experience.

You should ask yourself, "Is there a way to allow my users to take multiple routes but still reach the same goal? Are there places that I could allow them to make meaningful choices to craft their own experiences?" These are often difficult questions to answer. But if you can address them with insightful design mechanics, you will see a great deal of value in the form of enthusiastic, loyal, and engaged users that are glued to the experience - from Onboarding all the way into the Endgame Phase. And remember, in order to be successful, this must go beyond providing a shallow *perception* of choice.

Also keep in mind, our brains hate it when we have no choices, but we also dislike having too many choices. The latter leads to decision paralysis and ultimately makes us feel stupid. This is an Anti Core Drive within Core Drive 2: Development & Accomplishment, which I also call the "Google+ Problem." In Google+, there is an impressive amount of technology and engineering hours behind each feature, but users feel lost, powerless, and end up leaving quickly.You should avoid this by letting users choose between two to three meaningful options at any given point so they feel empowered without being overwhelmed.

Don't forget the Boosters!

Finally, designing multiple Boosters as your rewards increases strategy and creative play within an experience. If users can choose different paths to obtain different power-ups that work together towards different goals, they can optimize on what combinations to use and paths to take.

The biggest innovation introduced by the iconic game Megaman (known as Rockman in non-American companies) in 1987 was that it allowed players to pick which stage and boss they want to challenge. This was contrary to the traditional linear design where players challenge through Stage 1, Stage 2, Stage 3 sequentially[239].

Besides allowing each player to play the game differently each time they come back (this was before games could "save" their progress), it allowed players to strategize their own optimal path to play the game based on booster abilities along the way. When Megaman defeats a boss, he absorbs the boss' ability and is allowed to use that ability on other stages and bosses. Some abilities are perfect solutions to other bosses and scenarios, which incentivize the players to carefully pick which bosses they want to fight early on and which bosses to fight later.

In the real world, when you see people figuring out how to take multiple layovers to maximize their Airline Miles points, signing up for various credit cards to optimize spending and rewards, or collecting a variety of coupons to reduce a $20 item to $1, you are seeing strong implementations of Core Drive 3: Empowerment of Creativity & Feedback in making Extrinsic Rewards more intrinsically motivating. The end reward is often nice (Core Drive 2 and 4), but it is often the *process* of strategizing and optimizing that is truly engaging the individuals.

---

[239]Wikipedia Entry, "Mega Man": http://www.yukaichou.com/megaman. Accessed 02/09/2015.

Left Brain vs Right Brain Core Drives: the Bigger Picture

When you want to hook users into trying your experience, extrinsic rewards via Left Brain Core Drives work fairly well. However, most gamification campaigns see immediate results from these efforts and end up sticking with the same techniques continuously, which ultimately leads to a stale and stagnant experience. This results in overjustification, dwindled motivation, and even burnout. It is very important to quickly transition into Right Brain Core Drives and start implementing elements such as Meaningful Choices, Social Bonding, Refreshing Content (Game Technique #73), and Variable Rewards into the experience. Failure to do so will threaten the long-term success of a campaign.

Beyond that, it is also critical to consider the full implications of implementing various White Hat and Black Hat Core Drives, which we will cover in more depth in the next chapter.

To get the most out of the book, Choose only ONE of the below options to do right now:

Easy: Try reciting the Left Brain Core Drives and Right Brain Core Drives without looking at any cheat sheets.

Medium: Think about how a company has engaged you through Left Brain Core Drives in the past by offering you a reward, and contemplate whether it affected your overall enthusiasm about the company itself after the reward campaign was finished.

Medium: Think about how you can add at least one of the Right Brain Core Drives into a project you have done in the past or are currently doing. Would that have improved motivation and engagement for the tasks themselves?

Hard: Try to design a full engagement campaign that lures users in with the Left Brain Core Drive of giving them a reward (Core Drive 4), and then start making users feel accomplished (Core Drive 2) while dangling new unlockables within the experience (Core Drive 6). Then transition into the Right Brain Core Drives by giving users Group Quests (Core Drive 5) that utilize plenty of creativity, meaningful choices, and boosters (Core Drive 3). Upon each Desired Action, serve them unpredictable rewards or content (Core Drive 7). After going through this design practice, do you feel a better grasp of all the things you can do when mastering the 8 Core Drives?

Share what you come up with on Twitter or your preferred social network with the hashtag #OctalysisBook and check out what ideas other people have.

Practice with a Buddy

Now that you have acquired a great deal of Octalysis knowledge (and I assume you still feel very positive about it since you have read all the way up to this chapter), it's time to practice explaining it to others. Part of using any knowledge is how well you can persuade and explain it to others. I've learned early on in my consulting career that it doesn't matter if become the best at what you do and if you can help people increase client metrics - if you can't emotionally persuade your value, all that knowledge becomes worthless. If you want your manager, your university Dean, your engineers, or your significant other to understand and cooperate with your new design skills (whether you call it Gamification or not), you better know how to communicate it well and convincingly.

Find someone who you trust (and won't look down on you if you mess up and sound unorganized) and practice telling them about the concept of Human-Focused Design (as opposed to Function-Focused Design), the 8 Core Drives, and differences in the nature of various Core Drives. Think about which Core Drives you should use to communicate these concepts (maybe some Unpredictability? Scarcity? Social Influence? Epic Meaning?). Observe if the person becomes truly emotionally excited about it, interested but mostly because you are a friend, or bored but still being polite about it.

Another great place to find an Octalysis Buddy is the Octalysis Explorers Facebook Group. If you haven't joined the group yet, consider doing so and find one other person to learn/practice together. As we have learned in Core Drive 5, collaborative play makes everything even more intrinsically meaningful.

Chapter 14: The Mysteries of White Hat and Black Hat Gamification

In the last chapter, we looked at how Left Brain Core Drives and Right Brain Core Drives differ in the *nature* of their motivation as well as their design methodologies, resulting in various short-term and long-term effects.

In this chapter, we will examine the fascinating intricacies of White

Hat and Black Hat Core Drives, and how to balance them within a design.

The White Hat Core Drives are represented by the Core Drives at the Top of the Octalysis diagram:

- Core Drive 1: Epic Meaning & Calling
- Core Drive 2: Development & Accomplishment
- Core Drive 3: Empowerment of Creativity & Feedback

The Black Hat Core Drives are represented by the Core Drives at the Bottom of the Octalysis diagram:

- Core Drive 6: Scarcity & Impatience
- Core Drive 7: Unpredictability & Curiosity
- Core Drive 8: Loss & Avoidance

Origins of the Theory

Up to this point in the book, you should have a fairly good understanding of how White Hat and Black Hat Core Drives function. In this chapter we will discuss when and how to use them for optimal motivational systems.

Though every single Core Drive in the Octalysis Framework has been researched and written about individually (including the differences between intrinsic and extrinsic motivation), I believe my work on White Hat versus Black Hat Gamification theory is fairly original and provides a unique design perspective.

I began developing the White/Black Hat concepts while I was studying the Endgame Phase of different games. I became curious as to why the majority of successful games were obsessively addictive for many months, and then experience a huge user dropout with large numbers of players moving on with their lives.

On the other hand, I looked at how a few games such as Poker, Chess, Mahjong, and even Crossword Puzzles stood the test of time and never got old for their players. Video games like Starcraft, World of Warcraft, Defense of the Ancients (abbreviated as DotA[240], eventually spinning off the even bigger hit, League of Legends[241]), and re-skins of similar shooting games like Counter Strike[242] or Call of Duty[243], continue to be popular and engaging no matter how many years a player plays them.

Upon further research and observation, I realized that there was a big difference in how these games were designed and what Core Drives motivated their users in the late Scaffolding and Endgame Phases. It seemed like the games that go viral but then have shorter shelf-lives utilize Core Drives that create obsession, urgency, and addictiveness. Players would become glued to the game but then towards the Endgame Phase, the joy and fun no longer persists as strongly, yet the player mechanically continues to grind through many hours "laboring" through them. Due to the Sunk Cost Prison covered in Core Drive 8, players feel demoralized, but are unable to quit.

Eventually, some people do find the strength to finally quit and move on with their lives. This is perhaps due to important responsibilities, or shift to newer games that hit them hard with epic Discovery Phase marketing. Once that happens, Social Influence & Relatedness dictates a big exodus of people finally leaving the game, in hopes of finding that joy and passion again.

But for the games that are quite timeless (until their own sequels come out), when players are in the Endgame phase, there seems to be a continuous sense of wellbeing and satisfaction, just like the joy one has when playing an instrument or being called to a purpose. Based on this research, I started labeling a few Core Drives

[240]Wikipedia Entry, "Defense of the Ancients": http://www.yukaichou.com/dota

[241]Wikipedia Entry, "League of Legends": http://www.yukaichou.com/LoL

[242]Wikipedia Entry, "Counter Strike": http://www.yukaichou.com/CS

[243]Wikipedia Entry, "Call of Duty": http://www.yukaichou.com/CD

"White Hat" and a few others "Black Hat," which borrows from my background knowledge in SEO (Search Engine Optimization[244]).

In Search Engine Optimization, "White Hat SEO" refers to designing and promoting your site the way search engines like Google intend you to do. As a result, they rank your site highly when users search for related terms. "Black Hat SEO" on the other hand refers to methodologies that dishonestly exploit the rules, rigidness, and weaknesses of the search engines to get your site highly ranked.

Needless to say, search engines hate Black Hat SEO, and have massive teams of engineers that continuously make the engines smarter and harder to exploit, while severely penalizing any website that is caught utilizing Black Hat SEO techniques. Sometimes the search engine companies even ban websites completely off their search results, defeating the purpose of the Black Hat SEO in the first place. In the realm of SEO, just don't do Black Hat – it's not worth it.

Unfortunately, our brains cannot continuously update themselves to become harder to exploit like Google can. Nor can we as efficiently blacklist people who constantly apply black hat motivation techniques on us (nor do we want to, since some of them have good intentions that ultimately benefit us). The end result is that we become subconsciously motivated by things that make us stressed, worried, and obsessed, while feeling that we are not in control of ourselves.

The Nature of White Hat vs Black Hat Core Drives

White Hat Core Drives are motivation elements that make us feel powerful, fulfilled, and satisfied. They make us feel in control of our own lives and actions.

---

[244]Wikipedia Entry, "Search Engine Optimization": http://www.yukaichou.com/SEO

In contrast, Black Hat Core Drives, make us feel obsessed, anxious, and addicted. While they are very strong in motivating our behaviors, in the long run they often leave a bad taste in our mouths because we feel we've lost control of our own behaviors.

The advantages of White Hat Gamification are obvious and most companies who learn my framework immediately think, "Okay, we need to do White Hat!" They would mostly be right, except there is a critical weakness of White Hat Motivation: it does not create a sense of urgency.

For example: if I approached you with great enthusiasm and exclaimed, "Go out and change the world today!" You may become very excited by this Core Drive 1 trigger and may echo, "Yes! I'm going to go out and change the world! But I'm going to first have a nice breakfast, brush my teeth, and get prepared for the day!" As you can see, there is no urgency with this level of White Hat excitement.

However, if I took out a gun and pointed it at your head, while quietly whispering, "Go out and change the world, or I'm going to kill you" - you are still likely to "change the world," but you are probably not going to enjoy your nice breakfast or brush your teeth while being pushed by my threatening Core Drive 8: Loss & Avoidance motivation.

Of course, at that point you also no longer *feel* good about changing the world. Once you can leave my grasp, you will likely stop caring and drop the noble cause altogether. That is, unless the Epic Meaning & Calling regenerates from within.

Black Hat Gamification creates the urgency that system designers often need to accomplish their goals and change behavior. Often this cannot be accomplished through White Hat Gamification alone.

If a company simply implements White Hat Gamification while the user is constantly exposed to Black Hat stimuli from other sources such as email, appointments, or distractions from Facebook, they will most likely not have the opportunity to test out the experience. Of course, this user will feel terrible also, because they will continue to procrastinate instead of doing the things that are more meaningful and make them feel good. Unfortunately, because of the nature of Black Hat motivation, they will continue behaving that way nevertheless.

Zynga and Black Hat Gamification

My theories on Black Hat vs White Hat Gamification can often be utilized to explain or predict why certain companies are successful or fail at different stages.

One such example is the social gaming company Zynga[245], which is known for games such as Farmville, Words with Friends, and Zynga Poker.

Zynga has mastered how to implement all sorts of Black Hat Game Techniques – of course, they don't have a framework to think about the techniques as "Black Hat." Instead, they consider it "Data-Driven Design[246]," which on the outset seems to be extremely clever and legitimate. Because of the Black Hat designs, all their immediate metrics looked good: Monetization, Viral Coefficients, Daily Active Users, User Addiction, etc. However, because people don't *feel* good playing Zynga games after awhile, when they *can* drop out of the system, they will.

This is especially true for the late Scaffolding stage as well as the Endgame phase, since all the novelty, creativity, and true sense of development run out during these phases. This makes it even harder for all their new re-skinned games - basically Farmville in a city, in a castle, in kitchen, and so on, to become long-term successes. When that happens, it is almost like the users are still playing the same Endgame – right in Onboarding phase!

---

[245] Zynga Official Website: zynga.com

[246] Mike Williams. Gamesindustry.biz. "Zynga's high-speed, data-driven design vs console development". 08/06/2012.

Because of these Black Hat mechanics, users quickly get tired if they have already been burnt out by the last Zynga game. Farmville 2 was doomed from the start unless they could implement much better White Hat designs into it to ensure long-term success.

Early in 2014, Zynga proved my Octalysis theories accurate when they decided to "double-down" on Casino Slot Machine games like Riches of Olympus[247]. Of course, since they were committed to stick with Black Hat game design (which shows quick data-driven results), the only long-lasting engagement element they could use was the Right Brain Core Drive 7: Unpredictability & Curiosity. Nonetheless, even if a person were addicted to gambling, they don't feel awesome about themselves and their activities. This could still lead to later burnout.

In a Venturebeat article that accompanied the *Riches of Olympus* launch, the journalist Jeffrey Grubb asked then Head of Zynga's Casino franchise, Barry Cottle, what he meant when he said Zynga was focusing on "quality in experiences and excellence in execution." Cottle explained that Zynga wanted to make things that look and feel good. Cottle specifically brought up the game Candy Crush Saga, which "has a simple puzzle mechanic that players respond well to due to the extra animations and special effects."[248]

If Zynga thinks extra animations and special effects is what made Candy Crush successful, it's no wonder they have their own graves dug out as a "game design company." If extra animations and special effects are so important, why would a game like Minecraft become so successful? The graphics for Candy Crush aren't even that stunning, compared to other games that look similar but don't have even a tenth of Candy Crush's success.

If you have been an active student of the Octalysis Framework, you will know that the reason why these games became so popular

---

[247] Jeff Grubb. *VentureBeat.com*. "Zynga sticks with what works: Riches of Olympus is its next mobile slots game". 02/06/2014.
[248] Ibid.

was due to their ability to retain Core Drive 3: Empowerment of Creativity & Feedback for the longest time. Most Zynga games do not have long lasting Core Drive 3, and therefore engagement will wane.

Of course, the two games that are consistently top-ranking within Zynga are *Zynga Poker* and *Words with Friends*[249]. If you notice, since they build on already timeless game designs like Poker and Scrabble[250], Zynga accidentally copied sound Core Drive 3 design without necessarily recognizing it. Both games elicit a higher level of strategy and problem-solving that other Zynga games lack. As a result, they demonstrate long-term success well into the Endgame.

With a good understanding of White Hat and Black Hat game design, you can begin to analyze and predict the strengths and longevity of any motivational system. If there aren't any Black Hat techniques, it is likely there won't be any breakout success; if there aren't any White Hat techniques, users will quickly burn out and leave for something better.

According to the Octalysis Framework, Zynga will never achieve long-term success unless they start building in more White Hat game techniques and continue to empower their users. Instead of putting so much emphasis on Black Hat manipulative techniques, they should design for more long term engagement.

Black Hat with a Clear Conscious

I want to clarify here, that just because something is called "Black Hat Gamification" doesn't mean it's necessarily bad or unethical. Some people voluntarily use Black Hat gamification to force themselves to live healthier and achieve their short term and long term goals. I would personally love to be addicted to eating more

---

[249]Words with Friends Page: zynga.com/games/words-friends

[250]Wikipedia Entry: "Scrabble": http://en.wikipedia.org/wiki/Scrabble

vegetables or confronting the tasks that I tend to procrastinate on. The point of it being called Black Hat is that, once designed well, we are more compelled to take certain actions quickly without feeling completely in control.

However, whether it is "good" or "bad" depends on the intentions and final outcome of those actions. We could use Black Hat designs to motivate people towards good behaviors or we could use Black Hat designs to motivate people towards evil. Similarly, some of the most infamous people in history motivate others with Core Drive 1: Epic Meaning & Calling (among other Core Drives) towards evil and genocide, even though the *nature* of the motivation itself is White Hat.

An example of Black Hat Motivation towards good behaviors is the SnuzNLuz[251] alarm clock app. SnuzNLuz automatically donates the user's money to a non-profit they hate if they hit the snooze button (the "wake me up 10 minutes later" button - for my foreign readers).

A more visually compelling (but illegal) concept is the Shredder Clock[252], which physically destroys your money when you press the snooze button.

---

[251] John Balz. *The Nudge Blog*. "SnüzNLūz: The alarm clock that donates to your least favorite charity".

[252] Charlie White. Mashable.com. "Money-Shredding Alarm Clock Is Completely Unforgiving [PICS]". 05/29/2011.

253

In these products, people are waking up because of Core Drive 8: Loss & Avoidance – they don't want to lose their money, especially to a non-profit they hate! (The SnuzNLuz also has a weird Core Drive 1 angle, as it does donate to a non-profit for a cause)

But people are okay with this Black Hat design, because it's for a goal *they* want. They are fine with designs that compel them to do things that they intend to do already but lack the willpower to do so.

What people hate is when companies, governments, instructors, or marketers utilize these Black Hat techniques to get them to buy things they don't need, succumb under tyranny, work overtime, and get grades they don't care about. Keep in mind that these people will often still perform the Desired Actions because, again, these tendencies are obsessive and/or addictive. They just won't feel good about the actions and will burn out or revolt as time goes on.

---

[253] Charlie White. Mashable.com. "Money-Shredding Alarm Clock Is Completely Unforgiving [PICS]". 05/29/2011.

Gamification, Manipulation, and Ethics

During my conference talks, I regularly get questions from people who ask me whether gamification is a form of manipulation and therefore unethical to use. While there is no "correct" answer on this topic, and while the focus of this book is on effectively designing for behavioral change rather than ethics, I will attempt to share my own thoughts on the issue.

My quick answer: yes, gamification is a form of manipulation. However, even though "manipulation" is a strong word with immense negative connotations, we regularly accept it in our daily lives and even expect it.

If you think about it, saying "please" is a form of manipulation. You weren't going to do something for your friend, but your friend said "please" in a sincere manner (Core Drive 5), and even though nothing tangible has changed about the transaction, you now willingly and happily agree to do it for them.

That's *manipulation.*

And when your friend says, "Thank You," that's an emotional reward that makes you feel like the action was worth it. If your friend offered you payment (somehow paying someone to do the activity is one of the only ways that people don't complain as "manipulation" these days), you may even become offended.

And in our society, we don't seem to have a problem with people saying "please" and "thank you." In fact, we expect that, teach that, and get mad when people don't do it. It makes our brains happy and improves our quality of life. We enjoy that sort of manipulation.

When you want your employees to work harder and you transform the work to become a lot more interesting and engaging (as opposed to paying them more) – is that exploiting them? What about providing them a stronger sense of purpose, accomplishment or autonomy?

I have a litmus test to determine whether gamification or human-focused design is ethical or not:

a) Is there full transparency on its intended purpose?

b) Does the user implicitly or explicitly opt-in to the system?

If you have an extremely charismatic friend who is trying to persuade you to go to a party that you are not interested in, you may reject him with a smile. He will then pour in a lot more energy, saying something like, "Come on! Everyone's doing it! You got to show up!"

Even if you still didn't want to do it, you are starting to be persuaded. But in no way do you think your friend is being unethical in doing so. There is full transparency in what he is trying to get you to do. You also "opt-in" by allowing your friend to persuade you, especially when you turn him down with a smile. You may or may not change your mind, but because there is transparency in his intention and you've opted-in to his continued persuasion, you don't feel negatively manipulated.

However, I believe that gamification is completely unethical when there is a hidden agenda that users are not aware of. For example, when users think they are signing up for something, but in reality they are signing up for something else. False statements, lies, and a lack of authentic transparency create unethical interactions.

As a stunning example of whether transparent manipulation is bad, consider the field of hypnotism. Hypnosis can be considered the ultimate form of manipulation because, supposedly, once hypnotized, a person is fully compliant with whatever the hypnotizer wants them to do.

However, it is not generally considered unethical because a) there is transparency in what the hypnotizer is trying to accomplish, and b) the person fully opts-in to being hypnotized.

At the end of the day, gamification is not mind control. When we see amazing case studies where gamification increased conversions by 100%, it's often only where these metrics increased from 8% to 16%. A crushing 84% of the users can and still choose to not engage with the Desired Actions. If an action does not create emotional or physical value for someone, they still won't do it. But good gamification design motivates those who are on the fence - those who are interested with the end-results but need a bit more motivation to push through.

The people who don't want a service to begin with won't sign up (unless the marketing is being dishonest). Just as you don't have to agree with people who say "please" to you, nor do you have to finally consent to your charismatic friend who is persuading you to do things you hate. If you truly don't want to go to your friend's party, you still won't do it.

When to Use White Hat Gamification Design

Because of their natures, there are dominant strategies to determine when and how to use either White Hat or Black Hat gamification. Since employee motivation and workplace gamification are about long-term engagement, companies should use White Hat designs to make sure employees feel good, grow with the enterprise, and are there for the long haul.

Workplace gamification is often about the top three Core Drives in Octalysis: creating *meaning*, providing a path to mastery, and ensuring meaningful autonomy. You may identify these as components of Self Determination Theory[254] and the concepts within *Drive*[255], which we will cover in more detail in the next chapter.

Most large corporations make the mistake in believing that, because they pay their employees, their employees *have* to do their work

---

[254] SelfDeterminationTheory.org
[255] Daniel Pink. *Drive*. Penguin Group, New York, NY. 2009.

regardless of exploitive policies, unappreciative bosses, and bad workplace culture. As a result, employees only work hard enough to get a paycheck (Core Drive 4: Ownership & Possession) and not lose their jobs (Core Drive 8: Loss & Avoidance).

One company that challenged this trend is Google[256]. Very early on, Google started with the assumption that every one of their employees was either an entrepreneur, or wanted to be an entrepreneur. As a result, if these employees did not feel "happy" being at Google, they would simply leave and start their own businesses instead, maybe even becoming a Google competitor.

Remember I talked about how Gamification is Human-Focused Design and that games were the first to master it because no one *has* to play a game? When you design an experience with the underlying belief that, the moment your experience is no longer engaging, people will leave your system - you will likely create much better Human-Focused Designs.

In the case of Google, they implemented many White Hat designs into their company culture.

The first thing Google did was implement Core Drive 1: Epic Meaning & Calling. Google is widely known for having the mission statement, "Organizing the world's information and making it universally accessible and useful" as well as the catchy slogan, "Don't be evil." Because of that, many talented engineers felt that, "I could earn a paycheck anywhere, but at Google, I'm creating an impact in the world. Not only that, I'm part of the good guys, and that's really valuable for me!"

In regards to Core Drive 2: Development & Accomplishment, besides the usual raises and promotions, Google realizes that not every engineer can become a manager, but every engineer needs to feel a sense of progress and development. As a result, they introduced

---

[256]David Vise & Mark Malseed. *The Google Story*. P93-96. Random House, New York, New York. 2005.

eight levels of engineers so that engineers who either shouldn't or don't want to become managers can continue to "level up." In 2013, Google even introduced a ninth level titled "Senior Google Fellow," allegedly because they needed a way to give legendary engineer Jeff Dean a promotion[257].

In terms of Core Drive 3: Empowerment of Creativity & Feedback, we discussed in Chapter 7 how Google introduced 20% time, which allowed employees to spend 20% of their time to work on anything they wanted, as long as the intellectual property belonged to Google.

They also use some Core Drive 4: Ownership & Possession by allowing employees to take full ownership of their projects (and of course taking home nice paychecks too). They utilize Core Drive 5: Social Influence & Relatedness by creating a university-like campus and a workplace culture that makes laziness and stagnation highly undesirable and disparaged within their healthy social dynamics.

All these examples are White Hat influences that help their employees to be engaged in the long run. Unfortunately, there seems to be a weakening of Google's playful culture as Google becomes much larger and restructures their policies to be more like those of other large corporations that are more efficiently focused on profits.[258]

When to use Black Hat Gamification Design

On the other hand, when people are doing sales or running eCommerce sites, they often don't care about long-term engagement and motivation (though they probably should). All they want is for the customer to come in, buy something as quickly as possible, and then leave.

---

[257]Quora.com Entry: "What are the different levels of software engineers at Google and how does the promotion system work?"

[258]Patrick Goss. TechRadar.com. "Page: 'more wood behind fewer arrows' driving Google success". 7/14/2011.

As a result, they often involve Black Hat Gamification techniques: "What's going to be the surprise launch tomorrow? The chance to get this deal will expire in four hours. If you don't buy, you will end up being worse off than others!"

In an earlier chapter we looked at how Woot.com became an extremely successful eCommerce site based on two Core Drives: Scarcity & Impatience, as well as Unpredictability & Curiosity. Because Black Hat gamification creates urgency, when you need someone to take immediate action or a transaction, Black Hat techniques often become the most effective solutions.

This dynamic also holds true for sales and fundraising. One of my clients, Morf Media, provides a gamified training platform designed to make SEC compliance training more engaging and fun for employees of financial institutions[259].

By nature, financial institutions are risk-averse (Core Drive 8), and they are not inclined to work with new technology companies. You can give them a great deal of White Hat motivation, and they will be interested, intrigued, even excited, but they will likely take forever to make a move because there is no sense of urgency to take on any perceived risk.

The key here is to convince the company that, none of their employees like doing SEC compliance training (hardly a difficult sell), and *every single day* their employees' aren't compliant increases their risk. Lawsuits are literally laid out ahead like land mines. In that sense, it is riskier to *not* work with Morf Media than it is to work with them. We've turned that Black Hat Core Drive 8: Loss & Avoidance around. (Note: we will likely explore the strategy and process of turning Anti Core Drives around in a future book).

---

[259]Morf Media Website: morfmedia.com

Black Hat Motivation within Fundraising

In the realm of fundraising, I regularly get approached by startup entrepreneurs who are looking for some support to help them navigate fundraising from angel investors as well as venture capitalists (I also get approached by many investors, but on an entirely different set of motivational challenges - mostly White Hat).

The thing about investors is that they are generally motivated by the forces of greed and fear. The force of greed - the intense desire to make a billion dollars (Core Drives 2 and 4); the force of fear - the apprehension of losing all their money (Core Drive 8).

At the beginning, the entrepreneur may promote many great attributes about the company, appealing to the investor's sense of Core Drive 1, 2, 4 and even 5 if there is a good social proof. (Here you see the value of remembering the numbers for each Core Drive. Don't worry if you don't remember these numbers now, but just take note that they are mostly on the White Hat side of things.) The investor starts to show a lot of excitement, and the entrepreneur feels like the deal is sealed.

However, as the investor gets closer and closer to writing a check, the fear of losing all their money begins to preoccupy them, which is driven by Core Drive 8: Loss & Avoidance. They start to ask for more metrics, traction, and further social proof. Often, six months go by, and still no funding is committed.

From my personal experience, investors generally only close deals quickly when they are *convinced* that they will lose the deal if they don't commit. If an entrepreneur *convincingly* tells the investor that a lot of people are already in on the deal, and if the investor does not act this week the round will be full, only then will they finally react. Black Hat creates urgency and closes deals.

When I was trying to raise $600,000 for my gamification startup straight out of college[260], I found the experience to be extremely difficult and sobering. We were a very young team, and this "gamification" thing seemed like a half-baked crazy idea.

After struggling for awhile to raise a modest amount of money to keep our small team afloat, we were finally able to secure $650,000 from three investors. At that point, I wrote an email to all our potential investors, who for over a year continually "wanted to see more" and "weren't sure about this gamification thing." I simply told them, "We are going to close the round, but thank you for your continuous (and non-existent) support!"

At this point, many of these investors who didn't want to commit for an entire year suddenly responded with passion, enthusiasm, and even anger. "Yu-kai. I thought we agreed that I could invest this much money in your company. Why are you telling me that you are closing the round without me?" I was thinking, "Well, you kind of had an entire year to do that..." but they oddly made it seem like I was burning bridges if I didn't take their money.

As a result, we tried to cap the round at $800,000 instead of $600,000, and we couldn't do it. We tried to cap it at $900,000 and couldn't. We tried to cap it at $1,000,000 and we still couldn't. Finally, I capped the round at $1,050,000, while rejecting some investor money, just to show that we were serious about the cap. (I've also heard this same experience retold many times by other entrepreneurs.)

This illustrates the irrational power of Core Drive 6: Scarcity & Impatience as well as Core Drive 8: Loss & Avoidance (while also serving as a fine example of the limits of White Hat motivation). All these "potential investors" clearly liked what I was doing. They were encouraged whenever I gave them good news. They saw that it could potentially make the world a better place. But they didn't acted until they saw that the deal was being taken away from them.

---

[260] If you are curious about some gamification companies I started during my younger youth, I document that in the post, "How Yu-kai Chou started in Gamification in 2003 and became a Pioneer in the Industry": http://www.yukaichou.com/lifestyle-gamification/started-gamification-2003/

With White Hat motivation alone, people will always be intending, but never actually doing.

For the curious, eventually my startup launched RewardMe, a product that gamified the offline commerce experience. RewardMe was performing eleven times better than the numbers our closest competitors published. (Sorry - since these companies are still in existence, I won't cite sources here in respect to their current success.) Towards the end of my time there, we even closed a $1.5 million sales deal with a national chain.

Startups are risky, and the unfortunate thing is, just having a stunning product doesn't mean a company will be successful. A few years after RewardMe's launch, we hit a combination of personnel, funding, and legal issues. I stepped down as the CEO, and eventually the company folded. If only I had my Octalysis knowledge back then, many things would likely be different, which is why I am hoping my readers learn these elements on motivation before they run into issues in their own companies.

Fortunately, by stepping down as the CEO of RewardMe, it freed up a lot of my time to further study gamification, human-focused design, and develop the Octalysis Framework.

Today, even though my Octalysis Group organization is becoming busier and busier, I'm a lot happier than when I was running a technology startup. That's because I am now mostly motivated by White Hat Core Drives, as opposed to the Black Hat Core Drives of constantly counting our runway before dying[261].

---

[261] StartupDefinition.com Entry "Runway": *The amount of time until your startup goes out of business, assuming your current income and expenses stay constant. Typically calculated by dividing the current cash position by the current monthly burn rate.*

Bad Shifts from White Hat Design to Black Hat Design

When you switch from White Hat motivation to Black Hat Motivation, you need to make sure you understand the potential negative consequences. As an example, there was a day care center in Israel that had a problem with parents being late to pick up their kids. Researchers Uri Gneezy and Aldo Rustichini decided to conduct an experiment and implemented a test policy where parents would be charged $3 every time they were late[262].

Now a typical economist will tell you that this penalty would result in more parents picking up their kids on time because they don't want to lose money. However, the plan ended up backfiring - even more parents were now arriving late. Worse yet, when the daycare center realized this wasn't working and decided to remove the penalty fees, more parents *continued* to be late.

The plan backfired because they transitioned the parents' motivation from Core Drive 1: Epic Meaning & Calling (as well as Core Drive 5) to a weak form of Core Drive 8: Loss & Avoidance. Originally the parents tried to pick up their kids in a timely manner because they inherently wanted to be *good* and responsible parents. They also didn't want to burden the daycare center and its staff, so they tried earnestly to show up on time.

But when the daycare center put a monetary value on tardiness, it basically told parents that it was alright to be tardy as long as they paid the modest fee. Parents who were in business meetings or were preoccupied were therefore able to justify being late because a business meeting is worth more to them than the $3. Loss & Avoidance against leaving that meeting early was more powerful than Loss & Avoidance for losing $3.

Returning to the concept of proportional loss, we see that despite

---

[262]Uri Gneezy and Aldo Rustichini. *Journal of Legal Studies* Vol. 29, No. 1. "A Fine is a Price". 01/2000.

Loss and Avoidance typically being a powerful motivator, the $3 fee was just too low to properly motivate the parents in this situation. Remember I discussed about how when you use Loss & Avoidance, the loss needs to be threatening? If the daycare center charged a lot more than $3, the Loss & Avoidance motivation would become more threatening and more parents would likely comply (begrudgingly of course, which would lead to switching day-care centers soon).

Currently, there are some daycare centers that charge a $1 late fee for *every minute* the parent is late. This design actively gets parents to be on time more often. This is not only because the loss is more threatening, but also due to the parents feeling a combination of Core Drive 6: Scarcity & Impatience, as well as a bit of Core Drive 3: Empowerment of Creativity & Feedback since they feel a stronger sense of agency over end results.

Careful Transitioning between White Hat and Black Hat

So now that we've covered the nature and differences between White Hat and Black Hat gamification, how do we blend that knowledge together into our designed experiences?

In general (with some exceptions), it is better to first setup a White Hat environment to make users feel powerful and comfortable, then implement Black Hat designs at the moment when you need users to take that one Desired Action for conversion. At that point, users will likely take the Desired Action, but won't feel very comfortable. This is when you transition quickly back to White Hat motivation to make them feel good about their experience.

An example of this is seen in the previously mentioned game Battle Camp. In Battle Camp, there are often scenarios where you are in a "Troop" with twenty-four other players and the whole group needs to battle a big boss. Typically, you would have eight hours to fight this boss, where everyone needs to come back every fifty minutes when their energy is recharged (remember this technique is called a Torture Break), and then use that energy to attack the boss.

At times, after seven and a half hours, the will boss still have 20% of his health, and you begin to realize that your troop will not be able to defeat him. At this point, you basically have two options. Option one: you lose to the boss, and twenty-five players all waste eight hours of their time, not to mention falling behind other troops that will be ranked much higher after they defeat their boss. Option two: spend $10 and purchase more energy in order to beat the boss.

Because it is such a devastating event when everyone loses eight hours of their precious time, there is a fairly high chance that you will feel compelled to take option two - buy the energy needed to defeat the boss, especially if you were also the leader of the troop.

Now, we see that you were motivated by Core Drive 8: Loss & Avoidance when making this purchase – again, very compelling, but you feel fairly terrible afterwards. After you defeat the boss, if that was all and nothing special happened afterwards, you would feel pretty demoralized and perhaps subconsciously wished you weren't playing the game anymore.

However, this is when the game starts to shower you with White Hat Motivation by showing you how great of an achievement you accomplished (Core Drive 2: Development & Accomplishment), and the rewards or trophies you have obtained (Core Drive 4: Ownership & Possession) because you have beaten the boss. On top of that, your teammate will often start cheering for you (Core Drive 5: Social Influence & Relatedness), "Wow! You spent real money just to save our troop. You are our hero!" Being sprinkled by all this emotional confetti, people often start to think, "Hmm, maybe that was $10 well spent after all!" And this eventually trains their brains to be more open to spending the next $10 to buy energy and defeating the boss when necessary.

No Buyer's Remorse from TOMS

Similar to the Battle Camp example, businesses should consider creating an environment of White Hat motivations, use Black Hat techniques to convert users, and then revert back to a White Hat strategy to make users feel more comfortable again.

The initial White Hat environment is for people to take interest and have a good opinion of your system in the first place. A venture capitalist wouldn't want to invest in a startup if he didn't first consider it world-changing and a smart investment (Core Drives 1 and 2), even if there was convincing apprehension that he may lose the deal. (Oddly enough, some investors still plunge under the pressure of Scarcity and Loss, even though they have previously determined it to be a worthless idea with no future).

Once people feel comfortable in your system but aren't necessarily taking the strong Desired Action, such as making a purchase, you can then use the Black Hat techniques within Core Drives 6 and 8 (and sometimes Core Drive 5), to close the deal. If the user ends up buying the product, you want to reassure them that, if true, this is indeed the smartest purchase possible (Core Drive 2), that legions of others also made the same decision (Core Drive 5), and that it positively improves the world (Core Drive 1). This will likely ensure that customers don't feel buyer's remorse.

When you buy a pair of TOMS Shoes and begin to feel a little regret for making an expensive purchase, they hit you with reaffirming information on how your purchase has made a tremendous difference to a poor child in Africa - one who couldn't afford a pair of shoes and had to walk barefoot to fetch water for her family. When you see that, you instantly feel good again about your purchase. Subsequently, whenever you see your shoes, it will remind you that you are a decent human being that benefits the world.

It is the same thing with donations to children in developing countries. When you make a commitment, the non-profit will continuously send you pictures, thank-you letters, sometimes even something written by the "adopted" child to make you feel that you have truly made an impact in their lives. Of course, there is nothing wrong with sending donors these pictures and letters for such a noble cause (unless they are falsely manufactured) as these donors are truly making a big difference in the lives of the less fortunate. In fact, it would be a mistake for any charitable organization to *not* show visual and social information on the impact they are making in the world. We would all like to see some Feedback Mechanics after taking Desired Actions.

As you design your experiences, never forget that if you want good Endgame design, you *must* immerse your users in White Hat Gamification techniques.

What about Core Drives 4 and 5?

You may have noticed that I mentioned Core Drive 4: Ownership & Possession and Core Drive 5: Social Influence & Relatedness a few times in this chapter (in a White Hat context), and may wonder where they fit into all of this. They are in the middle of the Octalysis model, so are they Black Hat or White Hat?

Generally speaking, Core Drive 4 and Core Drive 5 have the duality of being able to be either White Hat or Black Hat. Often with Core Drive 4: Ownership & Possession, owning things make us feel like we are in control, that things are organized, and our general well-being is improving. We feel powerful and enriched.

However, sometimes the stuff we own start to own us instead. You can imagine a person who buys an extremely rare vintage car, and then becomes afraid of taking it anywhere because he is afraid to damage it or rack up miles. At the same time, he also doesn't want to leave it at home because he's afraid it might get stolen.

There are also people who are so obsessed about building more wealth that they neglect everything else that matters, such as family, health, and friendships. Then there are people who compulsively need to organize things to the point where they can't really focus on more important things that would bring them happiness. At that point, Black Hat starts to take over and the individual no longer feels good about their behavior, but simply does it because they feel compelled to do it.

On the other hand, for Core Drive 5: Social Influence & Relatedness, we obviously enjoy and have fun when hanging out with our friends, building strong friendships, and expressing appreciation for each other. Even if we are making friends to network and build our careers (which adds certain Left Brain Core Drives such as Core Drive 2: Development & Accomplishment as well as Core Drive 4: Ownership & Possession), we feel pretty positive about the experience.

However, sometimes peer pressure can cause some of the worst moments in our lives. When we feel pressured by our environment to behave in certain ways or get into fights with our loved ones, it starts to drive us crazy in a way that few other things can.

In fact, from time to time, social pressure is so strong that people end up committing suicide simply because they cannot endure the judgment of others. For these people, choosing to end their own lives is easier than confronting the situation, even when it is something as trivial as being afraid to go home and tell parents about a failed test. You can clearly see the Black Hat influences that can arise from Core Drive 5.

At the end of the day, each of the Core Drives wields a tremendous amount of power, and a designer must think carefully about designing for ethical purposes - to make sure there is full transparency towards the Desired Behavior, matched with the users' freedom to opt in and out. If this is not carefully done, gamification design will fail the promise of making life more enjoyable and productive, and it would simply become a source of misery and bitterness - and then likely dropped altogether. No one wants that.

The cliché phrase is that, "with great power comes great responsibility." When you understand how to motivate and change behavior, you can improve the world by helping others achieve *their* life, career, fitness, and relationship goals. Conversely, you can wield this knowledge to get people more addicted to harmful substances, create bad habits, and perpetuate broken relationships[263]. Ultimately, when your experience design becomes extremely successful, you must look in the mirror and ask yourself, "Is this the impact I want to have in the world?"

To get the most out of the book, Choose only ONE of the below options to do right now:

Easy: Try to recite the three White Hat Core Drives and the three Black Hat Core Drives without looking at them. Are you able to explain their differences?

Medium: Think back on your own life and all the major decisions that you made: applying for schools, changing jobs, finding a significant other, moving to new locations. What Core Drives motivated you to make those decisions? Are they mostly for White Hat reasons, or Black Hat? Are you happier with the decisions that you made from White Hat Core Drives? Do you feel less comfortable with decisions that were driven by Black Hat Core Drives, but feel like you had little choice when the decision were made?

---

[263] I myself was once approached by one of the world's largest tobacco and beer conglomerates to run a few workshops with them. After discussing with my team, we decided that even though it would be a fairly lucrative relationship - if we were extremely successful at our jobs and more people became addicted to tobacco and alcohol, that wouldn't be the impact we wanted to have in this world. We ended up turning that particular project down. Of course, we were also only able to do that because we were blessed with many great clients that more directly benefits society so we didn't need to be driven by Core Drive 8: Loss & Avoidance.

Hard: Think of a campaign that you can design for your own project. Try to come up with ways to use White Hat Gamification to create motivation and desire, then switch to Black Hat Gamification to trigger important Desired Actions. Finally, understand how to transition user motivation back to White Hat Core Drives so they enjoy the experience fully and feel emotionally rewarded after committing the Desired Actions.

Share what you come up with on Twitter or your preferred social network with the hashtag #OctalysisBook and check out what ideas other people have.

Share your Life reflections.

If you picked the Medium Challenge above, share your life paths and choices as part of a self introduction to the Octalysis Explorers Facebook Group. Identify the Core Drives that motivated you along the way, and reflect on how you felt during those life choices. That way the community will get to know you better as well as learn a bit more about the 8 Core Drives through your experiences.

As you know, a community makes an experience engaging and fun, and it will make all the time you have invested into this book more fulfilling. Chances are, there will be others in the group that will also have similar life experiences and choices as you and can help you understand your life motivations more through the 8 Core Drives.

Chapter 15: Understanding Other Gamification and Behavioral Frameworks with Octalysis

Up to this point we have covered almost everything there is to learn in Level I Octalysis design. My goal for the book is to go deep on one methodology and framework (namely my own), and then once competency of that one framework is achieved, use it to understand other frameworks.

In 2012, when I attended the annual GSummit[264], the largest gamification conference in the world, I was thoroughly impressed by the ensemble of knowledgeable panelists and speakers. However, I imagined that the average attendee could be flustered by all of the various talks and frameworks presented at the conference - from Richard Bartles' *Four Player Types*, Mihayi Chiksenmihayi's *Flow Theory*, Nicole Lazzarro's *4Keys2Fun*, and a plethora of others!

At the end of the day, while the attendee feels pumped and inspired about the world-changing potential of gamification, they may still feel confused about what to do next. All these frameworks, when pieced together, seem to communicate an abstract knowledge about the brain. But the question of how we connect them together in a way that holistically reflects our minds is difficult to answer. It becomes even more challenging when one needs to determine which framework to use for various projects.

Because of this, I wanted to make sure that my readers have a deep understanding of my own model instead of a shallow knowledge

---

[264]GSummit Website: http://sf14.gsummit.com

of different concepts. However, I do not want my readers to be ignorant of other prominent gamification theories and key models in motivational psychology and behavioral economics, which are all great in their own rights. So in this chapter we will discuss these concepts and examine them using our "Octalysis Glasses."

One of the things I enjoy about the Octalysis Framework is that it helps me understand other experts' work better by putting their research and findings into perspective. As we all have the same brain, I believe that various studies on the brain and motivation can converge with each other to provide a richer understanding.

Hopefully your understanding of Octalysis will help you comprehend these other frameworks quickly. Of course, there are many excellent books that are highly recommended, if you're keen on diving deeper into those other frameworks.

Scientific Research and Game Studies

Every once in a while, someone asks me whether my Octalysis Framework was created based on a deep study of all the texts and scientific studies I've mentioned in this book.

In truth, Octalysis was 100% derived from my experience and study of games. I wish there was a more impressive origin, but in reality everything I needed to create the Octalysis Framework was found in my many years of playing and analyzing games. This is why I consider it a Gamification Framework, and not just mere psychological and behavioral studies that are independent of games, as viewed by others.

Once the Framework was created, I began to research behavioral economics, motivational psychology, and neurobiology to confirm (or extend) the principles behind the Core Drives. I knew that these Core Drives motivated us, but I didn't have scientific publications to back it up until much later. Luckily for me, most people who hear about my work on Octalysis can relate back to their own personal experiences and observations. This prompted them to give me the benefit of the doubt before I could scientifically prove *why* it works. A Core Drive 5 victory on *relatedness*.

On this point, let me explain why I believe studying games is legitimate enough to obtain a full grasp of motivational theories and behavioral predictions - feel free to disagree with me; I won't be offended.

As repeated in previous chapters, an important aspect of games is that you never *have* to play them. Again, you *have* to go to work and you *have* to do your taxes. They can be awfully dreadful but you still just have to grind through them. I call this "tainted motivation."

But with games, no one *has* to play them[265]. The moment a game is no longer fun, people leave it to do or play something else.

In a sense every game can be considered an experiment in motivation and behavior.

We receive most of our understanding of behavioral psychology from experiments where participants (often fifty to two hundred undergraduate students) are placed in controlled environments and tested for their reactions based on certain variables. The result of these peer-reviewed experiments become legitimate scientific research that gives us insight into the human mind.

On the other hand, every game can be thought of as a Petri dish where hundreds of thousands (if not hundreds of millions) of "test subjects" voluntarily modify their behaviors based on changes in the environment. These mass "experiments" naturally show us how certain experiences and mechanics are effective or ineffective at impacting human behavior.

One of the things I like to do is study "clones" of games in order to understand why some clones are flops while others become

---

[265] Much of my work can be understood through the differences between *can, have to, want to, compelled to, inspired to,* and *excited to* when it comes to Desired Actions.

more successful than the original. When two games look almost identical, but one (sometimes the less attractive one) becomes a breakout success while the other becomes a failure, it creates a great opportunity to study the subtle elements within the design that make a big difference. Sometimes the differences are as small as how many seconds pass before a message pops up, the order of challenges are introduced, or how well scarcity is controlled in the economy.

From my own research, these subtle differences are not well covered in gamification or even game design literature. But I have found them to be among the most important for the success of an experience - beyond graphics, animation, or even theme. At the end of the day, it is not whether they have certain game elements (theme, group quests, badges, power-ups), but whether those certain game elements are designed in a way that bring out our Core Drives.

Now, the challenge is that between two "similar" games there is never just one variable of difference. Often there are hundreds or even thousands of differences between games. As such, it requires a substantial amount of time and pattern recognition effort/analysis to identify the behavioral impact of each element to the point that it can be predicted and replicated.

This requires studying scores of games and years of serious observation before patterns can be easily recognized and predictions can be made on how behavior changes when game elements shift. You also need to go beyond the superficial changes to find what truly drives user behavior. This means digging into the experience and ultimately immersing yourself in those games to feel the forces of motivation first hand - which I must admit, consumed many joyful and some agonizing hours of my life.

One of the things I like to do when playing financially successful games is to try and play them as seriously as I can while purposely resisting the pressure from the game design to spend money. There were many moments where I had an extremely strong urge to spend a few dollars just to save my time, save my troop, get through frustration, or eliminate some unpredictability.

And so I pay special attention to those moments in a game when I clearly feel a powerful compulsion to spend money in order to solve my problems (as well as boost my happy brain chemicals such as dopamine, endorphins, and oxytocin[266])!

From these years of study I derived the 8 Core Drives and the accompanying concepts of White Hat/Black Hat and Left Brain/Right Brain Core Drives to demonstrate and reflect the tendencies and trends I've seen in games.

Later on I realized that each Core Drive had dozens of books dedicated to it and so I started reading more to understand their nature better.

Remember earlier we talked about how games are a combination of behavioral economics, motivational psychology, neurobiology, UX/UI (User Experience/User Interface) design, technology platforms, and the obvious game design dynamics? Again, you need all these elements to create a great game.

---

[266]Thai Nguyen. *Huffingtonpost.com*. "Hacking Into Your Happy Chemicals: Dopamine, Serotonin, Endorphins and Oxytocin". 10/20/2014.

In this chapter, we will see how Octalysis applies to a variety of behavioral psychology and game design theories. For those newly learning about gamification or behavioral design, this chapter may feel a bit advanced. Don't worry if you don't remember or understand all the other frameworks. If you ever stumble upon them again in future settings, this chapter would have prepared you to digest them in a most holistic manner.

Octalysis View of Self-Determination Theory

Up to this point we have mentioned Ryan and Deci's Self-Determination Theory several times. The Self-Determination Theory is a theory on motivation to understand our natural or intrinsic tendencies to behave in effective and healthy ways[267]. The theory demonstrates

---

[267] Self Determination Theory Website: selfdeterminationtheory.org

that people are not motivated purely through rewards and punishment, but are actually motivated more through three elements:
Competence, Relatedness, and *Autonomy*.

Competence is the need to feel self-efficacy and experience mastery.
Autonomy is the urge to be causal agents of one's own life and
control one's own choices. *Relatedness* is the universal want to
interact, be connected to, and experience caring for others.

Three Innate Psychological Needs Comprise The Self-Determination Theory of Student Motivation

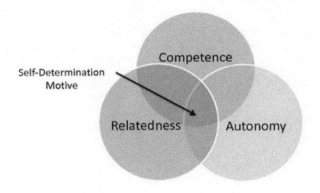

Source: Deci, E.L., & Ryan, R.M. (2000). The "What" and "Why" of goal pursuits: Human needs and the self-
determination of behaviour. *Psychological Inquiry, 11,* 227-268.

268

If you look at the theory from an Octalysis perspective, you will
notice that Competence is in line with Core Drive 2: Development
& Accomplishment. Following the same line of thought, Autonomy
lends itself to Core Drive 3: Empowerment of Creativity and Feedback, while Relatedness naturally falls within Core Drive 5: Social
Influence and Relatedness.

---

[268]Image Source: Edward L. Deci and Richard M. Ryan. *Psychological Inquiry, Vol. 11,
No. 4, 227–268*. "The "What" and "Why" of Goal Pursuits: Human Needs and the Self-
Determination of Behavior". 2000.

In the book *Drive*, Daniel Pink demonstrates a fourth component to this theory, which is *Purpose*. (He also re-terms Competence with the more appealing expression - Mastery[269].) Again, with our Octalysis Glasses on, Purpose can be seen as directly connecting to Core Drive 1: Epic Meaning & Calling

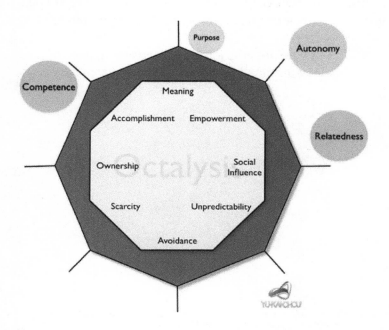

The diagram above illustrates which Core Drives the Self-Determination Theory corresponds to in a graphical way. What becomes very clear in the diagram is that these elements are also considered White Hat Core Drives. By focusing on *Relatedness*, the Self-Determination Theory also incorporates Right Brain (Intrinsic) Motivation through Core Drive 5: Social Influence & Relatedness.

The Self-Determination Theory is a very good model that recognizes the power behind positive, White Hat, and intrinsic motivation.

---

[269]Daniel Pink. *Drive*. P107-128. Penguin Group, New York, NY. 2009.

However, it does not necessarily explain why people are addicted to gambling or why exclusivity itself often drives our behaviors. Though the theory covers all the positive emotions within motivation, it does not include the "dark side" of behavior, which is demonstrated in the form of the Black Hat Core Drives (which are generally considered "non self-determined" motivations[270]).

This actually makes a lot of sense, given that the Self-Determination Theory focuses on motivating employees and students, especially towards creative work. For this purpose, the theory is a powerful framework to help guide companies towards creating long-term White Hat motivational environments for their workers.

We learned from the Chapter 14 that since employee motivation requires long-term engagement, we should generally apply White Hat Core drives to its design. That said, there are some Black Hat motivational techniques that companies also use to motivate their employees towards short-term productivity bursts (e.g. scarcity of opportunities, deadlines, social pressure, competition). The Self-Determination Theory does not focus on these, as this type of motivation could lead to long-term burnout if applied incorrectly.

With that said, a framework like Octalysis allows you to put the Self-Determination Theory into broader perspective and understand what it covers and what it doesn't cover in order to expand and fine-tune your understanding of human behavior.

Richard Bartle's Four Player Types

Another very well known study in the realm of game design is Richard Bartle's Four Player Types[271]. Richard Bartle is a game

[270]Yves Chantal and Robert J. Vallerand. *Journal of Gambling Studies. Volume 12, Issue 4, Pages 407-418*. "Skill versus luck: A motivational analysis of gambling involvement". Winter 1996.

[271]Richard Bartle. *Mud.co.uk*. "Hearts, Clubs, Diamonds, Spades: Players who suit MUDS". April 1996.

researcher who invented the first MUD (Multi-User Dungeon) game during the 1970's, which evolved into the role-playing games (RPGs) we know today. He realized that within a virtual environment there tends to be four main groups of players doing four distinct types of activities.

There are the *Achievers* who try to master everything there is to do within the game system. There are the *Explorers* that just want to go out and explore all the content in the world but aren't as focused on overcoming challenges. There are the *Socializers* who are really in the virtual world just to interact with each other, have conversations, and build companionship. And then there are the Killers - players that not only strive to reach the top, but take glory in beating down the competition in the process. Furthermore, they need to bask in their victories and be admired by all.

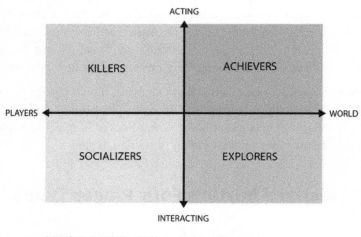

Richard Bartle, *Designing Virtual Worlds*

272

Many people who work in gamification as well as game design build on Richard Bartle's Four Player types. Game designer Amy Jo Kim

---

[272] Image accessed from Gamasutra.com. "Designing Computer-Games Preemptively for Emotions and Player Types." 06/19/13.

is known to use Richard Bartle's Player Types, evolving them into Kim's Social Action Matrix[273]. In this model, Kim assigns verbs and actions to various Player Types to determine how to design a fun and engaging environment within games. Those action verbs became: *Explore, Create, Compete*, and *Collaborate*. (Try to see how those action verbs correspond to various Core Drives.)

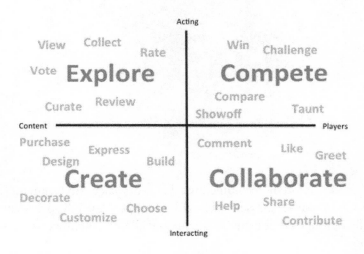

274

Andrzej Marczewski is also an influencer in the gamification field who has done extensive research to build upon Richard Bartle's Player Types for the enterprise workplace. He has derived six User Types to design for: Disruptors, Philanthropists, Free Spirits, Socializers, Achievers, and Players[275]. Each of these User Types are more motivated by different activities and experiences.

---

[273] Amy Jo Kim. AmyJoKim.com. "Beyond Player Types: Kim's Social Action Matrix". 02/28/2014.

[274] Ibid.

[275] Andrzej Marczewski. Gamified.uk. "User Types". Accessed 2/17/2015.

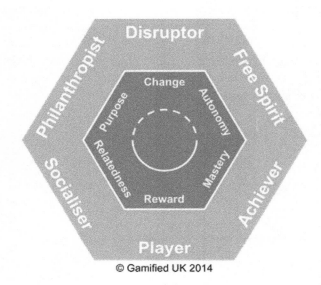

© Gamified UK 2014

276

This model is often recommended for workplace environments, as Richard Bartle himself has said that his Player Types may not be appropriate for environments outside of voluntary virtual worlds[277].

For simplicity's sake, let's take an Octalysis look at Richard Bartle's Four Player Types to understand what Core Drives motivate each player type. This will help you determine how to better design for these player types.

Achievers are driven heavily by Core Drive 2: Development and Accomplishment as well as Core Drive 6: Scarcity and Impatience. They're always trying to complete their next goal, which makes them feel accomplished when they do. Of course, to some extent they also care about using their creativity to overcome challenges, as well as accumulating the results of their success (Core Drives 3

---

[276]Andrzej Marczewski. Gamified.uk. "User Types". Accessed 2/17/2015.

[277]Youtube Video: "GSummit SF 2012: Richard Bartle - A Game Designer's View of Gamification". 9/27/2012.

and 4).

Explorers are dominantly motivated by Core Drive 7: Unpredictability & Curiosity, which drives them to discover novel content that they haven't seen before. There are also seeds of Core Drive 2, 3, and 6. They continuously use their creativity to find new ways to test every boundary that constrains them, and when they succeed, they are fulfilled by a sense of accomplishment.

Socializers are primarily motivated by Core Drive 5: Social Influence and Relatedness. They like to mingle with others and bond. To a smaller extent, they are also driven to think up clever ways to engage others more (Core Drive 3), they enjoy new or unpredictable information or even gossip (Core Drive 7), and sometimes becomes territorial with their friends (Core Drive 4).

Finally, *Killers* are primarily motivated by a mix of Core Drive 2: Development & Accomplishment and Core Drive 5: Social Influence of Relatedness. They not only need to strive for high goals, but they need others to recognize their accomplishments and acknowledge their superiority. In a smaller sense, they are also driven to come up with the best way to defeat the competition (Core Drive 3), avoid being killed or seen as weak themselves (Core Drive 8), and ultimately, to count their wins and victories (Core Drive 4).

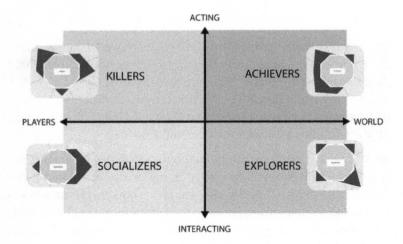

With the chart above, we can better understand what uniquely motivates these player types and can design appropriate Game Techniques for them. Later in your Octalysis journey, you will begin to invest a significant amount of effort in defining your own Player Types and designing systems that uniquely appeal to them with Level 3 Octalysis. (Unfortunately, we won't be able to cover that within the scope of this book.)

So what about the other Core Drives that are not covered above, namely Epic Meaning & Calling, and to some extent Loss & Avoidance?

Core Drive 1: Epic Meaning & Calling can be utilized by any of the Player Types: to achieve their goals of reaching a higher target, becoming more respected by their friends, exploring new areas, as well as defeating weaker players.

It is simply the context to be in the game environment in the first place. But since Richard Bartle was creating an open virtual world, there doesn't seem to be any real sense of higher missions beyond virtual world idealism.

Sometimes a smaller sense of Epic Meaning & Calling is created when users within a virtual world band together for a higher mission that they believe in. But this is independent of the player types studied here.

In Andrzej Marczewski's model, there is a unique user type within the workplace called *Philanthropists*, which are individuals who derive joy, hence play, from helping others. They are motivated by Core Drive 1: Epic Meaning & Calling, and companies should encourage behavior from Philanthropists to ensure more collaborative efforts and stronger teamwork. Unfortunately, most company environments punish Philanthropists while rewarding those who are exclusively going after their own extrinsic rewards. These *Players* in Andrzej Marczewski's model, are highly motivated by Core Drive 4: Ownership & Possession, where the aim is to maximize their bonuses, rewards, promotions, and pay raises.

In terms of Core Drive 8: Loss & Avoidance, there are always threats for not succeeding in any endeavor. Especially, as mentioned earlier, when *Killers* try to avoid being humiliated. However, there is no real player type that focuses on avoiding bad things. As we have learned, if you are only motivated by Black Hat Drives, you will not want to be in an open and voluntarily virtual world in the first place. That's often a different story for the workplace.

At the end of the day, these eight Core Drives motivate all of us to some extent, as we universally crave these Core Drives in different measures at different times. The Octalysis Framework allows us to understand whether certain Core Drives are stronger with certain people, so that we can be aware and design for these differences appropriately.

Nicole Lazzaro's 4 Keys To Fun

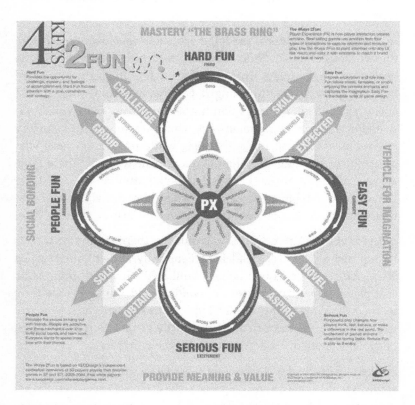

The *4 Keys to Fun* is another design framework created by game designer and President of XEODesign Nicole Lazzaro[278]. Lazzaro spent many years researching and designing engaging games. Based on her experience, she has derived four types of fun that engage people within games.

The 4 Keys to Fun are: *Hard Fun, Easy Fun, People Fun*, and *Serious Fun*.

---

[278]Nicole Lazzaro. XEO Design. "Why We Play Games: Four Keys to More Emotion Without Story" 03/08/2004.

Hard Fun is joy that is derived from overcoming a frustration and achieving the Win-State. This puts players in a state of *Fiero*, the feeling of triumph over adversity.

Easy Fun is the fun from doing interesting activities where you don't need to try very hard and can simply enjoy the relaxing and playful experience. This is commonly seen in games children enjoy with their parents, such as board games or drawing.

Serious Fun is fun that is engaging because it makes real world differences such as improving oneself, making more money or creating an impact in the environment.

Lastly, People Fun is fun that you have because you are interacting with other people and forming relationships.

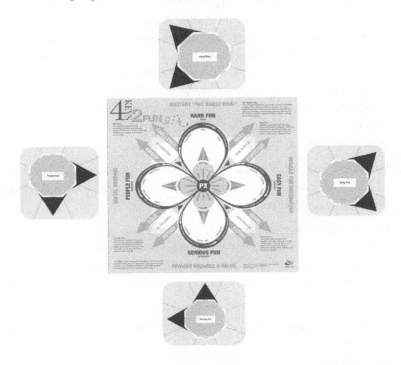

If you again try to understand this with your Octalysis Glasses on, you will see that *Hard Fun* is a combination of Core Drive 2: Development & Accomplishment, as well as Core Drive 6: Scarcity & Impatience – the difficulty and frustration of reaching the Win-State is what drive user motivation as well as the sense of achievement after accomplishing it.

Easy Fun is like a combination of Core Drive 3: Empowerment of Creativity & Feedback as well as Core Drive 7: Unpredictability and Curiosity. It's like playing with clay or Legos where you can do anything you want and can't really lose. Whatever you do you are winning because you are enjoying your time and seeing feedback from your creativity.

Situations with inherent randomness also inspire curiosity and make things fun and easy. Playing games like Yahtzee or watching a cartoon makes us enjoy our time without really needing to put in a lot of effort and focus. In fact, in the game design industry it is known that one of the best ways to make a game easier (penalizing hardcore competitive players but benefitting mainstream casual players) is to add more randomness and chance to the game[279]. A father can play a dice game seriously with his five year old daughter without always winning, but he likely needs to go easy on her if he is playing chess against her.

On the other hand, *Serious Fun* can be interpreted as a combination of Core Drive 1: Epic Meaning and Calling as well as Core Drive 4: Ownership and Possession.

Epic Meaning & Calling is derived when one is engaged with an activity because they see its real impact in the world. In the case of activities that are exhilarating because they make you money every time you engage them, it is the result of Core Drive 4: Ownership & Possession.

People Fun is generally a combination of the obvious Core Drive

---

[279] Jesse Schell. *The Art of Game Design: A Book of Lenses.* P183-184. CRC Press. Boca Raton. 2008.

5: Social Influence & Relatedness and to some extent Core Drive 8: Loss & Avoidance.

This is because when you are collaborating with people, you are under a bit more stress while you are trying to avoid looking bad, saying the wrong things, being shunned, or losing your position on a leaderboard. Fun competition also extends out of *People Fun*, and the thrill of *hide-and-seek* or *catch* is often derived from a moderate level of Core Drive 8: Loss & Avoidance.

Of course, I was motivated by a sense of "completeness" (Core Drive 4) to match up all 8 Core Drives with each type of fun corresponding to the 4 Keys To Fun model. If you feel that Core Drive 8: Loss & Avoidance isn't unique to People Fun, I am willing to accept that as well.

Mihaly Csikszentmihalyi's Flow Theory

I think it is a good time to move on to Mihaly Csikszentmihalyi's *Flow Theory*. Csikszentmihalyi is a world-renowned scholar in the fields of psychology and management science, and is best known for creating the *Flow Theory* which combines the factors of a user's skill level to the difficulty of the challenge.

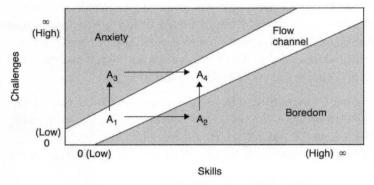

The Flow. After Mihaly Csikszentmihalyi, *The Flow (1990)*, p. 74

The *Flow* theory illustrates that when the difficulty of a challenge is too high compared to a user's skill level, the result is a sense of anxiety which may compel the user to drop out quickly. Similarly, if the user's skill level is dramatically higher than the difficulty of the challenge, the user will feel bored and may also drop out.

Only when the user's skill level is balanced with the difficulty of the challenge, do they enter the state known as *Flow*. During *Flow*, users become completely focused. They "zone in" on their activities, loosing their sense of self, as well as loosing track of time. This is a moment of euphoria, excitement, and engagement.

The tricky thing here is that, more often than not, the player's skill level increases as time goes by. If the designer gives the exact same experience throughout the 4 Experience Phases (Discovery, Onboarding, Scaffolding, Endgame) the user quickly ends up being bored because they've outpaced the difficulty level.

Even though the *Flow* theory by nature feels a bit different from the other models we've discussed, as it is less focused on classifying types, we can still use Octalysis to comprehend what's going on.

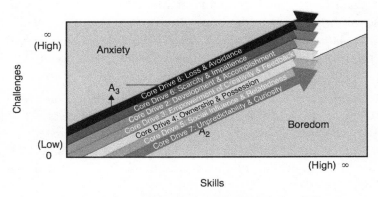

The Flow. After Mihaly Csikszentmihalyi, *The Flow (1990)*, p. 74

As you can see here, the zone at the top of the Flow is where the challenge is much more difficult than the player can handle. This is driven by a feeling of Core Drive 8: Loss & Avoidance, where users are really just struggling to survive. As we already know, this puts people in a state of extreme anxiety.

Now if you slightly decrease the difficulty relative to the user's skill level, we now enter the zone of Core Drive 6: Scarcity & Impatience. At this point the user feels challenged and occasionally frustrated. However, there is always a chance for them to overcome the challenge and achieve the Win-State, as long as they take action quickly and surpass a Moat (Game Technique #67) through skill or planning.

Right below Core Drive 6 we have Core Drive 2: Development & Accomplishment. This is the zone where the challenge is moderate and the user feels accomplished and competent. The user is in the

Flow and they feel like they are achieving their goals and building their confidence.

A little further down we have Core Drive 3: Empowerment of Creative & Feedback. This is at the heart of Flow where users are again tapping their creativity and adjusting their strategy to discover better ways to do things. This process puts many people in the state of Flow, especially when it rotates quickly between Core Drive 3 and Core Drive 2 - when their creativity lead to accomplishments.

Moving down one level from Core Drive 3, you have Core Drive 4: Ownership & Possession, which is often the mindless act of collecting things, organizing things, and putting things together - what you often do in Farmville-like games. This is usually a lot easier in terms of difficulty, relative to the user skill set and will relax the mind.

Most of the time to fulfill the Ownership & Possession Core Drive, all the user needs to do is to spend more time on it, to take actions based on moderate planning, or to organize their systems. There is no sense of anxiety. If not designed properly, this sometimes even creates boredom. Think about employees who do data entry work just for a paycheck; the task is not very difficult, but there isn't a strong level of engagement either.

Below Core Drive 4 is Core Drive 5: Social Influence & Relatedness. This is basically like going to a chat room. You don't need too much skill, you just say whatever you want to express yourself, and you can even troll others. This is often seen in the Water Cooler game technique we discussed in Chapter 9. The activity could still be quite fun, but it is mostly very easy. Even if you don't see feedback from your witty comments (Core Drive 3) and impress others (Core Drive 2) the feeling of relatedness, acceptance, and bonding with others will make the experience pleasant and relaxing.

If you look another level down, you could say that Core Drive 7: Unpredictability & Curiosity is at the lowest level of *Flow*. We mentioned earlier that adding chance and randomness is a good way to make a game easier. Most gambling games, sweepstakes, and lotteries don't require any amount of skill. You basically participate, take the Desired Action, and wait for the results. That's also why playing games that involve randomness like *Risk* or *Monopoly* (including the Chance Cards) often produce more laughter than pure skill-based games such as Chess.

Now you could argue that people engaged by Core Drive 7: Unpredictability & Curiosity are not really in a state of "boredom," especially if they're watching a movie or trying to finish a book. However, when you look at it from the perspective of skill versus challenge (the *Flow* chart), the user is not enjoying the activity because of skill usage. They are instead, entertained in a different way that drives pleasure.

In one of Csikszentmihalyi's charts, as seen below, he includes a state of "relaxation" as a result of having skills that greatly surpass the challenge. Core Drive 7 then does not result in boredom but rather appropriate relaxation.

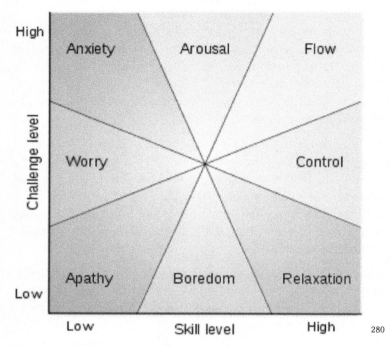

You can see here that within the *Flow* model, the only Core Drive that is missing is Core Drive 1: Epic Meaning & Calling. That's because Core Drive 1 is completely out of the context of player skill level compared to challenge difficulty, as those two factors are irrelevant when it comes to committing to something that is bigger than oneself. Core Drive 1 does not really fit into the *Flow* model but powers the reason why people may engage with any experience in the first place.

Fogg Behavior Model

BJ Fogg, a professor of human behavior from Stanford, created a model that boils down all behavior into three factors: *motivation,*

[280]Image from Wikipedia: http://en.wikipedia.org/wiki/File:Challenge_vs_skill.svg

ability, and a *trigger*[281].

Motivation is how much the individual wants to take the action or obtain the desired outcome. *Ability* is how equipped the individual is in taking that action; in other words, how easy or convenient it is for the user to perform the action. The third factor is a *Trigger*, or something that reminds the user to take action.

Fogg proposes that every action you take is a result of these three components coming together. If any one of them is absent, there can be no action.

He is an evangelist of what he calls "Tiny Habits." For instance, Fogg explained a system where every time he goes to urinate, he does two push-ups before washing his hands. Urinating is the trigger, and since doing two push-ups is so easy, you don't need a lot of motivation to do it.[282]

In this system, setting the goal at two push-ups instead of something more ambitious like eight or ten is very important. If you set your goal at ten, then at one point your brain will likely think, "I'm kind of busy or tired. I'm just going to skip this one time," which will then lead to another occurrence of skipping soon after. This weakens self-confidence and ensures that a positive habit does not form.

But when you design the goal to be two push-ups and you actually do them, you feel a sense of accomplishment (Core Drive 2), which builds up your confidence and allows you to eventually build a stronger habit.

In general, I like Fogg's Behavioral Model and often reflect on it within my own studies. The one area I differ with him on is his claim that the motivation piece is very difficult and unpredictable, and that companies or individuals shouldn't start with improving motivation. His conclusion calls for companies to focus on making

---

[281]Fogg Behavior Model Website: behaviormodel.org

[282]Youtube Video: "Forget big change, start with a tiny habit: BJ Fogg at TEDxFremont". 12/05/2012.

sure the activity is extremely easy and that there is an appropriate trigger to do it.

From this viewpoint, Octalysis puts a much stronger emphasis on the *motivation piece*. As Fogg expresses in his own model, when there is no motivation, it doesn't matter how easy the task is, people won't do it.

We saw from earlier chapters that if we adjust the difficulty with Octalysis design campaigns, it is primarily because we either want users to feel smart and competent (Core Drive 2), or we want to make users sense that the opportunity is exclusive and difficult to obtain (Core Drive 6). In whatever way you adjust the experience, Octalysis brings the focus back to motivation. Games don't necessarily make things easy - they make things motivating and engaging. In fact, one of the most respected definitions of a *game* is "the voluntary attempt to overcome unnecessary obstacles"[283]

Fogg himself says that, as you accomplish your tiny habits, your motivation increases because you feel accomplished, which, in turn, becomes a positive cycle that builds on itself. Eventually doing more push-ups feels easier and you don't require as much motivation to maintain that higher level of activity. This line of thinking is aligned with our understanding of Core Drive 2.

Fogg supports his strategy to focus on *Ability* by saying that, instead of "motivating" people to do what they don't want to, companies should focus on what people already want to do, and just make that easier.

That makes a great deal of sense. However, from my own design experience, we see that even if a user has the motivation to become healthy, they don't necessarily have the motivation to use your particular health app. Even if people want to connect with their friends, there is still no incentive for them to share your product with their friends unless you design for it. And even if people

---

[283]Jane McGonigal. *Reality is Broken*. P22. Penguin Group. New York, NY. 2011.

already want to do great work, they don't necessarily want to work hard for a micromanaging boss that treats them badly. In these cases, it is more productive to improve how the boss motivates his employees (via methods of appreciation, autonomy, clear purpose, etc.), instead of trying to make their dreadful jobs easier.

Tiny Habits work great for self-improvement goals from the individual standpoint, but it sometimes works less ideally with employee engagement or viral marketing systems. If you just focus on making things easier, users may or may not muster enough motivation to perform the new behaviors that you want to create.

The flip side of generating motivation by making things easier is to make things more difficult. From the viewpoint of Core Drive 6: Scarcity & Impatience, we've already seen through many examples that when something is too easy, people don't necessarily appreciate it.

What if you use the "make things easy" strategy for dating? Let's say you want a certain person to become your significant other (the Desired Action), so you ask the person out (a *Trigger*), but their motivation is still very low at this point because they are just trying to figure out if you are a desirable mate. At this point, if you did everything you could to make it extremely easy for the person to go out with you, such as constantly being free at their convenience any day of the week or sending dozens of texts a day so the person can respond easily (*Trigger* and *Ability* boost) - this would not work out very well according to my own experiences... I mean, my observations. Shhh. Don't laugh.

Sometimes holding back increases the anticipation and suspense, and as a result, creates motivation. The outcome is that despite the increased difficulty of the Desired Action, scarcity creates more of the desired behavior. We have seen in previous chapters that inconveniencing your users or walking away from a deal (if done right), can seriously boost motivation and actions too.

So while Fogg's Behavior Model itself is extremely useful in terms of understanding behavior and its implications, Fogg and I have slightly different conclusions on the actionable steps to improve the process. Namely, Fogg focuses on the *Ability* aspect of his model, while I focus on the *Motivational* aspect. Of course, I also work on improving the ease of each Desired Action, and I'm sure Fogg also spends time on improving motivation; our priorities just seem to be different.

With that said, it is true that most products are so complicated and difficult to use they make users feel stupid and demoralized (Anti Core Drive 2). This is especially an issue during the Onboarding Phase when users don't have enough motivation to commit much energy into figuring things out. As a result, it is still a high priority to make the activities so easy that users do not need to think hard about committing the actions is still a high priority.

In terms of *Motivation*, Fogg states that Motivation is derived from six factors: Seeking Pleasure, Avoiding Pain, Seeking Hope, Avoiding Fear, Seeking Social Acceptance, and Avoiding Social Rejection[284]. This is a mix of Core Drives 2, 4, 5, 7, 8, and the Hidden Core Drive 9: Sensation.[285]

For drives like Core Drive 6: Scarcity & Impatience, as well as with the Endowment Effect within Core Drive 4: Ownership & Possession, these are often not explained in other behavioral models. They are mental shortcuts we take in our heads and are academically known as *cognitive biases* and decision-making *heuristics*[286]. There is a list of dozens of heuristics[287], including Anchoring (everything is relative in my mind), Illusory superiority (I am surely above average), IKEA effect (I value what I built), and Loss Aversion (I

---

[284]BJ Fogg. *Behaviormodel.org.* "3 core motivators, each with two sides" Accessed 2/17/2015.

[285] As an optional exercise for the diligent Octalysis learner, can you figure out how these Core Drives match with BJ Fogg's motivation components?

[286]Wikipedia Entry, "Heuristics in Judgement and Decision-Making": http://www.yukaichou.com/heuristics. Accessed 02/17/2015.

[287]Wikipedia Entry, "List of cognitive biases": http://www.yukaichou.com/cognitivebias. Accessed 02/17/2015.

wouldn't risk $10 to earn $15) that we have discussed in several of the previous chapters.

Together, Fogg's six components of motivation plus a list of behavioral heuristics, become a fairly complete view of all our behaviors; though they may not explain why we would sometimes die for a greater cause - Epic Meaning & Calling. For my own design work, I have preferred to have a general framework that is more inclusive of our psychological Core Drives and how they foster and interact with each other. It's easier to simply utilize one framework instead of thinking about a list of exceptions when we design for engaging experiences.

Lastly, if we look at the *Trigger* component through Octalysis, that's the role of Feedback Mechanics within the Octalysis Strategy Dashboard - something we will cover in more depth in future writings[288]. Feedback Mechanics allow users to pay attention to what they need to do, often via a received email or text message, user interfaces that show actionable information, or friends that "Like" your new Facebook photo, prompting you to return to the site. These are all Triggers delivered by Feedback Mechanics.

All Feedback Mechanics also incorporate various Core Drives of motivation within them, based on what the trigger itself is. Points and Badges are Core Drive 2 Triggers, Countdown Timers are Core Drive 6 Triggers, Spinning Fortune Wheels are Core Drive 7 Triggers, and Friend-Likes are Core Drive 5 Triggers. When you design for Feedback Mechanics or Triggers, you need to understand whether they are meant to drive the users' curiosity, their sense of accomplishment, their internal social pressure, or other Core Drives. If not, the Feedback Mechanics become empty signals that do not trigger towards any Desired Actions.

---

[288]Yu-kai Chou. *YukaiChou.com.* "The Strategy Dashboard for Gamification Design": http://www.yukaichou.com/strategydashboard. 07/14/2014.

Jane McGonigal's Theories

As the final touchstone of this chapter, we will look at Jane McGonigal's theories. McGonigal is a game designer and author of the book *Reality is Broken*[289]. She's most known for two TED talks on the power of games within the real world.

McGonigal describes the four components behind how games make people better and more resilient: *Epic Meaning, Urgent Optimism, Blissful Productivity*, and *Social Fabric*.

There are a few components that we can easily match with Octalysis. Epic Meaning of course echoes Core Drive 1: Epic Meaning & Calling - something that makes you feel like you're changing the world. Social Fabric clearly aligns with Core Drive 5: Social Influence & Relatedness, which is about the trusting bond between people taking on the same quests.

Urgent Optimism is slightly trickier to comprehend through Octalysis Glasses. In *Reality is Broken*, McGonigal defines Urgent Optimism as, "the moment of hope just before our success is real, when we feel inspired to try our hardest and do our best."[290] In my own interpretation, this is the sense where as long as you act immediately, you can accomplish your objective and achieve the Win-State. In this sense, a gamer always trusts the game designer to provide a way to win, as long as the gamer is doing the right thing in taking prompt action towards the obviously designed objectives.

Now with our Octalysis Glasses on, *Urgent Optimism* is generally a combination of Core Drive 2: Develop & Accomplishment as well as Core Drive 6: Scarcity & Impatience. Core Drive 2 is present because the player is optimistic that they are capable of hitting the Win-State and feeling accomplished. On the other hand, Core Drive 6 also comes into play because the player can't wait forever to commit

---

[289] Jane McGonigal. *Reality is Broken*. Penguin Group. New York, NY. 2011.
[290] Ibid. P69.

the Desired Action - they have to do it now because it is urgent. Therefore, the White and Black Hat combination of these Left Brain Core Drives leads to a player who is truly engaged.

The last component is *Blissful Productivity*[291], which was originally coined by a team of computer scientists at the Indiana University who were studying the unusually high stamina of World of Warcraft players. McGonigal defines Blissful Productivity as "the sense of being deeply immersed in work that produces immediate and obvious results."

From my understanding, Blissful Productivity is the sense that you are growing, accumulating, or improving something as you spend more time on it. Sometimes the task itself could seem a bit monotonous, but as long as the player feels like there is progress, the process will generate a sense of bliss and delight within.

Often this is a combination of Core Drive 2: Development & Accomplishment, Core Drives 3: Empowerment of Creativity & Feedback as well as Core Drive 4: Ownership & Possession. The user is accumulating, growing, or organizing something (Core Drive 4), and is continuously shown feedback on those activities in order to adjust, optimize, and feel accomplished.

As you can see, these four Core Drive packages are great combinations that allow users to deeply enjoy games as well as experiences outside of games. As you progress further into your Octalysis Gamification learning journey, you will start to identify and define many more of these Core Drive combinations beyond these four components, and pioneer your own work as an experience designer. For instance, we can see from the above analysis that Core Drive 7: Unpredictability & Curiosity isn't very prominent, and we can think about how to add more suspense, surprise, and unpredictability into the experience beyond the four components.

---

[291]Jane McGonigal. *Reality is Broken.* P53. Penguin Group. New York, NY. 2011.

The World is Your Playground

We all have the same brains, so all the sound studies on our motivation and behavior should have a way to converge with each other. The main point of this chapter is not that Octalysis is superior to any other framework, but at least to me, it can be a very useful tool to help comprehend and navigate the other models in behavioral science, games, and gamification. In my own experience, it is both convenient and rewarding to be able to use one framework to analyze them all and help refine our understanding of behavioral design.

There are obviously many other splendid theories and models on human behavior out there. But to make this book's length manageable for the reader, we won't be able to flush them all out here.

I highly encourage avid Octalysis Learners who are filled by Core Drive 3 and Core Drive 7 to put on your Octalysis Glasses and study Nir Eyal's *Hook Model*, Andrzej Marczewski's *User Types*, or Daniel Kahnemann's *Prospect Theory* and *Four Fold Pattern*. Works by behavioral psychology pioneers such as Dan Ariely, Michael Wu, or Robert Cialdini don't necessarily have graphical models, but you can understand their research through the 8 Core Drives as well.

With a strong grasp of the Core Drives, you can illuminate the aspects of motivation that other works cover or don't cover and determine how to best use these other models and frameworks for optimal experience design.

To get the most out of the book, Choose only ONE of the below options to do right now:

Medium: Pick a new model on human behavior (make sure it is related to actions, not necessarily emotions), and try to analyze it with Octalysis Glasses. What 8 Core Drives are present, and what are absent? Based on that, can you draw conclusions on what that particular model specializes in and when best to utilize it?

Medium: Try to recite all the models and frameworks covered in this chapter. You will need to take some time going back and forth before fully memorizing them. Can you remember how each is analyzed through Octalysis? Did your knowledge on Octalysis help you understand (hence remember) these models better?

Hard: Analyze Nir Eyal's *Hook* Model and try to understand how Octalysis fits into the cycles of *Trigger, Action, Reward*, and *Investment*. Does each component rely on a few of the 8 Core Drives? (For instance, *Investment* is often using Core Drive 4 to build up the Endowment Effect). Think about how the Core Drives change as we go through each Hook cycle throughout the Discovery, Onboarding, Scaffolding, and Endgame Phases. (For instance, during the Discovery Phase, the Trigger is often an External Trigger from marketing materials built on Core Drive 7. During the Endgame, the Trigger becomes an Internal Trigger, where the user is motivated through Core Drives 4 and 8.) Try to fully immerse your Octalysis understanding into the Hook Model.

Share what you come up with on Twitter or your preferred social network with the hashtag #OctalysisBook and check out what ideas other people have.

Start Designing

You are getting close to the end of the book, and it is time to start designing your own project. Come up with a project related to Human-Motivation that you want to improve on.

Think about what are the *Quantifiable Metrics* you want to improve. Who are the *Users* you are targeting and what Core Drives motivate them? What are the Desired Actions you need them to perform? What mediums can you communicate with them, show them

Feedback Mechanics, and display Triggers? Finally, what are the *Rewards and Incentives* you can provide users?

Together, this becomes the Octalysis Strategy Dashboard that will be useful in any gamification design campaign. This will be a good foundation for Chapter 17. More information on the Octalysis Strategy Dashboard can be found on my blog at:

http://www.yukaichou.com/gamification-study/the-strategy-dashboard-for-gamification-design/

Chapter 16: Level I Octalysis in Action

Now that we have examined all the various components of Level I Octalysis, let's see how everything comes together. There are generally two methods to use Octalysis:

The first method is to analyze existing products to determine their strengths and weaknesses for motivation toward the Desired Actions. It allows us to identify what type of motivation is weak so we can introduce new improvements, often in the form of Game Design Techniques, to the experience. This is typically called an Octalysis Audit.

The second method is to create a brand new experience based on Octalysis and the 8 Core Drives. Through a very systematic process, we can create an engaging experience that will fulfill the goals of the experience designer.

Let's first look at the former.

Octalysis Review of Facebook

The first step of utilizing Octalysis as a tool is to decipher all the motivation Core Drives that are present in an experience. In Chapter 3, we briefly looked at Facebook through the lenses of Octalysis. Let's take a slightly closer look using your new familiarity with the 8 Core Drives.

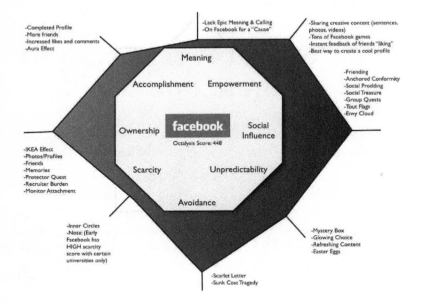

In general, Facebook is fairly strong in most of the Core Drives, hence the massive success it has today. At the center of Facebook there is Core Drive 5: Social Influence and Relatedness. People are consistently looking to stay connected with others to share their own experiences and check out what others are doing. Facebook deploys a great deal of Social Prodding, Social Treasures, and Conformity Anchors to create a more engaging experience.

On the other hand there is a high amount of Core Drive 7: Unpredictability and Curiosity in the experience. Every time a user goes on Facebook, they are looking for new and wondrous content that is worth viewing and sharing.

Hooked author Nir Eyal even implies that every time we go onto our Facebook (or Twitter) News Feeds, or when we "pull down" to refresh the News Feed updates, it's as if we are pulling the lever on a slot machine - something he terms "Rewards of the Hunt."[292] Every

---

[292] Nir Eyal. *Hooked.* Chapter 4: Variable Rewards - "Rewards of the Hunt". Kindle Version v 1.0. 2014.

time we commit the Desired Action, we are trying to see if we will be rewarded with more more interesting content. If we don't "win," we pull the lever to play again and see if we become luckier the next time.

There's also a strong sense of Core Drive 4: Ownership & Possession within Facebook. One of the core activities on Facebook is to accumulate and organize more photos of friends and experiences. In addition, since many people's Facebook profiles represent their social identity, there is a strong sense of ownership towards these profiles. True to Core Drive 4 principles, now there is an even stronger desire to organize and improve their profiles.

For some people, one of the joys of using Facebook is to constantly come up with creative and humorous things to say or content to share in order to get "Likes." This often utilizes Core Drive 3: Empowerment of Creativity & Feedback. The "Feedback" part of receiving likes is essential in any experience, as simply expressing creativity without receiving any feedback is actually a torturous experience.

Of course, when a person shares photos of their latest trip to Europe or a funny blog post that dozens or even hundreds of their friends are liking, they also feel a strong sense of Core Drive 2: Development & Accomplishment. This Left Brain White Hat Core Drive further makes a user feel good when they continue to commit the Desired Actions.

We also mentioned in Chapter 12 that there is a tremendous amount of Core Drive 8: Loss & Avoidance for Facebook, especially in the Endgame. This is because the Sunk Cost Prison prevents people from quitting due to all the time, friends, photos, experiences, messages, and game points accumulated on Facebook. Users are simply stuck with investing more of their time accumulating additional "valuables" that they are afraid to lose.

As mentioned in Chapter 3, the only two Core Drives that Facebook is lacking on are Core Drive 1: Epic Meaning & Calling, as well as Core Drive 6: Scarcity & Impatience. There is no real higher purpose that is greater than oneself when using Facebook. A rare exception is when people join Facebook Groups based on a higher mission or vision, such as some charity or cult groups. Of course, this type of motivation is certainly not dominant towards why people use Facebook, but only serves as an complementary experience alongside of Facebook.

We also mentioned how in the early days of Facebook, there was a tremendous amount of scarcity in the form of exclusivity as only students from a few selected universities like Harvard were allowed to join. During that time, Core Drive 6: Scarcity & Impatience was extremely high in the Discovery Phase, which also built up a strong sense of Elitism from Core Drive 1 during the Onboarding and Scaffolding Phases.

However, since Facebook opened up to everyone and their grandmothers, there is very little Core Drive 6 left. There isn't anything that you want but cannot have constantly being dangled in front of your face. Perhaps only when you are waiting for your friend to respond to your message or when Facebook has exclusive new features that are only offered to a small pool of users do you feel some sense of Core Drive 6. Oh yes, and that person you are stalking who refuses to accept your friend request and show you more pictures. I guess there is Core Drive 6 in that too, but it probably isn't the main "gameplay" experience of Facebook.

Of course, not having Core Drive 6 in this case is not a negative thing, because we learned that even though Core Drive 6 creates obsession by being Black Hat and Left Brain (Extrinsic Tendency), it is not ideal for long term engagement. If Facebook has already achieved strong engagement through other Core Drives (and earlier Core Drive 6 efforts), there is no need to add Core Drive 6 if it isn't trying to rapidly capture new users but to engage existing ones.

So based on the quick Level 1 Octalysis review above, we recognize that Facebook would be more successful if it had a greater element of Core Drive 1: Epic Meaning & Calling in it. People who are against Facebook often think of it is as a waste of time and a distraction to bigger, more important things. Plenty of people attempt to boycott or go on a "Facebook fast" because they don't want to waste their life on "silly" things. If Facebook could utilize its platform to get individuals to do more meaningful activities that help the world and contribute to society, then it would likely become even more engaging.

Of course, we see that Facebook already attempts to add in a thread of Core Drive 1 as they raise awareness and ask for donations to support natural disaster refugees. But those are usually one-off cases triggered by large world events that no one can ignore. It would be more meaningful if they build in more regular and streamlined experiences where users feel that every minute on Facebook actually contributes to the world. For instance, a top bar that continually displays an effort or group in less fortunate communities that is in dire need of help. It can also show a *trigger* button that allows people to donate their time or money to these causes.

Since the effort or group would change daily and would include details on exactly what they are going through, at the minimum people would feel more educated and aware of the world's problems each day they visit Facebook. Through massively increasing donations to groups, Facebook can truly say that they don't only change the world, but they also *save* the world as users login everyday.

Finally, it would likely benefit Facebook if it easily allowed people to find and seek help from mentors or homework buddies. This would make people think that being on Facebook is very "productive" and decrease their resistance of it.

The Score is a Smoke Screen

Over the years, a lot of people like to ask me what the Octalysis Score represents. You might have that question too as you look at some of the Octalysis charts. As we already know, scores tend to intrigue the mind, and everyone likes to find out about them. However, I usually try to stray away from spending too much time explaining the Octalysis Score because it is actually the least actionable element in the realm of Octalysis.

What's useful is using the Octalysis chart to determine which Core Drives are weak and need to be improved on, while understanding the nature of the dominant Core Drives in terms of being White/Black Hat and Left/Right Brain. The Octalysis Score itself is somewhat just fun and gimmicky. But since people keep asking, I thought I should share a bit on how I arrive at these numbers.

Generally, for each Core Drive, we assume a number between 0 to 10 based on "How strong does this Core Drive motivate towards the Desired Action." 0 Means that the Core Drive does not exist as a motivator within the experience. At the top end of the scale, 10 usually means that it is impossible to improve the Core Drive further, and almost all individuals who become exposed to the Core Drive will take the Desired Action.

After that, I take the square of all eight numbers and add them together. This means that the highest possible Octalysis Score is 800 (Ten squared multiplied by eight), and the lowest is 0. In my own ratings, most successful games are above 350, and most non-game products are below 150. In fact, most products that aren't sensitive to Human-Focused Design fall below 50.

However, since the scoring is relatively subjective, different people will come up with different scores for the same product. When people ask me how do I know the exact numbers assigned to each motivation, I just say that it is based on an intuitive feel after *experiencing* the system. However, the exact numbers aren't really that useful as I mentioned earlier, as long as you are not far off. It really doesn't do anything to your design whether you give a Core Drive a value of 2 or 3, as long as you know it is not a 7 or 8. As I said, Octalysis is a tool that allows people to design better based on their own sound judgements. (After all, sound judgement is required in all models, be it *SWOT Analysis*[293], BJ Fogg's *B=MAT*, or Boston Consulting Group's *BCG Matrix*[294]).

What's actually important in my mind is that you conceptually recognize things like: there is no *unpredictability* in your experience, or that you heavily rely on Black Hat Core Drives. Generally, just knowing which Core Drives are strong and which are weak can allow you to design appropriately for the experience, as opposed to spending precious time fussing over exact values.

One insight that can be derived out of the Octalysis Score formula, is that it is generally better being extremely strong in a few Core Drives, as opposed to having a little bit of everything. A score of 1 for all eight Core Drives will only result in an Octalysis Score of 8, whereas having two Core Drives that have the value of 9 will result in an Octalysis Score of 162. That is why it is so important to pick the *right* Core Drives that has the desired characteristics in your gamification design. If you are only going to pick a few Core Drives, you want to make sure that you are picking the most effective ones based on the specific scenario.

With that said, it is usually easier to improve on a Core Drive if it is completely lacking compared to ones that are already strong. It is usually fairly easy to add a little bit of unpredictability, a little bit of social, or a little bit of scarcity when there are none. But if there is already a high sense of Social Influence, it becomes much more difficult to further enhance that Core Drive. You usually need a true expert on that Core Drive doing a lot of design, research, and A/B

---

[293]SWOT Analysis stands for: Strengths, Weaknesses, Opportunities, and Threats. http://www.yukaichou.com/SWOT

[294]The well-known BCG Matrix is formally termed Growth Share Matrix and pioneered by the Boston Consulting Group:http://www.yukaichou.com/bcgmatrix

Testing to push out the Core Drive from a theoretical 8 to a 9.

Finally, I have noticed a tendency for students of Octalysis to "inflate" the values of Core Drives within their own projects (a Core Drive 4 bias - ha!). Everything appears to be a 7 to 9 in their projects, which is extremely unlikely unless your project is already more engaging than Facebook. Not surprisingly, Octalysis is more useful as a design tool if you are more realistic on the scale of motivation for each of the Core Drives.

As a thinking exercise, a value of 10 for Core Drive 1: Epic Meaning & Calling should be something that is so epically meaningful that people are willing to die for it. Similarly, a value of 10 for Core Drive 8: Loss & Avoidance should reflect something so threatening that people are willing to kill for it. With that in mind, I'm going to imagine your employee engagement campaign is far away from having all 8s or 9s on each Core Drive.

Most systems in the market are Function-Focused, and the majority of products I have seen have 0 on most Core Drives and only 1 or 2 on a few Core Drives. Successful products have 3 to 4 on a few Core Drives and a few 8 to 9s. Industry-dominating products might have one or two 9s and even a 10, but that should rarely be assigned.

At the end of the day, if you use Octalysis just to make yourself feel good about what you are doing, then there is very little room to find better ways to improve the experience.

It's difficult to absorb a waterfall when your cup is too full.[295]

Octalysis of the Speed Camera Lottery

One of the most famous analogue designs in the gamification world is The Speed Camera Lottery by *Volkswagen's Fun Theory*[296]. The

---

[295] Ramit Sethi's Brain Trust: iwillteachyoutoberich.com/braintrust

[296] TheFunTheory.com. "The Speed Camera Lottery." Accessed 03/20/2015.

goal of the campaign is to encourage drivers to obey the posted speed limits by making the Desired Action more engaging.

Originally proposed to the The Fun Factory by Kevin Richardson from San Francisco, the concept was implemented in 2010 by the Swedish National Society for Road Safety based in Stockholm, Sweden. Using existing traffic-camera and speed-capture technologies, the Speed Camera Lottery device would detect the speed of all drivers passing through it and take photographs of their license plates.

An LED board displayed the speeds to each passing driver, along with a thumbs up or thumbs down sign signifying whether they were obeying the law or not. Speeders that are photographed were issued a citation, with the proceeds going into a cash fund. On the other hand, drivers who obeyed the speed law would also be recorded and then entered into a lottery, where they would be eligible to win some of the money from the speeders.

This case study has been seen by many people within the gamification industry, and people often exclaim, "That's a really creative solution! How can I come up with creative solutions like that to solve my own problems?"

Here we see that, through the Octalysis process, one can *potentially* come up with creative solutions like the Speed Camera Lottery and more.

The Problem: Get people to drive under the speed limit

In every gamified campaign, one must first define the problem to solve, and how to measure success. If we take the problem of decreasing speeding drivers as an ongoing campaign, we can then analyze it through the 8 Core Drives of Octalysis.

Generally speaking, without any human intervention, driving within the speed limit is only motivated by Core Drive 1: Epic Meaning & Calling - driving safely and responsibly is for a cause greater than yourself. This has definitely caused many people to put some sort of limitation on their driving speed, making the roads safer overall.

The problem is, most people don't always equate fast driving to "dangerous" driving. For many, ignoring the speed limit is still worth it if the reward is the immediate gratification of arriving to their destinations sooner or feeling the thrill of going fast. As a consequence, most governments introduced Core Drive 8: Loss & Avoidance - fining people when they are caught driving over the speed limit. People want to avoid getting fined for fast driving, so they lower their driving speeds tangibly. This is what deters most people from driving dangerously.

However, law enforcement is a very expensive solution, especially if it needs to be ubiquitous. And because the odds of getting caught are relatively low when one speeds, many people are still not deterred from their occasional speeding habits.

Subsequently, another solution was introduced that utilizes Core Drive 3: Empowerment of Creativity & Feedback. You may have seen those speed detectors that don't give speeders a fine, but merely display what speed they were driving at. Since the driver is in control of their "score" and sees immediate feedback, this encourages many people to slow down even more when they see that their speeds are too high.

The issue here is that the Win-State is still not very clear to the driver. What was the speed limit again? Was I above it or below it? Remember that people often do not want to use their active brains to think if it is not necessary. If people have to calculate for themselves whether they hit the Win-State or not, many will get lazy and not bother. Also, it turns out that some people will also do the opposite of the Desired Action and try to see how high of a speed they can get recorded on the feedback device, which completely defeats the purpose of the design.

Speed Camera Lottery's Innovation

As a result, in comes the Speed Camera Lottery. The Speed Camera Lottery adds four additional Core Drives to solve this problem.

- Core Drive 4: Ownership & Possession. With the Speed Camera Lottery, a player can now potentially "earn" money if they score well and achieve the Win-State. In this case, the tangible reward of cash is itself a fairly strong motivator to get people interested in participating.
- Core Drive 7: Unpredictability & Curiosity. We have learned that, whenever there is a lottery or sweepstakes system, it involves Core Drive 7. A 10% chance of winning $100 often engages people more than a sure chance of getting $10, because they will continuously think about whether they will win or not. This anticipation makes things more exciting and engaging.
- Core Drive 2: Development & Accomplishment. Instead of being ambiguous about whether the driver hit the Win-State or not, the Speed Camera Lottery displays an obvious green thumbs up when drivers achieve the Win-State, and a red thumbs down when drivers fail to achieve the Win-State. This was further reinforced by displaying speeds at or below the limit in green, and displaying speeds in excess of the limit in red. This instant feedback mechanism allows the user to intuitively feel more successful and accomplished when achieving the Win-State.
- Core Drive 5: Social Influence & Relatedness. In the viral Youtube video that showcases the Speed Camera Lottery[297], we see that the Speed Camera Lottery is implemented on a busy street with lots of other drivers and passengers nearby. Beyond just the desire to do well and win some money, the driver would recognize that everyone around could see

---

[297] Youtube Video: "The Speed Camera Lottery - The Fun Theory". Accessed 03/20/2015.

whether they get a thumbs up or thumbs down. Even though the majority of the audience are mere strangers, we naturally don't like others to see us as "thumbs-down losers" that are disobeying the law. We would much prefer others to see that we are law-abiding citizens that are getting green thumbs-ups.

With four additional Core Drives designed into the experience, the Speed Camera Lottery was able to reduce the average speed of passing drivers by over 20% during their pilot run. Even though the Speed Camera Lottery isn't the end-all be-all solution due to a lack of Endgame design, we can see that by applying Octalysis and the 8 Core Drives to an existing problem, we are able to innovate and design new experiences that reinforce desired behaviors.

If there is one thing I want my readers to get out of this book, it is to constantly think about motivation and the 8 Core Drives instead of features, functions, and systems. When you start off with Human-Focused Design as opposed to Function-Focused Design, I'm confident that whatever you design will come out to be more appealing, more enjoyable, and more successful.

Octalysis of the Waze Navigation App

Beyond just a high level Octalysis overview of an experience, we can also analyze the experience separately throughout the 4 Experience Phases of a Player's Journey: Discovery, Onboarding, Scaffolding, and Endgame.

Somewhat inline with the Speed Camera Lottery, another sector in "gamified driving" is the navigation app *Waze*. As mentioned in Chapter 5, Waze is an immensely popular GPS app that is changing how we navigate traffic through crowdsourcing real-time traffic and road condition data. Often receiving an average five star rating by tens of thousands of users, its fans have taken the mundane experience of driving and turned it into an enjoyably immersive adventure with a rewarding social experience.

Let's take a deeper look into how Waze accomplishes this by applying Octalysis to its design and mechanics.

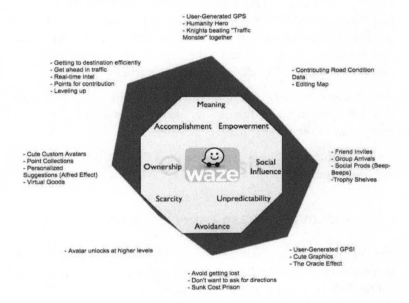

Most navigation systems simply provide directions as a means to an end (Function-Focused). They mostly motivate us through two Core Drives:

- Core Drive 2: Development & Accomplishment. Users continue to see progress towards the destination and feel very competent when they reach the Win-State efficiently.
- Core Drive 8: Loss & Avoidance. Users avoid the frustrating experience of getting lost or feeling confused.

But all navigation systems fulfill these two Core Drives, with some doing it better than others. As a new entrant into the industry, Waze needed to incorporate more Core Drives into their experience in order to create differentiating success.

Waze does this by enabling social components to create localized communities of drivers. While the company owns the map rights, the actual navigational system is driven by crowdsourced user data as drivers constantly contribute updates. These updates include road conditions, debris, traffic, presence of cops, and other specific details that are helpful to drivers using the app. This is somewhat akin to the spirit behind Wikipedia's community participation.

Waze's objective isn't just to provide people directions. hey want to create pleasant and fun driving *experiences* that bring more enjoyment to their users' daily commutes.

Let's dive into how Waze appeals to the 8 Core Drives throughout the 4 Experience Phases.

Discovery Phase experience for Waze

The Discovery Phase is where users decide to start trying out a certain experience. Many other gamification/game design frameworks define their first phase as *Onboarding* or *Identity*[298], which begins when users sign up to an experience. However, I believe that the user experience of a service does not start when people sign up to the service, but when they first hear about it. How they hear about it, in what context, motivated by what Core Drives will all affect how users behave during the Onboarding and Scaffolding Phase. As a result, we want to carefully analyze and craft the Discovery Experience of any service we are designing.

Many people discover the Waze app because of a mild form of Core Drive 7: Unpredictability & Curiosity. They heard about it somewhere, read about it through online media sites, or just

[298]Kevin Werbach. Slideshare.com. "Socialize14 keynote". Uploaded 07/04/2014.

stumbled upon it in the app store. Waze attracts users by displaying cute graphics and bringing out people's curiosity in being a user-generated navigation app. Since most GPS apps are centrally programmed and look overly serious, this prompts user curiosity, "Hmm! A user-generated GPS? How does that work?" The novel concept itself attracts people to become interested in trying out the experience.

Furthermore, Waze utilizes a strong sense of Core Drive 5: Social Influence & Relatedness. Because of the community ethos it has throughout the experience, the app encourages many users during Scaffolding and the Endgame to tell their friends about it. Prospective users are also heavily influenced by reviews and ratings from other users, which we know by now, heavily motivates Desired Actions due to the Conformity Anchor discussed in Chapter 9.

Along the two Core Drives that every navigation system has (2 and 8), there aren't many other Core Drives that are embedded in the Discovery Phase, so lets move on to examining the Onboarding Phase.

Onboarding Phase experience for Waze

Onboarding starts after users decide to give the experience a try and download the app.

I mentioned in Chapter 5 that one of the very impressive things Waze does is to bring in Core Drive 1: Epic Meaning & Calling during the Onboarding Experience. Instead of taking up a lot of time with text or video narratives, early versions of Waze simply show an Onboarding graphic of Traffic - a huge snake monster consisting of a road with cars stuck on it - combatting many cute and brave knight Wazers. Below, it displays the tagline "Beat Traffic, Together." This demonstrates that when users are driving with Waze, they are not just commuting to their destinations, but are actually helping an entire community of brave Wazers fight *Traffic*, which of course is something everyone hates.

The app then quickly demonstrates Feedback Mechanics that show "363 Wazers nearby" which is a display of Core Drive 5: Social Influence & Relatedness. The user needs to quickly know that this app is popular and there is activity within the app. She can also see cute icons of other drivers, some with crowns, others with helmets, and others have baby sucklers. This installs some Core Drive 7: Unpredictability & Curiosity along with some Core Drive 6: Scarcity & Impatience. "Hmm, I wonder how I can make my car avatar to look different."

Of course, the user is not likely to explore all the avatar settings the first time using the app, but instead will likely try to go somewhere with Waze. With big and round buttons and a clear navigation, Waze makes sure there is an element of Core Drive 2: Development & Accomplishment. This means that users feel smart and competent whenever they are interacting with the interface and searching for a new address. Remember: during the Onboarding Phase, it is critical to make users feel smart and not overwhelm them with too many features and functionalities, a mistake by many large corporations and startups alike.

Waze also allows users to accumulate Status Points while driving, appealing to Core Drive 4: Ownership & Possession, which is further enhanced by the personified car avatars. Even though users are shown unlockable avatars as they accumulate more points and level up (a Dangling element in Core Drive 6), I personally don't feel that it heavily motivates user behavior and is a bit more on the gimmicky side until later on in the Scaffolding phase.

At this point, the user probably isn't in the mood to contribute data, modify the map, and share road conditions to others. However, the experience thus far has been smooth and intriguing enough that many users would be open to move forward and move into the Scaffolding Phase.

Scaffolding Phase experience for Waze

The Scaffolding Phase is the regular journey of the user throughout the experience. Interestingly, this normally involves a repeated set of actions on a daily or weekly basis. Within Waze, once the user has a basic sense of how to navigate the system, they are driven to dive in further, explore, contribute, and achieve more until it becomes a daily habit.

As Waze properly functions, Core Drive 2: Development & Accomplishment kicks in even more as it navigates drivers through heavy traffic and takes them on little side roads that bypass dozens of cars stuck on the highway. This makes users feel smart and accomplished utilizing information that other people don't have access to in order to maneuver in traffic better.

Another key Core Drive that starts to build up more during Scaffolding is Core Drive 4: Ownership & Possession. As the user drives with Waze, it collects specific data about their habits and driving behavior. Thus the app is able to form a deep and individualized understanding of a user and customize their experience.

As an example of the *Alfred Effect* discussed in Chapter 9, Waze might ask the driver, "would you like to go to work now?" because it knows that the driver goes to work at 8:30 AM on weekdays. But at 8 PM on a Wednesday, Waze might ask, "Would you like to go to the gym?" because it knows that Wednesday nights are gym nights for this user. The personalized "Alfred Effect" motivates users to stay engaged and loyal with the app, even if other more advanced technologies come out. The user prefers to stick to the system that knows them over ones that are smarter.

Another powerful Core Drive within Waze during the Scaffolding Phase is Core Drive 7: Unpredictability & Curiosity. When a user is alerted about a disabled car stuck on the roadside, their minds suddenly become engaged. "Will it be there? Will it be there?" This is what I call the Oracle Effect (Game Technique #71), where a prediction about the future causes the user to become fully engaged to see whether the "prophecy" will become true or not. Often users will stay focused until *voila!*, they see the incapacitated car stuck on the shoulder - the prophecy is fulfilled! Even when the car isn't there, the user would think, "Bummer. Maybe next time I'll get to witness the alerted incident." When you pull the lever on a slot machine, sometimes you win, and sometimes you don't. That type of curiosity adds an extra layer of fun within the Waze's experience.

At one point, after continuously seeing and benefiting from reliable information contributed by others, users also start to think about exercising their Core Drive 3: Empowerment of Creativity & Feedback. Suddenly, the user is starting to share some of their own road information, tapping on a few large icons while driving to share that there was a policeman hiding at the bottom of a steep slope. (Note: this is not necessarily safe.) This gives users a "sense of agency" as they feel empowered to contribute what they want into the pool of helpful data.

We know that for Core Drive 3 to work, it needs quick "feedback" also, and feedback is often even stronger if it is mixed with Core Drive 5: Social Influence & Relatedness. What's emotionally rewarding about Waze, is that often, when you shared information with the community, you may receive a couple pop-ups that show people thanking you a few seconds later. (Again, this is not necessarily safe for either sharer or thanker; a gamification designer needs to think heavily about the ramifications of their designs). When users seemingly get instant feedback from other, appreciative users, they feel delighted and are prone to share more in the future. After every Desired Action must come a delightful moment.

Of course, there are still some Core Drive 6: Scarcity & Impatience designs in the system, as the app still dangles a path to mastery towards becoming "Waze Royalty." However, since the unlocked reward does not grant users more useful powers or actually represent an impressive status to others, from my observations, it does not heavily alter user behavior.

With Core Drive 8: Loss & Avoidance, people hate overpaying for commodities such as gas, beer, or groceries, so navigation services could really help people avoid overpaying by routing them to the least expensive locations along their way. In addition, when a person is trying to search for a restaurant "on the way" to a destination, most navigation apps show locations or detours that are really out of the way.

Waze allows users to avoid these pains by showing cheaper gas stations and shorter detours as users head towards their destinations. It even tells the user how long the detour is from the original route before the user commits to any location. This eventually leads to more Core Drive 2: Development & Accomplishment as people feel smart about not wasting much time or money in finding gas or a place to eat.

The Endgame Phase of Waze

The Endgame Phase starts when the user has been going through the activity loops for a long period of time and has done everything there is to do within their own perceptions. This is when we evaluate why they would still want to remain in the system and commit to more Desired Actions.

Luckily for Waze, the navigation functionality itself is a useful purpose that many people need on a daily basis. As such, people can't quit easily like they do with games. However, without diligent design, there may still be nothing that stops the user from migrating to other navigation services that offer similar Function-Focused benefits. This is where good Endgame design becomes very important.

During the Endgame, hardcore users who have been involved for a long time start taking more pride in being part of the community, which strengthens the Core Drive 1: Epic Meaning & Calling. As we know, the Alfred Effect within Core Drive 4 continues to grow, which also builds up Core Drive 8: Loss & Avoidance as users don't want to leave and lose the acquired system intelligence as well as the saved addresses and "favorites" in the system.

Also, at this stage, some Core Drive 3: Empowerment of Creativity can be utilized as people begin to actually use the available online map editor to update the map and make improvements. Of course, since the physical world is metaphorically "set in stone," there is still a limited amount of creativity that can be derived this process. Furthermore, there are only so many ways to say "there is a piece of trash or a police car here" (anything beyond the simplest ways would be too dangerous for driving), so Core Drive 3 is still very limited for a veteran user.

On the other hand, As long as Waze continues to offer faster routes than other competitors, Core Drive 2: Development & Accomplishment will likely remain strong in the Endgame. However, many other navigation apps are all touting that they are equally smart or smarter at finding faster routes to beat traffic. Regardless if that's accurate or not, the *perception* of that possibility along with some Black Hat Discovery Phase design, could quickly snatch users away from Waze if they depended on this alone.

Regarding Core Drive 5: Social Influence & Relatedness, even though the light social interactions within Waze remain fun in the endgame, the depth of interactivity and relationships don't necessarily expand. As people are driving, every friendship interaction is based on light touches, with people occasionally sending you Social Prods in the form of "Beep-Beeps" or a quick message. The level of friendship does not necessarily expand or become more meaningful through Waze.

Core Drive 6: Scarcity & Impatience as well as Core Drive 7: Unpredictability & Curiosity are also diminished, since the user has unlocked the high level avatars and the novelty factor (including the Oracle Effect since it has little variation) would likely have been reduced. This means that Waze does not have much Black Hat motivation within the Endgame Phase. Of course, the avatar levels in Waze are "percentile-based," which means you could lose your avatar status if you stopped using Waze while others diligently catch up. This means that there is still motivation to drive forward when a veteran user drops a rank after sluggish usage. Here we see that another potential side-effect of this gamified design may be that people would drive more with Waze on just to keep their ranks, even though it may not be necessary to drive in the first place. This may unintentionally impact the environment in a negative way.

From the analysis above, we can see that the Endgame experience of Waze is mostly focused on Core Drives 1, 2, 3, 4, and some 8. This is not necessarily bad, as we know the White Hat Core Drives stimulate longer engagement. As long as people are enjoying the experience, it is fine to have fewer Black Hat Core Drive designs. However, Waze's longer term success will depend on how well they appeal to Core Drive 2 - do users *really* feel smarter using Waze compared to other navigations apps - and Core Drive 3 - are there more ways to utilize creativity and see feedback without jeopardizing safe driving. Of course, if Waze can expand on Core Drive 5: Social Influence & Relatedness within their Endgame design, that would make it an even more compelling experience.

The Next Step: Identify Potential Improvements for Waze

Once we have analyzed the progressive experience of Waze, the next step is to come up with new creative ideas to enhance those 8 Core Drives. For simplicity sake, we will just go through a simple ten-minute Level I Octalysis brainstorm, which would be very instructive, but by no means exhaustive. For disclaimer sake, as of this writing, I have never worked with Waze before so this is not real consulting advice but simply a form of amusing brainstorming using the Octalysis Framework.

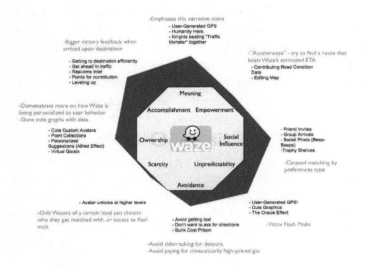

The first thing to improve in Waze through this quick analysis is to emphasize the Core Drive 1: Epic Meaning & Calling more. I mentioned earlier that the "Traffic Monster" onboarding image was there in the earlier days, but since then has been replaced by more social-related messages. Even if the company wants to emphasize the "playful fantasy" part of Core Drive 1, they should continue to provide the Epic Meaning of "helping a community beat traffic" throughout the Scaffolding, and Endgame experience. Unfortunately, Onboarding is the only place where many Feedback Mechanics elements are present.

To improve Core Drive 2: Development & Accomplishment, Waze should consider making every arrival to the destination a bigger Win-State. Play a victorious tune, show a popup that excitedly shows, "You have arrived safely. Awesome!" Maybe even show the image of the location like some other navigation apps do so the user knows what to look out for. All this is much better than the bland GPS voice of "You have reached your destination." I would probably use Waze more if every time I reach the destination, there is a 25% chance the mechanical female voice says, "You have reached your destination. You're awesome." Of course, that also adds a blend of Core Drive 7 Easter Egg design into it.

For Core Drive 4: Ownership & Possession, we mentioned that one of the great things about Waze is the Alfred Effect as it starts to offer personalized suggestions. The problem is, most users aren't aware that Waze is intelligently learning about their preferences until later on in the Scaffolding Phase. If more users knew about it, maybe fewer of them would drop out before they realized the feature was there. The app could consider adding an "Intelligent Score" for itself, where each time you drove with Waze, its intelligence score goes up as it is learning more and more about your preferences. This may have more contextual meaning than just points and builds some anticipation for what lies ahead in the experience.

Another idea with Core Drive 4 is to start showing cute graphics and charts that reflect the user's driving behaviors. Charts that reflect things like, "Did you know that you went to the gym 105 times this year and stayed there for a total of 5,775 minutes?" Or, "Did you know that you spent 9,422 minutes last year commuting to work?" These could really build more Core Drive 4 into the experience.

Even though information like this is not necessarily useful, people like it because it reflects who they are and makes them understand their behaviors better. This will increase their desire to to use Waze more often to ensure that the data, and hence insights, have more integrity in them and become more interesting.

Core Drive 3: Empowerment of Creativity & Feedback is actually rather difficult to design for since the point of a navigation app is to get users to their destinations as efficiently as possible. There isn't much room for creativity and meaningful choices that may divert the user or waste their time. However, one potential idea is to introduce a feature called "Accelerwaze," which allows users to try to beat Waze's predetermined "Estimated Time of Arrivals."

When you set Waze on a destination, it will tell you the most optimal way to get there, as well as the "ETA" if you took that route. Users could potentially choose to "challenge" Waze by saying, "I believe if I took this route instead, I would get there much faster than Waze's ETA." This would make the driving experience a bit more fun and dynamic, as well as allow Waze to learn about new driving routes in order to upgrade its own systems. People may even want to use Waze on destinations that they know full well how to get to, such as their daily commutes to work.

Of course, there are potential risks where, in order to prove that their routes are faster, drivers would drive more recklessly and run through red lights. For every motivating feature you design, you must consider the unintended consequences and negative ramifications before implementing it. Hopefully, these "Accelerwaze" drivers would be driving past many Speed Camera Lotteries and slowing down to potentially win prizes instead.

Octalysis allows you to ask the right questions and design for motivation with the 8 Core Drives. But just because you have a bunch of fun ideas doesn't mean they are all sound ideas. It is up to the designer's judgement to determine which features are sound and which ones need more refining.

Remember, we mentioned earlier that Waze's gamification system could incentivize people to drive unnecessarily more and hurt the environment? Luckily, there are ideas within Core Drive 5: Social Influence & Relatedness that also help reduce driving. Since Waze knows who commutes where every day, they can potentially introduce a carpool matching service where individuals can save on gas, energy and the environment. All while making a new friend. Waze could potentially match people by declared interest, industry, or even in the same company, to commute together on a regular basis.

If they really wanted to, Waze could even create a dating service and set up first dates as carpools. Of course, the joke here is that almost everyone would be getting second dates because the potential lovebirds at least have to carpool back from their commutes. Just don't be the one that is so terrible that the other person calls their friends to pick them up, so they don't have to go through the agony of being in a car with you again.

For Core Drive 7: Unpredictability & Curiosity, they could add interesting and delightful experiences to Endgame users, such as randomly telling users that a flash mob is in effect and ask them if they want to participate. If the user taps "Yes," it could reroute their car to a location such as a beach, where many other Wazers would gather. They could then implement interesting themes like, "Figure out why we brought all of you here."

Perhaps after a few conversations, people will realize that they all go to the gym twice a day and are hardcore health buffs. Once they figured it out, they could even earn a new "Health Buff" avatar that only people who showed up at this flash mob would get. Imagine if you are driving with the very limited Health Buff avatar and you suddenly see on the map another Health Buff is nearby. That type of Relatedness gets people even more connected to each other through the Waze app.

One of the concerns of meeting new people, whether it is for dating or flash mobs, is the safety of it. After all, there are people out there that are sometimes harmful, and Waze shouldn't risk their users getting a bad experience if perverts just used the app to find victims. This is where Core Drive 6: Scarcity & Impatience becomes useful.

Currently for Waze (early 2015), the only reason why people would level up is to unlock new status avatars. For most users who aren't really hung up on their avatars, there isn't much to look forward to when gaining more experience points. Waze could solve this problem by building in unlockable features such as the carpool matching and flash mobs, where only users with higher levels could set up more interest filters, preferences, and get better access to these features.

That way, everyone who "qualifies" to meet other members are proven and contributing members of the community. Waze even knows their driving history and where they frequent, such as where they live, where they work, and where they spend their weekends. It would be extremely difficult for shady people to sign up for Waze just to fulfill their harmful desires.

Finally, if the app has been doing everything well - getting users to accumulate points, the Alfred Effect, cool flash mob relatedness, carpooling with others, etc., Core Drive 8: Loss & Avoidance automatically sets in. Once people get used to a certain joyful driving experience, the thought of losing that for another plain and boring navigation system feels dreadful, and people habitually stick with Waze whenever they drive.

At this point, it is not necessary to design for more Core Drive 8: Loss & Avoidance game techniques since Black Hat Core Drives make users feel uncomfortable and therefore, not ideal for Endgame design. Since the app already has a strong and vibrant community, it is much better to focus on White Hat and Right Brain (intrinsic tendency) Core Drives.

As you can see, with Octalysis you are able to analyze your own product or experience thoroughly, as well as being able to use it to brainstorm other creative ideas to improve the experience. Of course, you rarely want to implement all the features that are planned, but it allows your thinking to have depth towards driving desired behaviors while allowing users to enjoy the process.

To get the most out of the book, Choose only ONE of the below options to do right now:

Easy: Check out Facebook, the Speed Camera Lottery, or the Waze navigation app. Review the analysis done in this chapter by experiencing through the various features. Does seeing these experiences with new Octalysis Glasses change the way you understand how they work?

Medium: Pick another product or experience that you have spent a significant amount of time on and which is also immensely popular. Try to run a Level I Octalysis Audit on it. Is it well designed within the context of the 8 Core Drives? How can you make it even better?

Hard: Find another project that is useful but struggling to get traction. Break down the experience into the 4 Experience Phases: Discovery, Onboarding, Scaffolding, and Endgame. For each phase, analyze what Core Drives, if any, are present in that project. Then, start brainstorming through how you can increase the presence of each Core Drive during each phase. This means you are actively thinking through thirty-two Core Drives. Do you feel like the project would become more successful if they implemented your design?

Share what you come up with on Twitter or your preferred social network with the hashtag #OctalysisBook and see what ideas other people have.

Prove your Mastery: Get the Level 1 Octalysis Certificate

With the knowledge you have from this book, you qualify to send a submission for a Level I Octalysis Certificate from my company the Octalysis Group, showing that you demonstrate a competent knowledge of Octalysis and the 8 Core Drives.

Despite many submissions, as of this writing only nineteen people have qualified for the Level I Octalysis Certificate. The value of one is what you make of it, but I know of at least one hiring manager that had interviewed an applicant just because she saw the Level I Octalysis Certificate on his resume. The pass/no-pass version (without feedback) of the certificate is free. For instructions on how to qualify for one, go to yukaichou.com/certificate[299].

---

[299] A/B Testing is an experiment where two interface versions with the same goals are randomly show to different site visitors, allowing the interface designer to understand which version has better metric conversions.

Chapter 17: Designing a project from scratch with Octalysis

Redesigning Yukaichou.com

As the finale of this book, I would like to go over a brief showcase of using the Octalysis Framework to design a project experience from scratch.

As mentioned before, most of my work for clients is confidential, so often it is not practical to showcase my design process in detail. However, I thought it would be appropriate and fitting to work through the design process for my own site YukaiChou.com, especially the new Premium Membership section that I would like to introduce in 2016 called "Octalysis Prime."

As a quick background, after I published the Octalysis Framework on my blog YukaiChou.com in late 2012, my site started to receive a great deal of traffic that led to most of my client work and speaker engagements. I then started to make my video series *The Beginner's Guide to Gamification*, which is planned to contain ninety ten-minute Episodes. However, it has progressed very slowly since it is just a time consuming hobby project for evangelical purposes, but not generating any revenue for me or my staff. As of this writing, I have finished 20 episodes online, though I do so many goofy things in the videos I'm often quite embarrassed to show people.

It came to a point where I feel a need to redesign my website again, partially because the design feels dated, but primarily because I now have a more complex set of Desired Actions for users as well as *rewards* to give out. Besides just focusing on clients and speaking engagements, I now have a book to sell (or offer as a reward), workshops to promote, foreign Octalysis Licensing Partners to attract, and premium subscription memberships to sign-up. The premium subscription program is called Octalysis Prime.

The goal for the Octalysis Prime program is for me to further enhance my research efforts on gamification design, behavioral economics, motivational psychology and more, while still being able to support my team of talented consultants, programmers, writers, and operational folks. Right now, even though I feel like I am likely one of the leading practitioners of gamification, there are so many things that I still long to explore and conduct research on.

For instance, I would love to dive deeper into *Chain Combos* of Game Techniques - what Game Technique combinations foster others Core Drives, and which ones suppress other Core Drives. Or research on how various player types respond to White/Black Hat and Right/Left Brain Core Drives, whether it is possible to use Octalysis to create better music, and how the Endowment Effect balance out the Scarcity Effect (in other words, do we value what we have, or do we covet what we don't have - and in what context is one effect more powerful than the other?).

These are all fascinating topics for me, but I am unable to investigate them further because of the continous client work I am committed to. I love working with clients and seeing my knowledge become fruitful, but I myself don't necessarily grow towards a higher level during that process (which means people learning from me aren't getting everything they could be potentially getting). As a result, I would like to create a way for me to investigate these wondrous questions, share my findings with the world, while still being able to support my team.

I fully believe my content can also transform peoples' lives into becoming more meaningful, fulfilling, fun, and enriching. It has definitely done that for me, and I would like the same thing to happen for the members of my audience. The difference is that my audience members can go straight to the crystallized benefits of my work instead of wasting years exploring and fumbling without direction. There's always a huge efficiency loss when you're a pioneer (but luckily a status and influence gain).

Before we dive into this last section, keep in mind that it is always risky to share the actual Game Design Techniques you have implemented for your own target market. When a magician shares the secrets behind their magic tricks, it instantly becomes lame and both sides lose - the audience is no longer entertained and the magician no longer has any business. I'm sharing this in a very genuine manner since I sincerely appreciate you reading my book and hope that you can make the world better with this knowledge, even if it means that I risk having a less successful online experience because of it. This is almost like a salesperson saying, "I am walking away from you right now because I calculate that you would stop me at the door and ask to sign the deal." Good luck, Mr. Salesperson.

With that said, let's check out how I would use the Octalysis Framework to redesign my own site.

The Octalysis Strategy Dashboard

At the beginning of every gamification campaign, the first thing I do is to define five items:

1) Business Metrics, which lead to Game Objective

2) Users, which lead to Players

3) Desired Actions, which lead to Win-States

4) Feedback Mechanics, which lead to Triggers

5) Incentives, which lead to Rewards

Octalysis Strategy Dashboard

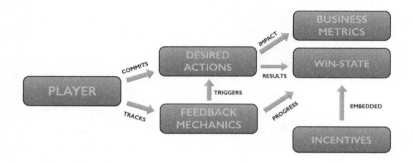

These come together to form the *Octalysis Strategy Dashboard*. Without understanding the business metrics, the users, and the desired actions, it is very difficult to see how effective a gamified design fulfills its objective.

Define Business Metrics

Below are the **Business Metrics** for my new site, in order of the *importance*:

- Increase sign-ups to the subscription plan
- Increase book purchases
- Workshop orders
- Increase consulting leads via the website
- Increase Email subscriptions
- Increase Social shares
- Increase video views for TEDx or Beginners Guide to Gamification
- Increase page views for the Octalysis Framework
- Increase overall views on my website

Notice that this list is based on quantifiable metrics for what creates a successful website, and less on my social and personal aspirations. Also, the ones on top are final metrics that would make a project successful, while the ones on the bottom are more of a "means-to-an-end" type of metrics.

Many clients would ask me, "Well, don't we need many viewers on the website before we can get purchases?" That's true, but one is to enable the other, not the other way around. This means that the enabled is more important than the enabler.

On every interface, you will realize that you can improve many different Business Metrics, but you can only optimize for *one* Business Metric with the limited real-estate and user attention span. As a rule of thumb, the question to ask is, if my top three Business Metrics are doing amazingly well, while the other Business Metrics are doing modestly, would this project still be successful. Since my goal is to scale my knowledge transfer without being pinned down by client work (while still generating revenue), I think my list is appropriate.

The Business Metrics then become the Game Objective. If these quantifiable numbers go up, then the gamification campaign is successful. If these metrics do not go up, then the gamification campaign is a failure. No fluffy things that can't be A/B Tested[300] or held accountable for.

Define User Types

The next step is to define who are my target Users, which ultimately become Players in the system if the gamified designs work:

- Company employees that want to use gamification or behavioral design to improve their organizations

---

[300] A/B Testing is an experiment where two interface versions with the same goals are randomly show to different site visitors, allowing the interface designer to understand which version has better metric conversions.

- Educators, nonprofits, and governments that want to use the knowledge to create a social impact
- Individuals who are passionate about gamification, games, or self-improvement

In Level III Octalysis, we would run separate Octalysis Charts to understand which Core Drives motivate each player type more, as well as define separate tracks of Desired Actions. However, since this is just a quick Level I Octalysis display, we will skip that and move ahead.

Define Desired Actions

The next step is to define the Desired Actions for the Users, which become Win-States once they commit to the actions. This is where we lay out all the little actions and steps that we want users to take in chronological order as part of a player journey.

Discovery Phase Desired Actions:

1) Learn about Yu-kai's content through a conference, social media, or friend referral

2) Land on an interesting content page within YukaiChou.com

3) Click on the Octalysis link

Onboarding Phase Desired Actions:

1) Skim the Octalysis article

2) Share the Octalysis article with friends

3) Watch Yu-kai's TEDx talk

4) Click on Yu-kai's About Me Page.

5) Fill in the email subscription form

Scaffolding Phase Desired Actions:

1) Receive weekly emails on great content

2) Open Weekly Emails

3) Visit YukaiChou.com and read articles weekly

4) Share articles with friends

5) Participate in the Octalysis Explorers Facebook Group

6) Buy and read Yu-kai's book

7) Watch all FREE episodes of the Beginner's Guide to Gamification

7) Sign up for Octalysis Workshops

8) Obtain the Level 1 Octalysis Certificate

Endgame Phase Desired Actions:

1) Sign up for Premium Subscription

2) Watch all available Beginner's Guide to Gamification Videos as well as past workshop recordings

3) Attend Weekly Office Hours

4) Learn a new Game Technique and apply it every week

5) Participate in exclusive discussion groups

6) View weekly Octalysis case studies on websites, games, or products.

7) Examine case studies and Showcases of actual member projects

8) Become an Octalysis Licensee in their region

9) Work directly with Yu-kai Chou and the Octalysis Group

These are the Desired Actions that form a logical player journey that extends all the way into the Endgame. The Endgame itself becomes the activities in Octalysis Prime, including Live Office Hours, exclusive discussion groups within a community, and weekly behavioral psychology content under the context of Octalysis. So if a user has invested a lot of time in Scaffolding and wants to take the next step forward, into the Endgame, it becomes a natural step to sign up for Octalysis Prime.

Every designed element needs to motivate users towards these Desired Actions. If it does not, the element is a distraction and should be thrown away. *Every Desired Action, when committed, leads to a Win-State.*

Define Feedback Mechanics

Feedback Mechanics are information delivery mechanisms that communicate to the user that their actions are meaningful. It allows them to track their progress towards the Win-State, feel the urgency of time, understand the unpredictable nature of the experience, and more. All Feedback Mechanics should become *Triggers* that promote the Desired Actions further, or else it should not be there.

The first step to understand possible Feedback Mechanics is to define mediums of interaction and communication. These are all the places I am able to actually plant these Feedback Mechanics as well as Triggers:

- YukaiChou.com Website
- OctalysisGroup.com Website
- Yu-kai's Book
- Email List
- Twitter and Facebook Group
- Speaker engagements
- Videos
- Workshops

The second step is to figure out what Feedback Mechanics I can insert into the site. This is what most people think about when they think "Gamification Design." These are the elements that allow communication of the 8 Core Drives that motivate behavior.

- Countdown Timers (Core Drives 6 and 8)
- Unlockable Content Page (Core Drive 3 and 6)
- Virtual Dice Roll Overlays (Core Drive 4 and 7)
- Little Tweet Bird on sidebar (Core Drives 5 and 7)
- Glowing Choice Overlay (Core Drives 2, 7)
- Embedded Videos (Core Drives 1, 5, and 7)
- Status Points via Captain Up or another Gamification Platform (Core Drives 2, 4, and 6)
- Hello Bar Top Display (Core Drives 1, 2, 6, and 7)
- Game Technique Collection Sets (Core Drives 2, 4, 6, and 7)
- Leaderboards via Captain Up (Core Drives 2, 5, 6, and 8)
- Certificates (Core Drives 2, 4, 5, and 6)
- Blog Posts to showcase members and announce information (Core Drives 1, 2, 5, 6, 7)
- Achievement Symbols via Captain Up (Core Drives 2, 3, 4, 6, and 7)
- Animated Popup Interfaces (Core Drives 1, 2, 5, 6, 8)
- Character Growth Charts (Core Drives 2, 3, 4, 5, 6, 8)
- Exchangeable Points that can be traded or redeemed (Core Drives 2, 3, 4, 5, 6, 7, 8)

As mentioned, this list is by no means exhaustive, but gives you a basic idea of the various elements I can use to insert game techniques as well as Core Drives to trigger users towards the Desired Actions.

Incentives and Rewards

The last item to define in the Octalysis Strategy Dashboard is Rewards, which is what the experience designer can give users when they commit the Desired Actions and arrive at the Win-State. The list below is in the order of abundance to scarce based on what the reward giver can issue:

- Status Points
- Achievement Symbols
- Social Community
- Feeling of accomplishment and progression
- Featured on the Emails
- Easter Egg Surprises
- Featured on the website
- Free eBook
- Featured on the videos
- Free Physical Book
- Signed Physical Book
- Discount on Workshops
- Spend personal time with Yu-kai
- Opportunity to work with Yu-kai
- Octalysis License

Beyond rewards, I also want to make Octalysis Prime itself rewarding and meaningful. Based on the brainstorming above, below are the programs I *can* provide once someone signs up to Octalysis Prime:

- Weekly Office Hours
- Chapter-by-Chapter Takeaways for books on Game Design, Motivational Psychology, and Behavioral Economics. These include books that were referenced a lot in this book and many more

- Access to all Beginner's Guide to Gamification videos and other workshop recordings. Since later videos will be locked, access to all videos would be a reward.
- 50% off every workshop, which can be hundreds or even thousands of dollars of savings over a period
- Weekly video/post about a new game technique, and encourage those to use it in their surrounding environment
- Accountability buddy to discuss the week's Game Technique usage
- Practical use-case teaching: how to negotiate a higher salary, how to use Black Hat to close deals, how to do parenting more effectively, how to deal with your coworkers, etc.
- Exclusive discussion groups
- Weekly case studies on Octalysis
- Weekly analysis of a website, game or product.
- Analysis of recent popular products and why they became successful
- Game technique combinations teaching
- The dynamic relationships between Core Drives
- Case studies and Showcase of actual member projects
- Live Streaming and Recordings of me researching on new games

I believe if I can implement all or a subset of the features above, it would be substantially valuable for the user.

Level I Octalysis Ideation Process

Once the Octalysis Strategy Dashboard is fully defined, the next step is to go through the 8 Core Drives and come up with new ideas that appeal to people's 8 Core Drives toward the Desired Actions. Below is a quick Level I Octalysis Ideation example:

Core Drive 1: Epic Meaning & Calling

- Messages (via Hello Bar and blog posts) that show users that they can transform their lives into something greater through the Octalysis movement. Earlier we mentioned that for Core Drive 1 to work, believability is very important. I wholeheartedly believe in my value proposition, and so the key is to communicate that in a believable manner.
- Showcase pro bono projects we do for world changing causes such as our campaigns with nonprofits to save the Amazon Rainforest. (Did you know at the current rate, the Amazon Rainforest will be *completely gone* within forty years?)
- Establish a sense of Elitism through the concept of "Good Gamification" as opposed to the subpar implementations that currently exist in the market.
- This idea just came to me as I was editing this chapter: for our Octalysis Prime offers, we could also do a "Save the World Weekly" campaign where each week we take one global problem and I showcase how to use Octalysis to design something that improves or solves the issue. At this point in my own design process, I would go up and add this to the offerings within "Octalysis Prime."

Core Drive 2: Development & Accomplishment

- Clear design that never lets users feel confused about what is the Desired Action. Use a combination of Glowing Choices and Desert Oasis.
- Constantly let users feel that they made the smartest choice being part of the Octalysis Prime program. Always provide so much value that every time they log in, they hit a delightful Win-State.

- Reward Captain Up points and badges when users commit light Desired Actions prior to signing up. High level players may get a discount for Octalysis Prime.
- Octalysis Prime members can increase their *Knowledge Scores* by viewing more content, and attending more sessions. High Knowledge Score members can earn certificates that will make a difference on their resumes.
- Perhaps extending beyond that, every subscribed user can start off with an empty Octalysis shape as their profile. As they increase their knowledge or activity in certain fields, that Core Drive will be visually expanded. In this case, some members who choose to engage all the Social Influence content as well as participate in community events, can be shown as specialists in Core Drive 5: Social Influence & Relatedness.

Core Drive 3: Empowerment of Creativity & Feedback

- A new and upgraded Octalysis Tool that people can use to design and analyze their own projects. At this point, I would go back to "Desired Actions" and add "Use Octalysis tool on own projects" into the Scaffolding Phase. Always keep in mind that the Octalysis Strategy Dashboard is a living document that grows based on more refined thinking.
- Member submission of their own work and receive feedback during Office Hours.
- Member voting on what products or campaigns I analyze next. This places a small sense of agency into the users' hands. Remember, Core Drive 3 is all about turning passive observers into active players.
- Chain Combos: if users sign up to Octalysis Prime as well as obtained other Achievement symbols on my site, they can obtain greater rewards that compound. During the designing

process, some ideas are vague. That's okay. Just know what you would ideally like to put into the experience and often you will find a great refined model later on.

- Each week, members will learn a new Game Technique that they will be encouraged to use in their own actual projects that week. They can share their experience with their accountability buddies or the community and gain feedback.
- "Specialists" in a certain Core Drive will be allowed to host sessions themselves and share their experience and research on certain topics.

Core Drive 4: Ownership & Possession & Feedback

- Collection Sets: Allow users to collect more Game Techniques, which will become the *key* to some higher level Octalysis magic later on.
- Earn the Level 1 Octalysis Certificate as well as other concrete career-boosting items.
- Use Easter Egg pop-ups to randomly give browsing users a free book, even signed. Remember, if you need to give out a reward, you can always go back to the Rewards/Incentives section of the Strategy Dashboard and pick from the list there. That's your arsenal to create delightful experiences.
- Show users how the Octalysis knowledge can benefit their health, productivity, happiness, and income. Sometimes people may view my work on Octalysis as too academic or theoretical, and so it's only for hardcore product managers or behavioral designers. However, it is important to communicate that this knowledge quickly translates to things that impact everyone into their daily lives, from negotiating a higher salary or raising funding for their organization, all the way to becoming a better parent

- A Personal Octalysis Report, where the Core Drives that motivate a person more are revealed - with tips and advice on how to use this knowledge.
- Exchangeable Points. Perhaps have some type of "in-game currency," perhaps called "Chou Coins." (Okay, don't laugh. This is just a brainstorming name, alright?) Users can accumulate Chou Coins and use them to unlock more scarce rewards and experiences within the Octalysis Prime experience.

Core Drive 5: Social Influence & Relatedness

- Entry Level Watercooler: Octalysis Explorers Facebook Group.
- Premium: Discussion Forum for hardcore users.
- Group Quest: Only after X users receiving the the Octalysis Certificate will the next level be opened. This will incentivize people to invite their friends to take on the challenge too.
- Accountability and Practice Buddy for Octalysis activities.
- Top Members showcase display. I don't want this to be a real competitive leaderboard, so probably won't show specific stats of the players nor their ranks, but merely randomly display members in the top 10%.
- Further Conformity Anchors, showing regional group scores may be interesting. Again, this incentivizes people to invite their friends to participate and improve the group rankings. What type of group rewards are to be given will need to be flushed out later.
- Use Twitter #hashtags for Octalysis (such as #OctalysisBook) to display a sense of relatedness between users. This can also work involving Instagram where every time someone sees an ad they identify the Core Drives in it on Instagram with #Octalysis labels.
- If I ultimately decide to go with the Chou Coins idea, then it opens up a new set of potential rewards and the ability to

introduce Social Treasures. Perhaps every day users have an opportunity to "tip" Chou Coins to someone they appreciate in the community, with each Chou Coin becoming two coins when tipped. Generosity takes a person further than self-consumption.

Core Drive 6: Scarcity & Impatience

- We want subscribers to feel committed. There should still be an admission process for signing up. But it can't be too difficult, to avoid creating any procrastination. Perhaps when they sign up to Octalysis Prime, they have to answer a question like, "In five sentences or less, share what you plan to do with the knowledge obtained from the membership." Of course, people who obviously have malicious intents would also be rejected, but this is mostly to set a barrier of commitment for those that want to be part of the war against boredom.
- Dangling: if there is additional content that members need to unlock or "earn," display lock-like feedback mechanics and provide users info on exactly how to unlock it. Even when people join Octalysis Prime, still make it a journey where things are paced out instead of overwhelming the user at once.
- Of course, a big part of Core Drive 6 design is making things challenging to the point where there is an actual sense of accomplishment (Core Drive 2) when completed. It is important to still make the Octalysis Certificates and other high-end rewards very difficult to obtain. That way they actually symbolize something meaningful.
- A Torture Break, Anchored Juxtaposition and Evanescent Opportunity Combo: there will always be content that is only reserved for premium members, but some of the new content I create for Octlaysis Prime will be free on my blog for one

or three days with a displayed countdown timer. After three days, it will be locked up for OP members only. However, a new Timer will appear, initiating a one year countdown. After a full year, the content will become publicly available - indefinitely. This means that if people want some of the Premium content and don't feel like paying, they either need to have enough diligence to be on my blog every day (another Desired Action), or have enough patience to wait an entire year before it comes out. As mentioned before, most free-to-play games monetize based on exchanging people's time with money.

- As mentioned before, since I want to have enough bandwidth to create all 90 Beginner's Guide to Gamification videos, later episodes will be locked and only accessible to OP members. Many viewers have also been collecting a set of secret key-words. My plan is that those with all the keywords from the free videos will get 50% off for the monthly subscription plan. People who then collect all of the keywords after that will get an *amazing reward worth remembering.*

- Create Daily 1-Hour Group Quests to get people to return often. The idea is to see if I could somehow pull off a daily activity, where if enough people take a certain Desired Action within a one hour period, something amazing happens. This requires further thinking and designing.

Core Drive 7: Unpredictability & Curiosity

- Goofy and unpredictable videos in The Beginner's Guide to Gamification. Part of the basic set of what's already in the current site is the Core Drive 7 strategy of constantly changing backgrounds for each sentence. It is a bit shaky for some people, but many people comment that despite their short attention spans, they always finish my videos because they want to see where I appear next. For the newer premium videos, I plan to be stationary while I switch scenes so my viewers won't feel dizzy anymore.

- Easter Egg elements in the site, such as the Icarus Badge or the secret Footer Link to a new set of navigation options. Currently on my blog, there are some secret Easter Egg elements, such as a secret door in the footer that leads people to an alternative world that unlocks new navigational items (along with unlocking the "Portal" badge). I would like to deploy more concepts like this in my new site.

- Set Mystery Boxes when users commit large Desired Actions. Whenever the user does a significant Desired Action, the dice rolling feedback mechanics can appear and certain rewards will be given. The variability of the rewards, assuming the Desired Action is not drawn out, may increase strong engagement with the experience.

Core Drive 8: Loss & Avoidance

- FOMO Punch. Remind users what they would lose every day when they don't have this Octalysis knowledge to employ within their lives.

- Addressing an Anti Core Drive: give users a guaranteed full refund if they did not obtain justified value from the service.

- The character growth chart and Chou Coins, if implemented would make it a bit harder for people to quit the system. However, I'm generally not interested in designing for the Sunk Cost Prison since I don't want anyone to think that they can't quit my site, just because they will lose many things that they have accumulated. If I am not delivering awesome value to my users, I don't feel comfortable that they are paying for it.

Repeating the Octalysis Process

Once you go through the 8 Core Drives, don't stop there. Do it again. More sophisticated ideas will often flow out. As a real example, after a few cycles of the process above, I derived a new type of player progress journey. This player journey intricately involves multiple Core Drives and could be a fun engaging experience throughout the Scaffolding and Endgame phases. The new concept is the below:

If possible, each Desired Action is assigned different Core Drives based on what a user can learn from those actions. For instance, participating in the community and helping others will increase a user's Core Drive 5 stats, while playing with the Octalysis Tool and coming up with creative solutions, will increases their Core Drive 3 stats.

Each player will start off with a basic octagon shape. Their octagon will eventually expand in the direction or directions where the corresponding Core Drives are being "leveled-up." Reading my Chapter-by-Chapter Takeaways from Daniel Pink's *Drive* will get experience points in Core Drives 1, 2, and 3, while taking advantage of a promotion at the very last minute will obtain Core Drive 8 points.

When each Core Drive levels up to a certain degree, specific boosters/power-ups and rewards will take place.

Here is a preliminary thought on how different leveled-up Core Drives might grant different benefits:

Core Drive 1: Yu-kai Chou and his team will help work on a non-profit cause pro-bono based on your request and votes. Or, half your monthly subscription fees will go into a non-profit cause

Core Drive 2: Turn your profile page into gold that is nicely textured and displayed to everyone you interact with. Your profile photo will have nice gold frames wherever you go on the site to show off your status

Core Drive 3: The ability to start researching and hosting your own sessions to the community, enabling you to express a great deal of creativity and receive immediate feedback. It will also allow you to build your personal brand.

Core Drive 4: Earn more Chou Coins for your Desired Actions. Perhaps every Desired Actions can earn a certain amount of Chou Coins to unlock more content. However, if your Core Drive 4 is leveled-up, you receive a 30% bonus on each Desired Action you perform.

Core Drive 5: The ability to moderate and lead the community. You will be able to mentor people, give support, perhaps be able to give out Social Treasures, and more. This will improve your ability to get helped from the community when you need it.

Core Drive 6: Penetrate through unlocked content faster. As an example, perhaps require less Chou Coins to unlock new content.

Core Drive 7: Unlock additional lucky dice rolls to obtain rewards such as Chou Coins. Perhaps every user gets a lucky dice roll every day or when they complete the Desired Actions. But people who have leveled-up their Core Drive 7 gets two lucky dice rolls to increase their odds of winning.

Core Drive 8: Even if you have stopped paying for Octalysis Prime, you will still get access for a few more months. This allows people to combat the "fear of missing out" or the Sunk Cost Prison. If they feel like they need to stop paying for a little bit, there wouldn't be any negative consequences.

With this preliminary concept, there is a strong reason for all the users to execute the Desired Actions while finding their own paths to level up in the experience. Socializers will get socializer benefits, while Achievers will get achiever status. Each can play the game differently.

If people start to master more Core Drives, it even allows for *Chain Combos* (Game Technique #40), which usually feels amazing when a person pulls it off. For instance, if a player achieved mastery in Core Drives 4, 6 , and 7: he will get more dice rolls to maximize the chance of getting Chou Coins; each time he wins, he would obtain more Chou Coins compared to others; and he needs fewer Chou Coins to unlock content. The three benefits compounded together would create hyper-powered gameplay that people can feel proud of.

Of course, I need to design for the other Core Drives too, so that being a leader or moderator of the community can also facilitate the gaining of rewards or unlocking new content. The experience design goes on.

Summary of Level 1 Octalysis in Action

As you can see, lots of new ideas can come out by thinking through the 8 Core Drives, setting a guiding roadmap to design for an engaging experience. Of course, the designing work is far from over.

When designing, it's great when lots of ideas go into the top of a brainstorming funnel. However, it is usually a bad sign when lots of ideas come out of the funnel towards implementation because it shows a lack of focus. Most companies can only implement a subset of the creative ideas in a timely manner.

There are other methodologies and processes to narrow down all the features to a feasible set within my own workflow, but this is somewhat beyond the scope of this book. I mostly want to explain how applying the 8 Core Drives allows us to creatively design for engaging experiences, when previously we only knew how to slap on badges. Beyond that, there are also things that need to be refined such as reward schedules, activity loops, balanced economies, and concept wireframes.

At the end of the day, Octalysis allows you to ask the right questions for your experience design, but you still need to answer them in a sophisticated and empathetic way. If you just treat Octalysis as a checklist, your design will only have the *shell* but not the *essence* within. Only if you utilize your creative intuition as well as sensitive empathy skills throughout the process will you come up with concepts that truly help increase all your Business Metrics and allow users to enjoy the entire process - from the Discovery Phase all the way to the Endgame.

To get the most out of the book, Choose only ONE of the below options to do right now:

Easy: Review this chapter again. There are many complex ideas within this chapter that assume a strong knowledge of the 8 Core Drives. If this book is your first encounter with the Octalysis Framework, it would likely be a rather challenging read. Don't worry, slow down, and take a deep breath. If you go back and read it again, I promise you it will make a lot more sense than it did the first time.

Medium: In Chapter 15, you were asked to come up with your own project and design for it. I laid down the foundation for you to create your own Octalysis Strategy Dashboard. Now that you have seen it in practice, start refining your Octalysis Strategy Dashboard and make sure each component is precise. This is essential for designing any gamification campaign, and will be even more critical when you one day utilize the powerful but nebulous Level IV Octalysis.

Hard: Now that you have seen me go through the design process myself, go through the entire process on your own project. Create the appropriate Octalysis Strategy Dashboard and go through each Core Drive over and over again until you have come up with a fun and dynamic experience. Did many more creative ideas - ones that appeal to our Core Drives and motivate us towards the declared Desired Actions - come out during this process?

Share what you come up with on Twitter or your preferred social network with the hashtag #OctalysisBook and check out what ideas other people have.

Become an Octalysis Hero

As you can see, I am completely passionate about sharing my studies and knowledge to the world in hopes of making it a better place. With that said, I have a great team that makes sure I protect myself and my intellectual property from those who seek to maliciously profit upon the Octalysis reputation and methodologies. My teammates have helped setup a licensing arrangement called the "Octalysis Hero" program, where individuals and companies can get properly trained to represent Octalysis and "save" their region from depressing boredom.

Anyone can use Octalysis for their own personal improvement, education purposes, or for non-profit causes. However, for those who want to generate profits based on it, they should look into signing up as an Octalysis Hero. If anything, we want to make sure each person's work does not reflect "Second-Hand Sushi Making" and hurt the Octalysis reputation.

As of 2015, we already have Octalysis Heroes in a few countries in Europe, and are excited to expand the good work further. For information on how to become an Octalysis Hero, check out: *octalysisgroup.com/licensing-octalysis-framework.*

Chapter 18: The Journey Goes On

We're finally here.

It has been a fun and meaningful two-year journey writing this book. I hope it has been equally fun and meaningful for you reading it.

This book is not an easy read. It is packed with complex psychological principles as well as design instruments that I have acquired over the past decade. Even though I have tried to make the content more intriguing and relatable by filling it with my own personal stories, being able to finish this book is a remarkable achievement for you, just as much as it is an achievement for me. You should give yourself a big cheer.

No, literally. You should put the book down, fling your arms in the air, and exclaim, "I finally did it!" This is actually an emotional reward when hitting the desired Win-State, and it does all sorts of good things to your brain chemicals, your health, and your happiness. Go ahead - do it. I'll wait for you. In fact, I'm doing it right now as I write this.

....

Now that there are two line breaks before this paragraph instead of just one, I trust that there has been enough time for you to actually do the self-cheer. A measly badge would not appropriately reflect the **epic win** you just bestowed upon yourself.

As I was finishing this book, I realized that one of the biggest fears of a writer is that no one will read his book after pouring out his heart and mind into the tiny confinements of letters, pages, and grammar rules. In fact, I even wonder if my wife or parents will ever get to read the text in this chapter, even though they have all enthusiastically stated that they will "of course" read my book when it comes out.

This reminds me of a story in the Bible[301], where Jesus performed miracles abundantly everywhere he went, but when he returned to his hometown in Nazareth (largest city in the north of present-day Israel), he performed very few miracles. People there recognized him as the "Carpenter's Son" that they had watched grow up. They couldn't muster enough faith for Jesus to perform miracles there[302]. Jesus left the town with a note that stuck with me, "A prophet is honored everywhere except in his own hometown and among his relatives and his own family."[303]

Regardless of whether my family will have enough stamina to finish my book, I am completely honored to have paragon readers like you who carefully study my work in order to create more good in this world.

What might be exhilarating to many but discouraging to a few, is that you are actually still at the onset of this exciting journey in learning how to make things fun and engaging. So far we have only covered Level I Octalysis, while there are many more levels and peripheral knowledge to learn, utilize, and master.

To be honest, when I first started writing this book, I was concerned

---

[301]Occasionally, I would get comments stating that my mentioning of the Bible is offensive, as if I were trying to impose my faith and my beliefs onto others. I have no such intention. Initially growing up as an argumentative atheist, my current faith is a very important part of me, and I have learned many valuable lessons from it, which I joyfully share with others. Strangely, it seems like if I instead proclaimed as a "Yoga enthusiast and Follower of Buddha," that somehow is more acceptable to those that are offended. We should all have the right to stand up for what we believe and not be judged simply because of it. For that, I thank Malcolm Gladwell for giving me the courage to stand strong in my beliefs through being a Bestselling Author who is not afraid to proclaim Christ.

[302]In the Bible, miracles seem to be powered by our faith. Jesus claims that if we just had faith the size of a tiny mustard seed, we would be able to move mountains. Even when Jesus heals people, he would say, "*Your* faith has healed you," as opposed to "I have healed you." As a result, in a town without faith, even Jesus does not perform miracles that he abundantly performs elsewhere.

[303]Bible. New Living Translation. Mark 6:4.

about whether I had enough content to write a full book. However, midway through writing it, I realized I actually needed to write three books instead of one. One on pure Octalysis design, which is this book. One on Lifestyle Gamification, which will likely be titled *10,000 Hours of Play*, and will focus on how to apply gamification principles to improve your life and turn everything into a game. The last one is a book tentatively titled *Subtle Differences* where I share all my research between two games/apps/systems that look almost identical to each other but where one is a fluke and the other a great success. I want my readers to observe the subtle differences that truly make something successful (hint: they focus more on appealing to the 8 Core Drives more).

Even with this first book, I initially designed it to have 29 Chapters. But when I started to actually write through the content, my personal stories, and other intriguing examples, it became clear to me that the book was becoming too bulky and I would have to divide it into two separate volumes. Instead of 29 Chapters, I reduced it to 18. This has created a need to write another future book on more advanced Octalysis Design via The Strategy Dashboard, 4 Experience Phases, and 8 Core Drives. The sequel will allow us to really learn to implement Level II or even Level III Octalysis into an experience from step one to completion. The nice thing is, I am already a third way into writing that book since I originally thought it would be part of this one.

Of course, your acquired knowledge in Level I Octalysis is by no means trivial. Level I Octalysis alone will allow you to create much better Human-Focused experiences on a day-to-day basis. You will begin to see everything differently, including your own motives. You will learn many other psychological and behavioral theories much quicker and more intuitively. You will also be able to close deals or negotiate your salaries better when you can appeal to the right human motivations. At the same time, you can develop an internal red flag response when an experience utilizes too much Black Hat technique where users will likely burn out soon - before it becomes too late to prevent the crash.

I regularly get emails from startups, product designers, and educators telling me that just reading my blog posts has changed how they do business and that they have seen immense improvements in their desired metrics. I urge you to not simply treat this book as a feel-good item that you just check off your to-do list. If you continue to pay attention to Human Motivation and the 8 Core Drives as much as I do, you will truly reap benefits from it on a daily basis. Octalysis is a design tool and a way of thinking. If you don't use the tool or don't follow the *way*, it becomes completely useless. Just another book to show off on your *trophy shelf*[304].

Lastly, if you feel that this book will benefit your life even a tiny bit, it is my hope that you share this knowledge with others, especially to those doing *good*. As you have seen, the understanding of human motivation and behavior is very powerful, but it could be used for changing the world for both positive and negative causes. If designed properly, people in these systems will all be enjoying their time more while executing the Desired Actions. However, whether people are joyfully performing tasks that benefit society or tasks that harm society completely depends on the objective of the experience designer.

It is my desire that this knowledge falls into the hands of more people who are creating positive change, meaningful work, and inspiring causes, as opposed to those who just try to profit off of others' misfortunes. As with anything, immoral people will use the best tools available to fulfill their objectives, and I myself am unable to stop that. But you can truly play a role in making sure my work also goes into very good hands that make the world a better place to counterbalance the mere profiteers. You would be making a true impact if you pass it forward - if you heard about the book

---

[304]We learned in this book that it is less ideal to give users the *Status* reward of the Trophy Shelf game technique from Core Drive 5. Generally, it is more engaging when utilizing the Core Drive 3 device Boosters/Power-ups so users can use their rewards to achieve greater heights.

from Twitter, please share it on Twitter; if you found the book on Amazon, please leave a review there.

At the end of the day, we know that because of Core Drive 1, we as humans prefer to be joyfully doing work that positively impacts the world, as opposed to joyfully doing work that makes the world worse - assuming all other Core Drives are equal. If there are an equal number of behavioral designers using Octalysis for selfish reasons compared to designers using Octalysis for beneficial reasons, end users will naturally be inclined towards the good.

I hope that you not only use the knowledge from this book for good, but can also pass on the torch to others who have similar aspirations. You would be making a true impact when you pass it forward (I have made it easy to leave a review on Amazon with this *Pretty Link* URL: http://www.yukaichou.com/octalysisbook). That way, my vision of making the world a better place through productive play, exhilarating work, and fulfilling camaraderie will finally become a reality.

It has been an honor writing for you, and I hope this won't be the last chance I get to communicate with you in our journeys. With or without me, your journey of interacting with others and motivating them will continue. I hope at one point our paths will converge again, perhaps on my website, my workshops, or in my next book.

I'm sure it will take us to even greater heights than ever before.

Wall of Gratitude

I'm completely in-debt to a great deal of people who made this book possible. More people than I can name. Regardless, I would like to express appreciation for those who shaped me to become who I am, which manifested into the content of this book.

Those who directly contributed to the book

I want to thank Wendy Lim (who prefers to be known as Average Joey), as well as Zen Trenholm, who have relentlessly combed through my book and fixed up many of my careless mistakes, as well as pointed out unclear or inappropriate content within my blind spots. I want to thank Jerry Fuqua for bringing his Ph.D. discipline into editing my book and making me a better writer. This book would have embarrassed me without me knowing it if it wasn't for you. Many thanks to Ping-Hsiang Chen for designing all the logos for my personal brand as well as the book cover of this book.

I want to thank Christine Yee and Monica Leonelle for helping out with research and content. I also want to thank Jun Loayza, Sergey Znutin, Michael Jensen, Victoria Pan, Solomon Rajput, Morlion Thijs, Belal Sweileh, Mike Finney, Mauro Ghibaudo, and Mark Welch for providing feedback as they read through the book. I want to thank Mario Herger for giving me the extra push to write this book. I also want to thank Dutch Driver for persistently asking about my book and motivating me to finish it via Core Drive 5.

Those who impacted who I am today

In extension, I want to thank my parents – my father for being my greatest role model for maintaining integrity despite any hardship, and my mother for providing me a boundless flow of love and empathetic sophistication. I want to thank my wife Angel for offering constant support towards my career, my lifestyle, and my spiritual health. Even though we are very different, together we make each other stronger, more resilient, and of course cuter.

I want to thank Lwazi Mabuza for being my first best friend since my South Africa days and helping me seed my unique confidence from early on. It is a true blessing that, after twenty-two years of *zero* communication, we get to become friends again through the wonders of technology. I want to thank my cousin Winston Wang for not only protecting my health as an acupuncturist, but also always being there for me as my closest friend during my moments of emotional weaknesses.

I want to thank Ping-Hsiang Chen again for teaching me my first lesson about charismatic leadership in 5th grade. Without you, I probably would have been the target of bullying throughout my student life. I want to thank Yi Chou for inspiring me with his relentless pursuit of playing better guitar, as well as demonstrating a more Core Drive 6 style of personal charisma. I want to thank Chris Schedler for persistently bringing me to Christ, despite facing my awkward rejections six weeks in a row. I wish I one day would have the same courage you had within me.

I want to thank Todor Gogov for making being a foreigner in Kansas not just bearable, but enjoyable. I want to thank Curtis Lo for helping me push through the last semester in South Pasadena High School. It surprisingly was the most difficult academic semester in my life. I want to thank Jun Loayza for being my best friend throughout UCLA and for most of my professional career. You have changed my life just as much as I have changed yours. I want to thank Stephen Johnson for making it possible for me to become a tech entrepreneur and truly pioneering some of the earliest gamification concepts together. Some of the best (and arguably worst) moments of my life were fondly spent with you. I also want to thank Joris Beerda, my student-turned Partner and Managing Director for the Octalysis Group, for keeping my company smoothly operating as I attempted to finish this book.

I want to thank Frank Jwong for being the first to believe in me and writing me my first check as an angel investor, as well as Vicki Young for taking the first big risk on a young entrepreneur like me. I want to thank DJ Martin for being my biggest emotional support as an investor during the darkest times of my life. I will try to help you out with anything within my powers for the rest of my life. I want to thank Bernie Grohsman for teaching me how to become a more persuasive consultant and picking myself up when I first transitioned from being a tech entrepreneur to a full-time consultant.

I want to thank Wayne Silby for being my role model and guiding many of my moral choices in life. I hope one day I can create as much positive impact in this world as you did and still do today. Finally, I want to give thanks to Jesus Christ the God of my faith for literally everything.

There are obviously substantially more people to thank throughout my journey, and I am unable to list everyone out here. However, my heart goes out to every one of you and I hope I have also made a positive difference in your lives. Never hesitate to reach out to me for anything I can help you with.

Last but definitely not least, I want to thank you the reader for reading my book and making my two years of dedicated grinding actually meaningful. Thank you for investing your precious time into what I have to say. I hope it has been impactful and meaningful for you too.

Thank you.